REVIVING ROMAN RELIGION

Sacred trees are easy to dismiss as a simplistic, weird phenomenon, but this book argues that, in fact, they prompted sophisticated theological thinking in the Roman world. Challenging major aspects of current scholarly constructions of Roman religion, Ailsa Hunt rethinks what sacrality means in Roman culture, proposing an organic model which defies the current legalistic approach. She approaches Roman religion as a 'thinking' religion (in contrast to the ingrained idea of Roman religion as orthopraxy) and warns against writing the environment out of our understanding of Roman religion, as has happened to date. In addition, the individual trees showcased in this book have much to tell us which enriches and thickens our portraits of Roman religion, be it about the subtleties of engaging in imperial cult, the meaning of *numen*, the interpretation of portents or the way statues of the divine communicate.

AILSA HUNT is Lecturer in Classics at the University of Cambridge and a Fellow of Newnham College, Cambridge.

CAMBRIDGE CLASSICAL STUDIES

General editors

R. L. HUNTER, R. G. OSBORNE, M. J. MILLETT, G. BETEGH, G. C. HORROCKS, S. P. OAKLEY,
W. M. BEARD, T. J. G. WHITMARSH

REVIVING ROMAN RELIGION
Sacred Trees in the Roman World

AILSA HUNT
University of Cambridge

CAMBRIDGE
UNIVERSITY PRESS

University Printing House, Cambridge CB2 8BS, United Kingdom

Cambridge University Press is part of the University of Cambridge.

It furthers the University's mission by disseminating knowledge in the pursuit of
education, learning, and research at the highest international levels of excellence.

www.cambridge.org
Information on this title: www.cambridge.org/9781107153547

© Ailsa Hunt 2016

This publication is in copyright. Subject to statutory exception
and to the provisions of relevant collective licensing agreements,
no reproduction of any part may take place without the written
permission of Cambridge University Press.

First published 2016

Printed in the United States of America by Sheridan Books, Inc.

A catalogue record for this publication is available from the British Library.

Library of Congress Cataloguing in Publication Data
Names: Hunt, Ailsa, author.
Title: Reviving Roman religion : sacred trees in the Roman world / Ailsa Hunt.
Description: New York : Cambridge University Press, 2016. | Series: Cambridge
classical studies | Includes bibliographical references and index.
Identifiers: LCCN 2016021106 | ISBN 9781107153547 (hardback)
Subjects: LCSH: Rome–Religion. | Trees–Religious aspects.
Classification: LCC BL805 .H86 2016 | DDC 292.2/12–dc23
LC record available at https://lccn.loc.gov/2016021106

ISBN 978-1-107-15354-7 Hardback

Cambridge University Press has no responsibility for the persistence or accuracy of URLS
for external or third-party Internet Web sites referred to in this publication and does not
guarantee that any content on such Web sites is, or will remain, accurate or appropriate.

for James Edward

CONTENTS

List of figures		*page* x
Acknowledgements		xi
1	Rooting in: why give time to sacred trees?	1
2	A brief history of tree thinking: the enduring power of animism	29
3	How arboreal matter matters: rethinking sacrality through trees	72
4	Arboriculture and arboreal deaths: rethinking sacrality again	121
5	Confronting arboreal agency: reading the divine in arboreal behaviour	173
6	Imagining the gods: how trees flesh out the identity of the divine	224
7	Branching out: what sacred trees mean for Roman religion	292
Appendix		295
Bibliography		302
Index		328

FIGURES

1	Tiberian sestertius, Tarraco.	page 221
2	Fresco from the *calidarium*, *villa di Poppaea*, Oplontis.	225
3	Detail from the *Anaglypha Traiani*, Rome.	256
4	Fresco from the *oecus* of *casa* VII.9.47, Pompeii.	257
5	Detail from the Arch of Constantine, Rome.	267
6	Fresco from the garden of *casa* VI.7.23, Pompeii.	272
7	Fresco from the Red Room, Villa at Boscotrecase.	273
8	Fresco from the *ekklesiasterion*, Temple of Isis, Pompeii.	274
9	Fresco from the *ekklesiasterion*, Temple of Isis, Pompeii.	275
10	Fresco from the *ekklesiasterion*, Temple of Isis, Pompeii.	276
11	Fresco from the *villa Arianna*, Stabiae.	278
12	Drawing of fresco from *cubiculum* b, *casa* IX.2.16, Pompeii.	279
13	Detail of relief from the amphitheatre at Capua.	281
14	Relief depicting the Temple of Vesta.	282
15	Relief depicting a sacrificial procession for Cybele, Cyzicus.	283
16	Detail from wooden furniture leg, *villa dei Papiri*, Herculaneum.	285
17	Detail from wooden furniture leg, *villa dei Papiri*, Herculaneum.	287

ACKNOWLEDGEMENTS

I grew up in a house called Yggdrasil in a remote North Yorkshire village, and whilst I spent far more of my childhood climbing trees than thinking about them, it was perhaps inevitable that it would one day come to this. I would like to start by thanking my family for all their love over the years and for their support of my academic work, caring about both successes and failures.

Transplanted from Yorkshire to Corpus Christi, Oxford, I discovered a brave new world of classicists, who all helped to transform my own intellectual world: in particular I am grateful to Stephen Harrison, Ewen Bowie, Neil McLynn, Martin Goodman, Anna Clark, John Ma, Tim Whitmarsh and Jaś Elsner. From Oxford to Cambridge, I then had my intellectual world blown apart by John Henderson, who supervised my MPhil research: his unique ability to see something interesting in everything was both infectious and inspiring. For my doctorate I was supervised by Mary Beard, to whom I am also deeply indebted. Mary takes no prisoners in intellectual terms, and I have learned so much from the sharpness of her thinking and her knack for bulldozing through irrelevancies and homing in on the pertinent question.

As this doctorate turned from a thesis into a book, I have been guided and encouraged by my examiners, Catharine Edwards and Andrew Wallace-Hadrill, and by Robin Osborne and Stephen Oakley, who read and improved the final manuscript. I am also grateful to Michael Sharp and the editorial team at Cambridge University Press, and to all the library staff in the Faculty of Classics. I wrote the book whilst I held an Isaac Newton Research Fellowship in Classics at Fitzwilliam College, Cambridge, and I will remember with fondness this my most recent academic home, the friendliness of the fellowship and the peacefulness of the college gardens and their old trees.

Acknowledgements

Last but not least, I want to thank my husband Richard. Throughout the years that have gone into this book I have leaned on him for strength, and he has been endlessly patient with my antisocial hours and frequent failures to see the wood for the trees. I have not always been easy to live with. I once dragged him and our unborn child to Tarraco just so I could see the home of my favourite palm tree.

This book is dedicated to baby James, who endured it both in and out of the womb. I am sorry it isn't a lift-the-flap book.

CHAPTER I

ROOTING IN: WHY GIVE TIME TO SACRED TREES?

In summer 2011, *Private Eye* featured in their 'Funny Old World' column a letter written by one Radnor the Wise. He had sent this letter to the *Surrey Advertiser*, in an attempt to address local concern about the Wiccan practice of draping a sacred tree in underwear.

> Some of your readers may be aware of the recent discovery of a tree in the Hurtwood forest, which was found to be covered in black underwear (both men's and women's panties, briefs, bras and ladies' stockings), and reported in the local Peaslake parish magazine. As a practising Wicca (with the ceremonial title of High Witch), I can confirm that there is nothing sinister in this practice, and users of the Hurtwood forest should have no fear. The decoration of sacred trees is a feature of our religion, and represents our faith in the virility and generosity of mother nature. The tree-dressing ceremony is conducted very early during an icy spring morning, and is followed by a tactile exploration of rebirth, rejuvenation and renewal which is the highlight of the Coven's annual calendar. A similar ceremony is held at Harvest time, followed by our annual barbecue and quiz night. I hope this ceremony shows how religion, fashion, feminism, and ecology can work harmoniously together in the modern day.[1]

Radnor is at pains to emphasise the intellectual sophistication and relevance of the tree-dressing practice, enacting as it does the potential intersection of religion, fashion, feminism and ecology in modern culture. He also takes care to frame sacred trees within the recognisably normal: what could be 'sinister' about anything followed by a barbecue and quiz night, that staple of Anglican social life and no doubt often advertised in the Peaslake parish magazine? Yet Radnor is fighting a losing battle here. For there is *nothing* sophisticated about sacred trees in the public imagination. To the contrary, sacred trees almost always find themselves stereotyped as the preserve of the weird and deluded, something very much marginal to the concerns of mainstream society.[2] For most

---

[1] *Private Eye* no. 1295 (19 August–1 September 2011): 15.
[2] These stereotypes persist despite increasing public concern in the UK for our arboreal heritage and future: consider the recent outrage over government proposals to sell land

people today, 'Funny Old World' is simply the only appropriate kind of space for giving any thought to sacred trees.

I begin with Radnor to emphasise how the urge to publish his letter in 'Funny Old World' stifles our intellectual openness to the idea of sacred trees. Be it a Wiccan sacred tree in a Surrey forest, the world-ash Yggdrasil with its central role in Norse mythology or the Bodhi Tree, an offshoot of the fig under which the Buddha is said to have reached enlightenment, our assumptions about the *weirdness* of sacred trees hamper our ability to engage seriously with their significance in any given culture. Indeed for students of the Roman world – the focus of this book – it is not only images of neo-pagans hanging bras on trees which might prejudice our approach to sacred trees. The figure of Sir James Frazer and his multi-volume *Golden Bough* loom large in the classicist's imagination, the very idea of sacred trees tainted by association with the scholar whom a recent biographer has branded an 'embarrassment' to the academic community.[3] As one of the most notorious of the nineteenth- and early twentieth-century academics who employed comparativist methods to understand 'primitive religion' – and held up sacred trees for the rich insights they provided into such primitive thinking – Frazer represents a type of scholarship on which current classicists have firmly turned their backs. The prominent role of sacred trees in this now discredited scholarship has blackened their reputation today, meaning that any scholar of Roman religion giving time to such trees runs the risk of being typecast as a Radnor of the academic world.

Yet for scholars of Roman religion to act on this instinct to steer clear of sacred trees is, I believe, a guaranteed way to impoverish our understanding of Roman religion. For it is the foundational claim of my book that trees provoked the inhabitants of the Roman world into grappling with challenging theological questions that took them to the heart of their understanding of where they stood

owned by the Forestry Commission (over half a million signed the Save Our Forests petition) or the Trees for Cities campaign (www.treesforcities.org). Lewis 1999: 291–292 provides a brief survey of the significance of trees in neo-pagan movements. Harvey 1997: 25–32 draws out the role of trees and tree-lore in modern Druidry, and later discusses how neo-pagan practices encourage the exploration and expression of ecological concerns (131–138).
[3] Ackerman 1987: 1.

What is a sacred tree?

in relation to the divine. Yet before we can explore this claim further a basic question needs to be answered: what do I *mean* by a Roman 'sacred tree'?

What is a sacred tree?

My answer offers a loose definition which has little to do with the sacred tree in the popular imagination. For me, a Roman sacred tree is any tree which intersects with Roman religious thought and practice. Sometimes such trees are easy to spot: the famous *ficus Ruminalis* in the Roman forum is, Pliny the Elder tells us, considered *sacra* (sacred; *Nat.* 15.77). Yet the vast majority of Roman sacred trees are not 'labelled' in this way. When we see inhabitants of Lydia inscribing prayers of confession to Zeus of the Twin Oaks, the Arval priesthood sacrificing for the sake of pruning their grove or Augustus transplanting a palm so that it stands alongside the *penates* in his *conpluvium*, in all these cases we stand in the presence of what I will be considering sacred trees. Roman sacred trees were everywhere and there can be no hard and fast rules for identifying one, nor can we expect agreement within the Roman world as to whether a particular tree was sacred or not. Indeed my understanding of Roman sacred trees presupposes a very flexible model of sacrality, the like of which are influential in some contemporary theoretical approaches to the study of religion. Bell, for example, defines the sacrality of an object as 'the way in which the object is more than the mere sum of its parts and points to something beyond itself'.[4] To many contemporary scholars of religion there might seem little controversial in taking a similar kind of broad-brushstroke approach to what makes a tree sacred in Roman culture, yet within scholarship on Roman religion this is a far from standard approach. For to date, scholars of Roman religion have relied on a one-size-fits-all model of Roman sacrality.

The official line is that objects become sacred by being dedicated or consecrated to a god, a process which must be performed by a Roman magistrate and take place within Roman

---

[4] Bell 1997: 157. Smith 1982: 55 also reflects this idea that what is significant about a sacred object is not the object itself, arguing that 'there is nothing that is sacred in itself, only things sacred in relation'.

territory.[5] Roman sacrality thus boils down to a transfer of property to the divine, making the object inviolable. This view has been repeated *ad nauseam*, with ideas expressed by Wissowa in 1912 still being regurgitated a hundred years later.

So erfolgt die Überweisung durch den Akt der Dedication, durch den sich der Verpflichtete des Eigentumsrechtes an der gelobten Sache entäußert und sie an die Gottheit aufläßt.[6]

The sacred was not a 'magic force' placed in an object, but simply a juridical quality possessed by that object. Like all public or private property, the property of the gods was inviolable, the more so because its owners were terribly superior to men and their vengeance was inexorable.[7]

The Latin word *sacer* of course means 'holy'; but is derived from the terminology relating to ownership ... Votive offerings, or statues, could be consecrated ... and thus legally conveyed into the possession of the divinity.[8]

By dedicating an object, one ceased to own it; and by transferring it into the sphere of divine law, one invested it with godly power, transforming its very nature and turning it into a *res sacra*, with important implications for its juridical status.[9]

By contrast, the argument continues, objects dedicated by private individuals were not legally sacred.[10] Rather they had 'an ambiguous status', as Galvao-Sobrinho puts it, for whilst 'they may have been juristically profane ... they were not deprived of religious force'.[11] Also left in limbo were objects consecrated by a Roman magistrate in Italy, but not in Roman territory itself, and thus considered quasi-sacred.[12] As their legalistic language signals – and as they themselves openly admit – these scholars' construction of Roman sacrality is tightly modelled on definitions of the word

---

[5] I follow Nisbet 1939: 209–212, Bodel 2009: 21–22 and Galvao-Sobrinho 2009: 131 and 156 in emphasising that Roman authors often used *dedicare* (to dedicate) and *consecrare* (to consecrate) interchangeably (e.g. Fest. 321M). Scheid 2003a: 24 and 64–66 discusses consecration regulations and conceptual changes in what counted as Roman territory after the Social War. Orlin 1996: 162–172 analyses evidence for how dedications were legally authorised (Liv. 9.46.6–7; Cic. *Att.* 4.2.3; Cic. *Dom.* 127–130).
[6] Wissowa 1912: 385.
[7] Scheid 2003a: 24.
[8] Rüpke 2007: 8.
[9] Galvao-Sobrinho 2009: 131. For further reiterations of the orthodoxy see Gall 1975: 39; Schilling 1979: 49; Dubourdieu and Scheid 2000: 60.
[10] Wissowa 1912: 385; Nisbet 1939: 210; Scheid 2003a: 64; Bodel 2009: 22.
[11] Galvao-Sobrinho 2009: 151.
[12] Scheid 2003a: 64 and Lambrinoudakis 2005: 304 note the use of the legal term *pro sacro* (quasi-sacred) in this context.

What is a sacred tree?

sacer found in the Roman jurists, like that of Aelius Gallus, as quoted by Festus:

> Gallus Aelius ait sacrum esse quocumque modo atque instituto civitatis consecratum sit, sive aedis, sive ara, sive signum, sive locus, sive pecunia, sive quid aliud, quod dis dedicatum atque consecratum sit: quod autem privati suae religionis causa aliquid earum rerum deo dedicent, id pontifices Romanos non existimare sacrum. (Fest. 424L)
>
> Aelius Gallus says that something consecrated in whatever way and by a mandate of the state is sacred, whether a temple, altar, statue, place, property, or any other thing which is dedicated and consecrated to the gods: but any of those things which private individuals dedicate to a god for their own religious observance, that the Roman pontiffs do not consider sacred.[13]

Paramount authority is given to this one adjective *sacer* (as defined in the jurists) in scholarly accounts of what it means for something to be sacred in Roman culture.[14]

Yet when engaging with Roman conceptions of the natural world, this legalistic model of sacrality falls short. After all, Ovid can call a lake *sacer* with no hint of a suggestion that it had been consecrated by a Roman magistrate (*Fast.* 3.264). In response, scholars have drawn a distinction between objects formally transferred to the gods' possession through consecration, and natural objects or

---

[13] In quoting this text, scholars are of course ignoring the fact that its very existence suggests that 'popular' thinking about what made something sacred was rather different. Justinian (*Dig.* 1.8.6) and Gaius (*Inst.* 2.5) are also frequently cited. For open scholarly reliance on the jurists see e.g. Schilling 1979: 49, Scheid 2003a: 24 and Rives 2012: 166. Smith 2004: 105 discusses how the work of Durkheim has also given impetus to the understanding that 'the structure of property and the structure of sacrality are parallel'.

[14] Within the jurists' texts, definitions of *sacer* often feature within wider discussions of objects or places whose status is of religious significance in Roman culture: *res sanctae* and *res religiosae* are also defined, with *res profanae* sometimes forming an additional category. See Dumézil 1970: 130–131 and Rives 2012: 166–169 for discussion of this tripartite or tetrapartite division. Following this format, some modern 'textbooks' on Roman religion also provide an overview – alongside discussion of *sacer* – of the terms *sanctus* ('anything which it was a religious offence to violate'), *religiosus* ('objects or places marked by death'; 'places left to the *di manes*') and *profanus* ('anything not sacred'), to borrow definitions from Scheid 2003a: 25. Cf. Dumézil 1970: 129–133; Schilling 1979: 49–50; Rüpke 2007: 8–9. By replicating the categorising tendencies of the jurists in this way scholars reinforce the implication running throughout their discussion that Roman sacrality can be neatly pinned down, although strictly speaking it is only *sacer* which they understand to indicate what 'being sacred' meant in Roman culture. Fugier 1963 provides a very rare example of engagement with the adjective *sacer* which is not purely derivative of the jurists, dividing it into multiple categories: '*sacer* = cultuel, rituel', '*sacer* = qui est consacré', '*sacer* = numineux', '*sacer* = magique'.

spaces, which, it is argued, were understood to be the possession of the gods automatically: trees and wooded spaces play a prominent role in this latter category, alongside rivers, lakes, hills and fields.[15] This leads to broader definitions of Roman sacrality than those encountered so far, characterised by a 'distinction between the sacred as defined by human authority and the sacred as more or less spontaneously perceived'.[16] Yet, at the same time, this distinction is downplayed by reusing the language of consecration to elucidate what makes natural phenomena sacred. To use Bodel's words:

> Natural phenomena (rivers, trees, meteorites, etc.) were regularly regarded as consecrated (*pro sacro*) without formal dedication by a human agent.[17]
> Many natural settings were thought of as having been claimed directly by the gods and thus, in a sense 'auto-consecrated'.[18]

In short, whether dealing with a sacred statue or a sacred lake, the orthodox scholarly position insists that their sacrality depended on their being understood as in some way consecrated to, and hence the property of, a particular deity. As for explaining *why* Roman thinkers might have understood lakes or trees or mountains to be automatically consecrated to the gods, no reasons are given beyond gestures to a 'divine presence' or their numinous quality.[19] Turcan, for example, thus breezes through his explanation of what makes a forest sacred: 'The forest belonged to the gods. To the ancients it gave that frisson of the supernatural.'[20]

---

[15] See e.g. Gall 1975: 54–55; Scheid 2003a: 73–74; Bodel 2009: 22.

[16] Rives 2012: 165. Dumézil 1970: 130 also argues that '*sacer* describes that which is reserved and kept apart for the gods, whether by nature or by human agency'.

[17] Bodel 2009: 22. On the blurring of this distinction cf. Sabbatucci 1952: 91–92, who argues that the idea of *sacer* meaning 'offerto ad una divinità' leads organically to 'un estensione di questo significato al *sacer* che definisce un possesso divino nello spazio'.

[18] Bodel 2009: 24. Cf. Scheid 2003a: 63 and 73. For a similar account of the sacrality of mountains, groves, springs, etc. in Greek culture, see Larson 2010: 57–58: humans respond to the 'pre-existent holiness' of such places (57), which were 'often regarded as inherently sacred' (58).

[19] Scheid 2003a: 73. Rives 2007: 89–92 also provides examples of how 'the natural world ... would for many people have been shot through with the presence of the divine' (92).

[20] Turcan 2000: 39. Sometimes even less explanation is forthcoming: Rives 2012: 178, relying on a reading of Cato, *Agr.* 139, writes that 'the grove was simply perceived as sacred', even though it 'had not been formally consecrated to a particular god'. Even Fugier 1963, who is more prepared than many to think outside of the box about Roman sacrality, echoes the idea that arboreal sacrality depends on a 'frisson of the supernatural'. Writing of the *ficus Ruminalis*, for example, she first notes that on one level its sacrality depended on its connection with Romulus and Remus, but then subordinates

What is a sacred tree?

The vague terminology of 'frisson' sits uneasily with the fact that the underlying model of sacrality in operation here is a legalistic one concerning property, an incongruity which suggests just how much is being forced when scholars try to apply juristic models of sacrality to the sacrality of natural phenomena in Roman culture. Indeed this incongruity is quite glaring, but it is only recently that allegiance to these juristic models has come under any attack from scholars of Roman religion. What has attracted attention in particular is not the irrelevance of these models to the sacrality of lakes or forests, but the fact that the jurists' elitist and top-down approach to sacrality clearly represents one particular way of thinking about and ordering the world: it is hard not to suspect that the world of Roman sacred objects and places was a lot less tidy in the experience of those less interested in definitions.[21] Bodel, for example, noting the sheer number of private dedications in the Roman world – which on a strict juristic model of sacrality must be considered of no religious significance – has recently challenged the relevance of the jurists to lived experiences of Roman sacrality. He argues that it was not being legally consecrated by a magistrate which made an object sacred, but someone *conceptually* setting it apart for the gods.[22] Thus Bodel denies the jurists definitive authority over what it means to be sacred, yet at the same time perpetuates the fundamental tenet of their model of sacrality: 'what matters for the religious status of an object is ... its conceptual placement within the framework of the rules of *property*' (my italics).[23] His 'new' understanding of sacrality thus takes only a very small step away from the standard juristic model, and in fact replicates that of another jurist, Trebatius, as quoted in Macrobius, who defines the sacred as *quicquid est quod deorum habetur* (whatever is considered to belong to the gods; 3.3.2).

---

this to the fact that, at a more elementary level, 'ce qui crée le sentiment de sacralité ... est une impression constituée de crainte et d'attirance – d'un mot, une impression "numineuse" – éprouvée devant l'arbre' (83).

[21] Rives 2012: 165 also acknowledges that non-technical writers 'tend to employ the words *sacer*, *sanctus*, and *religiosus* in fairly loose and overlapping ways'. Sabbatucci 1952: 91 was much more of a lone voice in the 1950s when he questioned the value of a legalistic approach (although he did not develop the idea in any detail).

[22] Bodel 2009: 26–30.

[23] Bodel 2009: 27.

7

Rives too is sceptical of the value of the jurists' construction of sacrality. In an imaginative (but precariously grounded) argument, he claims that in archaic Rome *sacer* was applied to 'anything spontaneously perceived as having some inherent connection with the divine'.[24] Then, once the elite came to regard this 'as a potentially disruptive factor in Roman society', they tightened their control over the category of the sacred, resulting in the kind of definitions we find in the jurists.[25] Thus Rives diminishes these definitions to a distortion of what sacred really meant to most people. Yet by presenting the 'real' sacred as something felt to have an 'inherent connection with the divine' – the examples he gives being mountains and groves – he echoes the traditional emphasis on the numinous quality of 'auto-consecrated' natural features, an emphasis itself rooted in attempts to apply universally the juristic model of sacrality as consecration. Roman sacrality is still crying out to be freed from the mould into which the jurists poured it.[26]

On one level, common sense alone should prompt us to a more fluid understanding of Roman sacrality. We do not expect the English word 'sacred' to have a simple definition or the same connotations in different contexts; even the *Oxford English Dictionary*'s entry for sacred, which naturally attempts to boil down the adjective to its essential meanings, consists of fifteen sub-entries, followed by a list of special collocations. So why impose a reductive definition of *sacer* on the Romans? Why, moreover, should we restrict our understanding of sacrality in

---

[24] Rives 2012: 177.
[25] Rives 2012: 179.
[26] Nor is this juristic focus among scholars of Roman religion by any means restricted to discussion of *sacer*. Indeed a vicious (and lazy) circle has developed by which reliance on juristic texts leads to the characterisation of Roman religion as quintessentially legalistic, which then in itself seemingly justifies the use of such source material. Since Mommsen this characterisation has held sway, as this brief selection of quotations illustrates. At the beginning of the last century Warde-Fowler 1911: 120 branded the *pontifices* 'religious lawyers'; six decades later Ogilvie 1969: 35 observed that 'Roman prayers were phrased like legal documents'; at the start of the twenty-first century Turcan 2000: 4 was still insisting that 'the gods were to be approached like magistrates ... the formalism of words and gestures went hand in hand with a strict legalism'. More sophisticated work on the intersection of law and religion has recently made an appearance, e.g. Ando and Rüpke 2006, but in general scholarship on Roman religion remains hampered by the unquestioned assumption that cult practice and ideas about the divine were all bound by strict sets of rules.

the Roman world by tying it to this one adjective? Any meaningful discussion of Roman sacrality should, I argue, focus on the *notion* of sacrality, rather than the use of a specific word. It is vital that we relax our conception of what sacrality means in Roman culture, and it is my hope that the trees we will encounter in this book will jolt us into doing so. Consider the *ficus Ruminalis* which, as I have already mentioned, Pliny the Elder labels *sacra* (sacred; *Nat.* 15.77). He goes on to elucidate its sacrality in two ways: firstly it is sacred *fulguribus ibi conditis* (from the lightning-struck objects buried there). Sacrality, it seems, can be catching. Yet this fig, Pliny continues, is more sacred *ob memoriam* (because of its memorial power). As we come face to face with a tree which is sacred by degrees – sacred from contagious proximity to other sacred objects, but more so from the memories it embodies – we are forced to acknowledge that no property-centric model of sacrality could ever do justice to what makes this fig sacred.

Throughout this book, trees like the *ficus Ruminalis* will show us how we have distorted and simplified our understanding of Roman sacrality through unthinking reliance on the restrictive model of sacrality found in the jurists. This is, however, by no means the only way in which the trees we are about to meet will enrich our understanding of Roman religion. For these sacred trees – loosely understood as trees which *mean* something in religious terms to those engaging with them – provoked questions which went straight to the heart of Roman efforts to understand the divine. As this book draws out such questions, the trees on which it shines a spotlight offer us a way into Roman theological thinking in action. Yet before we can allow the trees to take centre stage and prove their theological worth, it is necessary to confront any doubt over the place of 'theological thinking' in a book on Roman religion.

Thinking theologically through trees

Midway through his book on the Roman religious experience, Warde-Fowler sums up his attitude to the intellectual capabilities of those whose religion he is studying: 'the Romans were not a thinking people'.[27] Since 1911, when Warde-Fowler's book was published, this attitude has changed far more on the surface than in practice. Recent conferences have aimed to put the 'belief' back into Roman religion – or at least to argue about whether this is advisable – but the assumption persists that Roman religion is better understood as an orthopraxy rather than an orthodoxy:[28]

> A Roman was free to think what he liked about the gods; what mattered was what religious action he performed.[29]
>
> Paganism was not credal, but a matter of observing systems of ritual.[30]

This distinction is both artificial and misleading. Beliefs and religious action – the 'doxy' and the 'praxy' – are deeply entwined, and shape each other's development. Religious thinking or belief expresses itself through action as well as words, and religious actions must be accompanied by some kind of thinking about what is taking place and why. The common claim that Roman paganism was about unthinkingly 'going through the motions' is unrealistic, not to mention condescending. Moreover, as Dowden's use of 'credal' here suggests, it is also a deeply Christianocentric – indeed Protestant-centric – claim. For such constructions of Roman religion are born of a long history of scholarship which is deeply imbued with Protestant assumptions. Taking for granted that Catholicism consists of unthinking performance of 'rites', and thus sidesteps the element of belief central to Protestant doctrines of salvation, it is almost instinctive for these scholars to present Romans as 'proto-Catholics' in their unthinking reliance on actions alone.[31]

---

[27] Warde-Fowler 1911: 114. Cf. Rose 1948: 9, who categorises the Romans as 'a much slower-witted people' than the Greeks, whilst Halliday 1922: 30 sees the early Romans as 'a practical and unspeculative people'.

[28] A conference entitled 'Belief and its Alternatives in Greek and Roman Religion' was held at St Andrews in 2010; 'Disbelief in Antiquity' took place at Corpus Christi College, Oxford in 2013.

[29] Ogilvie 1969: 2.

[30] Dowden 2000: 2.

[31] See discussion on pp. 50–51 for the vivacity of anti-Catholic tendencies in early scholarship on Roman religion. Such thinking also continues to thrive in more recent scholarship. Ogilvie 1969: 38 is particularly overt about this, with his criticism of Roman pagans and their 'Catholic descendants'. Turcan 2000: 13 also boldly claims that 'the Roman attitude continued to impregnate the Catholic religion, at least until the advent of modernism or the Vatican II Council'.

Thinking theologically through trees

Slightly more nuanced approaches have also been advanced. Linder and Scheid, for example, argue that we do not need to exclude belief entirely from our portraits of Roman religion, but rather to acknowledge that, in Roman eyes, acting was believing:

La croyance romaine était avant tout un acte; c'était un savoir-faire et non un savoir-penser ... chez les Romains, croire c'était faire, c'était exécuter correctement les obligations cultuelles, ni plus, ni moins.[32]

Yet this is to sidestep the issue, and *does* push Roman belief or 'theological thinking' out of the frame; belief is retained in name only, reconfigured as action. Rüpke, by contrast, does allow 'thinking' a place in his portrait of Roman religion, but in such a way as to end up relegating it to the margins. Part one of his *Religion of the Romans* contains adjacent chapters entitled 'Religious Action' and 'Thinking about Religion', but only the first of these chapters is later expanded upon, with the whole of part two ('Religion in Action') covering topics like sacrifices, curses, temples and festivals; thus Rüpke undermines the significance of thinking in Roman religion by sheer volume of words alone. The book's structure also makes absolutely no attempt to integrate religious action and religious thinking: the content of the 'Thinking about Religion' chapter boils down to analysis of authors like Cicero and Varro, with 'religious thinking' presented as the preserve of an elite and academic niche, rather than something which structured and made sense of everyday lived experiences of Roman religion.[33] Thus, this book screams Rüpke's own stated belief that 'in the case of polytheistic religions, action, not belief is primary'.[34]

Moreover, when it comes to sacred trees, another factor exacerbates this ingrained tendency to treat Roman religion as the antithesis of a 'thinking religion'. This is a scholarly emphasis on the Roman 'soft spot for primal Golden Age simplicity', the cultural myth of a time in Rome's past which was characterised by rustic

---

[32] Linder and Scheid 1993: 50. Cf. Scheid 2005, in which he reasserts the same argument throughout: 'chez les Romains faire c'était croire' (282). Scheid's emphasis on Roman ritual savoir-faire has been hugely influential, with the phrase 'croire c'est faire' now considered a 'formule', as Prescendi 2007: 12 puts it.

[33] Cf. Dowden 1992: 8 and his claim that 'belief only became important for small, untypical sectors of the population'.

[34] Rüpke 2007: 87.

simplicity, moral purity and closeness to the gods.[35] Golden Age discourse seems to encourage scholars to presume that, in Roman eyes, sacred trees were also bound up with this idealised world of a morally simpler rustic past. Grimal, for example, believes that Rome's sacred trees could not fail to evoke Golden Age ideas:

> Dans Rome même, la présence des arbres sacrés rappelait à chaque instant le mythe de la vieille Rome 'arcadienne', ville de bergers, qui trouvera dans l'*Enéide* sa plus belle illustration.[36]

If sacred trees *were* part and parcel of Golden Age discourse – a discourse in which *rusticitas* (rusticity) equals *simplicitas* (simplicity) – then it is easy to see why scholars would presume that sacred trees must have been a simplistic phenomenon in Roman eyes. Yet there is little reason to follow Grimal's line of thinking here. Why presume, first of all, that sacred trees had to be perceived as something rural or rustic in Roman culture? The *ficus Ruminalis* was, after all, a landmark in the very heart of Rome which helped to construct urban Romans' sense of communal identity. More important, however, is the simple fact that sacred trees are markedly absent from Golden Age discourse. Certainly motifs prominent in this discourse emphasised that Golden Age Romans had a different attitude towards their trees: acorns were a staple food in those distant days (Ov. *Met*. 1.106; Juv. 6.10; Tib. 2.3.69; Lucr. 5.939–940); trees had not yet been cut down to make boats (Ov. *Met*. 1.94–95; Tib. 1.3.37; Cat. 64.11–18); it was even said that early men were born from trees, especially oaks (Juv. 6.12; Virg. *Aen*. 8.315; Stat. *Theb*. 4.275–281).[37] All these motifs paint a picture of a closer and more respectful relationship with trees than that enjoyed by inhabitants of the current age, but they do not suggest that these trees were considered sacred. Rather the thrust of these motifs is to emphasise a morally simpler way of life in which men were reliant on a hearty diet of local acorns and cut off from a world of morally polluting luxuries by their inability to sail.

---

[35] Dowden 2000: 104. For detailed discussion of this Roman soft spot see Evans 2008: *passim*, and especially 83–92 on the prominence of agricultural motifs and nostalgia for the countryside within Golden Age discourse; see also Lovejoy and Boas 1965: 41–70.

[36] Grimal 1943: 177.

[37] Campbell 2003: 330–353 provides useful lists of references for common motifs within creation and Golden Age narratives in Greco-Roman literature: for the motif of tree-born

Thinking theologically through trees

In fact only a handful of passages could be made to suggest that Roman thinkers associated the distant rustic past with a more *religious* attitude towards trees. One would be *Aeneid* 8.349–354, in which Evander tells Aeneas of the *religio* (religious awe) which causes his people to fear a nearby grove as the home of an unknown god; another would be Pliny's reflection that trees used to be the temples of *numina* ('numina'; *Nat.* 12.3), which prompts him to add that even today 'simple rural districts' (*simplicia rura*) dedicate trees of exceptional height to a god.[38] On other occasions we encounter a similar urban pose in which Roman thinkers associate *contemporary* rural living with religious responses to trees. Fronto, for example, informs the emperor Verus that on hearing of his recovery from illness (an illness in fact brought on by overeating), he offered thanks at every hearth, altar, sacred grove and consecrated tree, because he was 'living the rural life' (*rure agebam*; *Ver.* 2.6). The tone of this letter is tricky to gauge, but it is hard not to suspect that Fronto is writing to Verus at least somewhat tongue-in-cheek; there is certainly a generous hint of self-mockery as well. In similarly self-conscious fashion Tibullus – daydreaming about the simplistic and idyllic rural life he *could* be leading – pictures himself venerating a wreathed tree trunk (1.1.11–12). Wreathed trees are also presented by Apuleius as a 'stock' rural scene: making an elaborate claim for why he should be allowed time to give a speech on entering a city, he calls to mind how it is the way of religious travellers to stop for a moment on seeing a 'beech tree wreathed with skins' (*fagus pellibus coronata*; *Flor.* 1). Although these isolated passages do associate sacred trees and simple rusticity, we must not ignore their rhetoric and urban poise – their constructed image of 'rustic religion' – and blow them out of proportion. Even if we do want to acknowledge a wistful Golden Age tinge, or a sense of nostalgia

---

humans see 343; on the prominence of acorns and the absence of seafaring in Golden Age discourse see 343 and 345–346, respectively.

[38] As Evans 2008: 91–92 points out, we must not directly equate Virgil's portrait of Evander's community with Roman images of the Golden Age; there are many uncomfortable tensions within this brief snapshot of Evander's simple community, which is explicitly distanced from the Golden Age by the fact that Evander himself narrates, as a past event, Saturn's Golden Age in Latium (8.324–325). The difficulty of translating the slippery and multivalent *numina* will be discussed in detail at pp. 177–190.

for a simpler rural life, to *some* depictions of sacred trees, we must not let this lull us into presuming that such trees were thought of as a simplistic phenomenon.

In short, by claiming that sacred trees reveal Roman theological thinking in action, I intend not only to challenge the instinct to think of sacred trees as a simplistic 'Funny Old World' phenomenon, but also to overturn the persistent assumption that Roman religion had little to do with thinking. Rather, by examining what people both said and did in response to sacred trees in the Roman world, I aim to tease out the thinking these responses presupposed or prompted. And as it is a major claim of my book that such trees urged people to ask and explore questions about where they stood in relation to the divine, I term this thinking 'theological'. It is worth pausing at this word for a moment, however, as 'theology' is a term which fosters disagreement among scholars of Greco-Roman religion. To many the word suggests a rationalised, philosophical (and often Christian) *system*; whether it is of any use in understanding the diverse intellectual world of Greco-Roman paganism is becoming a matter of intense debate.[39] For me, however, the answer to this lies simply in the type of questions with which we see Greco-Roman thinkers engage, which we would not, in any other context, hesitate to call theological. What is the divine like? How does the divine manifest itself in the human world? What is the right relationship between humans and the divine? On the level at which theology is, to borrow the words of Eidinow, Kindt and Osborne, 'the articulation of conceptions, representations and questions about gods', it is surely hard to deny theology to the Greeks and Romans.[40] Indeed, where I expect far

---

[39] Leading the way here will be the forthcoming proceedings of a conference on 'The Theologies of Greek Religion', held in Cambridge in 2012 (Eidinow, Kindt and Osborne in press). In their introduction Eidinow et al. discuss the Christian connotations of the word 'theology', before proposing five different 'senses' or 'strengths' in how the term could usefully be applied to Greek religion, with a particular emphasis on whether these different strengths have to invoke the category of 'belief'. See also Kindt 2012: 188 for reflection on the connotations of systematisation and Christian thinking felt to be present in the word 'theology'.

[40] I would also follow Eidinow, Kindt and Osborne in press to the next 'strength' of theology which they propose, in which 'certain verbal or pictorial representations of gods, or certain practices, suggest, in a more or less underdetermined and vague way, certain possible sets of beliefs about gods'.

Thinking theologically through trees

more scepticism is in response to my claim that *trees* can prompt the articulation of such conceptions and questions about the divine. That said, it is more than time to turn to some trees. Consider a few examples, all of which will return to the limelight later in the book. Returning home from diplomatic service, Titus Pomponius Victor deposited a stone tablet high up in the Alps, inscribed with a prayer invoking *Silvane sacra semicluse fraxino* (Silvanus 'half shut up' in the sacred ash; *CIL* 12.103). How can a deity be 'shut up', let alone 'half shut up', in a tree? What kind of relationship did Victor imagine to exist between Silvanus and this particular tree, or perhaps the whole *genus* of ash? These questions I am, for now, going to leave hanging, and turn from the Alps to the grove of Dea Dia, a few miles outside of Rome. It is 8 February 183 CE and the priests who manage this grove are facing a crisis: a fig tree has sprouted from the roof of Dea Dia's temple. In response they sacrifice to many deities, including Adolenda Conmolenda Deferunda. Unsurprisingly attested only here, this goddess's name means Needing to be Burned, Needing to be Chopped Up, Needing to be Taken Down, and presumably captures the actions necessary to remove the troublesome fig, albeit rearranged in alphabetical order. But what kind of deity is this 'gerundive goddess'? And why did the removal of the fig prompt the Arvals to 'coin' a new goddess and offer her a one-off sacrifice? From the Alps to Rome, I move now to Delphi. Here the Athenians had once dedicated a bronze palm, which not only boasted showy golden dates, but also had a gold image of Athena attached to it, along with shield, spear and owls (Paus. 10.15.4; Plut. *Nic.* 13.3 and *De Pyth. or.* 397F). This striking statue only comes to our attention because of an omen involving crows pecking at its gold, but its unusual form certainly prompts further questions for us. What did this hybrid Athena-cum-palm say about the identity of the Athena imagined and worshipped here at Delphi? My final stop in this brief spin around the Roman world is the city of Tarraco, in Hispania Citerior. Here a palm tree had unexpectedly sprung up on an altar of Augustus. What did this mean? Was it just a 'fluke of nature'? Or did the fact that this was a palm – a type of tree imbued with victory associations – and on Augustus' altar, make it a portentous message of divine support for the emperor?

No doubt the Tarraconians implied as much when they informed Augustus himself about the palm, but unfortunately, he was unimpressed. Quintilian reports his snide reply: it is obvious how often you light fires on *my* altar (*Inst.* 6.3.77). Nevertheless, as soon as Augustus was dead, the Tarraconians minted coins with images of the altar and its protruding tree (for an example see Figure 1). What did they hope to say with this bold coinage, and what was it about Augustus' death and deification which allowed, or perhaps prompted, them to say it?

The handful of trees we have now briefly met have all given us glimpses of people 'thinking theologically' through trees, grappling to understand what trees might tell them about the nature of the divine and their relationship with it. They have also all had something to say about concerns at the heart of Roman religious discourse, be it the interpretation of portents, the impact of considering an emperor as in some way divine, or the way that statues of the gods communicate. Trees, then, can hardly be marginal to studies of Roman religion. Yet the assumption that Roman religion was not a 'thinking religion', combined with the instinct to view sacred trees as the preserve of the simplistic and deluded, means that scholars have never allowed trees to provoke *them* into serious thought about Roman religious thinking. Ferguson, for one, nicely captures the unthinking and dismissive attitude reserved for sacred trees. I quote here, in full, his discussion of the phenomenon:

Trees were sacred: Pliny has a long section on the subject. There was a sacred fig-tree on the Palatine. Augustus put a palm-shoot among his household gods; the emperors had a grove of laurels at Veii, plucking a branch to carry in triumph and replanting it; the Flavians had their own oak. Groves were especially sacred; witness Vergil or Ovid or Lucan.

> *In this grove, on this hill with its leafy summit*
> *some god lives – though I do not know who it is.*[41]

If we brush over sacred trees in this way – asserting their sacrality as a blanket and uninteresting rule, followed by a few unanalysed examples – then of course they *will* appear a simplistic and marginal element of Roman religion. But if we only allow sacred trees

---

[41] Ferguson 1970: 66. Ferguson gives no reference, but the lines he is translating are Virgil, *Aen.* 8.351–352.

Thinking theologically through trees

the space, approaching them as a phenomenon rooted in Roman religious thinking and practice, then, time and time again, they will take us to the heart of Roman grappling with no less a question than where they stood in relation to the divine.

Nor is this the end of what trees have to offer modern scholarship on Roman religion. So far I have focused on the factors which have led trees to be ignored in this scholarship, but trees are not its only victims. In many ways trees have simply had the rough end of the stick within a pattern of scholarly thought which relegates Roman religious thinking about their natural environment to a few pages of discussion at most. The stigma of the likes of Radnor and Frazer has exacerbated the fate of trees, but they are not alone: what of rivers, say, or lightning? The very language used to describe Roman thinking about the environment cuts it down to size. With terms such as 'cults of the land' or 'farm cult' scholars express that thinking about the environment is something which takes place in a locationally restricted sphere, a world apart from the urban sophistication of the religious thinking of Varro or Cicero or Tacitus.[42] The environment, it is implied, only registered on the radar of Roman thinkers when they were in the countryside, or during a few increasingly obscure festivals which were something of a throwback to Rome's early agricultural and pre-urbanised days, such as the *Cerealia* or *Robigalia* (with their respective concerns of cereal crops and wheat rust).[43] Thinking about the environment is thus at best a minor element of Roman 'theological thinking'. By virtue of being both non-urban and chronologically primary it is also very much a simplistic element: 'in the country', Ferguson observes, 'ancient religions persist when the more sophisticated town-dwellers have outgrown them'.[44]

Alongside the assumption that Roman intellectual engagement with the natural environment was a 'countryside phenomenon', North's influential article 'Religion and Rusticity' has also cemented the idea that the religious experiences of those

---

[42] Beard, North and Price 1998: 50; Turcan 2000: 37.
[43] Beard, North and Price 1998: 46 note the common scholarly assumption that, in the Roman republic, these 'agrarian festivals' were fast becoming 'antiquarian survivals', with no contemporary significance for urban-dwelling Romans.
[44] Ferguson 1970: 65.

inhabitants of the Roman world who happened to live in the countryside are well and truly lost to us.[45] Consequently, Roman religious thinking about the environment is felt to be something of a dead-end subject: citing a sacrificial prayer from Cato's *De agricultura*, mentioning a festival like the *Robigalia*, gesturing to the religious aura of groves (backed up by Seneca *Ep*. 41.3) and reciting Servius' list of 'specialist' agricultural deities, featuring the likes of Vervactor (First Plougher) and Subruncinator (Weeder; *G*. 1.21) would be deemed more than sufficient coverage.[46] Ovid's account of the *Parilia* (*Fast*. 4.721–805) also provides too tempting an account of a 'rural festival' for some to ignore. Awareness of its distinctively urbane and intellectual treatment at the hands of Ovid leads to cases of special pleading, so that the *Fasti* passage *can* give us access to the elusive world of 'rural religion': 'even reinterpreted by the poet', Turcan insists, 'this prayer conveys intensely the major concerns of the peasant trying to survive'.[47] Sweeping claims about the presence of the divine in the environment also commonly feature in this scholarship – 'Catullus, Vergil, Tibullus, Ovid are instinct with the power of the divine in the countryside'; 'the natural world ... would for many people have been shot through with the presence of the divine' – followed by a roll call of features such as groves, pools, caves and mountains to reinforce the point.[48]

[45] North 1995.
[46] Vervactor, Subruncinator and the ten other deities who constitute Servius' list are treated as classic examples of *Sondergötter*, or 'specialist deities', whose name corresponds precisely to their one function or sphere of interest. That these deities are only mentioned by Servius is not taken into account, nor is any reflection offered on the nature of Servius as a source; indeed this passage has been much abused by scholars of Roman religion, as I argue in a forthcoming essay.
[47] Turcan 2000: 42. Rüpke 2007: 114, on the other hand, does distinguish between the *Parilia* as a 'purification festival especially popular in rural areas' and its 'urban version', despite only having one source for both, namely the Ovidian passage.
[48] Ferguson 1970: 66; Rives 2007: 92. Ferguson's five-page section (1970: 65–69) on religion in the countryside covers Roman consciousness of the divine in trees, rivers and mountains, and makes the most of Servius' list of agricultural gods. Scheid 2003a: 48–50 and 73–75 devotes three pages to a list of the festivals (like the *Robigalia* and *Cerealia*) which constitute what he calls 'the agrarian cycle' and another three to the divine presence in groves, caves, pools and springs. Rives 2007: 89–92 gives over four pages to exploring how Romans 'perceived the presence of the gods in the natural world' (89). Seneca on groves is given most attention here, with springs, rivers, pools, caves and rocks dealt with in one paragraph. Turcan 2000: 37–42 discusses a few prayers in Cato's *De agricultura*, like that accompanying a sacrifice to purify an estate (*Agr*. 141); he

Sources and methodology

North is of course right about the difficulty of reconstructing lived experiences of religion in rural areas; and in my call to bring trees into the limelight I am hardly advocating that we attempt to do so. Rather, I want to make the obvious point that people who live in cities think about their natural environment too. You did not have to live on a farm to wonder what it means when a palm shoots up on an altar of Augustus. You did not have to live on a farm to worry about what to do when the *ficus Ruminalis* dies. The trees featured in this book stand as an exemplary case which urges us to stop pigeonholing and undermining Roman thinking about the natural environment, to acknowledge how often Romans asked questions of the world in which they found themselves and to recognise that these questions were not only challenging to answer, but theologically urgent too.

Roman religion: sources and methodology

In my whirlwind tour of the kinds of theological questions trees could raise in the Roman world, our evidence came from literary texts, inscriptions and a coin. This sample is characteristic of my book's scope, in which I embrace texts in Greek and Latin, prose and poetry, alongside epigraphical and visual material from across the Roman world, with the aim of producing the thickest possible description of the thinking which trees prompted about the divine. Yet a word of justification is perhaps needed for my heavy use of literary texts, and in particular poetry. Whilst most classicists would find nothing amiss in a historian of Roman religion citing, say, Tacitus or Varro, texts in verse more often raise eyebrows. The same also goes, to a lesser extent, for prose which flaunts its fictionality: is Lucian's *Vera historia* really a *suitable* source for a historian? Such worries seem to stem from an assumption that a historian 'extracts' value from a text by searching for any historical truths about its cultural context which it is 'concealing',

---

also enjoys Servius' list of agricultural deities as an illustration of 'the Roman sense of operational realism' (38), padding out Servius' list with further examples preserved in Augustine (as though this were an unproblematic source!); festivals like the *Parilia* and the *Cerealia* also feature.

19

and that in texts like Ovid's *Amores* these truths are far more concealed than, say, in Tacitus' *Annals*. The prevalence of this attitude among those engaging with Roman religion reveals how few academics have truly responded to the call of a much-lauded book now over two decades old, Feeney's *Literature and Religion at Rome*. Responding to a tendency among scholars of Roman religion to approach Latin literary texts only on the look-out for concealed or distorted nuggets of religious information, Feeney urges us to stop asking 'how religion is transmuted into literature'.[49] Instead we need to recognise that literature is itself a form of religion. Literature is what I would call a 'theological voice' (and a powerful one at that) which, in tandem with other voices, built up Roman religious discourse. Writing literature was one way of articulating and engaging with theological questions; reading literature was another. Thus, when I engage with sacred trees through Roman literary texts, I approach those texts as a form of theological thinking in action. It is of course vital to be sensitive to generic nuances and literary conventions when exploring the thinking expressed in these texts; but being 'literary' in no way weakens the value of these texts' theological insights.

As well as embracing a rich variety of literary texts, epigraphic evidence and visual sources, my book is also geographically wide-ranging in scope: a fig in the Roman forum sits alongside a bronze palm at Delphi and an ash in the Alps. Indeed the sample of trees showcased so far deliberately reflects the way this book embraces the culture both of the city of Rome and of its empire; this broad embrace also raises a vital question of terminology.[50] So far I have talked unreservedly of how trees enrich our understanding of *Roman* religion, but to what degree can, say, the response of the Tarraconians to their palm meaningfully be

---

[49] Feeney 1988: 1. Harrison 2007 makes a similarly persuasive call for how we should think about the intersection of Greek literature and religion: 'the various imaginary worlds of Greek literature themselves *constitute* Greek religious experience' (374). Jenkyns 2013: 208 provides a recent anti-Feeney voice: the problem with thinking about gods through Latin literature, he claims, is that they are 'mostly literary gods' (208); for Roman thinkers, 'no poet significantly modified their religious experience' (210).

[50] Rome of course had an empire long before it had emperors, and I use the term 'empire' here in this sense. Whilst Cato and Nonnus represent the chronological extremes of authors examined in this book, the majority of sources considered are late Republican or of the first two centuries CE.

Sources and methodology

understood as Roman? In recent years scholars have been keen to distance themselves from the idea that all inhabitants of the areas conquered by the Roman army quickly adopted Roman culture and identified themselves as Roman through a smooth process of 'Romanisation'.[51] In particular, those interested in the religious culture of the Roman empire have been warned against the temptation 'to produce a version of provincial religion which closely resembles the cults of the Roman republic'.[52]

Nevertheless, the theological questions with which the inhabitants of the Roman empire grappled when face to face with trees can, I argue, meaningfully be understood as Roman religious thinking. As the small city state of Rome expanded its territories into Italy and then the wider Mediterranean world, a new culture developed in tandem.[53] This culture was not Roman in the sense of being the culture of elite Roman citizens imposed on all people under their political sway; rather it was a multicultural, radically diverse and often internally contradictory culture which was always evolving, and in so doing continually shaped the identity of Roman citizens, as well as the empire's other inhabitants.[54] Some might find Hingley's metaphor for the dynamic process by which this Roman culture evolved helpful here; he speaks of Rome as the 'catalyst in the transformations

---

[51] For example, Millett 2002: 35–41, esp. 37, and Wallace-Hadrill 2008: 9–14. Mattingly 1997: 8–10 discusses how the term Romanisation has produced more 'heat' than 'light' (8), whilst Hingley 1996: 39–45 offers a historiographical sketch of the term. Keay and Terrenato 2001: ix–xii aim to reappropriate the term Romanisation from its 'value-laden' use in the past, and particularly its connection with colonialist ideology (ix).

[52] Woolf 2009: 244. See Rüpke 2011b for interesting reflection on what the term 'religion of empire' might mean, how it has been construed in past scholarship on Roman religion and how today we might meaningfully talk of a 'religious koine' in the empire: his suggested model revolves around the ideas of 'action', 'content' and 'media'.

[53] As Moatti 1997: 59 put it, through her conquests Rome discovered the other, and in so doing 'sa pensée va s'en trouver transformée'.

[54] Purcell's 2005 model of the Roman 'diaspora' has done much to ensure that we no longer imagine Roman citizens clustered in Rome, but rather woven into the fabric of the empire. As I engage with the theological thinking prompted by trees in this 'new cultural universe' (a phrase borrowed from Keay and Terrenato 2001: ix), more often than not it will be from the perspective of Romans who were Roman both in the sense of their citizenship and in the sense that they contributed to, and were influenced by, the multicultural fabric of the Roman empire. Yet this focus is due only to the restrictions imposed by our sources, our inescapable reliance on literary texts authored by elite Roman citizens, and certainly does not mean that I privilege some kind of 'purely Roman' thinking.

Rooting in

that occurred across Italy and then throughout the empire'.[55] Another insightful model for thinking about this cultural change is Wallace-Hadrill's concept of cultural 'bilingualism'. Reacting against a scholarly tendency to approach cultural change in the Roman empire in terms of either a fusion of existing identities or resistance to that fusion, Wallace-Hadrill proposes his model of bilingualism or multilingualism.[56] Inhabitants of the Roman empire were often literally bilingual or multilingual, but also culturally so: his model encourages us to see the Roman empire as made up of 'populations that can sustain simultaneously diverse culture-systems, in full awareness of their difference, and code-switch between them'.[57] Wallace-Hadrill's model is thus rather different from Hingley's, which frames Rome as the primary agency in the creation of this new culture. Both, however, agree on this: it was multiculturalism which was the distinctively *Roman* thing about the vibrant and ever-evolving culture of the Roman empire.

Greece became a Roman province in 146 BCE. Yet of all the nationalities which made up the Roman empire, it is the Greeks whom we often find it hardest to think of as in some way 'Roman': what Alcock terms 'the problem of Roman Greece' is largely a conceptual problem of our own.[58] For when it comes to Roman Greece, we cannot fail to be aware that this was a nation with a powerful cultural 'back story', a long and fêted history of cultural and literary achievement, which was now coming into contact with the catalyst for cultural transformation that was

---

[55] Hingley 2005: 55. Cf. Woolf 1997a: 347, who writes of this cultural change that 'the process might be compared to the growth of an organism that metabolizes other matter and is itself transformed by what it feeds on'. Hingley 2005: 55–56 goes on to argue that 'The use of the term "Roman" for the constellation that formed the empire is justified by the fact that these highly variable individual cultures were incorporated into an entity that called itself by this term.' Cf. Keay and Terrenato 2001: ix, who also emphasise that this 'new cultural universe' called itself Roman.
[56] Wallace-Hadrill 2008: 13.
[57] Wallace-Hadrill 2008: 27–28. Bendlin 1997: 62 also adopts a linguistic model to describe religious change within the Roman empire, suggesting that provincials 'chose to model their religious discourse on a semantics which was influenced by Rome'. Bendlin's model shares much with Hingley's, with Rome framed as the key catalyst or influence in the creation of a new culture. See Osborne and Vout 2010: 238 on the limitations of such linguistic models.
[58] Alcock 1993: 1. Alcock 1993: 8–17 provides a potted history of Greece under Roman rule.

Rome. Indeed Spawforth has recently argued that under Roman influence Greek culture, far from being diluted, in fact experienced an active 're-Hellenising', thanks to a focus on reliving the Greek past which was designed to hold up the idea of 'classical' Greece as a store of cultural excellence shared by Romans as well as Greeks.[59] Add to this Horace's much quoted *Graecia capta ferum victorem cepit et artis intulit agresti Latio* (captured Greece conquered her savage conqueror and brought the arts to rural Latium; *Ep.* 2.1.156–157), and it is easy to see the attraction of the idea that Greek culture was particularly resistant to transformation within the Roman empire.[60] Yet whilst the cultural outputs of Roman Greece were clearly Greek, they were not the same as the outputs of fifth-century Athens; they were in some way Roman too, but articulating the nature of this new cultural reality is far from easy.

This book comes face to face with this conceptual problem when considering theological thinking about trees from the Roman world which happens to be expressed by Greeks, and/or written in Greek. It can be an intellectual stretch to think of this as 'Roman' religion. Yet 'Roman religion', in my terms, is shorthand for the diverse religious experiences of those living within the Roman world. This book investigates the religious thinking of the empire, in all its colourful difference. Differing perspectives on religious practice, or the nature of the divine, are – I argue – meaningfully studied together because of the way they contribute to the multicultural world of the Roman empire, enjoying the potential to influence and feed off each other. Referring to religious thinking expressed in Greek as 'Roman' may sometimes jar a little, but the benefits of studying these different perspectives side by side far outweigh the drawbacks of using the term. With sensitivity to the

---

[59] Spawforth 2012: 2. We have also long accepted that elements of 'Greekness' could make Roman citizens almost *more* Roman: being 'Hellenised' was a mark of social standing and a tour of Greece an almost mandatory part of elite Roman education, on which see Rawson 1985: 10 and Alcock 1993: 16.

[60] This idea of a push and pull between a distinct Greek culture and a distinct Roman culture runs counter to the model I have favoured of the Roman empire as a space for mutual cultural transformation. As both Woolf 1994 and Wallace-Hadrill 2008: 17–28 have pointed out, we tend to think of Hellenisation and Romanisation as competing processes, but in fact these two forces worked interdependently, as once-distinct cultures rubbed off on each other to produce something new.

cultural nuances and points of reference informing a Greek passage, the limitations of the term can be transcended.

It is also helpful to reflect on recent scholarship's valuable emphasis on how 'permeable' the categories of 'Greek' and 'Roman' were in the Roman world, especially when it comes to religion.[61] Greek religion powerfully informed religion in the Roman world: that Augustus was initiated into the Eleusinian mysteries is just one incident which should remind us what a 'negotiable boundary' there was between Greek and Roman religion.[62] Greek religion also came with the authority of age and a rich literature of myths and hymns: Greek religious traditions, practices and imagery provided a model through which thinkers in the Roman world conceptualised their own religious practices and thought through their own theological questions. In short, it is not intellectually beneficial to think of 'Greek religion' and 'Roman religion' as separate categories.

A final word of caution about one particular Greek is now needed. Some of the Greek authors featured in this book flaunted their multilingual approach to their cultural environment: think of Plutarch, the Greek with Roman citizenship who wrote biographies pairing up famous Greeks and Romans.[63] Yet Pausanias – who has a weighty presence in this book – might seem to many a devotee of a 'purely Greek' past, as we imagine him traipsing round Greece, cataloguing its old glories, apparently so impervious to present reality that he left many Roman monuments out of his otherwise comprehensive descriptions.[64] Indeed Pausanias has even been characterised as defiantly resistant to Roman rule and culture.[65] Certainly we know nothing about his readership and

---

[61] Alcock 2002: 86. Cf. Woolf 1994: 118 and Beard, North and Price 1998: 225.
[62] Beard, North and Price 1998: 223.
[63] As a particularly vivid example of this multilingualism, Swain 1996: 146 discusses how Plutarch's cultural double vision enables him to present even Flamininus' notorious political interference in Greece as both domination ('Greek' view) and liberation ('Roman' view).
[64] For this characterisation of Pausanias see Elsner 1992: 17–18 and Rutherford 2001: 41. Arafat 1996: 212–213 explains away the exclusion of Roman monuments as Pausanias' choice to focus on classical originals.
[65] Elsner 1992: 5. A lot of energy has been expended on trying to gauge the level of Pausanias' hostility to Roman rule: see Habicht 1985: 117–125, Arafat 1996: 202–215 and Pretzler 2007: 28–29. Many discuss Paus. 8.27.1, which refers to residents of Greek

A plan for growth

cannot assume his book was used as a handy travel guide by religiously minded Romans on their grand tour of Greece. Yet whilst Pausanias may seem to be stuck in the past in religious terms, we can also understand this as his personal way of constructing his religious experience of the present, what Elsner has termed 'a sanctified present-past'.[66] Pausanias paints a picture of what religion in Greece meant to him in the second century CE, and as such his voice has to be present in a study of religion in the multicultural empire we call Roman.

Considering my broad understanding of 'Roman religion', it should come as no surprise that my interest in Roman sacred trees celebrates variety and disagreements in the thinking which trees prompted across the Roman world. This book expects no 'orthodox' Roman position on what it means for a tree to be sacred. Yet at the same time, we will find that unifying themes and concerns do emerge from the thinking prompted by trees across the cultural expanse of the Roman world. Consequently my discussion of sacred trees will not be divided on geographical or chronological lines; rather the sacrality of trees will be explored thematically, with the book structured around the kinds of theological questions which trees raised in the Roman world.

A plan for growth

Today our thinking about Roman sacred trees has come to a standstill: Ferguson's 'trees were sacred' sums up the unwillingness which permeates scholarship on Roman religion to push our thinking about such trees. A plan for growth is thus badly needed. Yet before we can attempt a fresh start, it is important to understand why we have arrived at this standstill. Figures like Radnor cannot be held solely responsible for this academic aversion to Roman sacred trees. In fact it is Frazer and company who have done the real damage

---

cities who were removed κατὰ συμφορὰν (ἐπὶ) ἀρχῆς τῆς Ῥωμαίων (by the disaster of (/ during) Roman rule): arguments rage over whether ἐπί should be inserted here, making this disaster take place during Roman rule, rather than Roman rule itself being the disaster. Habicht 1985: 120 and Arafat 1996: 202 argue for ἐπί, Swain 1996: 353 against.

[66] Elsner 1992: 20. Cf. Alcock 1993: 202, who writes that, for Pausanias, 'sacred places and images became crucially important ... as a channel by which that past became immanent in the present'.

here. For in the nineteenth- and early twentieth-century scholars of comparative religion and the first scholars of Roman religion – then developing as a discipline in its own right – placed sacred trees on a pedestal. For them sacred trees provided vivid proof of their major claim that in all primitive cultures, that of Rome included, religion began with an animistic stage. Whether you turn to Tylor's famous *Primitive Culture* (1871), rarely read works like Mrs Philpot's *The Sacred Tree* (1897) or specialist studies of Roman religion like Carter's *The Religion of Numa* (1906), the story told is the same. When confronted with a tree, a primitive thinker would mistake its agency for an internal spirit animating the tree. This then led him to worship the material tree, something these Protestant-centric scholars delighted to mock as Catholic-style idolatry.

The methodology and priorities of this early scholarship are today distinctly unfashionable, thanks to which sacred trees have become something of a baby thrown out with the bathwater: indeed sacred trees are almost invisible in modern scholarship on Roman religion. Yet ironically, the very limited engagement we do have with Roman sacred trees is practically dictated by the intellectual legacy of the early scholarship in which sacred trees enjoyed their glory days. Distaste for the materiality of sacred trees is still very much present today, whilst the idea that trees were considered sacred because of an 'animating spirit' also returns, albeit in somewhat modified form. We need only think here of Turcan's 'frisson of the supernatural': trees are sacred, as another contemporary scholar puts it, because they have a 'divine aura' to them.[67] This long and colourful history of scholarly thought about sacred trees is my subject in Chapter 2, as I set out the intellectual precedents which inform current assumptions about Roman sacred trees. In particular I show that, from the comparativists to the present day, it has gone unquestioned that Roman religious conceptions of trees were primitive and simplistic because they centred on a particular understanding of both their matter and their agency.

My next aim is to turn this kind of thinking on its head. For in fact, it is thanks to their status as living material objects that trees so often raised theological questions for Roman thinkers. One of

---

[67] Turcan 2000: 39; Rives 2007: 91.

A plan for growth

the most pressing was this: what did it mean to consider as sacred a material object which happens to be alive? In Chapter 3 I begin to tackle this question, asking how the matter of a tree mattered to Roman conceptions of its sacrality. The famous *ficus Ruminalis* plays a prominent role here as an example of a tree whose sacrality was ambiguously bound up with its material identity, thanks to the fig's vulnerability and the inescapable fact that it will eventually die. Chapter 4 then continues to push this same question. As living objects, trees cry out for arboricultural care and human interference. Yet this obvious truth sits uneasily with the scholarly consensus that to consider an object sacred in Roman culture meant treating its matter as inviolable. Challenging this consensus, Chapter 4 puts pressure on Roman understanding of what it meant to interfere with the matter of sacred trees, focused in particular through a rich body of inscriptions from the Arval grove.

In Chapter 5 I tackle from a different angle the fact that trees are alive. The behaviour of trees may often seem outside of human control, and here I explore how this unpredictable behaviour enriched Roman understanding of ways in which the divine might express itself in the natural environment. The idea of portents looms large in this chapter, as I consider how Roman thinkers might try to distinguish between natural and divine causation in arboreal behaviour, not to mention the difficulty of deciding what such behaviour meant, if it was deemed of divine significance. This new theme – how the divine can be 'read' in the natural environment – is then developed in Chapter 6. Here I examine the diverse ways in which trees were imagined to stand as 'points of contact' between the human world and the divine world. Why call Jupiter 'of the Beech'? Why plant a fig in the shrine of Rumina? Why say that the laurel is sacred to Apollo? The trees encountered in this chapter, each in their own way, fleshed out Roman imagination of the nature and identity of individual deities.

For scholars of Roman religion, the image of Radnor and friends decorating a tree in underwear is, in many ways, not much of a laughing matter. For our instinct to relegate sacred trees to 'Funny Old World' has impoverished our understanding of Roman religion. Be it the niceties of negotiating imperial cult, the purpose of sacrifice or the significance of a cult site's layout, trees turn out to be a surprisingly good way of thinking about many aspects of Roman religion, in all its micro-level detail. Yet this is only the beginning of what trees have to offer us. Going far beyond these individual contributions, trees also urge us to revive the way we approach Roman religion, how we think about it 'in the round'. Thinking about trees encourages us to throw out the previously influential model of sacrality, which revolves around the ideas of consecration and property, and to adopt a far more flexible approach to what sacrality means in the Roman world. Trees also make us confront the way we have written the natural environment out of our portraits of Roman religion – and this is to miss out on much. For trees open up a picture of Roman thinkers engaging with their natural environment as theologians, as that environment challenged them with questions about how it might intersect with the divine and, the corollary of this, where they themselves stood in relation to the divine. Thinking about trees may not look like the most obvious of ways to get to grips with Roman theology, but their roots into Roman religion run deep.

CHAPTER 2

A BRIEF HISTORY OF TREE THINKING: THE ENDURING POWER OF ANIMISM

Tree thinking: getting back to roots

Today trees sit in a blindspot for scholars of Roman religion. Yet if we take a long view back over the history of scholarship on Roman religion, this sidelining of trees becomes an ironic coda to almost a century and a half of unmitigated scholarly enthusiasm for sacred trees. Why have sacred trees been pushed to the margins in this way? What effect has the sacred tree's fall from grace had on our own scholarship? Understanding the history of our thinking about sacred trees – the way it moulds our presumptions about their significance within Roman religion and dictates what questions we ask about them – is the major aim of this chapter.

From early in the nineteenth century until well into the twentieth century sacred trees were overwhelmed with scholarly attention, thanks to the way they were felt to speak to concerns at the heart of intellectual culture during this period. The nineteenth century saw thinkers much exercised by questions about the origins of mankind and human culture, and when it came to religious studies the central aim was to identify the most primitive form of religion and then to trace its adaptations and developments down to the present day.[1] Confidently titled books such as Caird's *The Evolution of Religion* (1893) or Allen's *The Evolution of the Idea of God* (1897) say it all. Certainly the search for the originary germ of religion was by no means entirely new – Hume's *Natural History of Religion* had argued in 1757 that this lay in people's fear of natural forces and consequent deification of them – but the nineteenth century saw an intensification of this particular

---

[1] On which see Lessa and Vogt 1972: 1; Sharpe 1975: 30; Gellner 1999: 10–11; Ackerman 2002: 2; Bonnet 2007: 1. Harrison sums up this mania for origins when she opens her *Introductory Studies in Greek Art* (1885) by observing how she and her contemporaries 'seek with a new-won earnestness to know the genesis, the *origines* of whatever we study' (2).

scholarly mode. No small part was played in this by the influence of Darwin's evolutionary theories, which sanctioned the rationale of pursuing an original idea and tracing its developments in linear, chronological fashion.[2] At the same time, this mode of scholarly enquiry was also deeply Christianocentric, as scholars pondered how it was possible that the most primitive religious thinking could eventually evolve into the sophistication of the Christian faith, something Caird sums up in laying out the central methodological questions for those who take 'the idea of development' as 'a key to the history of religion'.[3] Firstly we have to ask ourselves how religious consciousness develops, and secondly 'how the religious consciousness itself advances from one form to another, from the lowest awe of the supernatural which we can call a religion, to the highest form of Christian faith'.[4]

Besides the impetus from Darwinian theories, a flood of ethnographic material available through exploration of the farther corners of the British empire also provided nineteenth-century scholars with case studies to fuel their passion for primitive religious behaviour.[5] Until then they had relied on ancient cultures for such material, but now data from 'savage' communities understood to be at a primitive stage of development could be seen to corroborate their findings from the ancient world. Pervasive imagery of 'savages' as children reinforced their perceived role as substitutes for members of a chronologically originary culture.[6]

---

[2] Rose 1934: 4 describes the nineteenth century as the time of 'the promotion of Evolution ... from the status of a theory held here and there to that of a recognized and fundamental fact'. Gellner 1999: 10–11 notes how evolutionary thinking about society and religion during this period was greatly strengthened by Darwin's theories, but did not solely depend on them; indeed some formulations of these ideas predated *The Origin of Species* (1859).
[3] Caird 1893: 175.
[4] Caird 1893: 176.
[5] On which see Stocking 1987: 78–109 and Dorson 1968: esp. 332–333. The acquisition of such valued data could, as Young 1985: 18 notes, be framed as offering 'intellectual underpinnings for defences of imperialism'.
[6] For example, Caird 1893: 178 observes that 'the savage, like the boy, seems to live almost entirely out of himself', whilst Philpot 1897: 72–73 writes that 'to the modern mind ... the idea of man taking origin from a tree will seem in the highest degree fantastic, but to the primitive intelligence it probably presented no greater difficulty than the extraction of the new baby from the parsley bed does to the modern child'. For other examples see Caird 1893: 202 and 204 and Hartland 1891: 25. Müller 1901: 126–127 was unusual in his questioning of the value of comparing children and savages.

Moreover, whilst these 'savage' communities were welcomed as uniquely informative because their civilisation lagged so far behind that of European culture, Europe also had something to offer those on the hunt for primitive religion: European folklore and rural traditions were valued for the way they were felt to preserve remnants or 'survivals' of primitive behaviour and thinking.[7] Scholars found that they could build up and thicken their analysis of primitive religious ideas by examining them through these three lenses – ancient culture, modern savage culture and European folklore – and thus comparative religion was born.

Arboreal ardour

One feature which seemed to recur whichever of the lenses the comparativists looked through was a religious response to trees which they termed 'tree worship'. As Barlow put it in 1866, 'most nations, if not all, would appear, at some time or other, to have had a sacred tree'.[8] A veritable craze for the 'sacred trees' which received this worship spread through the academic world. At first this was particularly intense in Germany, where the craze was fuelled by a vogue for defining German national identity and distinctiveness in terms of their woodland past. German racial hardiness was ascribed to their origins as men of the woods and their racial purity to the barrier of dense forests enclosing the fatherland. Tacitus' *Germania*, with its ferocious Germans decimating Roman forces in impenetrable forests, was adopted as the definitive account of their pristine identity, whilst the robust oak became

---

[7] It was Tylor 1871a: 14–15 who first introduced the term 'survivals', defining them as 'processes, customs, opinions, and so forth, which have been carried on by force of habit into a new state of society different from that in which they had their original home … [which] thus remain as proofs and examples of an older condition of culture out of which a newer has been evolved' (15). See Preus 1987: 136–137 and Sharpe 1975: 54–55 on the role of 'survivals' in Tylor's thinking. Interest in European folklore grew out of antiquarian investigation – known as 'popular antiquities' – which stretched back to the sixteenth century, with the Society of Antiquaries founded in 1717. This area of research was renamed 'folklore' by Thoms in 1846. For an overview of this development see Stocking 1987: 53–56.

[8] Barlow 1866: 97. Lubbock 1870: 206 too observes that the worship of sacred trees is 'one among many illustrations that the human mind, in its upward progress, everywhere passes through the same or very similar phases'.

a favoured symbol of Germanness.[9] These racial ideas both motivated and found support in *Altdeutsche Wälder*, a collection of German woodland folk tales produced by the Brothers Grimm between 1813 and 1816, after which tree-focused explorations of national identity appeared at a noticeable rate.[10] It is into this cultural context that Mannhardt then launched his influential two-volume *Wald- und Feldkulte* (1875–1877), a work which blended German nationalistic enthusiasm for trees with comparativist enthusiasm for tree worship. Mannhardt paired a first volume on trees and vegetation in German folklore with a second in which he examined survivals of *Baumkultus* (tree worship) in modern European customs, emphasising its ancient roots by opening the volume with a chapter on Greco-Roman *Baumkultus*.

Mannhardt's fascination with both ancient tree worship and the tree worship latent in contemporary European traditions reflected – and indeed strongly influenced – wider comparativist interest in tree worship, which was predominantly British.[11] Popular anecdotes reminded these scholars that as recently as the sixteenth century a Finnish pastor had to get locals drunk on brandy before they would chop down their sacred tree, and in the form of survivals tree worship was felt to be very close at hand.[12]

---

[9] Schama 1995: 75–134 explores in depth a 'virtual oak-fetish' in late eighteenth- and early nineteenth-century Germany (103).

[10] This tradition was still going strong in 1935 when Kober's unambiguously titled *Deutscher Wald, Deutsches Volk* appeared.

[11] Allen 1897: 138, Philpot 1897: 58 and Frazer 1911: 47 all acknowledge a debt to Mannhardt. See Sharpe 1975: 50–51 on Mannhardt's influence and Stocking 1995: 139 on Frazer's particularly strong debt to Mannhardt, among other scholars on whose work he built. Stocking 1987: 56 also notes how German scholarship became 'the ultimate court of appeal' for early British comparativists, whilst Dorson 1968: 44–48 discusses interaction between early British and German 'folklorists'. In comparison with Germany, there was a far less pronounced national aspect to British scholarly enthusiasm for sacred trees. Frazer 1911: 7–8 opens a chapter on tree worship with nostalgic reference to the time when 'a squirrel might leap from tree to tree for nearly the whole length of Warwickshire', and Philpot 1897: 164 similarly reflects on the recently abandoned custom of placing mistletoe on the altar at York Minster at Christmas time, which, she argues, is 'a direct legacy from the Druids'. Yet, in general, British investigations into sacred trees did not foreground a picture of their own past as arboreal devotees. This, however, is not to deny a nationalistic aspect to many other areas of British comparativist studies: Celtic folklore, a hugely popular area of enquiry, was often spun so as to contribute to nationalistic agendas in Scotland, Wales and Ireland, on which see Dorson 1968: 392–439.

[12] Ouseley 1819: 397–398 and Jennings 1890: 43 record this anecdote. Illustrating this reliance on 'survivals' by those investigating the phenomenon of tree worship, Philpot 1897: vii insists that 'no other form of pagan ritual ... has left behind it such persistent

Getting back to roots

These ranged from the well-known May Day celebrations to far more obscure instances, such as the belief in Devon and Cornwall that oaks are inhabited by elves, or the practice on 'out-of-the-way Swedish farms' of pouring milk and beer over tree roots.[13] Arguments over whether Christmas trees were a recently imported German custom or actually a remnant of an ancient Egyptian tree cult also constituted a lively point of debate.[14] Indeed these scholars saw tree worship in so many aspects of both contemporary European and ancient cultures that it easily led to scholarship with a *farrago* feel, as seen in the contents list for chapter six of Jennings' *Cultus Arborum*:

Usefulness of the Ash-tree – Its position among Sacred Trees – The Queen of Trees – Mythology of the Ash – Scotch Superstitious Usages – The 'Ash Faggot Ball' of Somersetshire – Pliny and others on the Serpent and the Ash – The Ash as a medium of cure of complaints – Anecdotes – Phallic Associations – The New-birth – Ireland and the Ash – The Juniper-Tree – The Madonna and the Juniper – The Elm-Tree – Mythology of the Elm – The Apple-tree – Mythological Allusions to the Apple-tree – The Pine tree – Wind Spirits – German Superstitions – The Oak-tree – Universal Sacredness of the Oak – The Oak of the Hebrew Scriptures – Classic Oaks – Socrates and his Oath – Greek Sayings – The Trees Speaking – Sacred Ash of Dodona – Legend of Philemon and Baucis – The Hamadryads – The Yule Log – St Boniface – Mysteries connected with the Oak – Christmas-trees.

Others added into this mix examples of tree worship from contemporary 'primitive' cultures. In just five pages Tylor turns from 'the negro woodman', to the oak of Dodona, to current folk tradition about an old tree in the Rugaard forest.[15] Likewise we find Frazer comparing Ovambo women's belief that branches of a certain tree attract rain with the European custom of drenching trees when they are cut at Whitsuntide, whilst a south Slavonian peasant suddenly reminds him of Virgil's story of Polydorus.[16]

---

traces', whilst Jennings 1890: 3–4 also emphasises that sacred trees 'linger among the last vestiges of heathenism long after the advent of a purer creed'.

[13] Philpot 1897: 65 on elves. Tylor 1873: 228 on milk and beer pouring (this anecdote is not mentioned in the very first edition of *Primitive Culture*).

[14] Barlow 1866: 95 and Jennings 1890: 84 argue for Egyptian origins, Philpot 1897: 165 for German provenance.

[15] Tylor 1871b: 197–201.

[16] Frazer 1911: 46–47 and 32–33. Frazer's chapter on tree worship (1911: 7–58) is packed with material from contemporary 'primitive' cultures.

33

A brief history of tree thinking

Few scholars did not express their enthusiasm for sacred trees through such a comparative model. By far the most influential exception was Boetticher, who in 1856 published his *Der Baumkultus der Hellenen nach den Gottesdienstlichen Gebräuchen und den Überlieferten Bildwerken*.[17] Boetticher understood himself to be investigating a phenomenon at 'die Ursprünge des Polytheismus', but he was not searching for religion's most primitive form.[18] Nor was he a fully-fledged comparativist. He devoted his attention to Greek, and despite the title, briefly to Roman *Baumkultus*; that of other ancient cultures he restricts to 40 pages of his 544-page book, and contemporary practices make no appearance at all. Having begun working life as an apprentice in the construction industry, Boetticher then studied at the Bauakedemie in Berlin, the first step on his academic career as an expert in architectural ornaments.[19] Alongside many books on his specialism he also published on medieval wooden architecture, before turning his hand to ancient Greek religious architecture.[20] From here it must have seemed an organic step to his book on Greek *Baumkultus*. In sacred trees Boetticher saw combined in one entity both his old-time interests in architecture and wood, and his more recently developed interest in Greek religion. Boetticher's book on *Baumkultus* was thus the culmination of a personal academic journey, not a product of contemporary scholarly and cultural trends, and his interpretation of sacred trees was correspondingly idiosyncratic and 'architectural'. Boetticher understood trees as an essential preliminary for any cult practice, providing the wood for sacrifices and the branches used in other rites:

Denn nur wenn man weiss dass die Götterverehrung mit den Zweigen eines heiligen Baumes ganz untrennbar verknüpft ist, wie kein Gebet ohne dieselben ausgeübt werden kann, dann begreift man erst vollkommen was Kultus der Bäume sei,

---

[17] Seidensticker was another, far less influential exception; his *Waldgeschichte des Alterthums* (1886) focused on defining ancient terminology for wooded spaces, including those considered sacred.

[18] Boetticher 1856: 2.

[19] *Neue Deutsche Biographie* 1955: 412.

[20] Two books on this latter topic were written in the decade leading up to his work on *Baumkultus*, which was the culmination of his publishing career: *Andeutungen über das Heilige und das Profane in der Baukunst der Hellenen* appeared in 1846 and *Der Hellenische Tempel in seiner Raumanlage für Zwecke des Cultus* in 1849.

Getting back to roots

dann erklärt sich die Verwendung ihrer Zweige, Früchte und Hölzer in den heiligen Riten, dann erschliesst sich die Ursache warum man die Stiftung von Sacra und Kultusstätten von der Möglichkeit abhängig machen musste der Gottheit heiligen Baum pflanzen und zu den Kultriten benutzen zu können.[21]

In addition to this central claim, Boetticher saw trees as an originary form of both temples and idols, primitive natural versions of elements of cult sites which would later be manmade.[22] Boetticher's arguments were of fairly limited influence on the comparative interpretations of tree worship which appeared throughout the latter half of the nineteenth century, but as a weighty assertion that *Baumkultus* stood at the heart of Greco-Roman religion, Boetticher's work had a resounding impact and indelibly marked Greco-Roman sacred trees on the comparativists' map.[23]

Arboreal analysis

The study of comparative religion provoked intense religious discomfort within the Protestant culture of nineteenth-century Germany and Britain, not least among its practitioners, many of whom were closely linked with the Church.[24] For in an academic world where the aim of the game was to trace the development of religion from its earliest origins to the present day, where all religious ideas – even the most sophisticated Christian ones – could be traced back to primitive, deluded thinking, it is easy to see how the fear grew that contemporary religion would also be seen as 'a mere survival', to use James' terms, or an 'atavistic relapse into a mode of thought which humanity in its more enlightened examples has

---

[21] Boetticher 1856: 13.
[22] Boetticher 1856: 8 and 16.
[23] Boetticher's understanding of trees as primitive idols was echoed by Barlow 1866: 97 and Philpot 1897: 28, and can still be encountered today, as seen for example in Dowden 2000: 34. Likewise his portrayal of trees as precursors to temples influenced both Seidensticker 1886: 144 and Jennings 1890: 4. (Philpot 1897: 14 also imaginatively describes a tree in the Indian kingdom of Travancore as 'the cathedral of the district', appearing not to notice the irony of her description of the tree's end, chopped down by a Christian missionary and used to build a mere 'chapel' on the site.)
[24] See Engel 1983: 1–6 on the 'overwhelmingly clerical society' which was nineteenth-century Oxbridge academia (1) and Winstanley 1940: 83–96 on the Anglican monopoly of Cambridge University, which was 'practically a preserve of the Church of England' (83).

outgrown'.[25] To borrow Lang's blunt phrasing in his *The Making of Religion* (1898), comparativism could swiftly lead to the 'inference that religion is untrue'.[26] Everything, therefore, was at stake in how the comparativists dealt with such implications.[27]

Tylor adopted one approach: passing the buck. Since his observations are 'made rather from an ethnographic than a theological point of view', or so he pleads when introducing the first volume of *Primitive Culture*, 'there has seemed little need of entering into direct controversial argument, which indeed I have taken pains to avoid as far as possible'.[28] Despite this non-confrontational approach, by the end of the volume Tylor still felt uneasy enough about the reception of his work to re-emphasise his position: 'While dwelling at some length on doctrines and ceremonies of the lower races, and sometimes particularizing for special reasons the related doctrines and ceremonies of the higher nations, it has not seemed my proper task to work out in detail the problems thus suggested among the philosophies and creeds of Christendom.'[29] Farnell was slightly more prepared than Tylor to face up to the implications of comparative work on religion. He acknowledges the worrying idea that 'the solidarity of the human family appears stronger than we might have supposed', but comfortingly adds that to presume all higher races passed through all savage stages would be to ignore 'the possibility that it was just by avoiding some particular detrimental institution that some of the higher peoples were able to proceed on their path to progress'.[30]

---

[25] James 1902: 495 and 490. As Stocking 1987: 188 argues, the fact that the comparativists were prepared 'to defend a natural rather than a supernatural causation' when it came to cultural development suggests that many had already experienced a 'considerable prior weakening of religious belief' before setting out on such an intellectual path.

[26] Lang 1898: 51.

[27] Ackerman 2002: 2 understands comparativist focus on ancient cultures as a 'transparent ruse' designed to deflect attention from the implications of their research, but scholarly expertise and the need to investigate the earliest forms of religious behaviour were surely factors of at least equal weight here.

[28] Tylor 1871a: 21.

[29] Tylor 1871a: 386. Preus 1987: 153 notes how 'the gentle Tylor does not try to drive theology from its corner'.

[30] Farnell 1905: 12. Cf. Caird 1893: 202–204, who also found a way of framing these implications in a fairly positive light. He observes how 'even the rudest religious systems have represented in them – though, no doubt, in a shadowy and distorted way – all the elements that enter into the highest Christian worship' (202) and for him this is not a

Getting back to roots

A more respectable route for Christianity's development is thus kept clear. By 1896, however, far more challenging views were coming from the mouth of no less prominent a figure than the president of the Folk-Lore Society. In his presidential address for that year Clodd boldly elucidated Christianity's debt to ancient paganism regarding the eucharist, baptism and the doctrine of the virgin birth: the massive furore which erupted over whether the presidential address should even be published reveals the intensity of the comparativists' concern about their public theological standing.[31] Nor was Clodd the first to articulate Christianity's debt to the pagan past. Several years earlier the more idiosyncratic Waring, disturbed by the realisation that 'all our modern Christian doctrine has its roots in Pagan thought, and has not been given by supernatural revelation to man', announces that we should give up on Christianity, and instead give 'the Religion of Christ' a trial.[32] In this careful move, Waring emphasises that the results of comparative investigation do not force him to turn his back entirely on his Christian faith, but do urge him to adopt a radically anti-traditionalist and anti-doctrinal approach to that faith; he turns his back on the history of the Church, not on Jesus. In short, even with the most non-confrontational of scholarly approaches, the advent of comparative religion meant that traditional Christian faith could never look quite the same again.

Yet despite this uneasy relationship with the Church, comparativist research was still deeply Protestant in tone and ideology. Indeed one way in which scholars deflected the worrying implications of their research for the Church – which for them meant the Protestant Church – was to align Catholicism and primitive savage

---

matter for theological concern but rather a warming thought, a realisation that 'humanity lives already in the most immature' (203–204).

[31] Dorson 1968: 251–256 discusses this controversial speech. Clodd relied heavily on Frazer for his data in this address, a figure whose *Golden Bough* likewise provoked no small controversy, especially thanks to its alignment of Jesus' resurrection with other 'savage' models of the sacrifice of a fertility god. See Farnell 1905: 6 on the 'mistrust, even hostility' provoked by Frazer's attempts 'to trace what may be called the anthropological genesis of the central idea of Christianity itself'. Stocking 1995: 147–148 discusses the conflict between Frazer's theories and Christian doctrine, but also the potential for Christian accommodation of Frazer's views; the *Golden Bough* 'could also be read as universalizing Christianity' (148).

[32] Waring 1870: 37–38. Although this work, *An Essay on the Mythological Significance of Tree and Serpent Worship*, is printed anonymously, an insert within the copy held in the

practices as the common enemy.[33] Whilst this hardly eradicated concerns about Christianity's relationship with primitive thinking and the savage past, it did distract attention from that relationship by focusing instead on an organic connection between primitive religious practices and Catholic practices (both often disparagingly termed 'rites').[34] According to Waring, for example, modern Catholicism is a living repository for 'Pagan ceremonial' and primitive thinking:

> As the Church of Rome, the mother of all our modern churches, adopted the great mass of Pagan ceremonial in her worship, so in her theological fancies she embodied much more than was worth retaining in the ancient mythological thought, except for astute purposes of superstition.[35]

Indeed it is thanks to 'its maintenance of rites more naturally belonging to barbaric culture' that Tylor suggests current Catholic practice (or 'the Roman scheme') as an excellent source of material for those wishing to investigate religion in primitive cultures.[36]

  Cambridge University Library listing 'books by the same writer' suggests Waring to be the author.
[33] Anti-Catholic bias often screams from the pages of comparativist works: consider Keary's observation (1882: 504) on the medieval church that 'like the tree Yggdrasill, Catholicism had many different roots in many different places; some were in heaven, but some were, we cannot question it, on earth, and some perchance in hell'. See Dorson 1968: 14–15 and 65 for discussion of 'anti-Catholic rage' among the early antiquarians (65).
[34] See Smith 1990: esp. 1–53 for insightful discussion of how Protestant-centric scholarship on the origins of Christianity aligned elements of early Christianities distasteful to their theological outlook with the theology of Catholicism: 'it is the Protestant catalogue of the central characteristics of Catholicism, from which it dissents, which provides the categories for comparison with Late Antiquity' (43). Phillips 2011: 18 also briefly discusses how Catholicism's association with the city of Rome helped to reinforce this alignment.
[35] Waring 1870: 37. Cf. Philpot 1897: 162, who writes: 'We owe the survival of many pagan customs largely to the Roman Church, whose settled policy it was to adapt the old festal rites to the purposes of the new faith, and to divert its rude converts from the riotous festivities of their unconverted friends by offering them the more orderly rejoicings of a Christian holy day.' Influential on such thinking was a book from the previous century, Middleton's *A letter from Rome, Shewing an Exact Conformity between Popery and Paganism: or, the Religion of the Present Romans to be derived entirely from that of their Heathen Ancestors* (1729): the book's title succinctly sums up the thrust of his argument!
[36] Tylor 1871b: 407. These scholars also inherited from the early antiquarians the idea that some contemporary 'primitive' traditions, normally considered 'survivals' of primitive non-Christian thinking, actually developed out of an early stage of Catholicism. As Bourne, in a work originally published in 1725, memorably put it (reprinted in Brand 1777: v): 'the popular Notions and vulgar Ceremonies in our Nation' can be traced back to 'the Times when Popery was our established Religion', customs which, 'like the

Getting back to roots

Such claims were fleshed out with multiple examples of the organic connection between primitive religion and Catholicism: Catholic use of candles in worship derives from an Egyptian feast of lights in honour of the tree goddess Neith, whilst the practice of placing flowers on graves on the *jour des morts* is 'a surviving relic of a very ancient form of Manes-worship'.[37]

As these scholars looked to align primitive and Catholic religious practices, tree worship also seemed a particularly promising point of contact. Indeed Dalyell actually caught some Catholics in the very act of tree worship, recording in his *Darker Superstitions of Scotland* how 'superstitious papists' consider sacred a row of trees near a chapel of St Ninian.[38] More commonly, however, tree worship was presented as a parallel *form* of what Protestants referred to as Catholic 'idolatry' (be this of statues, icons or other material objects). Tree worship was, for example, often given a role in universal narratives of how idolatry develops:

> Anyone who has watched the progress of idolatry must have observed how rapidly minds, at a certain stage of enlightenment, weary of the unseen, and how wittingly they transfer their worship to any tangible or visible object. An image, a temple, a stone or tree may thus become an object of adoration or pilgrimage, and when sanctified by time, the indolence of the human mind too gladly contents itself with any idol which previous generations have been content to venerate.[39]

> Most nations, if not all, would appear, at some time or other, to have had a sacred tree, and from the worship of sacred trees, to have proceeded to the adoration of idols formed from their wood. This was the opinion of Winckelmann and Caylus, it was also held by Pausanias, and is alluded to in the Bible (Isaiah xl. 20).[40]

Indeed tree worship and Catholic idolatry were blurred in the Protestant imagination as such similar kinds of act that a shared

---

Penates of another Troy', were 'snatched out of the smoking ruins of Popery'. (Bourne's *Antiquitates Vulgares* was reprinted and expanded in Brand's *Observations on Popular Antiquities*.) Bourne does not confront the incongruence between this idea and the more common suggestion that such popular practices are 'survivals' of early non-Christian religion.

[37] Waring 1870: 12; Allen 1892: 62.
[38] Dalyell 1834: 400.
[39] Fergusson 1868: 2. Jennings 1890: 3, whose work on tree worship often takes the form of a patchwork of excerpts from other authors, singles out this passage for citation. Cf. Boetticher 1856: 16, as discussed briefly on p. 35, with his characterisation of the tree as 'das ursprünglich erste Gottesbild', and for the continuance of such thinking in modern scholarship see chapter 6, n. 81.
[40] Barlow 1866: 97 (expanding the quotation cited on p. 31).

A brief history of tree thinking

language developed to describe the two practices. Thus Ouseley, writing of 'trees reputed Sacred in classical antiquity', explains how a tree or stump can easily become 'an object of idolatrous worship'; likewise, having turned to 'the Pagan Arabs of early ages', he describes at length the worship of a particular 'tree-idol', a date known as Aluzza.[41] Lubbock too, having encountered a sacred tree in Congo, describes 'the Gentiles adoring it as one of their idols', whilst Keary shows slightly more hesitance in referring to trees treated as 'half-idols' in savage cultures.[42]

Also crucial to this shared language was the term 'fetish'. Nineteenth-century scholars often used the idea of 'fetish worship' synonymously with animistic worship, in particular what they saw as the lowest, most materialistic stage of animistic worship.[43] The term 'fetish' was also characterised as something quintessentially Catholic, the history of the word having an important role to play here. Introducing the term in his book *Du culte des dieux fétiches* (1760), De Brosses openly acknowledges that he has adopted the word from some Portuguese sailors: these men, having observed the reverence paid to certain objects by inhabitants of the Gold Coast, referred to the objects as 'feitiços', a term they also used of their own prayer beads and crosses.[44] The term caught on like wildfire, with De Brosses' academic successors keeping alive its Catholic roots by arguing, as Keary does here, that contemporary remnants of 'fetich belief' are most visible in Catholic practices:

> The last faint echoes of this belief are found in the uses of objects such as the *relics* of the Roman Catholics, the very feitiços from which the belief has received its name. The bone of the saint, the nail from the true Cross, are fetiches of this sort.[45]

---

[41] Ouseley 1819: 362, 363, 369 and 371.
[42] Lubbock 1870: 306 and Keary 1882: 65. Tylor 1871b: 204 confirms the presence of tree idols in the Congo.
[43] Thus, Lang 1898: 160 defines fetishism as 'the belief in the souls tenanting animate objects', whilst in Tylor's words 1871b: 132 fetishism conveyed 'the doctrine of spirits embodied in, or attached to, or conveying influence through, certain material objects'. Usage of the term fetish did, however, vary from author to author and we may well sympathise with Robertson-Smith 1889: 192 when he brands it 'a merely popular term, which conveys no precise idea, but is vaguely supposed to mean something very vague and contemptible'.
[44] De Brosses 1760: 10. See Sharpe 1975: 18 on the significant turning point which De Brosses' book represented in the history of 'comparative religion'.
[45] Keary 1882: 88. Farnell 1905: 45 likewise claims that we need only glance at Catholic practices to 'recognise the fetichistic value of the sacred objects, relics, crucifixes'. Even Müller 1901: 63, who was unfashionably opposed to the term fetish, contributed to the

Adding to the Catholic colouring of the term, these scholars also presented fetish worship as a first step on the path towards idolatry; fetishism was a stage of thought which, according to Tylor, 'passes by an imperceptible gradation into Idolatry', the organic continuity between the two so strong that Farnell can call idolatry 'a higher form of fetichism'.[46] What kind of objects might be treated as fetishes in savage societies? The simple answer is that any material object would do but, perhaps unsurprisingly, trees often featured among the examples given. De Brosses himself gave trees first place in his list of potential fetish objects, whilst we find Keary emphasising, with typical Protestant disgust, that the 'tree fetich was a thing prayed to *of itself*' (my italics).[47] Thus it was that the idea of fetishism – a term used of the earlier stages of idolatry and of tree worship, and which came saturated with Catholic connotations – only further aligned primitive tree worship with idolatrous Catholic mistakes about matter in the Protestant imagination.

It can be no surprise, then, that all the moral disgust which Protestants instinctively felt for Catholic idolatry as the worship of something material was replicated in their response to tree worship, this alternative form of idolatry for non-Catholics.[48] For Farnell stone and tree worship are 'crude and repulsive facts', whilst Philpot writes of the 'crude worship of the god in the anthropomorphised tree'.[49] Strongly predetermined by their abhorrence for Catholic idolatry, these Protestant-centric comparativists

---

framing of it as a quintessentially Catholic concept when he objected that the Portuguese sailors only interpreted the practices they saw in this way because 'they themselves were fetish-worshippers in a certain sense'.

[46] Tylor 1871b: 132; Farnell 1905: 44. This common understanding of the organic link between fetishism and idolatry is again opposed by Müller 1901: 65–66, whilst Keary 1882: 32 also observes that Christian veneration of an icon is not quite the same as fetishism, 'however ignorant the Christian may be'.

[47] De Brosses 1760: 18; Keary 1882: 82.

[48] This instinctive Protestant disgust is seen, for example, when Caird 1893: 202 treats 'crude' and 'materialistic' as synonyms, commenting on 'the crudest and most materialistic conceptions of supernatural powers'.

[49] Philpot 1897: 33; Farnell 1905: 10. Indeed it could be a real shock when such 'crude' practices appeared in ancient cultures which the comparativists had held up, for their non-religious achievements, as examples of striking civilisation. Farnell 1905: 10 captures this emotion when he describes how, with the discovery of Greek reverence for animals, stones and trees, it felt like 'the sacred edifice of Hellenism was attacked'.

visibly shuddered when considering the degradation that was worshipping a tree.

What was it, then, that prompted primitive people to such a barbaric act? At times, the comparativists made tree worship seem so straightforward that analysis was apparently superfluous. Consider the case of the 'wanzy tree' in Abyssinia:

Every tribe of the Galla nation in Abyssinia worships avowedly as a God, the Wanzey tree.[50]

Mr. Bruce mentions in his travels, that in Abyssinia, the wanzy-tree is avowedly worshipped as God, and Mr. Salt has confirmed this statement.[51]

Several testimonies insist that this tree is simply worshipped as a god, a statement which apparently needs no unpacking or exploration. Nor is it just the wanzy tree whose worship is characterised in this way. Frazer also writes, without qualification, of a pear tree which is 'adored as a divinity' by the Circassians and a Hindu basil shrub 'worshipped daily as a deity'.[52]

When the comparativists did engage a little more with the thinking which led to tree worship, their beauty, as well as the practical benefits derived from their shade, fruit and material, were all put forward as motivating factors. Fergusson, for example, waxes lyrical on this theme:

There is such wondrous beauty in the external form of trees, and so welcome a shelter beneath their over-arching boughs, that we should not feel surprise that in early ages groves were considered as the fittest temples for the gods. There are also, it must be remembered, few things in nature so pleasing to the eye as the form or colour of the flowers which adorn at seasons the whole vegetable kingdom, and nothing so grateful to the palate of the rude man as the flavour of the fruits which trees afford. In addition to these were the multifarious uses to which their wood could always be applied. For buildings, for furniture, for implements of peace or war, or for ornament, it was indispensable. In ancient times it was from wood alone that man obtained that fire which enabled him to cook his food, to warm his dwelling, or to sacrifice to his gods. With all their poetry, and all their usefulness, we can hardly feel astonished that the primitive races of mankind should have considered trees as the choicest gift of the gods to men, and should have believed that their spirits still delighted to dwell among their branches, or spoke oracles through the rustling of their leaves.[53]

[50] Ouseley 1819: 394.
[51] Barlow 1866: 101.
[52] Frazer 1911: 55 and 26.
[53] Fergusson 1868: 1–2. This passage is later cited by McLennan 1869–1870: 212. In similar vein Barlow 1866: 84 and 101 emphasises that 'any tree pre-eminently distinguished

Other explanations placed less emphasis on the pragmatic benefits trees provided. Taking a symbolist approach, Barlow explains how the tree functions as a symbol of the divine scripture without which we cannot live: this 'primitive doctrine', he goes on to argue, is 'dimly traceable' in acts of tree worship within savage cultures.[54] The idea of totemism was also occasionally introduced to explain the prevalence of sacred trees in primitive societies.[55] All these explanations, however, fade into insignificance in light of the comparativists' devotion to animistic interpretations of tree worship.

Observing that trees are alive – so the argument goes – primitive people were led to assume that they must be pervaded or 'animated' by some kind of spirit or divine power, which demanded their worship. Hugely influential in securing this interpretation of tree worship its prominence was Tylor's hefty *Primitive Culture* (1871), and its well-known argument that animism was the fundamental basis of all religions. Tylor saw 'belief in Spiritual Beings' as a 'minimum definition of Religion', further arguing that religion develops from the mistaken understanding that the natural world and its features are animated by such spiritual beings.[56] In the worldview Tylor describes, it would be strange if trees – considering that they are so obviously alive – were not misinterpreted in this way. Or so at least King argues:

> For the origin of the mysterious reverence with which certain trees and flowers were anciently regarded, and of tree 'worship', properly so called, we must

by its majesty and grace became the object of religious reverence' and that 'trees of grateful shade', being a resort for prayer and meditation, 'obtained thereby a certain sanctity'.

[54] Barlow 1866: 80. On the symbolist approach see also Allen 1897: 138, who discusses the close relation of sacred trees to Christian symbolism of the tree of the cross and the true vine.

[55] McLennan 1869–1870 is the notable proponent of totemistic explanations. For him, the idea of tribes having an original animal or plant totem with which they identified explains the sheer number of animal and vegetable gods in ancient societies (although plants and trees are practically squeezed out of his discussion in preference for animals). See Sharpe 1975: 74–77 on McLennan's influence as the figure thanks to whom, he argues, 'totemism ceases to be an entertaining curiosity of primitive life, and becomes a full-blown theory of the origin of religion'.

[56] Tylor 1871a: 383. Tylor 1871b: 100–101 understood these spiritual beings to range 'from the tiniest elf that sports in the long grass up to the heavenly Creator and Ruler of the world, the Great Spirit', a breadth which enabled him to assert a unity to all religious conceptions from the most primitive to the most civilised.

go back to that primaeval period into which comparative mythology has of late afforded us such remarkable glimpses; when the earth, to its early inhabitants, seemed not only 'apparelled in celestial light,' but when every part of creation seemed to be endowed with a strange and conscious vitality. When rocks and mountains, the most apparently lifeless and unchanging of the world's features, were thus regarded and were personified in common language, it would have been wonderful if its more lifelike – the great rivers that fertilised it, and the trees with their changing growth and waving branches, that clothed it – should have been disregarded and unhonoured.[57]

The pervasive popularity of such constructions of tree worship is seen when we find similar arguments in niche academic works which we might suspect to be rather distanced from 'mainstream' comparativist arguments, like Thiselton-Dyer's *The Folk-lore of Plants* (1889):

The fact that plants, in common with man and the lower animals, possess the phenomenon of life and death, naturally suggested in primitive times the notion of their having a similar kind of existence ... On this account a personality was ascribed to the products of the vegetable kingdom, survivals of which are still of frequent occurrence at the present day. It was partly this conception which invested trees with that mystic or sacred character whereby they were regarded with a superstitious fear which found expression in sundry acts of sacrifice and worship.[58]

Unsurprisingly, Tylor himself also placed tree worship and tree spirits on a pedestal for their excellent 'illustrations of man's primitive animistic theory of nature'.[59] In *Primitive Culture* he offers many such illustrations, like that of the 'negro woodman' who, when he cuts down trees, does so 'in fear of the anger of their inhabiting demons'.[60] Frazer's *Golden Bough* also echoes *Primitive Culture* in this way, with eighty-nine pages devoted to examples of animistic tree worship, like that of the Wanika of Eastern Africa who 'fancy that every tree, and especially every coco-nut tree, has its spirit'.[61] By sheer weight of examples, animism and sacred trees became firmly aligned in the nineteenth-century academic imagination.

---

[57] King 1863: 211–212. (This passage is later cited, with some inaccuracies, by Jennings 1890: 3.)
[58] Thiselton-Dyer 1889: 1–2.
[59] Tylor 1871b: 196.
[60] Tylor 1871b: 197.
[61] Frazer 1911: 7–96; Frazer 1911: 12.

Indeed talk of tree 'spirits' or tree 'demons' represents but a tiny sample of the imaginative range of animistic interpretations of sacred trees found in nineteenth-century scholarship. Consider the language of Philpot, Jennings, Barlow and Boetticher:

> Most if not all races, at some period of their development, have regarded the tree as the home, haunt, or embodiment of a spiritual essence.[62]

> Their beauty when single, their grandeur as forests, their grateful shade in hot climates, their mysterious forms of life, suggested them as the abodes of departed spirits, or of existing agencies of the Creator.[63]

> [I]n the veneration paid to trees, both in Europe and in Asia, under the supposition that those of beautiful growth were more especially the favourites of deity, and the haunts of blessed spirits, or even of God himself, which notion the Bible in some places countenances, any tree pre-eminently distinguished by its majesty and grace became the object of religious reverence.[64]

> Für die ursprüngliche heilige Bedeutung des Baumes wie sie bis hierher dargelegt worden ist, insbesondere für den Glauben wie die Gotteskraft demselben eingeboren sei und seine Substanz erfülle, liefert ferner die Verwendung seiner Zweige in den heiligen Riten und gottesdienstlichen Bräuchen ein so recht einschneidendes Zeugnis.[65]

The perception of a living force in trees meant that primitive people might see them as materially assimilated with 'die Gotteskraft', or as the 'home', 'haunt' or 'embodiment' of anything from a 'spiritual essence', to 'departed spirits', to 'blessed spirits', to 'God himself', to whatever is meant by 'existing agencies of the Creator'. Here Barlow and Jennings also nicely illustrate how animistic interpretations of sacred trees often blended with the idea that their beauty and shade prompted their worship. Indeed Jennings' reference to 'departed spirits' also gestures to another 'hybrid' theory of tree worship, notably argued for by Allen: adopting Spencer's arguments that all religion arose from the instinct to worship dead ancestors, Allen presented tree worship as an 'aberrant and highly specialised offshoot' of ancestor

---

[62] Philpot 1897: 1.
[63] Jennings 1890: 2.
[64] Barlow 1866: 84.
[65] Boetticher 1856: 313. The presence of animistic thinking even in Boetticher's idiosyncratic take on *Baumkultus* reveals the incredible pervasiveness of such ideas, whilst both Boetticher and Barlow provide an important reminder that animistic thinking did not begin with Tylor; rather it was through Tylor that animism received its official stamp of scholarly approval.

worship, claiming that tree worship always stemmed ultimately from the belief that trees were inhabited by the souls of dead relatives.[66]

Although a giant of the field, Tylor was certainly not the only influence in cementing the dominance of animistic interpretations of sacred trees: Mannhardt's *Wald- und Feldkulte* (1875–1877), which appeared hot on the heels of *Primitive Culture*, was also formative. He opened the first volume of this work with a chapter identifying examples of what he saw as a widespread animistic motif in German mythology and folklore, that of the tree soul ('die Baumseele'). After this, he went off in search of other German animistic conceptions of the natural world, traversing woodlands and fields thronged with a variety of humanised natural entities or 'Vegetationsdämonen', such as the 'Blumenmädchen' and 'Moosfräulein'.[67] In volume two Mannhardt widened his gaze to European culture, but beginning in Greco-Roman antiquity. This volume's opening chapter on 'die Dryaden' explicitly paralleled the dryads and hamadryads of Greek and Roman poetry with the concept of a 'Baumseele', the subject of the first chapter in volume one. Indeed for Mannhardt dryads and hamadryads were, like the tree-soul, yet another way in which animist thinkers represented the tree's inner 'Naturlebens'.[68] Mannhardt's championing of dryads and hamadryads caught on like wildfire and gave huge impetus to the idea that trees were a *quintessentially* animistic phenomenon.[69]

Moreover, after Tylor and Mannhardt it was not long until further support for animistic interpretations of sacred trees was understood to arrive, in the form of an ethnological report on the

---

[66] Allen 1892: 125. Allen sums up his 'main idea' as follows: 'sacred trees and tree-gods owe their sanctity to having grown in the first place on the tumulus or barrow of the deified ancestor' (xii). Sharpe 1975: 34–35 discusses Spencer's influence on Allen. Cf. Keary 1882: 66–67, Thiselton-Dyer 1889: 10–11, Philpot 1897: 72 and Frazer 1911: 29–33 for discussion of what was seen, to use Keary's words, as 'that common superstition that the souls of the dead have gone to inhabit trees' (66–67).
[67] This interest in 'Vegetationsdämonen' built on his earlier book *Die Korndämonen* (1868), as Mannhardt 1875: 609 himself notes.
[68] Mannhardt 1875: 20.
[69] Only a few years later, Philpot 1897: 58 was confidently claiming that it is in hamadryads that 'the idea of an actual tree-soul is most clearly exemplified'. Beer 1983: 105 interestingly suggests that Darwinian theories also encouraged speculation about 'hybrid' or 'intermediate' forms such as dryads.

savages of Melanesia. In 1891 Bishop Codrington presented to the world the 'mana' of the Melanesians, a word he understood to refer to 'a supernatural power or influence', something which 'works to effect everything which is beyond the ordinary power of men, outside the common processes of nature'.[70] This 'influence' was rather different from Tylorian animism, a theory to which Codrington never fully signed up. Indeed he insisted that his investigations among the Melanesians found no evidence of 'a belief in a spirit which animates any natural object, a tree, waterfall, storm or rock, so as to be to it what the soul is believed to be to the body of a man'.[71] It is ironic, then, that 'mana' was welcomed by the academic world as a firsthand insight into animistic responses to the natural world. Indeed Codrington's *mana* rapidly became famous as such, and by 1897 animistic interpretations of trees had become so dominant that in the preface to *The Sacred Tree* Philpot announced her subject matter simply as 'the worship of the spirit-inhabited tree'.[72]

Once scholars had ascertained that the key to understanding primitive tree worship was animism, the next question for these evolutionary-minded comparativists was obvious: how did tree worship develop? Here scholars fixated on one major development. To begin with, they claimed, tree spirits were understood as fully assimilated with their trees, the result being that the material tree itself was worshipped. As Robertson-Smith put it, when tree worship is 'pure and simple', the tree 'is in all respects treated as a god'.[73] That the comparativists saw tree worship of this type as a mistake primarily about matter is revealed through their reliance on the word 'direct' to explain what was at stake here: primitive people treated trees as 'direct objects of worship', engaging in 'direct and absolute tree-worship' or the 'direct cult of trees'.[74]

[70] Codrington 1891: 118–119.
[71] Codrington 1891: 123. On Codrington's uneasy response to Tylorian animism see Stocking 1995: 42–43.
[72] Philpot 1897: vii. Throughout Philpot's book, animism is *the* explanatory tool for understanding the sacrality of trees: even the use of tree parts in divining rituals is due to their supposed animation (103).
[73] Robertson-Smith 1889: 185.
[74] King 1863: 212; Tylor 1871b: 202, echoed by Philpot 1897: 21–22; Robertson-Smith 1889: 187.

A brief history of tree thinking

From such a primitive position the next step was to conceive of the spirit as rather more separate from the tree, living in it but not materially assimilated with it, and to direct worship towards the spirit rather than the tree. This advance was often explained by leaning on the difference between the relationship of a soul to a human body and that of a lodger to a house: thus Frazer observes that 'the tree is regarded, sometimes as the body, sometimes as merely the house of the tree-spirit'.[75] After becoming a 'lodger', the final step in the tree spirit's development was to grow yet further independent; instead of being linked to one tree alone, it becomes associated with several trees or even a whole wood, and thus the spirit matures into 'a god of trees'.[76]

In an evolutionary framework, temporally later always equals an advance, and considering the Protestant-centric bias of the scholars constructing this narrative, it is no surprise to find that their moral approval lay with the later and less materially restricted conceptions of the tree spirit. Indeed they underlined the moral and theological significance of the progression from incorporate to indwelling tree spirits, and from there to a smaller number of 'tree gods', by framing it in terms of a universal narrative which explained how primitive animistic thinking eventually evolves into a position from which people could accept the Christian faith. This narrative made a gradual reduction in the number of divine entities, and an increasingly personal conception of them, the crux of religious development: an animistic stage, with impersonal spirits everywhere you looked, should

---

[75] Frazer 1911: 40. This was the distinction at the back of Philpot's mind, for example, when she wrote of trees being understood as 'the home, haunt, or embodiment of a spiritual essence' (1897: 1). Indeed such a distinction is pervasive in comparativist scholarship on sacred trees. Barlow 1866: 99, for example, distinguishes between 'the spirits that inhabit trees and their successors, the sprightly fairies, who sometimes dance around them'. Similarly, for Mannhardt 1877: 44, it was crucial to determine whether a tree was a 'Schutzgeist' or a 'Sitz des Schutzgeistes'. Robertson-Smith 1889: 85 was confident enough to plump for one interpretation only: 'the god inhabited the tree or sacred stone not in the sense in which a man inhabits a house, but in the sense in which his soul inhabits his body'. Tylor 1871b: 196 proposes a slightly more subtle distinction, but still relying on the soul–body analogy: he distinguishes a tree 'inhabited, like a man, by its own proper life or soul, or as possessed, like a fetish, by some other spirit which has entered it and uses it for a body'.

[76] Frazer 1911: 45. For a similar argument see Philpot 1897: 27, who notes that this narrative 'received special development' in the religions of Greece and Rome.

Getting back to roots

blur into a polytheistic stage with anthropomorphic gods, before finally the light of a monotheistic position could be reached.[77] Frazer illustrates how the tree spirit development narrative was slotted into this universal model:

> When a tree comes to be viewed, no longer as the body of the tree-spirit, but simply as its abode which it can quit at pleasure, an important advance has been made in religious thought. Animism is passing into polytheism ... As soon as the tree-spirit is thus in a measure disengaged from each particular tree, he begins to change his shape and assume the body of a man ... But this change of shape does not affect the essential character of the tree-spirit. The powers which he exercised as a tree-soul incorporate in a tree, he still continues to wield as a god of trees.[78]

Since the issue at stake here is essentially how savage communities could, given enough time, convert to Christianity, the act of identifying the boundaries between incorporate, indwelling and entirely independent tree spirits was deeply charged. Philpot's language reveals this when she distinguishes the idea 'of the tree-god whose worship became organised into a definite religion' and that 'of the tree-demons or tree-spirits whose propitiation was degraded into or never rose above the level of sorcery and incantation'.[79] Only those animistic conceptions which could lead to a religion organised around a single god would pass the first of evolution's hurdles; other conceptions were travelling against evolution's upward flow, degraded and unable to rise above a level of thought so primitive it does not even warrant the label religious. Having set the idea of tree worship on a pedestal as quintessential proof of primitive man's animistic understanding of the world around him, the questions these scholars prioritised when engaging with tree worship, and their often emotionally charged responses to it, were driven both by their academic penchant for evolutionary narratives and their instinctive Protestant repugnance for material objects of worship.

---

[77] Tylor 1871b: 305–306 vocalises this structural narrative, which was implicit in most comparativist works on religion: 'Animism has its distinct and consistent outcome, and Polytheism its distinct and consistent completion, in the doctrine of a Supreme Deity.' The increasing personalisation of concepts of god is a strong theme in Keary's narrative of religious development, e.g. 1882: 39 and 81.
[78] Frazer 1911: 45.
[79] Philpot 1897: 22.

Tree thinking: propagating the tradition

In 1905 Baddeley published an article entitled 'The Sacred Trees of Rome', which opened with the following pronouncement: 'That tree worship is one of the most primitive forms of worship is a matter of ordinary knowledge.'[80] In 1905 the study of Roman religion was also finding its feet as a discipline in its own right. More and more scholars, like Baddeley, were paying the subject individual attention rather than allocating it a small space in broad comparativist studies of religion, or allowing it to play second fiddle in studies of Greco-Roman religion.[81] By 1905, as Baddeley reveals, the comparativists had also made their impact: it was 'ordinary knowledge' that sacred trees would have a place in any picture of early religious behaviour. It must have seemed indisputable to these early scholars of Roman religion that Roman sacred trees were simply waiting for their focused attention. Nor did this conviction stem purely from the understanding that they were studying an ancient, primitive culture like any other, and hence it was bound to boast sacred trees. In fact, comparativist scholarship had already singled out the culture of Rome as being unusually rich in primitive, animistic conceptions of trees.

Why this reputation? One factor to bear in mind is that Roman religion was understood to be *particularly* primitive. Contributing to this understanding was a deep-seated Hellenic bias among nineteenth-century scholars, which often led to Roman culture being treated as the less sophisticated cousin of Greek culture, but Roman religion also found itself framed by nineteenth-century scholars as a religion 'of the rudest and most primitive type' because it was seen to enjoy an organic connection with the Catholic Church.[82] As we have seen, the

---

[80] Baddeley 1905: 101.
[81] Hartung's *Die Religion der Römer* (1836) was the first book to treat Roman religion as an independent subject. See Scheid 1987: 303–305 for discussion of how Hartung prompted a flurry of enquiries into Roman religion, with the momentum really picking up pace shortly before the turn of the nineteenth century.
[82] Allen 1897: 369. In Bettini's 2012: 15–16 words, Rome is seen as the '*ancilla*' of Greece (16). See Habinek 1998: 15–33 on nineteenth-century Hellenic preferences and their intellectual legacy and Phillips 2000: 345 on the nineteenth-century 'intelligentsia's conviction of the ineffably noble quality of Hellenic culture'. This bias has had a long-reaching effect, and scholars of Roman religion have a history of treating their area of expertise as somehow 'inferior' to and more primitive than Greek religion: thus we

comparativists were quick to colour all primitive religious practices as quintessentially Catholic, but this was particularly easy to do with the practices of ancient Rome, the city now famed as the seat of the Catholic Church.[83] A perceived continuity between Roman paganism and modern Catholicism meant that the former could not be anything but deeply and deludedly primitive, especially with regard to its understanding of material objects: sacred trees were bound to flourish in such an environment! This expectation was, moreover, amply confirmed when comparativist scholars encountered in the literature of the Roman world multiple figures whom they saw as classic *exempla* of animistic responses to trees, and it is thanks to these figures that Rome's reputation for sacred trees was truly secured. Most popular of all such literary texts was Ovid's *Metamorphoses*, with its portraits of young women like Daphne who metamorphose into trees. These transformation myths were understood to preserve the 'memory' of Rome's primitive animistic conceptions of trees: as Tylor puts it, they are to be valued for preserving 'vestiges of philosophy of archaic type', and for Philpot too they 'demonstrate the survival of very ancient modes of thought among races who had otherwise reached a high degree of civilisation'.[84]

---

find Rose 1948: 9–11 writing that 'the Romans were a much slower-witted people ... their theology and philosophy, when they had such things at all, were simplified adaptations of Greek thought ... [W]e can quite easily find, almost on the surface as it were, remnants of a very early and simple type of thought which, in Greece, we have to dig deep to recover.'

[83] See pp. 37–39 on the alignment of Catholicism and religious primitivism by scholars of comparative religion. Indeed, like the comparativists, the early scholars of Roman religion continued to view Roman paganism and contemporary Catholicism as organically linked: thus Warde-Fowler 1911: 25 observes that 'to this day the Catholic church in Italy retains in a thinly-disguised form many of the religious practices of the Roman people'. This is also the principle underlying the arguments of Conway 1933: 1–25 in which multiple aspects of ancient Italian religion are compared to modern Catholic practices.

[84] Tylor 1871b: 200; Philpot 1897: 78. Of all Ovid's arboreal transformations, that of Daphne was firm favourite. Tylor 1871b: 200 singles out Daphne and the sisters of Phaethon for preserving this archaic stage of thought; Thiselton-Dyer 1889: 243 also makes Daphne a prime example of 'the olden heathen mythology' in which every tree was 'the abode of a nymph'; Philpot 1897: 77–80 too starts with Daphne, before going on to mention the sisters of Phaeton, Baucis and Philemon, Phyllis, Melus, Lotis and Attis. Only Müller 1901: 440–441 seems to have had enough of Daphne, mocking the 'ethno-psychological mythologists' who want to compare the story of her transformation to the thinking of people in Samoa or Sarawak.

Such arboreal transformations were particularly beloved of scholars who, within their animistic interpretations of tree worship, emphasised that souls of the dead were understood to pass into trees. Boetticher, for example, argued that belief in the dead living on in trees was 'der verhüllte Sinn' of all Ovid's arboreal metamorphoses.[85] Eclipsing Ovid here, however, was Virgil and his story of the dead Polydorus, apparently transformed into a shrubby thicket of cornel and myrtle trees (*Aen.* 3.22–48).[86] As Aeneas tried to uproot a tree from this thicket, the transformed Polydorus groaned in pain and black blood and gore flowed from the tree. This haunting figure was never far from comparativist minds, distracting Frazer, for example, from his discussion of South Slavonian tree beliefs:

> A tree that grows on a grave is regarded by the South Slavonian peasant as a sort of fetish. Whoever breaks a twig from it hurts the soul of the dead, but gains thereby a magic wand, since the soul embodied in the twig will be at his service. This reminds us of the story of Polydorus in Virgil.[87]

Allen, who championed the idea that tree worship arose from a belief in souls of the dead inhabiting trees, predictably makes much of the story of Polydorus, showcasing this 'typical and highly illustrative myth' as *the* example by which he introduces his theory of tree worship.[88] The influential Mannhardt also made space for Polydorus in his *Wald- und Feldkulte*: when arguing that the folklore motif of a bleeding tree indicates that the tree is understood as 'beseelt', the first example he turns to is that of Polydorus.[89] Yet when it comes to bleeding Roman trees, Polydorus has to compete with Erysichthon for pride of place. For Ovid's account of how the vicious Erysichthon attacked an oak inhabited by a nymph takes much of its poignancy from his emphasis on the trembling, pale and bleeding tree (*Met.* 8.741–779), and as such Erysichthon's oak was well loved for its illustration of primitive animistic conceptions of their trees; as early as Grimm it was held up as a prime

---

[85] Boetticher 1856: 254.
[86] Virgil's depiction of Polydorus' transformed state is ambiguous; he refers to bushes (23), a wood (24) and two individual trees (27 and 31).
[87] Frazer 1911: 32–33.
[88] Allen 1892: 34.
[89] Mannhardt 1877: 20–21.

Propagating the tradition

exemplum, even in a discussion which was primarily focused on *German* cautionary tales against tree felling.[90]

The dying 'tree nymph' who cursed Erysichthon from within the oak which he had so viciously attacked, and the dryads who danced around it in happier days, were also crucial to this particular story's popularity.[91] For the shadowy dryads and hamadryads of Greco-Roman mythology also found themselves held up as a quintessentially animistic phenomenon. Philpot sums up the majority opinion when she claims that in the hamadryads 'the idea of an actual tree-soul is most clearly exemplified'.[92] Indeed, dryads and hamadryads became a shared point of cultural reference with which to make sense of instances of tree spirits in other cultures. Thus in the late eighteenth century Marsden noted in his history of Sumatra (as later repeated by Lubbock in 1870) how the locals

> superstitiously believe that certain trees, particularly those of a venerable appearance, (as an old jawee jawee or banyan tree) are the residence, or rather the material frame of spirits of the woods: an opinion which exactly answers to the idea entertained by the ancients, of the *dryades* and *hamadryades*.[93]

Tylor too takes the idea of dryads as a conceptual model for understanding tree worship in other cultures, referring to Buddhist areas of Southern Asia where a 'dryad' is reckoned capable of marriage with a human hero.[94] As well as being taken as a blueprint for understanding distant cultures like that of Sumatra and Southern Asia, dryads and hamadryads were also valued for the way they

---

[90] Grimm 1835: 653. Mannhardt 1877: 10–11 and Philpot 1897: 62–63 also pay special attention to Erysichthon, with Mannhardt 1877: 11 exemplifying how Ovid's Erysichthon account finds itself prioritised over that of Callimachus in this scholarship. Just as Grimm includes Daphne in his account of German anti-tree-felling myths, so Dalyell 1834: 405 needs no more than a quick gesture to the transformation of Attis into a pine and to Syrinx to observe, as a general rule relating to plants in *all* times and cultures, that 'sanguinary streams have escaped from their wounds'.

[91] It is for the dryads that Tylor 1871b: 207 turns to the story.

[92] Philpot 1897: 58. To reinforce this portrait of hamadryads as 'tree souls', Philpot emphasised that etymologically their name means 'spirits whose life was bound up *with* the life of the tree' (58; my italics). This was a common move (cf. e.g. Mannhardt 1877: 8), with scholars turning to the scholiast on Apollonius Rhodius 2.479 (who notes that hamadryads are born and die ἅμα ταῖς δρυσί (with their trees)) and Servius' similar note on *Ecl.* 10.62 for further support. See pp. 190–196 for detailed discussion of dryads and hamadryads, as presented in the literature of the Greco-Roman world.

[93] Marsden 1783: 253; Lubbock 1870: 283.

[94] Tylor 1871b: 197–198.

paralleled another culture closer to home, known for its animistic conceptions of trees: this was the culture of Germany, whose arboreal mythology and folklore had been made famous thanks to both Grimm and Mannhardt.[95] Indeed in *Wald- und Feldkulte* Mannhardt explicitly paralleled German belief in 'die Baumseele' with the Greco-Roman dryads – 'Dryaden sind die typischen Gegenbilder der deutscher Baumgeister' – a comparison which consolidated their renown as perfect illustrations of animistic tree worship.[96]

All these Roman 'arboreal figures' – dryads and hamadryads, Polydorus, Erysichthon, girls like Daphne who metamorphosed into trees – loomed large in the comparativist imagination. For these scholars, making reference to figures like Daphne or the hamadryads was not simply about dipping into a pool of classical knowledge which was the preserve of the educated elite; rather Roman examples were valued and foregrounded on the understanding that they embodied the *essence* of primitive beliefs in other cultures, providing 'classic' *exempla*, or in Tylor's words 'perfect types', of particular aspects of animistic tree worship.[97] In principle, all primitive cultures were worth investigating by comparativists wanting to illustrate a particular phenomenon or idea, but when it came to tree worship, the 'primitively Catholic' culture of Rome came high on the agenda. Indeed the fact that the comparativists so championed Roman material in this way prompts us to acknowledge that the distinction I drew at the start of this section between the comparativists and the early scholars of Roman religion will always be rather blurry.[98] Nineteenth- and early twentieth-century intellectual life was deeply interdisciplinary, with subject boundaries and areas of expertise felt far less acutely than in current academic circles, where interdisciplinarity is often a conscious *aim* for

---

[95] Grimm often relied on the concept of dryads in his journeys through German mythology, once describing the legendary Holda, for example, as 'a dryad incorporated with that tree' (1835: 456) and elsewhere treating the idea of a 'dryad, whose life is bound up with that of the tree' as synonymous with an 'elvish tree-wife' (432).
[96] Mannhardt 1877: 212. Both Philpot 1897: 55 and 67 and Thiselton-Dyer 1889: 89 reveal a debt to Mannhardt's focusing of scholarly attention on the dryads.
[97] Tylor 1871b: 207.
[98] See Calame and Lincoln 2012: 7–8 on the role of Greco-Roman antiquity as 'un point de référence déterminant' in comparativist scholarship (7).

Propagating the tradition

scholars.[99] Frazer nicely illustrates this 'overlap' between studies of comparative religion and Roman religion in claiming that a question about the Roman cult at Nemi triggered the *Golden Bough*, a book which, by the time it appeared in all twelve volumes of the third edition, feels very much the work of a comparativist.[100] Or consider, on a far smaller scale, the way that Jennings borrows a term from Roman cult to articulate the nature of a Bengali custom, which he describes as the honouring of *'lares rurales'*.[101] This shared language reminds us that the comparativists and the scholars of Roman religion inhabited a shared mental world.

This shared mental world also encouraged an open use of comparativist data and approaches among the first scholars of Roman religion. Thus Baddeley, when he wants to elucidate Roman religious responses to the oak, states that 'precisely what the cotton-tree is to the Khonds, the oak or acorn-bearer was to the Latin and Sabine'.[102] Although to us this may well look like a scholar of Roman religion 'adopting' another discipline's material and methods, for Baddeley it was simply utilising the most up-to-date methods of religious interpretation, as developed by his colleagues. Indeed scholars of Roman religion boasted that a comparativist approach was of unique benefit to tackling their particular source material, as Carter here explains:

In fact we cannot go back appreciably before the dawn of primitive history, but there are certain considerations which enable us at least to understand the phenomena of the dawn itself, those survivals in culture which loom up in the twilight and the understanding of which gives us a fair start in our historical development. For this knowledge we are indebted to the so-called 'anthropological' method, which is based on the assumption that mankind is essentially uniform, and that this essential uniformity justifies us in drawing inferences about very ancient thought from the

---

[99] See Young 1985: 127 and Phillips 2011: 12 on the interdisciplinarity of nineteenth-century academia. This lack of awareness of disciplinary boundaries was cemented by fledgling scholars all receiving a similar university education, of which the nearest equivalent today would be obtained in a classics department.

[100] Beard 1992: 218–219 discusses how Frazer flaunts his comparativeness. Indeed, by the third edition of his *Golden Bough* Roman cult at Nemi seemed to many only an artificial way into his real subject matter: see Dorson 1968: 287, Ackerman 1987: 240–241 and Beard 1992: 219–220. Smith 1973 offers a compelling critique of Frazer's logic in interpreting evidence for the cult at Nemi.

[101] Jennings 1890: 15.

[102] Baddeley 1905: 103.

very primitive thought of the barbarous and savage peoples of our own day. At first sight the weakness of this contention is more apparent than its strength, and it is easy to show that the prehistoric primitive culture of a people destined to civilisation is one thing, and the retarded primitive culture of modern tribes is quite another thing, so that, as has so often been said, the two bear a relation to each other not unlike that of a healthy young child to a full-grown idiot. And yet there is a decided resemblance between the child and the idiot, and whether pre-historic or retarded, primitive culture shows everywhere strong likeness, and the method is productive of good if we confine our reasoning backwards to those things in savage life which the two kinds of primitive culture, the prehistoric and the retarded, have in common. To do this, however, we must have some knowledge of the prehistoric, and our modern retarded savage must be used merely to illumine certain things which we see only in half-light; he must never be employed as a lay-figure in sketching those features of prehistoric life of which we are totally in ignorance. It is peculiarly useful to the student of Roman religion because he stands on the borderland and looking backwards sees just enough dark shapes looming up behind him to crave more light. For in many phases of early Roman religion there are present characteristics which go back to old manners of thought, and these manners of thought are not peculiar to the Romans but are found in many primitive peoples of our own day.[103]

Carter's initial unease about taking insights from 'the retarded primitive culture of modern tribes' to shed light on that of a 'prehistoric primitive culture' like Rome soon dissipates. For the limited sources available to the student of primitive Roman religion leave him stranded at a 'borderland', straining at data which always seems tantalisingly out of reach and only observable in the odd remnant of religious practice, preserved through conservative traditionalism.[104] Comparative religion, and its analysis of uniformities in religious behaviour across cultures, holds out hope of reconstructing more of that nebulous past, through cautious employment of information gleaned from the study of living 'savages' alongside analysis of Roman sources. A few years earlier Granger had similarly and more bluntly praised the comparative method: 'Where one set of records is imperfect, we can sometimes fill up the gaps by reference to the fuller accounts of another set.'[105] This he demonstrates in practice – to give some tree-focused

---

[103] Carter 1906: 4–5.
[104] Recently Davies 2004: 4 has argued that scholars still misleadingly insist on their being stranded at this borderland in order to reinforce their model of Roman religion as one of perpetual decline: 'any "genuine" religion was deferred backwards (conveniently) into the past (just) before any useful documentation was begun'.
[105] Granger 1895: 129.

examples – by setting Pliny's thoughts on tree souls alongside those of 'modern Arabs' on tree 'angels' or 'jinn', or comparing Suetonius' account of Vespasia and a portentous cypress with a fifteenth-century story about a shoemaker in Basle.[106]

Early scholarship on Roman religion was also – and if anything more so than that of the comparativists – deeply Christianocentric. Certainly, there was less need for these scholars to pussyfoot around their relationship with the Church, given that the study of Roman religion in isolation would have been felt to have fewer direct implications for contemporary religion than the work of the comparativists.[107] Yet at the same time, these scholars always had an eye to the fact that the pagan religion of Rome would one day cede to, or grow into, Christianity. Scholarly portraits of Roman religion thus often took the form (explicitly or implicitly) of an evolutionary narrative: such a framework is hard to miss when Conway, for example, entitled the final chapter of his work on Roman religion 'The Road to Christmas'![108] Predictably enough, the explanation of how Roman religion evolved also mirrored the comparativists' favoured universal narrative of a development from animism to polytheism and finally into monotheism, with these scholars placing particular emphasis on this being achieved by means of increasingly personal conceptions of the divine.[109] Bailey, for example, comments with seeming approval that, even in Rome's early stages, there were some deities which had 'so far emerged into personality as to have attained to the status of god rather than spirit'.[110] How far Roman religion ever developed along this trajectory from animism to polytheism (let alone

---

[106] Granger 1895: 96 and 99.

[107] Granger 1895: vi–vii stands out from the crowd when he cautiously introduces his plan to compare elements of Roman religion and contemporary Christianity, noting 'venerable precedents for dwelling upon the continuity of the religious experience' (vii).

[108] Conway 1933. Indeed Conway 1933: 7 is unusually open about his Christian bias, as seen again when he writes of 'an extraordinary festival which does not appear to be, in fact, religious at all, at least not in any Christian sense'. See Scheid 1987: 310 for a discussion of the 'classic scenario' in which scholars of this period present Roman religion as having 'a natural tendency towards Christianity'.

[109] See Carter 1906: 6; Warde-Fowler 1911: 119–120 and Bailey 1932: 66–71 for classic accounts of the insistence within scholarship on Roman religion that 'development of personality ... was the first step from animism to anthropomorphism' (i.e. polytheism; Bailey 1932: 71).

[110] Bailey 1932: 68.

A brief history of tree thinking

monotheism) was, however, a matter of debate, with many less approving than Bailey.[111] The ingrained evolutionary mindset of these scholars prompted them to rely on subdivisions to the tripartite model in order to track Roman religious development more precisely, with the early end of the scale felt most in need of subdivision. Thus, Wagenvoort caught a 'glimpse of a transition from pre-animistic to animistic thought' in *Aeneid* 8.347, whilst Granger distinguished this transition with the labels fetishism and animism: 'Where the Roman religion rises above fetishism, it does not go beyond the lower stages of animism.'[112]

As well as adopting their predecessors' comparativist and evolutionary approach, scholars of Roman religion also took to heart their obsession with animism. Carter nicely sums up the orthodox position when he insists that animism 'explains better than any other theory certain habits of thought which the early Romans cherished in regard to their gods'.[113] Seized upon as conclusive justification for understanding early Roman religion as animistic was the Latin word *numen*.[114] Set on a pedestal as the 'characteristic conception of Roman religion' (to use Altheim's words), this neuter noun was understood to indicate a genderless and characterless 'divine spirit', the like of which all primitive cultures understood to animate their natural surroundings.[115] Thus Rose, in

---

[111] Warde-Fowler 1914: 29–54 also went further than many in his chapter entitled 'Jupiter and the *Tendency* to Monotheism' (my italics).

[112] Granger 1895: 212; Wagenvoort 1947: 79. See Sharpe 1975: 66–71 for discussion of Marett and his controversial introduction of the term 'preanimism', on which Wagenvoort here relies; Marett suggested that there was a stage of religious consciousness prior to Tylor's animistic stage, in which primitive men worshipped impersonal forces, but had not yet developed the idea of a spirit.

[113] Carter 1906: 6. Halliday 1922: 89 similarly argued that 'the roots then of Roman religion appear to lie in animism'.

[114] This word *numen* had already enjoyed some favour among nineteenth-century scholarship on religion's earliest days, especially with regard to trees. Boetticher 1856, for example, made frequent use of the term: in trees 'wurde des Gottes Numen wie in einer sichtbaren Hülle hausend geglaubt' (8), a belief which he later summarises by means of the term 'Baum-Numen' (187). Otto's *Das Heilige*, which adopted the word *numen* to express the perception of the mysterious which was to him the irreducible religious experience, no doubt would have seemed to cement *numen*'s significance: ironically, though, Otto 1923: 125 himself insisted that perceiving an object as animated 'does *not* in itself lead to myth or religion'.

[115] Altheim 1938: 192. See pp. 177–190 for detailed discussion of the way scholars of Roman religion have constructed what *numen* means and my unease with those constructions.

his inimitable way, places *numen* at the heart of Roman religion's earliest days:

> A great deal of what the good Bishop says of his Melanesian parishioners could be taken over with little change when we speak of the earliest Roman ideas ... The Romans, like the Melanesians (and Polynesians) of modern times, believed in 'a supernatural power or influence', which they called *numen*, plural *numina*.[116]

Nor is Rose alone in aligning Roman thinking with that of the Melanesians. Wagenvoort also illustrates how *numen* was taken as a straightforward synonym for Codrington's *mana*: 'in *numen* we have therefore an originally general word for *"mana"*'.[117] Thanks to the word *numen*, Roman religion was held up as a *quintessentially* animistic religion, even on a par with that of the famous Melanesians.

Consequently, and bearing in mind that the comparativists had already shone a spotlight on Roman examples of animistic responses to trees, it can come as no surprise that the early scholars of Roman religion made a beeline for what they saw as examples of Roman animistic tree worship. Indeed, of all possible ways to illustrate early Rome's animism, none was more favoured than the presumed omnipresent practice of tree worship: to borrow Wagenvoort's words, 'formerly, it was believed that in a sacred grove, and in *every* tree of the wood, there dwelt a *numen*, an impersonal power' (my italics).[118] Baddeley's explanation of the 'universal prevalence of tree-worship' in Roman culture also holds no surprises, as he echoes King's talk of a 'strange and conscious vitality' perceptible in arboreal life, and leans on the concept of hamadryads:

> And if we consider well, this universal prevalence of tree-worship is not at all surprising. The tree is an organic form of force in the natural world. Tree-worship is a simple deduction from this especial manifestation of it. Sharing with ourselves and the animal creation the alternating phenomena of life, health, maturity, sickness, and finally that of death, it is but natural the possession of some sort of spirit should have been ascribed to trees, a spirit partaking of the character of a conscious being. This

---

[116] Rose 1948: 13.
[117] Wagenvoort 1947: 75. Cf. Bailey 1932: 133 and Rose 1934: 11 on this standard position, as much later echoed by Nock 1972: 604. Smith 2002: 198–201 provides a potted history of thinking about *mana*, 'a complex, century-long drama in which a word was transformed into an incarnate power only to be reduced to a word again' (199).
[118] Wagenvoort 1947: 79.

is why we read that the Hamadryad's life was bound up with her tree! She cried out when the axe threatened, she was hurt when the tree was wounded, she died with the fallen trunk. To the tree was, therefore, assigned a spirit which came into being with it, and would perish along with it.[119]

In general, however, the Roman figures so beloved by the comparativists – Daphne, Polydorus, Erysichthon, the hamadryads – are oddly absent from this early scholarship on Roman religion.

Rather it was a connection between the word *numen* and trees on which these scholars fixated, repeatedly calling upon a handful of passages from Latin literature. The first was *Fasti* 3.295–296, in which Ovid suggests the reader might perceive a *numen* in a grove on the Aventine.[120] A passage from Pliny was also cited as proof of both the antiquity and persistence of Roman perceptions of wooded spaces as numinous (*Nat.* 12.3).[121] Taking the passages completely out of context, these scholars assumed their message was simple and did not stop to engage with the fact that both deal with woods rather than individual trees, or the number of ways Pliny uses *numen*, or the playful tone of the Ovidian passage, let alone to consider any other uses of *numen* in an arboreal context (all of which I intend to put to rights when grappling with arboreal *numina* in Chapter 5).[122] Instead Granger forced these passages to spell out a general rule: 'The black shadows of the groves of ilex brought the cry to the lips of him on whom they stole, "a spirit is here".'[123]

A passage of Cato was also made to do duty as a complement to the *numen*-focused extracts above, in which he instructs those who want to prune a grove to pray and sacrifice to an entity to be addressed as *sive deus sive dea* (either god or goddess; *Agr.* 139).

---

[119] Baddeley 1905: 101–102. Granger 1895: 104 similarly privileged 'the wood fairies' as a way of illustrating the essential nature of early Roman religion. Following in the footsteps of scholars like Allen, Granger 1895: 99 also claimed that some Roman sacred trees were felt to be 'a kind of home for the dead'.

[120] For example, Granger 1895: 95; Bailey 1932: 41 and 133; Rose 1935: 237; Pfister 1937: 1279; Wagenvoort 1947: 79; Rose 1948: 15.

[121] For example, Granger 1895: 96; Pfister 1937: 1280 and Wagenvoort 1947: 79. See pp. 184–185 and 187–188 for further discussion of scholarly reliance on these passages.

[122] See pp. 177–190.

[123] Granger 1895: 95. Indeed the idea that perceiving a *numen* was the instinctive response to an awe-inspiring grove so infiltrated the early twentieth-century consciousness that Lawrence of Arabia, reminiscing about the splendours of Azraq and the Wadi Rum, wrote: 'of Azrak, as of Rumm, one said *numen inest*' (Lawrence 1926: 423).

Scholars showcased this seemingly nameless and genderless deity as an illustration of the impersonal nature of the divine force associated with trees and as confirmation of the significance they had attributed to *numen* being a noun of neuter gender.[124] Also called upon was a moment from Evander's tour of 'proto-Rome' (*Aen.* 8.349–352), in which he evokes the awe-inspiring religious power of a nearby grove, inhabited by an unknown deity: 'here is exactly the feeling of early animism', Bailey observes.[125] Analysis of Roman sacred trees revolved so tightly around these 'proof passages' that no room was left for questioning the animist orthodoxy. Instead, together these passages were made to tell of an originary stage in Rome's religious history, when all trees and wooded spaces were perceived to be animated by an impersonal divine force. Indeed the inability of these scholars to see Roman sacred trees in *non* animistic terms is nicely summed up in Bailey's bafflement over the *ficus Ruminalis*: it was clearly a sacred tree, he writes, but he cannot understand why there is 'no trace of any worship of itself or its indwelling spirit'.[126]

Unsurprisingly, the 'tone' and bias of this early scholarship on Roman trees is also reminiscent of the work of the nineteenth-century comparativists. An instinctive Protestant antipathy to the idea of worshipping something material is still palpable: note the snide change of term when Wagenvoort comments 'there was a time when the priest addressed his prayers – or rather his conjurations – to the tree'.[127] Worship of a material tree was magic, not

---

[124] For example, Granger 1895: 95, Bailey 1932: 43–44 and Wagenvoort 1947: 80. The impact of this passage on the scholarly imagination can be seen when Baddeley 1905: 101 digresses into a reverie about certain sacred trees which survived long after Cato's day, musing that their 'leaves (for those who had ears to hear) still murmured the same mysterious music, "Sive Deus, sive Dea", heard of old when the leaves sang together in the forest, by Latian shepherd and Sabine maiden'. It was also singled out for mention by Tylor 1871b: 207. For further brief discussion of this passage see p. 13.

[125] Bailey 1932: 41. The passage is also cited by Wagenvoort 1947: 79 and Ogilvie 1969: 13.

[126] Bailey 1932: 44. The weighty influence of Farnell 1896: 14 and his claim that, in Greek culture also, trees were worshipped as 'the shrine of the divinity that houses within it' provided further support for animistic interpretations of Roman trees. Cf. Nilsson 1925: 111, who also characterised early Greek religion as animistic: 'every spring, every tree, every natural object has or at least may have its daimon'. Rose 1935: 243–249 discusses whether a δαίμων (daimon) is similar to *mana*, whilst Dumézil 1970: 19 mocks 'prominent Hellenists, won over by the contagion' of animist enthusiasm, who wanted their own equivalent to *mana* and hence picked δαίμων.

[127] Wagenvoort 1947: 81.

'real' religion. Like their evolutionary-minded predecessors, these scholars were also fond of tracing developments in Roman arboreal thinking in terms of the metamorphosis of tree spirits into tree or wood gods, as we earlier saw outlined by Frazer. Silvanus is the chief representative of such wood gods, with Granger keen that we keep sight of the early stages of Silvanus' development and his original lowly nature:

> The wonderful life of the trees was thought to be due to wood spirits, silvani, whose life was bound up with that of the trees they inhabited. As time passed, all these wood spirits seemed to melt into one great divinity: 'the mighty god and most holy shepherd Silvanus' ... But we must not let this later development blind us to the fact that we are dealing here simply with a wood fairy.[128]

Even Jupiter is not immune from narratives which told of his development from such humble origins. Bailey suggests that Jupiter Feretrius, who had a temple on the Capitoline, 'may have been in origin the spirit of a sacred oak', whilst Warde-Fowler more confidently proposes that there must have been an ancient oak connected with Jupiter's cult on the Capitoline, wondering only whether it was regarded 'as the dwelling of the numen or as the numen himself'.[129] What starker illustration of how animistic tree worship dominated scholarly understanding of Rome's early religious development, than having the conviction to paint Jupiter himself as a former tree spirit? Having absorbed the obsession of their predecessors and colleagues with both animism and animistic tree worship – both of which were felt to be particularly prevalent in the Roman world – there was simply no room for these scholars to doubt that the portraits they were painting of Roman religion's earliest days should also be bristling with sacred trees.

Tree thinking today

From the mid twentieth century onwards trees have stood at the margins of scholarly portraits of Roman religion, if not outside the

---

[128] Granger 1895: 102. Only a few years later, Visser 1903: 11 was applying exactly the same model to Greek sacred trees: 'Höher aber und erhabener ist der ewige Geist, der frei von einem Baume zum anderen gehen kann, und schliesslich zum Waldgott wird.'
[129] Warde-Fowler 1911: 130; Bailey 1932: 44.

frame altogether. This sidelining of trees was not, I believe, particularly conscious: rather gradual disillusionment with the early scholarship which first championed Roman sacred trees meant that these trees simply slipped out of fashion. For as the twentieth century progressed, scholars of Roman religion increasingly began to worry about the value of comparativist and animistic approaches to their subject, whilst embarrassment at the Christianocentric and imperialistic nature of early work on Roman religion spread. Sacred trees thus came to be seen as part and parcel of a scholarship on which we should firmly turn our backs.

These changes in scholarship on Roman religion did not take place in isolation, but rather were part of a wider revolution in anthropology and religious studies. Many view Durkheim's *Elementary Forms of Religious Life* (1912) as a turning point, the beginning of the end for the dominance of the comparativist approach. Durkheim was, like his predecessors, interested in studying the religious thinking of the most primitive people he could find (namely Australian aborigines), but he insisted on studying one such culture alone, and extrapolating universal rules from it, rather than embracing as many primitive cultures as possible.[130] The work of Malinowski also helped to knock the comparativist method off its pedestal. His functionalist approach to anthropology prioritised detailed study of an individual culture (undertaken through fieldwork), asking what function a given custom had within that particular culture.[131] Thus, an etic approach to culture slowly yielded to an emic one, helped along by increasing unease about the value of investigations into 'savage' thinking undertaken by elite white males who were strongly implicated in a colonial regime.[132] Scholars also began to tighten up the rules on what was believed to be a valid or meaningful comparison: Boas and Kluckhohn in particular wore away at the comparativist conviction that 'gaps' in cultures could always be filled by reference to others at a

---

[130] On the innovations in Durkheim's approach see Lessa and Vogt 1972: 2, Sharpe 1975: 82–86 and Gellner 1999: 12.
[131] On Malinowski see Sharpe 1975: 175–176, Gellner 1999: 16–17 and Harris 1968: 166–167 (the latter with specific reference to Malinowski's criticism of the idea of survivals).
[132] On this shift see Gellner 1999: 19–20.

similar stage in development.[133] In addition, the theory of social evolution – on which works like Tylor and Frazer utterly depended – also fell out of favour because of its associations with imperialistic cultural prejudice, whilst in tandem the dangers of Christianocentric 'confessional' approaches to culture were also highlighted.[134]

In many ways, scholars of Roman religion were slow to react to this seismic shift in cultural studies. Rose, arguably one of the most impervious to these changes in thinking, was in 1949 still praising what scholars of Roman religion could get out of 'the harvest of investigations into the lives and thoughts of the more backward of mankind'.[135] Today, however, the idea of a 'comparativist' approach is something of a dirty word, its fall from grace evidenced by the fact that 'comparison' most often features in scholarship on Roman religion when attempts are made to rehabilitate it.[136] A recent collection of essays, recognising that comparativist approaches have now 'tombées l'une après l'autre en disgrâce', suggests new models for a meaningful use of comparison: in particular contributors emphasise that comparison can (and should) be more interested in difference than similarity.[137] The historian of religion J. Z. Smith has also been influential in nuancing classicists' ideas about the value and use of comparison, arguing that a comparison should be 'a disciplined exaggeration in the service of knowledge'.[138] Detienne too

---

[133] On Boas' critique of the comparative method, see Harris 1968: 258–259 and Lessa and Vogt 1972: 5. Sharpe 1975: 187–190 discusses Boas' insistence, like that of Malinowski, on the priority of fieldwork, and his wide-ranging influence on others in the field.
[134] On which see Lessa and Vogt 1972: 4; Sharpe 1975: 142; Whaling 1984: 177–178; Gellner 1999: 11.
[135] Rose 1948: 12. Cf. Rose 1934: 23.
[136] Attitudes towards evolutionary models for approaching Roman religion have also changed with time. For much of the twentieth century scholarly works on Roman religion were often structured in a consciously evolutionary framework – consider the major divisions in Altheim 1938: 'Ancient Italy', 'Ancient Rome', 'The Roman Republic', 'The Augustan Age', 'The Empire'. Indeed in 1955 Beaujeu wrote his history of Roman religion still confident in the idea that 'par une sorte de loi d'évolution interne tout polythéisme tende vers le monothéisme' (30). Today this kind of chronological approach has been replaced by a thematic one in most 'textbook-style' accounts of Roman religion.
[137] Calame and Lincoln 2012. See in particular Calame and Lincoln 2012: 10 and Scheid 2012a: 112.
[138] Smith 1990: 52.

has published a self-styled manifesto in which he tackles the idea that 'on ne peut comparer que ce qui est comparable'.[139] He insists that today's comparativist work must be collaborative, arguing that historians and anthropologists need to work together, and to dare to construct comparables which are not immediately obvious.[140] To those questioning the purpose of drawing such comparisons, he simply answers 'il s'agit de voir ce qui se passe'.[141] These scholars' model of comparison is clearly a far cry from the collect-and-cite mentality of Tylor, Frazer and their colleagues.

In tandem with comparativism's decline, throughout the twentieth century scholars also began to put increasing pressure on the value of animistic interpretations of Roman religion, and by 1969 Bayet was able to acknowledge that previous scholars had been led to 'exagérer les aspects animistes de la religion romaine'.[142] One critique which had a major impact was Dumézil's chapter (originally published in 1966), which aimed to prove that '*numen* is unfit to fill the role to which H. J. Rose has assigned it': in other words, *numen* cannot be made the cornerstone of claims that Roman religion enjoyed an animistic stage.[143] Dumézil argued that *numen* is never used in Latin literature to mean an 'impersonal spirit', but is always to be understood with reference to a personal deity – *numen* is always shorthand for *numen dei* – thereby pulling the rug from under the animists' feet. Dumézil's influence provided crucial momentum to the gradual changes in thinking through which animism simply went out of fashion. Alongside these major changes in thought about the value of comparativism and animism, unease about the Christianocentric nature of past scholarship on Roman religion, as well as its imperialistic condescension towards other cultures, sharply increased. In 1969, Bayet

---

[139] Detienne 2000: 11.
[140] Our aversion to taking such intellectual risks with particular regard to Roman religion is interestingly discussed by Bettini 2012: 21–22, who outlines some conceptual stumbling blocks to our taking a 'regard éloigné' approach to Roman religion, as comparativist models demand.
[141] Detienne 2000: 15.
[142] Bayet 1969: 108.
[143] Dumézil 1970: 18–31 (30). As one of the last vigorous champions of *numen* (the substantial first chapter of his *Ancient Roman Religion* is simply entitled 'Numen'), Rose became a favoured target for the 'anti-animists'. Before Dumézil, Rose had also found his interpretation of *numen* under strong attack from Weinstock 1949.

was still writing his portrait of Roman religion with an eye to the eventual 'triomphe du monothéisme chrétien', but in more recent years warnings to beware looking at Roman religion through a Christian lens have become commonplace, with advances in the discipline linked to our 'jettisoning Christianizing baggage'.[144] And whilst in 1906 Carter could muse that there is 'something pathetically amusing' about our understanding Roman religion better than the Romans did, such attitudes have gradually been replaced with more of a Geertzian 'actor-oriented' approach to Roman culture.[145]

In short, the idea of Roman sacred trees is rooted in scholarship which is now dismissed for being comparativist, animistic, Christianocentric and imperialistic; consequently, it simply would not cross the minds of many scholars today that trees could have any real significance for their understanding of Roman religion. Those, on the other hand, who are more open to the idea of Roman sacred trees tend to accept uncritically that such a phenomenon exists, and then quickly move on as though the weight of attention it has received in the past renders further analysis superfluous: 'trees naturally inspired religious feeling'; 'trees were sacred'; 'all forests were by default sacred'.[146] Moreover, when these scholars do engage in a little more depth with the religious significance of trees in Roman culture, ironically they reveal

---

[144] Bayet 1969: 13; Tatum 1999: 288. For examples of such warnings see Dowden 2000: 1–4 and Ogilvie 1969: 1, warnings which both ironically fail to act upon. Davies 2004: 3–7 charts a slow reduction in Christian expectations in recent approaches to Roman religion, noting in particular the coining of the term 'civic paganism', which encourages us away from thinking about religion in terms of 'communion with the divine'. Yet, he warns, much of our framework for thinking about Roman religion still forces it to behave according to Christian principles; in particular, we are obsessed with asking whether Romans believed in, or were sceptical of, particular aspects of their religion. Ando 2009: 177 also shares this particular concern, observing that a recent tendency to move away from *radically* distinguishing Roman religion and Christianity does not stop scholars from thinking about features of Roman religion as analogues to Christian concepts, his chief example being Scheid's claim that, in Roman culture, to believe is to act. Davies also suggests that the notion of religion as a category may be a misleadingly Christian concept, a worry echoed by Rüpke 2007: 5–6.

[145] Carter 1906: 36.

[146] Ferguson 1970: 66; Birge 1982: 10; Lowe 2011: 104. As exemplified by these three scholars, Henderson 1995: 113 notes that the idea of 'primeval Baumkultus ... leaves a still deep imprint on our text-books', despite the lack of detailed attention the phenomenon receives.

Tree thinking today

themselves to be rooted firmly in the mindset of their predecessors' scholarship, no matter how professedly distanced from it. First of all, sacred trees are an undeniably *primitive* phenomenon: Nisbet and Rudd illustrate this when, commenting on Horace's relationship with a pine tree in *Odes* 3.22, they encourage any bemused readers that 'by using his imagination an urban rationalist can still recapture ... a sense of the sanctity of trees'.[147] Nor is this all: sacred trees are also presented as an undeniably animistic phenomenon, even if this is not as overtly acknowledged as it once was. The same *numen*-focused passages so favoured by the early scholars of Roman religion (Ov. *Fast.* 3.295–296 and Pliny *Nat.* 12.3) are still cited to illuminate Roman religious conceptions of trees. Lowe, for example, breezes through both passages in one sentence, adding into the mix also Seneca *Ep.* 41.3:

> The mere sight of old, dense trees could provoke religious awe, indicating that a *numen* resided there: Ovid says so when creating a suspenseful atmosphere; Seneca claims the same phenomenon as evidence for Stoic pantheism; and according to Pliny, the very silence of groves inspires as much reverence as chryselephantine statues.[148]

Lowe also calls on 'Cato's all-purpose prayer for cutting down trees' as straightforward proof 'that all forests were by default sacred', whilst Turcan turns to the anonymous deity living in Evander's grove.[149] The comparativists' tendency to treat all these passages as self-explanatory illustrations of what was at stake in considering a tree sacred has in no way abated.

Nor is it only through reference to these favoured passages that Roman sacred trees find themselves framed as an animistic phenomenon in contemporary scholarship. Animist thinking still deeply colours scholarship on Roman sacred trees, even if it is

---

[147] Nisbet and Rudd 2004: 257. It is hard not to suspect that a similar attitude prompted Ferguson's claim (1980: 18) that 'any African will understand' why mountains were 'numinous spots' for the Romans. Consider also how Turcan 2000: 39 presents sacred trees as a remnant from a period of 'traditional religion' in Rome.

[148] Lowe 2011: 101. Glay 1971: 18, Hughes 1994: 170 and Dowden 2000: 111 cite the Ovid passage; Ferguson 1970: 66; Glay 1971: 18; Hughes 1994: 170; Dowden 2000: 94; Rives 2007: 91 turn to Pliny. See pp. 184–188 for detailed discussion of contemporary reliance on all three passages.

[149] Turcan 2000: 39; Lowe 2011: 104.

A brief history of tree thinking

not overtly acknowledged as such, or expressed as forthrightly as Ogilvie did nearly fifty years ago:[150]

> In the hot, sunny climate of Italy ... a copse of trees inspires grateful respect. The Romans thought of them as sacred places in which a spirit dwelt.[151]

In more recent years such thinking persists, but finds itself expressed in slightly more muted language; spirits are no longer fashionable.

> The forest belonged to the gods. To the ancients it gave that frisson of the supernatural, even when traditional religion was tending to collapse.[152]

> [There] was a strong association of the divine with trees.[153]

> The implication here is that someone who does not even bother to acknowledge the divine aura of a special stone or tree must have utter contempt for the presence of the gods in his land.[154]

> [I]n the *Georgics* ... repeated allusions to divine powers when introducing wild trees imply that they are all numinous.[155]

Turcan's 'frisson of the supernatural' and Rives' 'strong association of the divine' or 'divine aura' are no more than descriptive ways of writing *mana* or *numen*. The language of tree spirits has been updated to that of 'sense' and 'aura', whilst Lowe's choice of the word 'numinous' also signals an unbroken chain of connection with past animist scholarship.[156]

---

[150] It is rare to find scholars openly reinstating the animist tradition with reference to Roman religion, as does Lomas 1996: 166: 'the most ancient of all forms of religious belief attested in Italy is the animist tradition of *numina*'.

[151] Ogilvie 1969: 13. Ogilvie's emphasis on the Italian climate also reminds us of the claim made by some comparativists that trees were considered sacred thanks to their refreshing shade.

[152] Turcan 2000: 39.

[153] Rives 2007: 75.

[154] Rives 2007: 91.

[155] Lowe 2011: 102. Elsewhere Lowe 2011: 100–101 echoes the comparativists' penchant for explaining the sacrality of trees by virtue of their beauty and shade. There are only 'two aesthetic models for the sacredness of trees in ancient Rome': 'on one hand is the 'monumental tree', a single tree notable for its size, beauty, or location; on the other is the 'dark mass', a grove notable for its age, density, shade, or silence'.

[156] Indeed the idea that trees had a 'divine aura' seems almost instinctive to many classicists, even though it is rarely discussed at any length. Thus Steiner 2001: 86, for example, in a discussion of the power of aniconic images in Greek culture, makes easy reference to the way a 'sacred aura' prompted 'the perceived affinity between a god and a tree'. Nor is such loose thinking restricted to trees: Rives 2007: 92 identifies the 'sense of the uncanny that Seneca expresses so well' as a force urging Romans to 'sacralize' various features of the natural landscape.

Tree thinking today

Unlike the comparativists, however, these scholars' engagement with Roman sacred trees is little more than glancing. For any sustained engagement with such trees we have to turn to Dowden's *European Paganism*, which, within the book's far wider scope, has bucked the trend of sidelining trees in studies of Roman religion. Unfortunately, it has not bucked the trend of simplifying the significance of such trees. Dowden continually undermines the academic import of his subject by littering his discussion with phrases such as 'obviously' and 'quite simply', making any exploration of the phenomenon feel superfluous.[157] Dowden's understanding of pagan religious responses to trees also sounds disturbingly familiar, again revealing the insidious influence of the traditional interpretation of sacred trees established by the comparativists. Starting from an animistic approach to sacred trees – even noting that 'the word *mana* is loosely used in this context' – Dowden works with a dichotomy between worshipping the tree itself and worshipping its internal spirit, framing this distinction in terms of an evolutionary advance.[158] As he puts it, the advantage of the notion of an arboreal spirit was that it provided

a way of accommodating the worship of a brute tree into a religious universe now more accustomed to personal divinities. Trees, stones and springs talk a different religious language from gods and nymphs; we must beware the infiltration of personalities and god-language into raw ecology.[159]

Dowden is in fact particularly attached to this mode of understanding:

The function of these myths and legendary associations is to translate the brute religious importance of the tree into the language of anthropomorphic and heroic religion.[160]

We should not be too impressed by Greek and Roman poetic anthropomorphism. The perception that the tree itself is a vehicle of power logically precedes the

---

[157] Dowden 2000: 34 and 96–97.
[158] Dowden 2000: 34. Such a dichotomy also makes its presence felt more broadly in thinking about Roman religious engagement with the natural world. Rives 2007: 90, for example, notes that there are 'two different ways that people in the Roman world interpreted their awareness of the divine in nature ... [T]hey might regard a particular topographical feature like a spring or a river as a deity in itself, and so make offerings to it ... [or] they might regard a certain place as the dwelling of a deity.'
[159] Dowden 2000: 35.
[160] Dowden 2000: 68.

69

creation of a place for it within an anthropomorphic system. First, powerful tree; then, personal gods; then, mopping up the trees by turning them into residences for the personal god.[161]

Despite insisting early on in his book that we must not slip into a Victorian-style Christianocentric approach to thinking about pagan religion, Dowden here reveals a deeply Protestant and anti-materialistic mindset in his painting of 'tree worship' as 'brute' and 'raw'.[162] Dowden's instructions that we 'must beware' and 'should not be too impressed' by Roman presentation of their conceptions of trees also condescendingly depicts Romans as attempting to cover up the materialistic nature of their 'tree worship'. Furthermore, Dowden exposes both an assumption that religion must evolve and an allegiance to the idea that the progress of religion can be tracked through a series of increasingly personal gods, both practically articles of faith for nineteenth-century comparativist scholars: for Dowden a tree spirit represents one step along the upwards path of accommodating 'brute' tree worship into a new and more anthropomorphic religious environment. In the last 150 years of scholarly engagement with sacred trees, very little, it seems, has changed.

Indeed Roman sacred trees have never been allowed to escape relegation to a simplistic, primitive stage of religious thinking, meaning that scholarly engagement with them today often feels intellectually distant from constructions of 'mainstream' Roman religion. An analysis of how trees contributed to the *complexity* of Roman religious thinking as a whole is long overdue, with the trees showcased in this book's first chapter providing an inkling of just how much is being overlooked here. Without further ado, then, I wish to turn to a fresh analysis of the religious significance of trees in the Roman world. Yet in so doing I will not entirely lose sight of the concerns of the comparativists and their methodological successors, the early scholars of Roman religion who so championed the Roman sacred tree. For in rethinking what was at stake in Roman constructions of arboreal sacrality, these early scholars'

[161] Dowden 2000: 34.
[162] Dowden 2000: 2. Smith 1990: 34 notes how Protestant anti-Catholic apologetics still underlie much contemporary research in religion.

Tree thinking today

fascination with the materiality and 'animation' of sacred trees will turn out to be of pivotal significance, albeit in modified form. This is because Roman intellectual grappling with what it meant for a tree to be sacred was in fact dominated by a nexus of issues arising from their existence as material objects and their apparent autonomous agency. Yet in exploring this nexus of issues I will turn traditional thinking about Roman sacred trees on its head. For a driving aim of this book is to reveal how trees fuelled the complexity of Roman theology, and did so by posing questions prompted by those very qualities, namely their materiality and agency, which in the past have led only to their characterisation as religiously simplistic.

CHAPTER 3

HOW ARBOREAL MATTER MATTERS: RETHINKING SACRALITY THROUGH TREES

After his conversion to Christianity, Arnobius found time to reflect on the thinking behind his former pagan self's veneration of idols, stones and trees:

> venerabar, o caecitas, nuper simulacra modo ex fornacibus prompta, in incudibus deos et ex malleis fabricatos, elephantorum ossa, picturas, veternosis in arboribus taenias; si quando conspexeram lubricatum lapidem et ex olivi unguine sordidatum, tamquam inesset vis praesens, adulabar, adfabar et beneficia poscebam nihil sentiente de trunco, et eos ipsos divos, quos esse mihi persuaseram, adficiebam contumeliis gravibus, cum eos esse credebam ligna lapides atque ossa aut in huiusmodi rerum habitare materia. (*Ad. nat.* 1.39.1)

> In my blindness I used to worship statues recently brought out from the furnace, gods made on anvils with mallets, bones of elephants, paintings, ribbons on ancient trees; if ever I caught sight of a stone anointed and meanly dressed with olive oil, I used to adore it as if it had an internal force, I used to address and demand benefits from an insentient tree trunk, and I afflicted with serious insults those very gods, whom I had persuaded myself existed, since I used to believe them to be bits of wood, stones and bones, or to live in the matter of things of that kind.[1]

Two factors were at play in his idiocy. The first was a deluded 'animistic' conception of such objects: he would worship an idol or stone or tree 'as if it had an internal force' (*tamquam inesset vis praesens*). Nineteenth-century lauding of 'animism' as the interpretative key to tree worship was, we see, no innovation. The second factor was a category mistake which resulted in Arnobius conceiving of gods either as synonymous with bits of wood, stones or bones, or as inhabitants of such objects.[2] Sulpicius Severus also

---

[1] Simmons 1995: 94–130 presents the evidence for what we know of Arnobius' life and discusses his conversion from being an actively anti-Christian pagan, suggesting that Books 1 and 2 of the *Adversus nationes* stand as 'retractations of the anti-Christian propaganda which Arnobius himself incorporated in his attack upon the faith' (122). See Edwards 1999: 198–199 for an overview of the difficulties in dating the *Adversus nationes*.

[2] Later in the *Adversus nationes* Arnobius indulges in an exposé of similar pagan category mistakes, urging us to laugh at Thespians worshipping 'a branch as Cinxia' (*ramum pro*

characterised pagan tree worship as a ridiculous category mistake. In his *Life of St Martin*, we read how the hero Martin had succeeded in destroying a pagan shrine, but once he moved to attack its associated tree found himself facing organised opposition.[3] Exhorting the pagans to comprehend the beneficial nature of cutting down this tree, Martin assured them that:

> nihil esse religionis in stipite; deum potius, cui serviret ipse, sequerentur; arborem illam succidi oportere, quia esset daemoni dedicata. (13.2)
>
> There was nothing religious in the tree trunk; rather they should follow the god which he himself served; that tree ought to be cut down, since it was dedicated to a demon.[4]

Terming the tree a mere *stipes* (trunk), Martin downgrades it from an organic whole to a lump of wood, and by juxtaposing *stipite* (trunk) with *deum potius* (god, rather) drives home the gulf between these two entities. Sulpicius thus uses Martin's speech to critique tree worship chiefly as a category mistake, but also hints at an animistic interpretation of such worship; for the locational nature of *nihil ... religionis in stipite* (nothing religious in the tree trunk) imposes on the pagan bystanders the belief that the tree boasted an internal *vis* or force. In framing tree worship as either an animistic mistake, a category mistake or a mixture of the two, both Arnobius and Sulpicius make the materiality of trees the crux of their theological critique. Mistakenly understanding a material tree either to be a god or to house a divine force was the root of the problem, and once the apologists have exposed this mistake as the cornerstone of pagan 'tree worship', they gleefully conclude that such worship is left without any theological foundation.

Cinxia), Pessinuntians 'a flint as the Mother of the Gods' (*silicem pro Deum Matre*) and Romans 'a spear as Mars' (*pro Marte ... hastam*; 6.11.1), to give but a few examples. In Arnobius' use of *pro* I see a blend of its common meaning 'in place of' (*OLD* §6) with its more technical meaning of 'as' or 'the equivalent of' (*OLD* §9).

[3] Stancliffe 1983: 15–47, 111–133 and 72 discusses Sulpicius' conversion and monastic life, the debated chronology of St Martin's life and her arguments for dating the *Vita* to 396 CE. Cutting down sacred trees became a fixed feature of Christian expositions of pagan error, e.g. Prudentius *Symm.* 2.1005–1014. As Lane Fox 1986: 44 puts it, 'The triumph of Christianity was accompanied by the sound of the axe on age-old arboreta.'

[4] Fontaine 1967: 740–749 discusses this passage, suggesting that this pine was sacred to Cybele (741–742) and that Martin forces the pagans to enact a mock version of the ritual cutting down and parading of a pine during worship of Cybele on 22 March (747). For further discussion of the limited evidence for this ritual see Chapter 6, n. 63.

Arnobius may try to give his account of pagan tree worship a certain authenticity by focalising it through his former pagan self, but it is clearly naive to believe that this accurately represents how he used to think about arboreal sacrality. That a pagan thinker would have objected to Arnobius' construction of arboreal sacrality is surely beyond reasonable doubt, but harder to ascertain is what form pagan dissent from such constructions would have taken. What counter-arguments would pagans have advanced against this mocking reductionist account of their 'tree worship'? Would Roman pagans have empathised *in any way* with Arnobius' insistence that his former religious conception of trees centred on an understanding of their matter? As Martin tried to chop down their pine, would pagan observers have cried out that, on the contrary, there was some *religio* (something religious) in that particular material tree? Or would they have shaken their heads in disbelief at someone who thought *they* thought a tree's *religio* was bound up with its matter?

Offering confident answers to these questions will always be frustrated by the Christian authorship of the apologetic texts which provide much of our evidence for pagan–Christian debate in the early centuries of Christianity's growth. It is, however, both intriguing and informative how these texts reveal that the apologists could also find themselves on the receiving end of pagan scorn about their wooden objects of worship: for in pagan eyes Christians were something far worse than tree worshippers, that is, cross worshippers. As such accusations are reported (and dismissed) in the work of the apologists, we catch a precious glimpse of pagan involvement in a live and heated debate about what really was at stake in the 'worship' – as it seemed to outsiders at least – of a material object like a cross or a tree. Such debate can, for example, be seen in Minucius Felix's *Octavius,* a Ciceronian-style dialogue staged between a pagan and a Christian.[5] The pagan speaker first notes that a man put to death for his crimes and the 'death-dealing wood of the cross' (*crucis ligna feralia*) are fitting

---

[5] See Powell 2007 on the use Minucius Felix makes of the Ciceronian dialogue form and for a useful overview of what (little) we know of Minucius Felix himself. Beaujeu 1964: xliv–lxvii discusses the difficulties of dating the *Octavius* and various hypotheses put forward, as well as its debated (chronological) relationship with the works of Tertullian.

'objects of worship' (*caerimoniae*) for such evil wretches (*Oct*. 9.4). When the Christian speaker gets his chance to respond he begins with a lengthy criticism of imperial cult, before turning to the claim that Christians worship the cross (29.2–5). To this the response is simple: *cruces etiam nec colimus nec optamus* (we neither worship nor hope in crosses). Yet pagans, he continues, cannot be so sure of this. For as they consecrate 'wooden gods' (*ligneos deos*; i.e. wooden statues of gods) they might easily end up worshipping the wooden crosses on which sculptors moulded those statues (16.6). As idolaters, pagans are by default cross worshippers.

Very similar mud-slinging also makes itself felt in Tertullian, reassuring us that this is not just an idiosyncratic exchange dreamt up by the rather idiosyncratic Minucius Felix. I here lay out an argument which appears twice in Tertullian's works, in almost identical form. He begins with a striking challenge: whoever thinks Christians are 'worshippers of the cross' (*crucis ... religiosi*, *Apol*. 16.6; *crucis ... antistites*, *Ad. nat*. 1.12.1) will find himself 'our fellow worshipper' (*consecraneus ... noster*, *Apol*. 16.6; *consacerdos ... noster*, *Ad. nat*. 1.12.1). From here, instead of directly countering the claim that Christians worship crosses, he points out that pagans worship far less shapely pieces of wood; the Pharian Ceres, for example, is but a 'crude stake' (*rude palum*, *Apol*. 16.6 and *Ad. nat*. 1.12.3). Nor is it only such simple, indeed almost aniconic, wooden statues which are subject to Tertullian's criticism; unbeknownst to pagans, *all* their statues of deities derive their origins from wooden crosses, moulded as they are on this sculptural support (*Apol*. 16.). Thus they end up consecrating the cross, from which the consecrated god originated (*Ad. nat*. 1.12.10). Even the trophies and military standards beloved of the Roman army reveal that pagans are the real cross worshippers. For Tertullian presents the army as venerating such 'crosses' (*cruces colit castrensis religio*; the religion of the camps worships crosses, *Ad. nat*. 1.12.14), the banners and images draped on them reduced to honorific necklaces and petticoats (*Ad. nat*. 1.12.15–16). At one point during this rant Tertullian does argue that the characteristic of the cross is that it is a sign made from wood (*Ad. nat*. 1.12.1) but, surprisingly perhaps, this claim is almost submerged by his central argumentative strategy, which is to turn the accusations of cross worship back on the pagans. Clearly *neither* side wanted to be seen as the worshippers of something as material as a cross, as both hurl the same accusations at the other. And whilst Tertullian (definitely) and Minucius Felix (most probably) tell us more about Christian thinking than they do about pagan thinking, one thing we can take away from these passages is that pagan thinkers would have had plenty to say about what made 'tree worship' (and its conceptions of arboreal matter) different from the cross worship (and its conceptions of wood) of which they accused the Christians.[6]

Yet, as we saw in the preceding chapter, the history of scholarship on Roman sacred trees has sided with the apologists in its outraged insistence on the simplistic and deluded understanding of arboreal matter evident in pagan tree worship. This in itself constitutes one pressing reason to rethink how arboreal matter matters for Roman conceptions of sacred trees. Yet we need not worry that we are being swayed by Christian priorities in making arboreal matter central to an investigation into trees' sacrality: the very nature of trees urges us to do so. Trees, after all, are organic objects. Unlike other objects which may be considered sacred – say temples, altars or statues – trees are living agents, as seen in their ability to grow and bud, to shed their leaves and change their colour. As living objects trees are also far more vulnerable than most objects, susceptible to destructive natural forces and human interference. Crucially trees can die, whereas non-organic objects can only decline or decompose. This material vulnerability must have affected Roman understanding of trees' sacrality, raising questions about the nature of human interference with those trees and the position this put you in vis-à-vis the divine. What did it mean when a sacred tree inevitably died, and what were you to do in response? Did humans have a duty of care towards sacred trees during their lifetime, and if so, how problematic was this, considering the frequently violent nature of arboriculture? As organic

---

[6] We do not know for certain that Minucius Felix was Christian, but many scholars assume from the *Octavius* that he must have been, chiefly because the Christian wins the argument; Powell 2007, for example, argues for the 'unfair' formulation and presentation of the pagan Caecilius' arguments in this dialogue.

objects, trees defy simple conceptions of what it means for a material object to be sacred.

In short, the foundational question which underlies the next two chapters is to ask how arboreal matter matters to Roman thinking about the sacrality of trees. As well as exploring various ways in which arboreal sacrality and materiality intersected in Roman eyes, I will focus on the questions which trees' material vulnerability raised for those who considered these organic objects sacred, in particular concerning the nature of arboricultural interference with a sacred tree and the significance of a sacred tree's death. Mindful of our history of thinking about the sacrality of trees, in particular the apologists' claims that pagans equated trees with deities and the enduring scholarly construction of pagan 'tree worship' as unmediated worship of a material tree, I will start by pushing at the very rare cases in which we see anything in the Roman world which might come close to Tylor's idea of 'direct and absolute tree-worship'.[7] Questioning what these cases of 'tree worship' tell us about Roman understandings of how matter matters to a particular tree's sacrality, from here the discussion will broaden into an exploration of other ways in which matter is at the heart of what makes a tree sacred in Roman culture; these range from the inscription to Silvanus 'half shut up in a sacred ash' to Virgil's depiction of a laurel which is 'especially sacred' in its foliage. Next, taking the *ficus Ruminalis* as a test case, I will consider how the organic vulnerability of this memorial tree shaped thinking about the relationship between its sacrality and its matter. In this section I will begin to put pressure on the nature of human intervention with a sacred tree and what it means when a sacred tree dies. These issues then come to the fore in Chapter 4, where I engage with the theological thinking which informs Roman arboricultural care for sacred trees and their responses to dead sacred trees, focusing my discussion through a detailed reading of the inscriptions of the *fratres Arvales*, found in the grove of Dea Dia.

A major aim of these two chapters is to begin to fill in a gap in our current understanding of Roman religion, recently bemoaned by Ando as a lack of 'sophisticated and sympathetic explanation

---

[7] Tylor 1871b: 202.

for the theology of idols and sacrality of material objects'.[8] Indeed, as we have seen, the history of scholarship on Roman religion has predisposed scholars to distrust anything which might seem like a 'material conception' of the divine, and thus it is that the sacrality of material objects in Roman culture is crying out for sensitive and nuanced investigation: the most sophisticated work in this area to date has focused on statues of the divine, or the 'theology of idols' in Ando's terms.[9] In this and the following chapter I intend to build further layers of complexity into an emerging scholarly interest in the sacrality of matter in Roman culture, by exploring what it means to conceive as sacred an organic, living material object.

Tree worship

Arnobius may be confident that he used to believe an insentient tree trunk *was* a deity, but was any practising Roman pagan ever convinced that a tree was a god? Or to phrase the question slightly less provocatively, did Romans ever worship trees? Starting from the viewpoint of the apologists and the comparativists, with their Protestant-centric idea of 'direct and absolute tree-worship', may seem counterintuitive: yet since their insistence on the animistic worship of a material tree has, to date, been the prime way of thinking about what makes a tree sacred in Roman culture, I choose to start by responding to their lead. What evidence, if any, is there of 'tree worship' in the Roman world? And if we do find cases of 'tree worship', what do they tell us about the significance of a tree's matter for Roman understanding of its sacrality? As I explore how meaningful Tylor's idea of 'direct and absolute tree-worship' would be for Roman thinkers, we will find ourselves shading in some of the area left blank by Arnobius' stark dichotomy between the belief that a tree is a god and the belief that a

---

[8] Ando 2008: 25.
[9] Indeed Ando's rallying cry for more sophisticated analysis of the sacrality of material objects disappointingly leads into a focused discussion of one cult statue alone. For further discussion of scholarship on the 'theology of idols' see pp. 80–81 and 262–265. Glinister 2000 makes an unusual and important contribution to the emerging debate in her consideration of 'sacred rubbish'.

Tree worship

tree is a lump of wood. Rarely discussed passages from Pausanias, Silius Italicus and Fronto will reveal that Roman thinking about 'tree worship' favoured infinitely more nuanced and complex options between these two extremes.

I begin with a story Pausanias tells of certain displaced citizens of Boiai, who were searching for a new home. An oracle had told them that Artemis would direct them to a suitable location, so when a hare suddenly appeared before them they joyfully adopted it as their guide. Soon the hare dived into a myrtle tree and they chose to found their city on that spot. Concluding this brief narrative, Pausanias adds:

καὶ τὸ δένδρον ἔτι ἐκείνην σέβουσι τὴν μυρσίνην καὶ Ἄρτεμιν ὀνομάζουσι Σώτειραν.
(3.22.12)
and they still worship that myrtle tree and call [it] Artemis Saviour.

How are we to understand this intriguing phrase? The myrtle is clearly identified as a sacred tree, with σέβουσι expressing that it is of religious significance to the citizens of Boiai.[10] Indeed this verb commonly takes deities as its object and finds itself translated as 'to worship'.[11] Is this myrtle, then, being worshipped? What would it mean to say this in Roman culture? Crucial to understanding this phrase in more depth is to distinguish two ways of reading it. Is Pausanias telling us that the citizens of Boiai worship the myrtle tree *and* call Artemis Saviour (an epithet offered in thanks for her intervention in directing them to a new home)? Or did they worship the myrtle and call *it* Artemis Saviour (with the tree as the implied object of ὀνομάζουσι)?[12] The first interpretation paints the religious response to the tree as distinct from the response to Artemis Saviour; here the tree is of religious significance in its

---

[10] For my definition of a sacred tree see p. 3.
[11] LSJ ad loc. It seems common to assume that the verb 'to worship' (with Greek and Latin equivalents being, for example, σέβειν, *adorare* or *colere*) means to treat as a god; one thing the following discussion will draw out is that uses of these verbs in relation to trees cannot mean to consider the tree somehow as a 'straightforward equivalent' to a deity.
[12] I do not believe this phrase could support the meaning 'they named it *after* Artemis Saviour', despite an apparent parallel in Pausanias' 'Menelean plane', named after its supposed planter (8.23.4), for here we have no equivalent 'Artemidean' epithet. If we take the myrtle as the object of ὀνομάζουσι then it is hard to understand καὶ Ἄρτεμιν ὀνομάζουσι Σώτειραν as merely indicating the tree's association with Artemis: the claim appears stronger than that.

own right, even if this was prompted by the sign it embodied, a sign which was engineered and overseen by Artemis. This would, surely, come very close to Tylor's idea of 'direct and absolute tree-worship'. By contrast, the second interpretation paints the grateful response of the citizens of Boiai to Artemis Saviour as subsumed into and focalised through their response to the tree: they worship the tree, calling it (and in some way thinking of it as?) Artemis Saviour.[13]

This latter reading of the myrtle's significance may seem conceptually odd to us: how could the citizens of Boiai imagine a tree to be – in some way – Artemis? However, Greco-Roman discourse about the nature of statues of the divine provides an illuminating parallel, which would support this way of thinking about the myrtle. For statues of deities often hovered in a grey area between *being* the deity in question and *representing* that deity in Greco-Roman thinking, as has become a topos of scholarly observation since a ground-breaking article by Gordon in 1979.[14] As Gordon noted, Greek and Roman authors had a tendency to write 'Artemis' when referring to what we would call 'a statue of Artemis'; conceptual boundaries between statue and deity were not rigidly observed.[15] In this intellectual context, the citizens of Boiai calling a tree Artemis Saviour should, perhaps, not overly surprise us. Indeed Elsner has emphasised how much Pausanias in particular grappled with the ambiguous status of divine statues: in him we find 'a much more dynamic interpenetration of image and referent, representation and prototype, than we usually allow for in discussions of mimesis'.[16] Thus a tree understood to 'be Artemis' could slot into Pausanias' conceptual world with less difficulty than we

---

[13] Taking the standard nineteenth-century animistic approach to tree worship, Boetticher 1856: 52 presumed that the citizens of Boiai had recognised Artemis *in* the tree: 'Wenn die Boiäer in jenem Myrtenbaume die Artemis Soteira erkannten, ihn mit diesem Namen benannten und rituell verehrten.'

[14] Gordon 1979. Steiner 2001: 79–104 and Stewart 2003: 35–45 tackle the complex range of options embraced by this grey area, whilst Platt 2011: 77–123 deepens this debate with her exploration of the 'mutual dependence of epiphany and representation', showing how 'the bond between gods and their cult statues is, like epiphany itself, continually shifting and elusive' (122). Ando 2008: 21–42 also provides sharp discussion of how Roman pagans engaged with 'the problem of theorizing … what sort of thing a material god might be' (22).

[15] Gordon 1979: 7.

[16] Elsner 2007: 44.

might at first imagine: calling the myrtle Artemis would express an understanding of it as a kind of instantiation of Artemis, but leaving its precise relationship with the goddess obscure.[17] The matter of this myrtle tree would share with statues of the divine a deep-seated ontological ambiguity.[18]

In short, those looking for 'direct and absolute tree-worship' in the Roman world could not hope for much more than Pausanias' ἐκείνην σέβουσι τὴν μυρσίνην (they worship that myrtle). Indeed, if read according to the first interpretation then this would seem to be a clear indication of at least one tree which was worshipped in the Roman world. Yet Pausanias' Greek also raises the option that the citizens of Boiai did not see themselves worshipping a tree so much as a tree-cum-goddess. Certainly, his tantalisingly brief phrase does not give us enough of a handle to plump confidently for one or the other interpretation. However, that Pausanias might have been thinking about this myrtle in statue-like terms is suggested when, on another occasion, he discusses what it means to 'worship a tree'. This time we are in Corinth and Pausanias is narrating a sequel to the tale of how Pentheus, hiding in a tree to spy on female devotees of Dionysus, was discovered by them and mercilessly torn to pieces. Some time after his death, Pausanias relates, the Corinthians were instructed by the Pythian priestess 'to find that tree and to worship it equally with the god' (ἀνευρόντας τὸ δένδρον ἐκεῖνο ἴσα τῷ θεῷ σέβειν; 2.2.7). For this reason, he abruptly concludes, they made two statues of Dionysus from the tree.

This little-known sequel to the story of Pentheus' infamous death raises a huge number of questions. How did the Pythia intend the Corinthians to fulfil her puzzling instruction to worship a tree equally with Dionysus? Was there something about the

---

[17] For further discussion of a blurring between trees and statues in the Roman world see pp. 255–265.
[18] It may be objected that we are here talking about a tree, not an anthropomorphic image of Artemis. However, it does not seem that it was the anthropomorphic 'verisimilitude' of a statue of a deity which helped to secure this 'dynamic interpenetration of image and referent'. Ando 2008: 22–26 and 41–42, for example, has persuasively shown how aniconic divine images could also be assimilated with the deities they 'represented', focusing on the case of the goddess Cybele, who 'somehow was, and yet was not coextensive with' a black stone (42).

specific tree in which Pentheus hid that meant that no alternative would do for the Pythia?[19] The time gap between the incident and the Pythia's instructions (which, we are told, came 'later' (ὕστερον δέ)), not to mention the disturbed mental state of the women who were presumably its only witnesses, would have made identifying the tree no mean feat. Yet suppose the tree had been discovered. What were the Corinthians supposed to do then? Was the Pythia telling them to worship the tree and Dionysus separately, but with equal intensity? Or was the Pythia's cryptic remark a command to assimilate the material tree and Dionysus mentally, to worship the tree on the understanding that thus they were somehow worshipping Dionysus too? All we can say for definite is that, for the Corinthians, the way to fulfil the Pythia's command was to make statues from the tree. But how is this worshipping a tree equally with a god? One thing here is certain: the Corinthians must have chopped up, or at least carved, the tree to make these statues, suggesting that one thing they did *not* believe the Pythia was instructing them to do was to recognise the tree *as* the god.[20] To me it seems most likely that the Corinthians reasoned as follows: making statues from the tree allowed them to worship the matter of the tree and Dionysus together.[21] Taking

[19] Another story recounted by Pausanias suggests a broadly similar understanding that only certain trees will do for cult statues. Here we see the Plataeans going to a grove, enticing crows with chunks of meat, and then observing on which tree a crow alights with their grabbed portion of meat; they then proceed to make a statue (for use in the festival of the Daedala) from that specific tree (9.3.4).

[20] Thus, I would disagree with the kind of interpretation of the passage Bennet puts forward: the Corinthians are told to honour the tree 'as if it were the god' (1917: 85). This seems to me overly simplistic, and does not engage with the awkward implications of the Corinthians' first action being to hack the tree about. Birge 1986: 28 has not grappled with the starkness of the command 'worship the tree equally with the god' when she concludes of this passage that 'to worship a tree equally with a god one does not consider the tree a god but rather the possession of a god'; nor, moreover, does Pausanias provide any support for the idea of Dionysus owning the tree.

[21] This would not entail that the statues were understood to *be* Dionysus, only that worship directed towards them constituted worship of the deity they 'depicted'. Boetticher 1856: 215, looking as usual through an animistic lens, confidently explains that pagans made statues from sacred trees because of an original belief in deities being assimilated with trees; such wooden statues consequently retained the sacred tree's 'ursprüngliche Eigenschaft'. He further adds that this is why oracles encourage the production of statues from sacred trees, and although he provides no supporting examples here, we might imagine the Corinthian episode was one he had in mind. Arguments about wooden statue production like that of Boetticher were common in scholarship of this period – cf. Philpot 1897: 32, who paints idolatry as 'a childish deduction' from the idea that 'the

Tree worship

the Pythia's 'equally' to denote chiefly the manner of their worship, making these wooden statues of Dionysus allowed them to worship the tree and Dionysus through a response to the same objects, and by means of the same actions, namely offerings and sacrifice. As the citizens of Boiai could be seen to have combined their worship of a myrtle and of Artemis through a statue-like tree, so at Corinth statues of Dionysus made out of a tree combined the worship of both god and tree through one entity; such a blurring of image and referent is, as Elsner argued, something we come to expect in a Pausanian worldview.[22] This tree was not, as the comparativists would have had it, a god: but the 'god' was made out of a tree.

Pythian instructions are supposed to be baffling, and the subtext to Pausanias' story is one of debate and bafflement among the Corinthians as to what on earth it means to worship a tree. Indeed, the fact that one of our rare attestations of 'tree worship' in the Roman world comes in the form of a Pythian command suggests just how alien this concept must have been to many Roman thinkers. Pausanias, however, is not quite the only author to grapple with what tree worship might mean in the Roman world. Silius Italicus too explores this question when describing the visit of a certain Carthaginian, named Bostar, to the Libyan grove and oracle of Jupiter Ammon in the third book of his *Punica*. That we are engaging with a portrait of Carthaginian religious practice through a Latin poem on the Punic Wars should alert us to the likelihood that any 'tree worship' featured will be characterised in a reductionist way, as both barbarian and primitive.[23] Yet, even if what we see here is a constructed image of the religion of the other, it

---

dead piece of wood retained some at least of the power originally attributed to the spirit dwelling in the living tree' – and still have a legacy today (see Hughes 1994: 174). Scholars who think in this way about the production of wooden statues do not confront the irony or implications of the violence involved in turning a tree into a statue if you also believe that the tree once housed a god or spirit.

[22] See p. 80.

[23] Indeed Parke 1967: 249 emphasises the distance between Silius and the reality of Carthaginian religion: 'Silius was completely out of touch with the real contemporary oracle of Ammon and depended ... on a mixture of literary reminiscence and his own imagination.' See Bagnall and Rathbone 2004: 271–277 on archaeological excavations at the Ammoniac oasis. Liebeschuetz 1979: 167–182 also comments on the Rome-centric and Stoic colouring of the depictions of gods and cults in Silius.

still illuminates the types of relationship between a material tree and a deity which Silius' own religious thinking enabled him to imagine. It is, then, with the aim of teasing out Silius' thinking about such relationships that I approach Bostar's report of his visit to the Libyan grove.

Bostar begins by describing how an old guide instructed him to prepare before putting his request to the oracle:

> has umbras nemorum et connexa cacumina caelo
> calcatosque Iovi lucos prece, Bostar, adora. (3.675–676)
>
> Worship in prayer, Bostar, these woodland shadows,
> and tree tops touching the sky and groves trodden by Jupiter.

The command *adora* with woodland shadows, tree tops and groves as its direct objects suggests that Bostar was being asked to engage in a form of 'tree worship'. But what exactly was he being asked to do? We might instinctively want to know whether Bostar was expected to worship the trees *themselves* (the sting is always in this seemingly innocuous word), or whether the trees stand as an intermediary for communication with a more distant divine entity, who is the 'real recipient' of the religious response expressed. With our Protestant-centric intellectual heritage, unease is often felt over the first option, as registered in Duff's rendering of these two lines as follows: 'Bostar, bow down in prayer before these shady woods, this roof that soars to heaven, and these groves where Jupiter has trodden.'[24] Making the phrase locational, the interposition of 'before' creates a comforting buffer between the trees and the worship offered. Indeed such unease could be expressed by Roman authors too, as when Fronto writes to the emperor Verus to inform him how he responded to news of the emperor's recovery from ill health.[25]

---

[24] Duff 1934: 165.

[25] The overall tone of this letter is hard to gauge. Fronto may paint a picture of his gay abandon on Verus' recovery, but Verus' illness, which delayed his Parthian campaign of 162 CE, was apparently brought on by over-eating, and in the rest of the letter Fronto takes a more didactic stance in urging him not to over-indulge. (Cf. the much more scathing account of Verus' illness in Julius Capitolinus *Ver.* 6.7, as Champlin 1980: 113 does. Brock 1911: 57–59 notes the unsurprising fact that Verus is portrayed more favourably in letters than in histories.)

Tree worship

respiravi igitur et revalui et apud omnes foculos, aras, lucos sacros, arbores sacratas, nam rure agebam, supplicavi. (*Ver.* 2.6)

So I breathed again and regained strength and worshipped at every hearth, altar, sacred grove and consecrated tree, for I was living the rural life.

Fronto locates his supplication *apud* (at) hearths, altars, groves and trees: like Duff's 'before', Fronto's *apud* provides a buffer which ensures that trees are not taken as the direct object of his supplication. The collocation of hearths, altars, groves and trees also frames the groves and trees as altar-like intermediaries for communication with deities, rather than the intended recipient of Fronto's supplications. Moreover, Fronto distances *himself* from the whole response with the phrase *nam rure agebam* (for I was living the rural life): with gentle self-mockery he presents his actions as the kind of thing you would only do when far from Rome, when you are living a rural, 'Golden Age-style' idyll.[26] This kind of behaviour at trees is hardly a norm for sophisticated urban Romans.

Unlike Duff and Fronto, however, Silius does not seem to shy away from presenting an image of 'direct tree-worship' in the instructions given to Bostar. There are no prepositional buffers following the command *adora* (worship!) in Silius' text. As his account of Bostar's visit to the Libyan grove continues, however, a more complex picture emerges of what 'tree worship' in this grove might entail, in which religious responses to the trees blur with worship of Jupiter Ammon. Indeed, we have already had our first hint of this in the phrase *calcatosque Iovi lucos* (groves trodden by Jupiter). Was it perhaps the trees' relationship with Jupiter, through his use of the grove as a stomping ground, which was to motivate Bostar's adoration of them, rather than the trees *per se*? Further questions about the relationship between Jupiter and the trees arise as the old guide's instruction of Bostar continues, in the form of a potted history of the grove: after Jupiter sent a dove to mark the spot for his temple, a grove of oaks suddenly sprang up from the soil, staggeringly tall on their very first day of growth. From that moment onwards, the guide continues, *arbor numen habet coliturque tepentibus aris* (the trees have 'religious power'

---

[26] The tone and nuances of this passage have already been discussed on p. 13.

and are worshipped on glowing altars; 3.691).[27] Jupiter plays no obvious role in this image of 'tree worship' in the grove; the guide is explicit that it is the trees which have something religious about them and which receive the sacrificial honours.[28] But were the trees the *only* concern of those performing the sacrifices? Did Jupiter have a role to play beneath the surface? After all, Jupiter was said to have sent the dove which triggered the chain of events leading to the grove's emergence. If he was the root cause of the grove's existence and its awe-inspiring appearance, did not a religious response to the grove also constitute a response to him?

Bostar certainly goes on to suggest a conception of the grove in which Jupiter's power is articulated through the trees. After he has made his request of the oracle, he reports the following miraculous occurrence:

> inde ubi mandatas effudi pectore voces,
> ecce intrat subitus vatem deus. alta sonoro,
> collisis trabibus, volvuntur murmura luco,
> ac maior nota iam vox prorumpit in auras. (3.696–699)

> Then when I had poured out from my chest my question as instructed,
> behold, the god suddenly enters the priest. Deep rumbles
> roll through the resounding grove, with tree trunks crashing together,
> and now a voice, greater than any known, bursts forth into the air.

Silius presents Jupiter's inspiration of his priest and the noisy reaction of the grove as parallel responses to Bostar's question: the behaviour of the trees is an expression, writ large, of the presence of the god in the priest.[29] With the god apparently manifest in the

---

[27] The logic of the Latin prompts us to read singular for plural here, as Duff 1934: 165 does in his translation.

[28] Cook 1903: 403 reads this line as Silius showing us 'one tree of especial sanctity in which the deity resided and before which altars were kept burning', but the complex word *numen* cannot simply be understood as a synonym for deity (on which see discussion on pp. 177–190, with pp. 189–190 specifically on the Silius passage). (The instinct of scholarship of this period to interpret sacred trees in an animistic framework is also blatant in Cook's observation.) Overall, Silius' striking depiction of the trees and their *numen* has generated surprisingly little interest: Tylor 1871b: 206 breezed over a reference to the passage as straightforward proof of tree worship in 'Semitic regions'; Spaltenstein 1986: 260, in his commentary on the book, ignores *numen* and thinks to comment only on *tepentibus* (glowing).

[29] Cf. Seneca *Oed.* 574–577, in which the arrival of Hecate, similarly summoned by a priest, makes a wood shudder and bristle, with tree trunks cracking apart. Schrijvers 2006: 103 emphasises that Silius' Jupiter thunders more than most.

trees and a divine voice emerging from among them, it seems that any religious actions directed towards those trees could hardly be seen as expressing religious concern *solely* for the trees *qua* trees. Indeed no straightforward 'tree worship' took place in this grove. For Silius vacillates between presenting the trees as prompting religious responses in their own right, and hinting at how Jupiter's relationship with, and articulation through, those trees prompted their worship. As in Pausanias' account of the Corinthians making statues of Dionysus from 'Pentheus' tree', once again worship of tree and god blend into one action.

Unsurprisingly, any suggestions of Roman tree worship, which we have encountered so far, have little to do with tree worship as it is painted by the Christian apologists or nineteenth-century comparativists. There is no simple 'category mistake' equation of a tree and deity. Rather, what we have seen are responses to trees where the worship of a material tree seems to articulate worship of a deity too. Questions about the degree to which a material tree might be assimilated with a deity are subtly raised here, both in Silius' portrait of Jupiter's epiphany in the trees of his grove, and in Pausanias' framing of tree worship as something conceptually similar to offering cult to statues of the gods (with all their hesitation between being and representing the deity concerned). This is hardly to say that the material tree is worshipped as a god, but rather that the nature and degree of 'material overlap' between the tree and the god is left as an open question.

At this point, a striking imperial inscription demands our attention. For, whilst this inscription does not contain such an overt image of tree worship as found in Pausanias or Silius, it does articulate worship of a deity whose material relationship with various trees is very much called into question. Heading home from diplomatic service in Alpine regions, Titus Pomponius Victor left inscribed for posterity the following verse prayer:

> Silvane sacra semicluse fraxino
> et huius alti summe custos hortuli
> tibi hasce grates dedicamus musicas
> quod nos per arva perque montis alpicos
> tuique luci suave olentis hospites
> dum ius guberno remque fungor Caesarum

tuo favore prosperanti sospitas
tu me meosque reduces Romam sistito
daque Itala rura te colamus praeside
ego iam dicabo mille magnas arbores. (*CIL* 12.103)

Silvanus, half shut up in the sacred ash,
and supreme guardian of this mountain garden plot,
let me dedicate to you these thanks in verse,
because you defend me with your prospering favour
through fields and through Alpine mountains
and the hosts of your sweet-odored grove,
while I dispense law and perform the Caesars' business.
See to it that you lead me and my family home to Rome
and grant that with you as my guardian I might work Italian fields;
straightaway I will dedicate a thousand huge trees.

How can a deity be *half shut up* in a tree? The strange phrase suggests an element of unease on Victor's part about the idea of Silvanus being materially assimilated with the tree, as he opts for a middle-ground compromise.[30] Victor goes on to inform us that Silvanus has protected him as he journeys through fields and mountains: if he is in some way materially restricted to a tree, this at least does not seem to limit his sphere of influence in Victor's eyes. Another possibility is that Victor was not using *semicluse* (half shut up) in a physical sense, but as a metaphorical expression of Silvanus' interest in the ash, or indeed the whole genus that *fraxinus* (ash) indicates. Is Silvanus *semicluse* (half shut up) in every ash tree? Alternatively, might Victor be imagining a statue of Silvanus, made out of ash, which guards the garden plot?[31] If this is the case, then this is not only an intriguing addition to the complex of relationships imagined between deities and their statues in the Greco-Roman world.[32] It is also interesting that Victor's

---

[30] In their commentary on this inscription Chapot and Laurot 2001: 356 ignore the theological implications of *semiclusus* (half shut up) by emphasising solely how it imitates Catullan neologisms based on *semi-*, and is no more than a 'jeu littéraire'. Indeed their dismissal of the challenging *semicluse* is characteristic of how little theological justice is done to Silvanus in modern engagements with the evidence for this god, on which see pp. 251–254.

[31] I am grateful to Robin Osborne for this particular suggestion.

[32] For further discussion of Greco-Roman discourse about these relationships and its impact on Roman thinking about the sacrality of certain trees see pp. 80–81 and 262–265. If we are here in the presence of an ash statue, then the epithet *semicluse* (half shut up) would put Victor near the middle of the spectrum on which, at one extreme, a statue and a god are presented as coterminous, whilst at the other, the statue is purely representative of the god.

Tree worship

language frames the wooden statue – if that is what it is – as a tree; what would be important about such a statue of the god Silvanus is its tree-like appearance, its visual evocation of the ash and Silvanus' relationship with it.[33]

The relationship Silvanus enjoys with trees is also the focus of the second half of the poem. Here Victor's promise to dedicate a thousand trees on Italian soil sits uneasily, indeed almost comically, with the idea of Silvanus being materially restrained in the Alps. Was the point of this gesture anything more than symbolic?[34] Or would Silvanus now be *semicluse* (half shut up) in the newly dedicated trees, as he was in the *sacra fraxinus* (sacred ash)? What type of trees would Victor choose to dedicate, and would any do for Silvanus, this generic god Woody, or did they have to be ash? Much of what Victor is striving to express in this enigmatic prayer centres on the relationships between Silvanus and particular trees, but he is coy about whether he articulates these relationships in terms of material assimilation. Indeed the wriggle room in the striking epithet *semicluse* (half shut up) allows Victor to have his cake and eat it. The epithet's connotations of physical restraint are inescapable, but its semi-commitment to the idea of Silvanus being materially restricted manages to blend an image of Silvanus as somehow coexistent with a tree, or several trees, with snapshots of him enjoying a lifestyle and significance seemingly independent of any particular tree. Was Victor worshipping a god or a god-cum-tree? The epithet *semicluse* (half shut up) helps him to evade the question.

At this point, I wish to pause briefly at a Roman response to trees which might seem to paint them as recipients of worship: this is the pouring out of wine, like a libation, on their roots. Of course for most trees, water suffices, but so great was the *honor* (honour) for planes, Pliny tells us, that they are nurtured with wine, 'this having been discovered to be very beneficial to their roots' (*conpertum id*

---

[33] Cf. my discussion of a myrtle tree/myrtlewood statue, depicted by Pausanias, on pp. 263–264; Pausanias' language suggests that, in his eyes at least, the divide between a wooden statue and a living tree, rooted in the earth, can be much narrower than we might imagine.

[34] Chapot and Laurot 2001: 356 insist the promise is made 'de façon hyperbolique', whilst Dorcey 1992: 18 takes the promise at face value, noting that Victor must be a wealthy man.

maxime prodesse radicibus; *Nat.* 12.8). The word *honor* can indicate religious or non-religious respect, making it hard to say to what degree, if any, Pliny understands the pouring of wine on planes as a religiously motivated act. Did religious awe for the plane prompt a response adopted from other rituals, namely the pouring out of wine? Or did general respect for the plane, whose useful shade Pliny has just praised, ensure it got the best fertilising treatment, which just happened to mean wine? Much depends on how Pliny understood the phrase beginning *conpertum id* to relate to the rest of his sentence: does it explain why people first decided to pour wine on planes, or was it a discovery incidental to the planes being treated to a libation-style watering? The idea of pouring wine on planes is in fact something of a topos in literature of the Roman world.[35] In one Greek epigram we meet a chatty plane who jokes that she alone finds a bath of wine helps her to stand up straight again, having been knocked over by the wind (*AG.* 9.247): no hint of the action being religiously significant here. Macrobius also recounts how Hortensius once tried to walk out on a court-case with

---

[35] Evidence for non-alcoholic 'offerings' to trees is far scarcer. Pliny tells us that the hair of the Vestal virgins is 'carried' (*defertur*) to an ancient lotus, which for that reason is called the 'hairy' lotus (*capillata*; *Nat.* 16.235), but this is *not* to say the hair is an offering for the tree. (Boetticher 1856: 96 somehow understands the Vestals to be consecrating their hair cuttings at the tree.) Cf. Gellius' description of how the *flamen Dialis*' nail cuttings have to be buried under a tree (*NA.* 10.15.15). Our only unambiguous portrayals of pagans leaving offerings on or near trees, as though they were intended for the tree, come within scathing portrayals of the religion of 'the other'. Thus, Christian apologetic likes to cut out the involvement of a deity when painting pictures of pagans placing offerings on trees (e.g. Prud. *Cont. Symm.* 2.1010–1011; Arn. *Ad. nat.* 5.16). Aelian too openly mocks the Persian Xerxes for 'honouring' (τιμῶν) a plane by hanging it with expensive ornaments, as well as leaving it a bodyguard as though it were a woman he loved (*VH.* 2.14). He calls Xerxes 'the plane's slave' (δεδούλωτο δὲ πλατάνῳ,), styling the offerings 'pointless' (εἰς ὥραν οὐδέν) and scathingly questioning what 'good' (καλόν) this could possibly be for the tree. (Commenting on this passage, Stubbings 1946: 63 accuses Aelian of lacking empathy with the 'religious awe' inspired by shady trees in arid countries.) These instances should be distinguished from the common motif in the *Anthologia Graeca* of dedicating an object to Pan *on* a tree. Teleso stretched a skin on a plane tree for Pan, along with his staff, cheese-pails and dog collars (6.35), Teucer dedicated a lion skin to Pan on a pine (6.57), Glaucon and Corydon fixed a steer's horns to a plane as an offering for Pan (6.96). Telamon too hung up a skin and staff on a plane for Pan (6.106), Xenophilus hung a boar's hide for Pan on a beech (6.168), certain goat-herds dedicated to Pan a picture of their miraculous escape from a lion attack and displayed it on a thick stemmed oak (6.221). Himself associated with wild, wooded spaces, it seems that, aside from their practical role, these trees' significance in the offerings to Pan rested in what they said about the nature of the god receiving them. Rouse 1902: 50–51 briefly discusses these offerings.

Tree worship

Cicero in order to 'water' his planes with wine: again no indication that Hortensius saw this as a religious duty, and using *inrigare* to describe the watering colours the action as one of arboricultural care (3.13.3).[36] Nor is it only planes which get treated to a drink from time to time. The consul Passienus Crispus had a tree in a grove of Diana which he loved so much that he made a habit not only of lying under it and pouring wine on it, but also kissing and embracing it (*Nat.* 16.242). In Pliny's eyes this response is clearly excessive, but he colours it more as amatory than religious excess.[37] Martial also presents a similar excess taking place within one of Caesar's houses: in an idealised image of a tree which grows inside the house, under which fauns play and a dryad hides, he describes how at wine-heavy parties the shade of the tree grew 'more luxurious' (*laetior*; 16) from poured-out wine (9.61.5–16). The term *laetus* used to describe the tree post-wine bath does have connotations of 'blessed': yet the adjective also means 'flourishing', and could perhaps play on the supposed benefit of wine to the tree's health. In short, the motif of pouring out wine on trees does visually frame them as though they were receiving 'worship'. Yet only Pliny and Martial encourage us in any way to view this action in religious terms, by use of the multivalent *honor* (honour) and *laetior* (more luxurious/blessed). Perhaps the borrowing of this ritual action was more a way of expressing the special status of planes (those kings of the tree world), or the tree which Crispus idolised, or the tree which enjoyed so prominent a place in Caesar's house. The motif could be read as a hyperbolic way of articulating that some trees have VIP status; these trees are simply too good for water.

To sum up, the glimpses of Roman tree worship encountered in Pausanias, Silius Italicus and Victor's prayer hardly warrant Tylor's adjectives 'direct' and 'absolute'. To the contrary, worship of a tree has been seen to blur with worship of a god, in ways which raise – and leave hanging – challenging questions about the

---

[36] Ovid also briefly alludes to planes' love of wine at *Rem.* 141.
[37] As noted by Beagon 1996: 302. Pliny expresses more surprise at the kissing and embracing than Crispus' other actions, but it seems to me that Dowden 2000: 73 leans on this distinction too heavily when claiming that Pliny would have seen Crispus as 'a normal person' if he had stopped at wine pouring. Many years ago Ouseley 1819: 390 wondered whether we see in Crispus' 'libation or affusion with wine, something of a religious ceremony'.

nature and degree of possible material overlap between a tree and a deity. Chasing these glimpsed snapshots of tree worship has also driven home the rarity of the idea in Roman culture, and so from here I wish to move forwards to ask new questions about ways in which matter might be at the heart of what makes a tree sacred. If a sacred tree finds itself no longer an organic whole, either a victim of natural forces or human violence, are its constituent parts still sacred?[38] Or at what stage of material decay, if any, does a sacred tree cease to be recognised as a sacred tree? And if you turn a sacred tree into something else, like a statue or a chair or a boat, does it continue to be sacred?

Sacred wood

We have already caught a hint that it can be the matter, not the form, of a tree which matters for conceptions of its sacrality in Pausanias' account of the Corinthians' tree-statues of Dionysus. For when asked to worship that tree they produced statues from it, proving that it was not what the tree stood for as an organic whole that mattered, but rather its constituent material. What poetic tradition tells us about the Argo also suggests a parallel way of thinking about arboreal sacrality, privileging the qualities of the wood from a group of prophetic trees over the form that wood takes. In Valerius Flaccus' retelling of this famous tale the Argonauts are on the verge of setting sail when Jason receives a night vision of the guardian of the ship (*tutela carinae*), who exhorts him as follows:

> Dodonida quercum
> Chaoniique vides famulam Iovis. aequora tecum
> ingredior, nec fatidicis avellere silvis
> me nisi promisso potuit Saturnia caelo. (1.302–305)

[38] We might compare how Pliny recommends a bitten-off piece of a lightning-struck tree as a cure for toothache (*Nat.* 28.45), or his account of the 'mad laurel', of which a piece taken on board ship will cause quarrelling to break out until you discard it (*Nat.* 16.239): is a tree's sacrality also like its medicinal or more magical properties, a kind of special quality which pervades all its components? Hughes 1994: 174 confidently observes, with no supporting references whatsoever, that 'Wood from sacred trees was believed to keep magical powers when fashioned into objects. It was therefore used to make statues of gods; staffs for augurs, speakers, and generals; military standards; scepters of office; heralds' wands; policeman's nightsticks; divining rods; and lot-tokens for oracles.'

Sacred wood

> You see a Dodonian oak and servant of Chaonian Jupiter.
> I am embarking on the seas with you, nor would Saturnia
> have been able to uproot me from prophetic woods
> without the promise of heaven.

Both a servant of Jupiter and a Dodonian oak from prophetic woods, this nebulous figure appears to be a kind of personification of the 'prophetic beam' which Athena fashioned for the Argo, the chief source for which being Apollonius Rhodius 1.524–527, where it is referred to as a δόρυ θεῖον (divine beam; 526).[39] Later in the adventure we are told that the *quercus* (oak) again intervenes when the crew needs to appoint a new helmsman, voicing her choice of Erginus (5.65–66).[40] Valerius thus suggests a way of thinking about the sacrality of trees in which the quality which makes a tree sacred pervades all its matter, remaining potent even after the tree's dismembering and reshaping. Yet the power of the Argo's wood must of course be set in context: the building of the Argo initiates a mythological narrative rich in magic and the dark arts, in which a prophetic beam hardly feels out of place; that this is a Greek myth may also contribute to its feelings of 'otherness'.[41] Do other Roman depictions of sacred trees reveal similar conceptions of their matter's significance?

A quintessentially Roman moment, the lead-up to Aeneas' foundational killing of Turnus in *Aeneid* 12, provides our next example. Here Aeneas finds his attempts to finish off Turnus stumped by a tree stump (12.766–790). Aeneas and his marauding invaders had cut down an oleaster, or wild olive, once sacred to Faunus – Virgil refers to it twice as *sacer* (sacred) and once as *venerabilis* (venerable) – in order to clear the plain for battle. Later on, having by chance hurled his spear at the place where the olive once stood, Aeneas found it gripped tight by the *lenta radice* (pliant root stock; 773). Seeing this, Turnus called on Faunus and Terra to remember his history of venerating them and to keep hold of Aeneas' spear. His

---

[39] Spaltenstein 2002: 135 insists the *quercus* (oak) mentioned is 'une pièce isolée', noting that the whole Argo is made of pine (1.123). Zissos 2008: 225 also links lines 302–303 back to the 'tradition of the prophetic plank'.
[40] Wijsman 1996: 45 argues that this must refer only to the beam, not the whole ship, again referring us to 1.302–305 and *AR*. 1.524–527.
[41] This is true despite Zissos' 2009: 351–352 rightful emphasis on Flaccus' Romanisation of the narrative.

prayer was answered: the remains of the olive stubbornly clenched Aeneas' spear until Venus intervened to retrieve it. So were the remains of this tree still sacred in Turnus' eyes? His prayer begging Faunus to act through the olive suggests that he understood its remains still to stand in special relationship with Faunus; Faunus' immediate response, actualised through the tree's remnants, seems to confirm that the relationship has not been broken.[42] Yet the sense of a unique relationship between the olive and Faunus is undermined by the fact that other deities also work through the woody remains. Turnus in addition asks Terra to hold onto the spear, perhaps because of her naturally close involvement with roots, whilst Venus demonstrates her power by unlocking the stump's grip on Aeneas' spear.[43] These deities are flexing their muscles, staging a power struggle over their ability to control the behaviour of a piece of wood in the human world: the sacrality of the former tree's material does not enter into *this* image of the stump's significance on a divine level, which rather slots into a picture Virgil builds up towards the end of the *Aeneid* of a world of relentless power struggles among both gods and men.[44] Nevertheless, the implication that Turnus is tragically deluded in believing in the continued power of the olive's remains and their unique relationship with Faunus still illuminates Roman thinking about the *potential* religious

[42] Many characterisations of this relationship are to be found in secondary literature. Some see Faunus as a 'wood spirit' e.g. Maguinness 1953: 107 and Dyson 2001: 20. Bailey 1935: 144 talks of Virgil's depiction of the 'open-air worship of Faunus *at* an ancient wild olive tree' (my italics). Recently Tarrant 2012: 79 depicted the tree 'as the embodiment of the god's worship'.

[43] Bailey 1935: 185 finds Faunus and Terra an 'unexpected combination', but the invocation of Terra does not seem out of place with this focus on roots. For the close co-operation of roots and earth/soil in another account of arboreal sacrality see Plutarch's depiction of how Romulus' spear metamorphosed into a cornel, with his emphasis that it was the fertilising earth which cherished the spear and sent up cornel shoots (*Rom.* 20.5).

[44] Indeed many have read the oleaster episode as a reflection of both the divine and human disorder which has reached fever pitch by this stage in the *Aeneid*. Thomas 1988a: 261–273 argues that a Roman audience would expect tree violation like Aeneas' to be avenged by the gods: that his attack on Faunus' *wild* olive is ultimately not avenged (Faunus only has temporary power over the stump) is a dark message about 'the price in spiritual loss attending the advent of civilization' (270). Dyson 2001: 221–231, heavily influenced by Frazer's theories about the cult at Nemi, sees similar symbolism in Aeneas' struggle with the oleaster: she reads it as a reference back to his removal of the 'golden bough' which, she argues, marked him out as the 'challenger' to Turnus' '*rex*'. Reckford 1974: 83 sees in Aeneas' uprooting of the oleaster a 'terrifying vision of the hero who is homeless itself and makes others homeless also'.

Sacred wood

significance of a tree's constituent matter; Turnus was deluded only because he was on the wrong side.

The demands of warfare would have left the Laurentines little leisure for considering a response to what was left of their sacred tree, but what if the tree had so decayed simply though the passage of time? A picture of a response to a tree in that situation emerges from Pausanias' account of his visit to a temple at Aulis:

πλατάνου δέ, ἧς καὶ Ὅμερος ἐν Ἰλιάδι ἐποιήσατο μνήμην, τὸ ἔτι τοῦ ξύλου περιὸν φυλάσσουσιν ἐν τῷ ναῷ. (9.19.7)

What is still remaining of the wood of the plane of which Homer made mention in the *Iliad*, they preserve in the temple.

With his allusion to the *Iliad* Pausanias expects his readers to recollect Homer's account of a portent witnessed by the Greek leaders gathered at Aulis, in which a serpent devoured eight baby sparrows and their mother, sheltering in the branches of a plane near a spring (*Il.* 2.305–316). Taking knowledge of this for granted, Pausanias pauses for a moment only to fill out the story of the Greeks' difficulties in sailing from Aulis, before carrying on with his guided tour. The next stop, he casually informs us, was the spring by which the plane grew. Thus he tacitly assumes the removal of the tree from its initial location by the spring to its final resting place in the temple.[45] Yet this is of no small significance, for the transferral of the presumably decaying tree to a place within the temple indicates a religious conception of the tree in which its matter played a crucial role. Pausanias' description of what he saw in the temple, 'what

---

[45] That Pausanias does not think to comment on the removal process *might* suggest it was, to him, a not unusual practice. Certainly Boetticher 1856: 46 is confident enough in the frequency of such removals to infer the general rule 'vom Holze eines vergangenen Baumes bewahrte man jedoch die Reste als ein Heiligthum auf', and later claims that 'man ... bewahrt das Holz jedes abgestorbenen Gottesbaumes als heilige Reliquie' (215), but there is precious little evidence to back him up. I know only of one other passage in Pausanias which could be used in support (2.9.7): here he tells us of a log which, through an oracle's advice, proved efficacious in ridding an area of wolves and was then moved into the sanctuary of Apollo Lycius. As we reflect on how unusual the actions of the Aulians were, we might wonder whether it was the plane's association with Homer which led them to treat it so deferentially. It is interesting that, by contrast, Pausanias depicts another 'Homeric tree' – a plane planted by Menelaus (8.23.4) – as still being alive; of course we do not know the actual age of the plane, but this would suggest that, if the Menelean plane died, it was replaced, rather than its remains being relocated to a temple.

remains of the wood of the plane', conjures up an image of something so decayed it is no longer recognisable as a tree; after all, he does not simply write 'what remains of the plane'. Nevertheless, the tree's matter has not ceased to be of religious significance; that is the message of its final resting place in the temple. We could easily imagine that what mattered about this tree was not its matter *per se* but what its physical presence *represented*, standing as a visual reminder of the portent witnessed by the Iliadic heroes. Yet if this were the case, the tree would first need to be recognisable as a plane (as opposed to a decaying lump of wood) and, more crucially, would need to be standing by the spring, its proximity to which is emphasised in Homer's account. That the Aulians did not simply plant a new plane at the spring when the old one decayed, but rather transferred its remains to the temple, speaks against an understanding of the tree's 'representative' significance, and for its matter being the religious issue at stake.

Finally, for a rather different conception of the relationship between a tree's sacrality and its materiality, I return to Virgil, and the laurel tree which he paints into his portrait of Latinus' palace.

> laurus erat tecti medio in penetralibus altis
> sacra comam multosque metu servata per annos,
> quam pater inventam, primas cum conderet arces,
> ipse ferebatur Phoebo sacrasse Latinus,
> Laurentisque ab ea nomen posuisse colonis. (*Aen.* 7.59–63)
>
> A laurel stood in the middle of the building, in its innermost rooms,
> sacred in its foliage and preserved for many years with awe,
> which father Latinus himself, having discovered it when first
> founding his citadel, was said to have dedicated to Phoebus,
> and to have named the Laurentine settlers from it.

Strikingly described as *sacra comam* (sacred in its foliage), this accusative of respect apparently limits the laurel's sacrality to its foliage and thus implies a materially focused understanding of its sacrality, attention being directed towards the leaves alone.[46] Yet Virgil goes on to say that Latinus consecrated the whole tree to Phoebus; this image of the tree emphasises its general sacrality,

---

[46] Fordyce 1977: 70 seems to find nothing striking in this phrase, simply commenting: 'i.e. its foliage is protected from the pruner's knife'.

and its status as such by virtue of a relationship with Phoebus rather than anything specific about its matter.[47] The two conceptions of the tree do not sit easily together, but were perhaps integrated by understanding the matter of one part of the tree, namely its foliage, as *particularly* sacred. Indeed Virgil appends to his portrait of the laurel an account of a portent which could explain that particular sacrality, namely that a large swarm of bees once settled on the top of the tree, prompting a prophecy of war and domination of the Laurentines' citadel.[48] Perhaps we are to imagine that it was the portent which first prompted Latinus to recognise the status of the tree by dedicating it, with its foliage standing out as especially significant. Or perhaps, on the understanding that the portent occurred after Latinus had dedicated the tree, we are to suppose that the arrival of the bees encouraged a revised understanding of the relative sacrality of the tree's components. In either case, Virgil constructs an image of the laurel's sacrality being so strongly bound up with its matter that it could in fact be concentrated in a particular part of the tree.

Whether it is articulated by preserving arboreal remains in a temple or in understanding a tree's foliage as 'more intensely sacred' than the rest, these varied snapshots have shown us multiple ways in which the sacrality of different trees was deeply entangled with their matter. This being so, the sheer vulnerability of arboreal matter prompts obvious and pressing questions, and indeed Turnus' laurel stump and the plane remains at Aulis have already started to raise such questions for us. How was the sacrality of a tree affected when its matter was damaged, or it went into decline from old age? What does it mean when a sacred tree dies? Could a replacement tree ever do? What were the theological

---

[47] Our glimpses of 'dedicated' trees so far (namely Latinus' laurel and those Victor promised Silvanus) do little to confirm the traditional view that dedication changed an object in material terms, by transferring it to the possession of the gods and thus making it inviolable, on which see pp. 3–7. The emphasis instead has been on the new relationship between deity and tree rather than any 'material transformation' in the tree. Scholars often assume that Faunus' wild olive also was dedicated (e.g. Maguinness 1953: 107 and Tarrant 2012: 284), but presumably only because it is described as *sacer* (sacred). For further discussion of our limited evidence for dedicated trees in the Roman world see pp. 227–228.

[48] Block 1981: 204 and Reckford 1974: 73 discuss the symbolism of the laurel and bees in this portent.

implications of humans interfering with the matter of sacred trees? Was arboriculture different from other kinds of interference? It is to the questions raised by the organic vulnerability of trees that I now turn, asking in particular how this vulnerability affected the sacrality of one tree which stood both at the heart of Rome and the heart of Roman identity, namely the *ficus Ruminalis*.

Memorial matter: the many faces of the *ficus Ruminalis*

Travelling towards the Psiphaean Sea with Pausanias as guidebook, you will find a wild olive known as the twisted ῥᾶχος (a local word for barren olive), so named from the time when the reins of Hippolytus' careering chariot got tangled up in it (2.32.10). Pausanias does not describe the tree's appearance, but if it had not lived up to its name and reputed mythological connection with a twisted and gnarled look, the stories told about it would surely have lost their credence. Such a tree, it seems, would be difficult to replace: only a twisted olive could authentically memorialise Hippolytus' fatal chariot ride. Doubtless the same also applies to a myrtle with holes in its leaves, reportedly so damaged when the frustrated Phaedra vented her rage on them (Paus. 2.32.3).[49] Nor is Pausanias alone in his fascination with such trees. Pliny also depicts a couple of trees whose appearance must have partly guaranteed stories about their origin and age. In a survey of trees of remarkable longevity (*Nat.* 16.234–240) he mentions a myrtle of conspicuous size on the elder Africanus' estate (234) and a lotus with mammoth roots spreading from the Volcanol to Caesar's *forum* (236). In the same survey he also introduces us to a plane at Delphi planted by Agamemnon whilst on his way to Troy, an olive to which Argus tethered Io, a wild olive from which came Hercules' first Olympic wreath and the olive Minerva produced at Athens (238–240). None of *these* trees, however, are mentioned for their impressive size or decrepit looks, and unlike the twisted olive, nothing made their appearance particularly striking. What was there, then, to guarantee accounts of their age?

---

[49] Birge 1994: 234–235 discusses Pausanias' noticeable penchant for trees which stand as 'a living memorial' to mythic events (235).

Memorial matter

Certainly trees do live to impressive ages: the Fortingall Yew, for example, is reckoned close to its two thousandth birthday. Yet should we imagine that Pliny believed all the trees his survey covers (over twenty in total) were as old as their supporters claimed? Whatever his opinion of the likelihood of a green-fingered Agamemnon having the time and inclination to plant a plane at Delphi, did he credit the plausibility of a tree existing since Agamemnon's day?[50] Pliny certainly distances himself from his reports of (often anonymous) claims about the age of these trees. 'Authorities say that' there is a plane tree planted by Agamemnon at Delphi (*sunt auctores*; *Nat.* 16.238); 'it is said that' the olive to which Argus tethered Io still exists (*dicitur*; *Nat.* 16.239); the olive produced by Minerva 'is reported' to survive (*traditur*; *Nat.* 16.240).[51] Not all the examples in Pliny's survey of ancient trees are introduced with such distancing scepticism, but the cumulative effect is undermining enough. Nor is Pliny alone in this hesitancy. For the outspoken Cicero, accepting that these trees had seen all their boasted years was laughable: only fools believe that Athens has an everlasting olive or that the palm which Homer's Odysseus said he saw at Delos is the one shown there today (*Leg.* 1.2).

Not all, however, were as stringently sceptical as Cicero. Certainly a more credulous response seems tangible when Pliny concludes his portrait of the olive which provided Hercules' first wreath with this apparently throwaway remark: *et nunc custoditur religio* (even today people keep up its 'veneration'; *Nat.* 16.240). Clearly this tree was of religious significance to some, but attributing such significance to a supposedly 'ancient' tree prompts nagging questions. Did this mean some believed it was the *actual* tree from which Hercules took his wreath? How much was at stake in the credibility of the tree's boasted age? How problematic was

---

[50] See Feeney 2007: esp. 80–84 on 'the question of the datability of myth' (80) and the dominant dating of Troy's fall to 1184/3 BCE by ancient writers; such a model would suggest an even earlier (if only slightly so) birth date for Agamemnon's plane. For similar examples of trees which memorialise their planter, compare the oaks reportedly planted by Hercules (Plin. *Nat.* 16.239) or the plane planted by Menelaus (Paus. 8.23.4).

[51] Pliny is more openly sceptical of the claim that a plane at Gortyn was the one under which Jupiter slept with Europa, attributing this to Greek 'inventiveness' (*fabulositas*; *Nat.* 12.11).

the almost inevitable process of having to replace such a tree? And how problematic was the alternative of letting the matter of a sacred memorial tree decay? Whilst the trees considered so far have been glimpsed in no more than snapshots, the *ficus Ruminalis*, a fig tree renowned for sheltering Romulus and Remus as they were suckled by a she-wolf, allows us to push these questions further. In so doing we approach from a new angle the live issue of how much a tree's religious significance was bound up with its material identity.

The secret history of the ficus Ruminalis

Occasionally Pliny highlights the age of trees by situating them in relation to the founding of Rome, an arboreal version of the *ab urbe condita* dating system. We are told that a lotus in the Volcanol was 'coeval' with the city (*aequaeva*; *Nat.* 16.236), whilst on the Vatican stood a holm oak even older than Rome, as evidenced by its accompanying Etruscan tablet (*Nat.* 16.237). Pliny normally prides himself on his comprehensivity, so the *ficus Ruminalis* is a glaring omission from this category of trees. Boasting a link to one of the most famous Roman images of their city's foundation, this tree must have been a prime contender among those trees jostling for the glory of being as old as Rome. So why Pliny's exclusion of the *ficus Ruminalis*? The natural historian's arboreal know-how is partly to blame. For as Pliny was well aware, fig trees are rarely long-lived, but rather known for their *brevissima vita* (extremely short life; *Nat.* 16.241), *senectus ocissima* (very fast approaching old age; *Nat.* 16.130) and *senescendi celeritas* (speed of ageing; *Nat.* 17.155). The *ficus Ruminalis*' conspicuous absence from Pliny's catalogue of ancient trees suggests his awareness that the fig known as the *ficus Ruminalis* in the Rome of his day was, in all likelihood, not the original fig which sheltered Romulus and Remus. After all, according to Pliny's close contemporary Tacitus, the suckling took place 830 years ago (*Ann.* 13.58), and who knew of such a veteran fig?

Pliny may exclude the *ficus Ruminalis* from his survey of notoriously old trees, but in a section on historically interesting fig trees he turns an insightful gaze on the tree and the nature of its

Memorial matter

sacrality (*Nat.* 15.77).[52] Unpicking Pliny's portrait of the tree in detail, I probe what importance he attributes to the material identity of this tree vis-à-vis conceptions of its sacrality.[53] Or, in other words, I ask how Pliny integrates his insistence on the *ficus Ruminalis*' sacrality with his acknowledgement of the minute chance that the fig which he knew had, as was boasted, been around since the days of Romulus and Remus.[54] First, however, I want to narrow down the location of the *ficus Ruminalis*: where would Pliny have gone to make an assessment of the age of this tree? The answer is not as simple as you might imagine. Quintus Fabius Pictor, Varro, Livy, Ovid, Plutarch and Servius all locate the *ficus Ruminalis* on the north side of the Palatine.[55] Whilst Ovid specifically positions the tree at the Lupercal, the others locate it either at the Palatine's foot, on the Germalus (the north slope of the Palatine) or at the point where the Tiber overflowed (in other words the Velabrum).[56] Considering the geographical proximity of these depictions, they should all be understood as expressions of the same tradition. Tacitus, however, ruins the uniformity of this picture. For him the *ficus Ruminalis* stands in the *comitium*, an assembly place within the Roman *forum* (*Ann.* 13.58). Conon, an Augustan grammarian, also locates a fig tree in the part of Rome which he calls the ἀγορά (or in Roman terms the *forum*), describing it as enclosed by the bronze gates of the βουλευτήριον (or again in Roman terms the *curia*; *Narr.* 48).[57] Conon does not specifically name the fig *Ruminalis*, but does single it out as witness to events from Romulus and Remus' lifetime, a strong indication

---

[52] Whilst not all authors depict this famous tree as sacred, Pliny is explicit that it was considered *sacra* (sacred).
[53] Pliny is currently enjoying something of an academic renaissance, as appreciation for his insights into the cultural and intellectual imagination of imperial Rome develops: Beagon 1992, Carey 2003, Gibson and Morello 2011 and Henderson 2011 do much to redeem the *Natural History* from 'a long career in the footnotes' (Gibson and Morello 2011: vii).
[54] An earlier version of some of this analysis was published in Hunt 2012.
[55] The references are as follows: Pictor as paraphrased in *OGR*. 20.3; Varro *LL*. 5.54; Ov. *Fast.* 2.411–412 and 421–422; Livy 1.4.4–6; Plutarch *De fort. Rom.* 320C; Plutarch *Rom.* 3.5–4.2; and Servius *A.* 8.90.
[56] Roman narratives of their city's history held that the Tiber used to flood the area later known as the Velabrum, before its draining by the Cloaca Maxima (e.g. Prop. 4.9.3–6); the historicity of these narratives has recently been challenged by excavations, on which see Ammerman 2006: 305–307.
[57] Conon's account is to be found paraphrased in Photius *Bibl.* 186.48.

that it was the *ficus Ruminalis* he meant. These two testimonies thus add another *ficus Ruminalis* to the map, standing in the *comitium* in front of the *curia*.[58]

Pliny appears to mention both figs, but which does he understand to be the *ficus Ruminalis*? An answer to this question will emerge as we go about unravelling the implications of his 'oscurissimo' depiction of the *ficus Ruminalis*.[59] I print the Teubner text below, followed by my own understanding of it.

colitur ficus arbor in foro ipso ac comitio Romae nata sacra fulguribus ibi conditis magisque ob memoriam eius quae, nutrix Romuli ac Remi, conditores imperii in Lupercali prima protexit, ruminalis appellata quoniam sub ea inventa est lupa infantibus praebens rumin (ita vocabant mammam), miraculo ex aere iuxta dicato, tamquam in comitium sponte transisset Atto Navio augurante. nec sine praesagio aliquo arescit rursusque cura sacerdotum seritur. (*Nat.* 15.77)[60]

A fig tree born in the very *forum* and *comitium* of Rome is cultivated, sacred because of the lightning-struck objects buried there, but more so because of the memorial tradition of that tree which, nurse of Romulus and Remus, first sheltered the founders of the empire at the Lupercal, called *Ruminalis* since under it the she-wolf was found offering her *rumis* (thus they used to call breast) to the infants, with the miracle portrayed in bronze nearby, as if the tree had of its own accord crossed into the *comitium* with Attus Navius as augur. Nor can it wither without being seen as an omen and being replanted by the care of the priests.

At first this depiction seems easy enough to follow. Pliny must be telling us that a fig in the *comitium* is considered sacred, partly because of the memory of the tree which sheltered Romulus and

---

[58] Such differing traditions are not unusual when it comes to myths about Romulus and Remus, which seem particularly susceptible to variation: see Wiseman 1995: 14 for a diagram of variants in Rome's foundation myth. There was similar controversy as to whether the *casa Romuli* stood on the Palatine or the Capitoline, on which see Balland 1984: 57–80, Edwards 1996: 30–37 and Rutledge 2012: 166.

[59] De Sanctis 1910: 79. Torelli 1982: 99 is alone in believing that 'the passage is clear enough'.

[60] Rackham 1945: 340 prints *qua* in place of *quae*, forcing us to understand the *nutrix* as the she-wolf rather than the fig. Yet *protexit* (protected) is more suited to the tree's sheltering role than the actions of the wolf, and her introduction a few words later (*quoniam sub ea inventa est lupa;* since under it the she-wolf was found) would be superfluous if she had already been introduced by *nutrix*. Latin usage does not restrict *nutrix* to human or animal agents; only a few chapters later Pliny describes acorn bearing trees as the first *nutrices* (nurses) of humankind (*Nat.* 16.1). Rackham also omits *in* before *comitium*, but a clause describing the putative actions of a tree now standing in the *comitium*, crossing *into* rather than *over* the *comitium* is far more pointed: my understanding of the subject of this clause is shortly to be argued in detail.

Remus at the Lupercal. As Pliny adds an etymological detail – 'it' is called *Ruminalis* from *rumis* – we would no doubt assume he is still talking about the Lupercal tree.[61] The next clause, however, 'with the miracle portrayed in bronze nearby', prompts a niggling question. I follow majority opinion in understanding this to mean a bronze statue of the suckling twins, the miracle just described in the preceding clause, but which tree is the bronze statue standing near? Is it the *comitium* fig or the Lupercal fig? Things get yet more obscure with the following *tamquam* clause: in light of what we have so far assumed the sentence to mean, this frustrates all attempts to extract meaning from it and especially to assign it a subject. We are left with the following reading: the *comitium* fig is sacred because of the memory of the Lupercal fig, called *Ruminalis* because under it a wolf offered the twins her *rumis*, with a bronze statue of the miracle standing nearby, as if 'something' had crossed into the *comitium* of its own accord, with Attus Navius as augur … We cannot leave our understanding of the sentence trailing off in such an unsatisfactory state. I therefore propose to rethink this sentence by establishing the subject and meaning of the *tamquam* clause, and then to reassess our understanding of the preceding clauses.

I start with the sentence's final three words, with the aim of explaining the unexpected introduction of the legendary augur Attus Navius: but to do so it is first necessary to fill in the story of another renowned fig. Verrius Flaccus tells of a fig in the *comitium* called the *ficus Navia*, closely associated with the story of how Attus Navius dissuaded Tarquinius Priscus from changing Romulus' system of tribes.[62] Tarquinius had tried to shake the augur's authority with a trick, asking him to predict whether he, the king, would be able to perform a secret task which he had in mind: this was to cut through a whetstone with a razor. Navius predicted that the king would accomplish the task and Tarquinius, much to his amazement,

---

[61] On the etymology cf. Plutarch *QR*. 57; this etymology is critiqued by Dulière 1979: 58–59. Wiseman 1995: 78 and Bruggisser 1987: 53–54 discuss alternative etymologies for *Ruminalis*.

[62] The details we extract from Verrius Flaccus as preserved in Festus 168–170L, Livy 1.36 and Dionysius of Halicarnassus 3.71.1–5. Unlike Torelli 1982: 99 I do not believe we can extract anything meaningful about this fig from the end of the extremely fragmentary Festus 170L.

found that he could. Dionysius of Halicarnassus adds to Flaccus' picture: won over by the augur's prowess, Tarquinius set up a bronze statue of Navius in the *forum* in front of the βουλευτήριον (i.e. the *curia*), near a sacred fig tree and the whetstone and razor which had been buried 'under a certain altar' (ὑπὸ βωμῷ τινι), called a φρέαρ by the Romans (3.71.5). In Latin this container was in fact called a *puteal*, as seen in Cicero's description of the covering over the whetstone and razor (*Div.* 1.33). But what was this 'altar-like' *puteal*? The *puteal* is certainly a sparsely documented structure: it may well have functioned as a covering for lightning-struck objects, as suggested by the phrase *fulgur conditum* (buried lightning-struck object) in a fragmentary reference of Festus to the *puteal Scribonianum* (448–450L) and by a fuller description of burying lightning-struck objects under the earth in the scholia to Persius 2.26.[63] Despite question marks over the precise nature of the *puteal*, we can at least be sure that it played a central role in the cluster of objects which commemorated Attus Navius' augury, and it is the location of this cluster to which I now return. Livy locates a statue of Navius and the whetstone by the steps to the left of the *curia* (1.36.5), and in a passing reference Pliny also locates a statue of Navius in front of the *curia* (*Nat.* 34.21). In short, the *ficus Navia*, along with its associated statue of Navius and buried whetstone and razor, are located very close to the *curia*, a spot disconcertingly close to that of the *ficus Ruminalis* as depicted by Tacitus and Conon.[64] Are we, then, to imagine two fig trees crowding in on each other by the *curia*? Pliny makes it clear that we are not, for there were never two separate fig trees at that spot, but rather one fig tree which underwent an identity shift. That Pliny understands the *comitium* fig tree as the one-time *ficus Navia* can be demonstrated through the combined force of four pieces of evidence.[65]

---

[63] On the nature of the *puteal* see Nash 1962: 259–261, Latte 1967: 81–82 and Coarelli 1985: 31–32; see Zetzel 2005: 169 for the Persius scholium. Glinister 2000: 65 discusses archaeological evidence for the burial of lightning-struck objects.
[64] Coarelli 1985: 28–38 discusses literary evidence for what he sees as a 'unità topografica' made up of the *puteal*, statue of Navius, *ficus Ruminalis* and a statue of the she-wolf (29).
[65] Over a century ago Baddeley 1905: 107 recognised that the *comitium* fig 'was at one time called "Navia" but later "Ruminalis"', without justifying his reconstruction of its history: his striking observation has been roundly ignored.

Memorial matter

The first of these we have just seen, namely the apparent coincidence of the two figs' location. Secondly there is the association of Pliny's *comitium* fig tree with buried lightning-struck objects. Pliny's *fulguribus ibi conditis* (lightning-struck objects buried there) sounds very much like a muffled reference to the whetstone and razor buried at the *ficus Navia*, with the identity of these objects perhaps not securely known by his day, but the *puteal* which most accounts place over them encouraging the assumption that they were the victims of lightning.[66] The third piece of evidence is provided by a survey of fig trees around the *forum* into which Pliny's depiction of the *comitium* fig tree develops: besides the *comitium* fig he also locates one at the *lacus Curtius* and one before the temple of Saturn, but makes no mention of a *ficus Navia* (*Nat.* 15.77–78). Strikingly this is despite Pliny's awareness of the existence and location of the statue of Navius (*Nat.* 34.21), which suggests that in Pliny's mental map of Rome the statue of Attus Navius still stood, but without its previously associated fig.

The fourth and crucial proof of Pliny's understanding of the *comitium* fig tree's 'secret past' as the *ficus Navia* lies in the phrase *tamquam in comitium sponte transisset Atto Navio augurante* (as if 'it' had of its own accord crossed into the *comitium* with Attus Navius as augur). Yet before extracting this proof, we first have to understand how Pliny saw this clause as a fitting conclusion to his monumental sentence. Its baffling nature stems chiefly from its lack of an obvious subject, with the four main options being the she-wolf, the Lupercal fig, the bronze statue group and the *comitium* fig. Taking the she-wolf as subject would not have any obvious pertinence, nor is it clear how a wolf moving of her own accord would have occasioned enough surprise to warrant the rather sceptical tone of *tamquam* (as if).[67] Likewise the Lupercal fig tree could not be the subject, for what would be the sense in saying that a tree at the Lupercal looked as if it had crossed to the *comitium*? What if the statue group were

[66] Petersen 1908: 447 too long ago suggested that the *fulgura condita* were Navius' whetstone and razor, but did not push this for what it might tell us about the nature and history of the *ficus Ruminalis* in the *comitium*: this observation has also been roundly ignored!
[67] Rackham 1945: 341 does take the she-wolf as subject, perhaps facilitated by his emendation of *quae* to *qua* (as discussed in n. 60, above) which elevates the wolf's role within the sentence.

the subject? There is nothing in Pliny's sentence to explain what might give us the impression that the statue had moved to the *comitium* of its own accord. Simply by a process of elimination, then, we conclude that the subject of Pliny's *tamquam* clause must be the *comitium* fig.[68] Yet reading this fig as the *tamquam* clause's subject is not just a 'last resort' option, but the only way to make sense of Pliny's monumental sentence; this will become clear as we unpack the implications of this fig being our missing subject for our understanding of the rest of the sentence. We already knew that Pliny opens his sentence with this tree, and now that he ends with it too. But what about the intervening clauses; to what do they refer? To help ascertain the relationship between the components of this paratactic sentence I divide it into five units of sense:

1. colitur ficus arbor in foro ipso ac comitio Romae nata sacra fulguribus ibi conditis magisque ob memoriam
2. eius quae, nutrix Romuli ac Remi, conditores imperii in Lupercali prima protexit,
3. ruminalis appellata quoniam sub ea inventa est lupa infantibus praebens rumin (ita vocabant mammam)
4. miraculo ex aere iuxta dicato
5. tamquam in comitium sponte transisset Atto Navio augurante.

We know that the first and fifth units describe the *comitium* fig, and the second clearly refers to the Lupercal fig, but what about units three and four? Both must, I argue, refer to the *comitium* fig, despite our initial assumption that unit three describes the Lupercal fig. For Pliny's whole sentence to have pertinence and coherence, we need sufficient information about the *comitium* fig to grasp what made it seem like it had moved to the *comitium* of its own accord, and that is what units three and four provide. These phrases explain how the *comitium* fig was identified as the *ficus Ruminalis* which famously stood at the Lupercal, thus creating the appearance that the *comitium* fig had migrated there from its 'original location'.

---

[68] Evans 1992: 79 also takes the subject of the *tamquam* clause to be the fig, but her overall understanding of this sentence is quite different from mine, as will be seen in following notes.

Memorial matter

First of all, the proximity of a bronze statue of the suckling twins close to the *comitium* fig (unit four) must have created a visually evocative whole, a tableau as it were of the original suckling scene, which would have encouraged association of the tradition of Romulus and Remus' suckling with the *comitium* fig.[69] (After all, the tree already had a pro-Romulan stance through association with the story of how Navius opposed Tarquinius' proposed changes to Romulus' tribe divisions.) The presence of the statue would also have visually mirrored the Lupercal *ficus Ruminalis*, itself accompanied by a bronze statue group of the suckling, according to Dionysius of Halicarnassus (1.79.8).[70] Just like the twisted ῥᾶχος, this *comitium* fig looked convincing! Yet the statue group did not effect the impression of the fig's migration on its own; public willingness to name the *comitium* fig tree *Ruminalis* (unit three) also helped to ensure that this fig was felt to be the famous *ficus Ruminalis*.[71] To paraphrase Pliny: the *comitium* fig poses, as it were, under the name of *Ruminalis*, with a statue of the twins in a supporting role, thereby giving the impression that it actually was the Lupercal *ficus Ruminalis* and had spontaneously migrated to the *comitium*. But why did the *comitium* fig take on this role? In addition to Pliny's explanations of the *comitium* fig's identity shift, we also have Ovid's testimony that in his day the Lupercal fig was in a state of decline, with only *vestigia* (remnants) of it left (*Fast*. 2.411).[72] This surely aided the *comitium*

---

[69] Evans 1992: 79 understands the miracle depicted in bronze to be the 'spontaneous transferral' of the tree, with *miraculo ex aere iuxta dicato* (with the miracle portrayed in bronze nearby) dependent on the subsequent *tamquam* clause for the identification of its *miraculum*. She does not suggest how she imagines this would have been achieved artistically, and it is an explanation I find wholly unconvincing. Evans' engagement with Pliny's text is prompted by her interest in statues of the wolf and suckling twins in Rome and she uses her reading of *miraculo ex aere iuxta dicato* to rule out the presence of such a statue under the *comitium* fig. Considering this driving concern behind her engagement with the text, it is unsurprising that the figs Pliny mentions and their significance in Roman culture do not receive sensitive attention.

[70] Controversies rage as to the appearance, location and number of Rome's statue groups of the suckling twins: see Evans 1992: 78–85 for an overview.

[71] It is telling that in Conon's brief portrait of the *comitium* fig, or at least as paraphrased by Photius, he chooses to state that the fig is 'pointed out' (δείκνυται; Phot. *Bibl*. 186.48) by the inhabitants of Rome; it is just the kind of memorial you show to your children or visitors, repeating its associated story.

[72] It is unclear how much of the fig is indicated by *vestigium*, but it is hardly thriving. When Tacitus describes a cypress which collapsed and then revived *eodem vestigio* he may be

fig's rise to prominence. The *comitium* was a common home for commemorative monuments, and by no means am I suggesting that the Lupercal fig's deterioration prompted an executive decision to 'transfer' its memories to a convenient fig in the *comitium* by erecting a statue of the suckling twins nearby.[73] It would surely have been less problematic to plant a new fig at the Lupercal than to try to relocate the public focus of such a location-focused tradition. Rather, what I am suggesting is that whilst the Lupercal fig was in decline the fig and statue group in the *comitium* were providing an alternative focus of attention as a visual instantiation of the suckling, and gradually and organically drew to this fig its new identity as the *ficus Ruminalis*.

What was the *comitium* fig doing before posing as the *ficus Ruminalis*? It was the *ficus Navia*: the fourth and final proof of this rests in the three words *Atto Navio augurante* (with Attus Navius as augur) Here Pliny makes it clear that he has not been duped by the apparent arboreal migration. Dryly he suggests that such migration would certainly have needed a supporter with powers like those of Navius, whilst slyly dropping in his awareness that, far from having migrated, the *comitium* fig now known as *Ruminalis* was once the *ficus Navia*. For when the supposed miracle of arboreal migration attempts to cover up the *ficus Navia*'s metamorphosis into the *ficus Ruminalis*, what better way to expose the truth behind the 'miracle' than by suggesting Attus Navius himself as its overseer?[74] Several scholars have inferred from Pliny's sentence that a 'leggenda del meraviglioso trasferimento' was doing the rounds, but I see no reason to suppose the existence of a 'legend' narrating

---

using this idiomatically to mean 'in exactly the same place' (*OLD* §2b), or he may be offering us a glimpse of evidence that an arboreal *vestigium* is no more than the hole left by an uprooted tree (*Hist.* 2.78). Could this be an arboreal parallel to *vestigium*'s meaning of footprint (*OLD* §1)?

[73] Lugli 1946: 87, to the contrary, does argue that the statue group would have been set up under the *comitium* fig 'per dare maggior valore al miraculo'. Torelli 1982: 97 characterises the *comitium* as 'an open-air place, filled with sacred memories'.

[74] This phrase further confirms that the *tamquam* clause's subject must be the *comitium* fig, for introducing Navius at this point would be irrelevant to any other potential subject. Torelli 1982: 99 takes the ablative absolute temporally, dating the 'ominous appearance' of the fig in the *comitium* to the reign of Tarquinius. Yet with the *comitium* fig understood as the *tamquam* clause's subject a temporal ablative absolute is meaningless: Pliny would be dating the *ficus Navia*'s transformation into the *ficus Ruminalis* to the very point when it first became known as the *ficus Navia*.

the tree's miraculous migration, for which we have no other evidence.[75] Pliny's *tamquam* phrase is not reporting an urban myth, but is rather a tongue-in-cheek witticism.[76] Two troubling aspects remain in my interpretation of Pliny's monumental sentence. If, as I have argued, Pliny was fully aware that the *ficus Ruminalis* in the *comitium* was at one stage the *ficus Navia*, why does he refer to the objects buried near it by means of the bland *fulguribus ibi conditis* (lightning-struck objects)? Why not broadcast his expert insight that these are actually Navius' whetstone and razor? The answer must lie in the phrase's position in the sentence: at this early stage, Pliny is focalising common opinion as to what makes the fig sacred, articulating the standard belief that its sacrality is partly due to its proximity to objects struck by lightning. It is only once we get to the snide *tamquam* clause that Pliny distances himself from those who believe these objects are generic lightning-struck objects rather than the whetstone and razor. Indeed it is vital that Pliny does not reveal the objects' true identity – and with this the original identity of the fig – early on in the sentence: for to give the game away at that stage would be to ruin his sentence's rhetorical effect. Instead, Pliny's refusal to acknowledge from the start the real identity of these buried objects means that as we progress through his protracted sentence we actively experience the revelation of the fig's former identity. Pliny teasingly takes us from the *communis opinio* to a point where we can, with hindsight, glimpse the fig's secret past as the *ficus Navia*, and with that realise the real nature of these anonymous objects.

The second troubling aspect is the way Pliny explains the epithet *Ruminalis*: the fig is so called because 'under it' (*sub ea*)

---

[75] De Sanctis 1910: 80. Coarelli 1983: 226 also believes in 'il mito del trasferimento', as Petersen 1908: 448 does in 'die Fabel von ihrer Wanderung', whilst Wiseman 1995: 74 suggests this miracle was a common explanation for the 'double tradition' about the fig's location. (Evans 1992: 79 and 82 also assumes the existence of such an arboreal legend, and one even visualised in statue form, according to her reading of Pliny.) Whilst all these scholars must recognise that the *comitium* fig is the subject of the *tamquam* clause so as to believe in the 'migration legend', they have not pushed this recognition and questioned the identity of the *comitium* fig before it became known as the *ficus Ruminalis*, nor have they asked what effect its identity shift should have on our understanding of its sacrality.

[76] Steiner 1955: 142 comments on Pliny's often tongue-in-cheek tone, whilst Goodyear 1982: 670 calls him 'a sceptic infected by traditional sentiment'.

109

the she-wolf offered Romulus and Remus her *rumis* (breast). On the understanding that Pliny is here talking about the *comitium* fig tree, this must come as a bit of a jolt to the reader. It is one thing to understand the *comitium* fig as in some way the *ficus Ruminalis*, but to claim that the twins were suckled under that very tree? After all, Pliny has just reminded us of the existence of the Lupercal fig tree, whose position by the Tiber makes a much more probable location for the suckling, since the twins being washed up by the Tiber is a recurrent feature of the myth. How, then, are we to understand his *sub ea* (under it)? The verb of the causal clause giving this etymology is indicative, so we cannot explain it away as a conjectured reason ascribed to those foolish enough to believe the *comitium* tree really is *the* Ruminal fig. Could we instead get round the difficulty by understanding *sub ea* as referring to the Lupercal tree? The *comitium* fig was called *Ruminalis* because of the tradition that, under that other tree just mentioned, the wolf offered the twins her *rumis* (breast)?[77] To me this reading seems rather forced, and prioritises making concessions to our own conceptual difficulties with the phrase over allowing Pliny's Latin to have its intended impact. For there is, I believe, a more informative way of understanding Pliny's disorienting *sub ea*. In a sense, the phrase refers both to the *comitium* fig and the Lupercal fig: through it Pliny makes us experience the very arboreal identity shift which he is describing. For once we have absorbed the full implication of the *tamquam* clause and its image of the *comitium* fig tree posing as the Lupercal *Ruminalis*, we are in retrospect torn between understanding *sub ea* as referring to the Lupercal fig tree or the *comitium* fig tree: thus we experience for ourselves the blurring of the two trees as the *comitium* fig became known as the *ficus Ruminalis*. Yet Pliny as pedantic academic also uses his jarring *sub ea* to make us feel the deceptive awkwardness of this identity shift, thus endowing the phrase with a tone similar to that of his *tamquam* clause. The 'fuzzy' nature of cultural traditions here comes face to face with the encyclopedic tradition and its drive to define, clarify and distinguish.

---

[77] After all, the Lupercal fig has just been described by that demonstrative pronoun in *eius quae* (of that tree which).

Memorial matter

Ironically, recognition of the flexibility of Pliny's portrait of the *ficus Ruminalis* has been hindered by just such an encyclopedic-style fixation among modern scholars when it comes to thinking about the history of the *ficus Ruminalis*. Scholars ceaselessly debate whether the Lupercal or the *comitium* fig is 'le seul et vrai figuier Ruminal' or 'la vera ruminale', with Evans scorning those who dare to think about the *ficus Ruminalis*' identity more fluidly and who 'call the tree in the *Comitium* the *ficus Ruminalis* even while admitting the tree was not the original'.[78] Did Roman responses to the *ficus Ruminalis* likewise privilege this concept of the 'original tree'? I am convinced that it had little validity at all. The *ficus Ruminalis* which Pliny locates in the *comitium* was obviously not, in material terms, the original tree which sheltered the suckling twins. Nor was it a youthful vivacity about the tree which gave the game away, but simply that it was nowhere near the Tiber. Nevertheless, this did not seem to affect conceptions of it as the/an authentic *ficus Ruminalis*. Admittedly, in both his *tamquam* clause and the multivalent *sub ea*, Pliny rather disingenuously undermines those who understand the *comitium* fig tree as *the* Ruminal fig, but this in itself highlights the unproblematic nature of this understanding for many Roman thinkers.

Indeed, even the hardened sceptic Tacitus can ascribe to the *comitium* fig the role of the 'original' tree, without any of Pliny's dry reserve:

eodem anno Ruminalem arborem in comitio, quae octingentos et triginta ante annos Remi Romulique infantiam texerat, mortuis ramalibus et arescente trunco deminutam prodigii loco habitum est, donec in novos fetus revivesceret. (*Ann.* 13.58)

In the same year it was considered a portent that the Ruminal tree in the *comitium*, which 830 years ago had protected Romulus and Remus in their infancy, had gone into decline with dead branches and a withering trunk, until it revived in new foliage.[79]

---

[78] Dulière 1979: 59, De Sanctis 1910: 80 and Evans 1992: 76. Others simply do not seem to notice that the *ficus Ruminalis* has two locations: Turcan 2000: 87, for example, confidently places the fig under which the twins were suckled in the *comitium*.

[79] This is not to deny any scepticism or cynicism to Tacitus' portrait of the fig. Segal 1973 persuasively points out the significance of Tacitus making the revivification of the Ruminal fig (with its associations of Rome in its archaic, purer days) the last image of *Annals* 13. By juxtaposing this image with the opening moments of Book 14, where

What's more, Pliny himself shows that he is more than capable of a similar mindset when he writes of the fig:

nec sine praesagio aliquo arescit rursusque cura sacerdotum seritur. (*Nat.* 15.77)
Nor can it wither without being seen as an omen and being replanted by the care of the priests.

The verb *arescere* (to wither) depicts a state of arboreal crisis which hardly holds out much hope for a tree's successful replanting. Yet Pliny's seemingly bizarre statement that a fig in this state is replanted by certain priests is not evidence that these were particularly green-fingered priests. Rather, it provides an insight into the way that each replacement tree was understood as the/a genuine *ficus Ruminalis*, as well as suggesting that such replacements were fairly commonplace. Pliny can talk of the troubled *ficus Ruminalis* being 'replanted' because as soon as a replacement was rooted in the ground then it *was* the *ficus Ruminalis*. The new tree immediately became the old *ficus Ruminalis*, and thus the latter was not 'replaced', but rather 'replanted'.

The sacrality of the ficus Ruminalis

The *ficus Ruminalis* in the *comitium* was certainly not the original tree under which Romulus and Remus were suckled: after all, how many figs live to be 830 years old? Nor was it even doing a good job of pretending to be that tree, standing as it was in the *comitium*, not at the Lupercal. But did this matter? Did it undermine the *comitium* fig's sacrality in any way, that it could not possibly be the same material tree as the one which had sheltered Romulus and Remus? To what degree, if any, was the sacrality of each *ficus Ruminalis* bound up with its material identity?

Pliny is explicit about what secures the *comitium* fig's religious significance: besides its proximity to certain lightning-struck objects, it is mostly 'sacred because of the memorial tradition' (*sacra ... ob memoriam*) of the Lupercal fig. Now at first sight this may seem an obstacle to my argument above that 'replacement'

Nero is blooming with 'metaphorical flowers of evil' (115), Tacitus – Segal argues – comments wryly on 'the discrepancy between the apparent and the actual meaning of divine signs' (113–114).

fici Ruminales were not really *felt* as replacements: each replacement was as good as the original tree. Certainly it would be an obstacle if Pliny meant by the phrase *sacra ... ob memoriam* that the *comitium* fig was sacred as a memorial to the Lupercal tree, enjoying a kind of secondary sacrality derived from another tree; and indeed many have understood the phrase in this way.[80] Yet this, I argue, is to misinterpret Pliny's Latin. For the phrase *ob memoriam eius quae* features not an objective genitive, but a subjective genitive: the tree was sacred not from memorialising the Lupercal tree, but because it had absorbed the memories which previously belonged to the Lupercal fig. In other words, it was sacred as a new focus for the community's memories of the suckling of Romulus and Remus, as a new instantiation of that memorial tradition.[81] On a first reading of the sentence we may instinctively interpret *memoria* to mean 'memorialising' rather than 'memorial tradition', but once again we experience here the way that Pliny forces us to alter our understanding of his monumental sentence in retrospect. For only reading the phrase *ob memoriam eius quae* as a subjective genitive could complement the full force of Pliny's claim that the *comitium* fig is called *Ruminalis* as if it were the Lupercal fig migrated to the *comitium*. Identifying the *comitium* tree as *the* Ruminal fig requires too strong an appropriation of the Lupercal fig's identity for it simply to stand as a memorial to the Lupercal tree.

So the *ficus Ruminalis* was sacred, on one level, as a visual and physical embodiment of a memorial tradition, and as such we might suppose that its sacrality was closely bound up with its matter. Yet we have also seen that the fig's frequent replacements

---

[80] For example, Hadzsits 1936: 308 and Evans 1992: 78. Boetticher 1856: 128–129 even argues that the *comitium* fig was genetically derived from the Lupercal fig: 'er war nach Plinius ein Pflanzreis von dem eigentlichen ruminalischen Baume am Tiber' (128). This understanding has little to do with Pliny's text, but is informative for the preconceptions it reveals. Boetticher must have believed it was something about the physical make-up of the *ficus Ruminalis* which made it sacred, fuelling his assumption that Romans would want to 'preserve' this matter by taking and planting cuttings to produce new *fici Ruminales*. Baddeley 1905: 107 similarly believes that Pliny's *rursus ... seritur* indicates that the fig was propagated. Cf. *Met.* 7.623 for a *possible* hint that Roman thinkers entertained the idea of inherited arboreal sacrality: here Ovid talks of an oak *sacra ... de semine Dodonaeo* (sacred from its Dodonian seed).
[81] *OLD* §7 for *memoria* meaning 'collective memory' or 'tradition'.

seem to have caused few problems for conceptions of its sacrality and value as a memorial tree, suggesting that each fig was of little importance *qua* tree; its particular material make-up was of no real religious concern. Indeed even pernickety Pliny only coughed over the relocation of the *ficus Ruminalis*, not any of the other replacements he alludes to in *rursus* ... *seritur* (is replanted). Pliny was unconcerned by regular changes in the material identity of the *ficus Ruminalis*, and only unsettled by the challenge to the credibility of the tree's memorial tradition posed by the tree's relocation. For here *was* a potential challenge to the fig's sacrality, dependent as it was on its preservation of cultural memories.[82] Yet the fact that this challenge was overridden – after all, Pliny's point is that for most people the *comitium* fig is sacred because it is *the ficus Ruminalis* – speaks loudly of how little the matter *or* location of this fig mattered for its memorial power. As such this fig makes a fascinating exception to the rightly influential idea that place was crucial to Roman public memorialising, and especially so when it came to construction of Roman religious identity through narratives about their past: in the words of Dupont, 'Roman memory ... was rooted in the sacred ground of the city. To walk around Rome was to travel through its memory, past Romulus' cabin, Cacus' rock and Egeria's wood.'[83] The *ficus Ruminalis*, with its vivacious

---

[82] Carey 2003: 138–141 discusses Pliny's awareness of the fragility of memory (as seen especially in his observation at *Nat.* 7.90). Pliny sees memory, Carey argues, as a 'construction of successive generations, as much as a passive reservoir to be referred to' (140).

[83] Dupont 1992: 74. On this theme see Edwards 1996: esp. 22–23 and 28–30, as she explores ways in which 'for Romans, places were especially significant as repositories for memory, both personal and national' (29), including discussion of the much-quoted Ciceronian tag, *tanta vis admonitionis inest in locis* (so great is the memorial force in places; *Fin.* 5.2). Beard, North and Price 1998: 167–210 also discuss the importance of the 'religion of place' in the Augustan period, with reflection on the way that sites and monuments of the city of Rome dominate Roman mythology, whilst Jenkyns 2013: 224–226 offers further discussion of the connectedness of Roman religion to particular places. In both these latter books, pride of place is given to Livy's story of Camillus' opposition to a proposal to move the population of Rome to Veii: how could they leave the city 'in which no place is not full of religious customs and gods' (*nullus locus in ea non religionum deorumque est plenus*; 5.52.2) (Beard, North and Price 1998: 167–168, Jenkyns 2013: 224). Many of the essays collected in Bommas, Harrison and Roy 2012 also add to discussion of the religious significance of what Bommas calls the 'memoryscapes' of Rome (xxxvi). We might contrast with the *ficus Ruminalis* Cicero's portrayal of a memorial tree whose location *is* presented as crucial (*Leg.* 1.2): standing by the *quercus Mariana* (Marian oak), Quintus assures us that as long as this

Memorial matter

memorial power, despite its shift in location, would make an awkward addition to Dupont's list and its emphasis on 'rootedness'.[84]

A sense of the insignificance of each fig's material identity also emerges from the subtext of Pliny's history of the *ficus Ruminalis* as a series of trees which shared one identity over time: this is the story of an individual memorial fig which supported more than one identity at a given moment. For as the *comitium* fig gradually shifted from being the *ficus Navia* to being the *ficus Ruminalis* it must have stood as a blurry mixture of both trees, with its dominant identity dependent on who was looking at it. Indeed Pliny articulates this dual identity in his assigning of two levels of sacrality to the tree: sacred because of the 'lightning-struck' objects buried there, but more sacred because of the memorial tradition of the Lupercal fig tree. This is a tree in a state of flux, with its identity as the *ficus Ruminalis* overriding its renown as the *ficus Navia*: the tree's previous identity may be slyly evoked by the pedantic Pliny,

---

tree lives on in the literary imagination, there will be a real oak called the Marian oak *huic loco* (in this place) and again *his in locis* (in this place).

[84] The *ficus Ruminalis* also raises questions about the degree to which the 'authenticity' of sacred objects was deemed significant in Roman culture. For a parallel to the insouciance which Pliny conveys about the authenticity of this Romulan fig, we might compare the fact that the *casa Romuli* also had two known locations, standing either on the Palatine or Capitoline hill (on which see Gransden 1976: 170, Edwards 1996: 32–42 and Rutledge 2012: 166; Balland 1984: 58 observes that the Capitoline hut often lies in the shadow of the Palatine hut within the critical tradition, but in general modern scholars are far more open to the idea of two *casae Romuli* in different locations than they are to the *ficus Ruminalis* having two locations). Clearly it was not possible for both to be the 'authentic' hut – and the fact that much of the tradition regarding this hut concerns occasions when it was accidentally burned down (e.g. Dio 48.43.4; 54.29.8) simply serves to accentuate the distance between any hut a contemporary Roman might see and Romulus' 'actual' hut – but did this matter? Apparently not. Particularly interesting here is Edwards' 1996: 34 persuasive analysis of the *casa Romuli*'s rebuildings: on one level this made the hut a 'fiction', but at the same time renewal of the hut actively demonstrated concern for the values it embodied, something which overrode any concern with 'authenticity'. Yet the seeming lack of concern over the hut's authenticity also sits rather uneasily with an emphasis elsewhere in the literary tradition on the preservation of the hut so as to give it an 'authentic' or at least primitive look (Dion. Hal. 1.78.11; Conon *Narr*. 48). If nothing else, the *casa Romuli* (like the *ficus Ruminalis*) reaffirms that our conceptual priorities may well be at odds with those of the Romans when approaching the 'authenticity' of this kind of sacred memorial object. It is surprising that, to my knowledge, Rome's eight *ancilia* have attracted no discussion in relation to the intersection between the perceived authenticity and sacrality of objects; Beard 1989: 49 touches on the fact that the 'divine object' was purposely made 'indistinguishable' from the eleven manmade shields, but I know of no discussion questioning whether this openness about eleven being 'non-authentic' copies affected their perceived sacrality.

but how many others remember its glory days? That different memorial traditions could share, and indeed compete for, the same arboreal base shows that the religious significance of a memorial tree was not dependent on its memories being embodied in any *particular* arboreal matter.

In fact, the *ficus Ruminalis* may well be concealing within its past another story of memorial traditions competing for one arboreal base. Ovid (*Fast.* 2.411–412) and Livy (1.4.5) tell us that the *ficus Ruminalis* at the Lupercal was once called *Romula* or *Romularis*, epithets which give the fig a more obvious 'Romulan' link than that of *Ruminalis*, and this testimony hints at a similar story of conflated associations within a single tree. For once, as we know from Varro, there stood a fig at the shrine of Rumina, a goddess associated with breastfeeding (*RR.* 2.11.5). One way to explain Ovid and Livy's testimony that the Lupercal *ficus Ruminalis* was previously known as the 'Romulan' fig is to posit that, at some stage, the fig at the Lupercal 'adopted' the identity of the fig at the shrine of Rumina. It experienced a similar transformation to the *ficus Navia*, only rather less drastic, in that the Lupercal fig managed to maintain its tradition of being the protectress of Romulus and Remus, but under a new name. The natural affinity of these figs (both associated with breastfeeding) could explain why over time their identities became conflated, whether this was prompted, perhaps, by their proximity (the location of Rumina's shrine is unknown), or perhaps by the decline of the fig at the shrine. Both the story of the *ficus Navia*'s transformation into the *ficus Ruminalis* and my hypothesis as to how the *ficus Romularis* might have morphed into the *ficus Ruminalis* tell us of Roman indifference over which material tree 'housed' a particular memorial tradition. As Pliny insisted from the start, the *ficus Ruminalis* in the *comitium* is sacred *ob memoriam* (because of the memorial tradition), not because of its material identity.

Yet this is clearly not the full story when it comes to thinking about the relationship between the sacrality of the *ficus Ruminalis* and its matter. For Pliny's portrait of the *ficus Ruminalis* also articulates religious concern which centres on each fig's material welfare, as encapsulated in his opening word *colitur*. Defying translation, to ask whether *colitur* means 'is worshipped' or 'is cultivated' is no doubt to get the wrong end of the stick. This deliberate pun on Pliny's part surely reveals that at times the distinction between cultivation and worship could be moot in Roman culture.[85] Both meanings, I would argue, are active in Pliny's use of *colitur*, showing us how practical arboricultural care could be felt to articulate a religious conception of the fig.[86] Indeed Pliny's use of *colitur* could nicely illustrate one potential response to a question which Smith frames as the central concern of scholars of religion: 'How are the actions in ritual to be distinguished from their close counterparts in everyday life?'[87] To an outside observer religiously informed arboriculture looks just like its 'profane' counterpart, but for those who have a religious agenda in engaging in arboricultural acts, those acts have a different colour or tone, and it is this colour which Pliny's *colitur* captures.

Interestingly, the blurring of religious response and physical care which is captured in *colitur* also makes its presence felt in Roman responses to other wooden objects associated with Romulus. Describing the wooden hut in which Romulus was believed to have lived, Dionysius of Halicarnassus tells us that those who have charge of these matters 'preserve it as sacred' (ἣν φυλάττουσιν ἱεράν; 1.79.11). This unusual use of φυλάττειν (preserve) suggests that caring for the hut helps to 'make the hut sacred', guaranteeing

---

[85] This pun likewise informs Cic. *Leg.* 2.45 and Ov. *Met.* 8.724. This is not to deny that *colere* can be used of trees without any apparent double meaning: religious responses seem most active in its use, for example, at Lucan 1.143 and Silius Italicus 3.691. Dowden 2000: 74 writes of Pliny's use of *colitur* that 'we should hesitate to translate this "is worshipped": it only means that it is respectfully and religiously tended. Friends, too, *coluntur*: they are "cultivated", not "hero-worshipped"'. Dowden's 'religiously tended' nicely captures the dual sense of *colere*, but I would not rule out resonances of worship. The comparison with *colere* used of friends is interesting. It is easy to see how practical care for a tree could 'bleed into' a religious response to that tree, but friends do not need us to care for them materially as a tree does; here *colere* must have subtly different nuances again.

[86] When Pliny mentions the *cura* (care) of the priests for 'replanting' every troubled *ficus Ruminalis*, this careful choice of word similarly suggests that their practical care for the fig could combine with more of an emotional concern for its well-being (*Nat.* 15.77). Likewise, his account of how certain *haruspices* instructed Livia to plant an ominous laurel branch also suggests a blending of religious and practical care in response to arboreal matter: the branch was to be *rite custodiri*, that is 'properly' (with overtones of 'ritually') preserved (15.136).

[87] Smith 2004: 147. Cf. Bell 1992: 7–8, who, like Smith, also questions how ritual actions compare to other forms of social action, and argues that 'acting ritually emerges as a particular cultural strategy of differentiation', a way of colouring an otherwise ordinary-looking act.

and publicly recognising its sacrality. Plutarch, too, is thinking on the same wavelength when he describes the care of a cornel tree which miraculously grew out of Romulus' spear.

τοῦτο δ' οἱ μετὰ Ῥωμύλον ὡς ὄν τι τῶν ἁγιωτάτων ἱερῶν φυλάττοντες καὶ σεβόμενοι περιετείχισαν. (*Rom.* 20.5)

Those born after Romulus walled it in, preserving it and honouring it as one of their most holy sacred objects.

The two participles φυλάττοντες and σεβόμενοι function as a complementary pair, together describing an action which sets the tree apart as one of their holiest objects; indeed Plutarch's participles read almost like a gloss on Pliny's *colitur*, a longhand spelling out of the Latin verb's resonances.

The way Pliny's *colitur* articulates religious concern for the fig's material well-being is also reinforced by his testimony that the tree cannot go into decline without this being considered a *praesagium* (portent), prompting the emergency services of certain priests who come to 'replant' it.[88] Tacitus too tells us that the decline of the Ruminal tree was considered a *prodigium* (portent; *Ann.* 13.58). But in light of Pliny's demonstration that the material make-up of the *ficus Ruminalis* was immaterial for conceptions of its sacrality as a memorial tree, how are we to make sense of such religious anxiety over the fig's material well-being? The key to reconciling these apparently contradictory approaches to the significance of the tree's matter again lies in the phrase *sacra ... ob memoriam* (sacred because of the memorial tradition). The *ficus Ruminalis* was sacred as an embodiment of a memorial tradition. Ensuring each fig's health was therefore important, but of far more importance was the avoidance of a hiatus in the succession of *fici Ruminales*, hence the speedy 'replantings' in the case of any fig's decline, and the perception of such a hiatus as a *prodigium* (portent).[89] Religious concern for the material well-being of the *ficus*

---

[88] Plutarch's cornel tree is also the recipient of rather melodramatic preservation: if ever it looks under the weather, people cry for water and all come running with buckets, as if to save a burning building (*Rom.* 20.6). Turcan 2000: 96 comments that the cornel was 'a much revered tree that was tended like a precious fetish'.

[89] Rutledge 2012: 166 compares the fact that the *ficus Ruminalis*' ill health was considered an omen with the careful tending and rebuilding of the *casa Romuli*, whose decline was also presented as ominous (on which see discussion on p. 161). Indeed the rebuilding of

Memorial matter

Ruminalis aimed not to preserve the matter of a particular tree, but the matter of *any* tree which, by its physical presence, would embody Rome's memories of the suckling infants. In short, the sacrality of each *ficus Ruminalis* was unaffected by its own material make-up, but inescapably dependent on *some* arboreal matter embodying the *memoria* (memorial tradition) which gave the tree its religious meaning.

Finally, I wish to consider briefly the other factor which Pliny singles out as contributing to the *ficus Ruminalis*' sacrality, namely its proximity to buried 'lightning-struck' objects. Here Pliny shows us how sacrality can be, as it were, contagious. The *ficus Navia* first became known as such and conceived of as sacred by association with the nearby whetstone, razor and statue of Navius, along with the memories they embodied. Over time, this fig grew into its new reputation as the *ficus Ruminalis*, with thanks again going (at least in part) to the 'contagious' proximity of a statue group. Yet this 'Navian sacrality' still remained a subsidiary stratum of the fig's religious significance, resulting in a tree which enjoyed degrees of sacrality – sacred because of its proximity to certain objects, but *more* sacred because of the memories it embodied – with Pliny capturing a snapshot of the fig as its sacrality was in a state of flux. As such this fig surely provides a sharp challenge to the scholarly consensus that the sacrality of an object in Roman culture depended on it being understood as consecrated to – and hence the property of – a god. There is simply no room for this kind of thinking in Pliny's account of what makes this fig sacred. Nor, I think, should we be too surprised that it is a *living* tree which has started to open up for us a much more fluid and multi-layered understanding of how an object might be sacred in Roman culture; sacred by means of association with particular objects, sacred because of the memories embodied in it and sacred in a way which is constantly adapting to change. As organic material objects, trees (and especially short-lived figs!) were particularly susceptible to change and challenges to their material continuity: Pliny's subtle and playful portrayal of the *ficus Ruminalis*'

the hut provides an even closer parallel once we acknowledge just how often the *ficus Ruminalis* was itself replanted.

secret past as the *ficus Navia* intersects with his portrayal of its sacrality to reveal what it means for something so vulnerable and organic to be considered sacred. The multi-layered sacrality of this memorial fig is vulnerably dependent on its memories being embodied in *some* arboreal matter, yet at the same time, remarkably resilient and flexibly independent of the matter of any *particular* tree. Pliny thus reveals a way of thinking about this fig's sacrality which is both pragmatic and intellectually flexible: the organic nature of this tree dictates an organic understanding of its sacrality.

CHAPTER 4

ARBORICULTURE AND ARBOREAL DEATHS: RETHINKING SACRALITY AGAIN

Pliny's use of the verb *colere* to encapsulate how some Romans respond to the *ficus Ruminalis* (*Nat.* 15.77) gives us a glimpse of a world in which arboricultural interference with a tree might articulate religious conceptions of it. Yet, on one level, Pliny aims in this passage to distract attention from human interference with the *ficus Ruminalis*, encouraging us to experience for ourselves conceptions of it as a continuous organic unity, which work against the subtext of its dependence on human care and occasional replanting. His focus thus leaves many questions to be asked about the nature of arboricultural interference with sacred trees, and its implications for our understanding of the significance of a sacred tree's matter. Yet to date these questions have not been asked: scholars from Boetticher onwards, reliant on the idea that Roman sacrality means the transfer of an object to the gods' property, have understood any interference with a sacred tree to be blatant sacrilege, even if not all follow Boetticher quite so far as to deem it punishable by death or exile.[1] Thus Thomas, in an influential article on tree violation in the *Aeneid*, articulates the standard view:

Every piece of relevant evidence from Greece and Rome, as from numerous other societies, conspires to demonstrate that the cutting of trees is a hazardous act, stigmatized by society and divinity alike.[2]

---

[1] Boetticher 1856: 195. For Frazer 1911: 9–10 the assumption that arboreal sacrality entails inviolability is so deep-seated that he turns it around to present the inviolability of a tree as 'proof' of its sacrality: 'Proofs of the prevalence of tree-worship in ancient Greece and Italy are abundant. In the sanctuary of Asclepius at Cos, for example, it was forbidden to cut down the cypress-trees under a penalty of a thousand drachmas.' Cf. Frazer 1911: 43, where he instinctively uses 'sacred and inviolable' as synonyms with relation to trees.
[2] Thomas 1988a: 263. Cf. Dyson 2001: 146: 'to harm any part of a tree without proper propitiatory rites was a dangerous act of impiety that invited retribution'. Morford, Lenardon and Sham 2011: 662 state that Silvanus was the deity you had to propitiate when felling trees.

Such 'evidence' can even be construed as a 'law', as when Hughes observes that 'a basic law found everywhere forbade felling trees or cutting branches'.[3] Indeed, if we add to this 'law' the common assumption that Roman thinkers considered trees sacred thanks to their perceived animation, then tree violation becomes an attack not just on divine property but on a divine spirit. Thus Thomas continues: 'tree spirits are obviously hard to detect, and any tree is therefore potentially numinous, any tree felling potentially hazardous'.[4]

Such assumptions are of course founded on juristic claims that being sacred meant belonging to a deity, reliance on which, as I have argued, stifles the complexity of what sacrality means in the Roman world. Yet it is not only a legalistic frame of mind among scholars of Roman religion which is to blame here. For this juristic mindset is also coupled with a narrow generic focus on poetic depictions of damaged sacred trees, a combination which reinforces the dogmatic and mistaken insistence that *any* interference with a sacred tree's matter was a matter of sacrilege: and it is to these poetic depictions that I now briefly turn. As Philostratus asks us to imagine a painting of the oak at Dodona, wrapped in ribbons, with the axe of the evil tree-cutter Hellus abandoned at its foot (*Im.* 2.33.1), so Roman poets often freeze the frame on images of violated sacred trees. Ovid's arrogant Erysichthon attacking a sacred oak is the quintessential illustration of this topos (*Met.* 8.741–779). Ovid overloads his account with language of religious condemnation for Erysichthon: he is *sceleratus* (evil; 754), wields a *manus inpia* (wicked hand; 761), and commits both a *nefas* (outrage; 766) and a *scelus* (crime; 774).[5] This outrage makes its

---

[3] Hughes 1994: 172. Bodel 1985: 24, in a section confusingly entitled 'The Roman Law of Sacred Groves', first notes that 'there is, of course, no single authoritative Roman law of sacred groves', but continues his arguments on the understanding that discrete pieces of evidence enable us to formulate 'certain principles ... widely, if not universally, followed throughout the Roman world'.

[4] Thomas 1988a: 263. Cf. Hughes' 1994: 172 sweeping observation that 'if a tree was felled, it was believed that its spirit, the dryad, died, and the god might leave the sanctuary', or Henrichs' 1979: 86 claim that in the 'earlier times' of Greek religion, 'would-be violators will have been deterred not by threats of legal action but by the prospect of a much more severe penalty exacted by the spirit who inhabited the tree, or the deity who protected it'.

[5] Hollis 1970: 132–133 briefly discusses the 'dominating impiety' of Erysichthon in Ovid's rather 'overblown' narrative (133). Griffin 1986 argues that hints of Erysichthon

visual impact as the tree trembled and groaned (758), went pale (759–760) and blood flowed from its wound (761–762): we can hardly escape how intensely this arboreal matter is in pain. As those more piously minded try to intervene, Erysichthon insists he will fell the tree, whether it is loved by the goddess or even is the goddess herself (755–756). Thrown out in the heat of the moment, this remark smacks of boastful exaggeration and hardly suggests measured evaluation of the level to which tree and goddess are assimilated. Nevertheless, that Erysichthon is prepared to countenance the tree *being* the goddess and still continue his attack makes yet more disturbing Ovid's depiction of the arboreal matter's pain. This is brought to a poignant climax when a dying nymph, who is *sub hoc ... ligno* (under this wood; 771), uses her final breaths to predict Erysichthon's punishment. Her vaguely articulated material relationship with the oak makes her a pathetic personification of suffering arboreal matter, the religious outrage of Erysichthon's crime again firmly tied to its material impact.[6]

Ovid's account became something of a blueprint for depictions of violated sacred trees in Latin literature, which emphasise the tree's material hurt through language of wounding and bleeding: consider Statius' snapshot of Atalanta's favoured oak, having suffered an attack which left it *multo proscissam vulnere* (lashed with many wounds), its branches gruesomely *rorantes sanguine* (dripping with blood; *Theb.* 9.595–597).[7] Ovid's Erysichthon also

being characterised as a giant make this 'a particularly heinous crime', as an 'earth-born' giant attacks a tree and its nymph (59).

[6] Griffin 1986: 60 misses the blurry nature of this material relationship when he observes that Ovid 'identifies the oak tree with the nymph who lives in it', as does Henrichs 1979: 88: 'the nymph is not merely a visitor of the tree, but identical with it'.

[7] Dewar 1991: 172 discusses Ovidian reminiscences in this passage of Statius, whilst Bruère 1958: 485–488 argues the same for Silius Italicus 5.475–516, which he reads as 'replete with echoes of the sacrilegious felling of a sacred oak by Erysichthon' (487). McKay 1962: 5–60 discusses various scholarly views on Ovid's originality in his depiction of Erysichthon, and in particular his debt to and relationship with the blueprint of Callimachus, who depicted Erysichthon's tree-attack in his *Hymn to Demeter* (17–117). As previously discussed, Erysichthon also made his presence felt in nineteenth-century comparativist scholarship, with its dominant focus on animist interpretations of sacred trees; see pp. 52–53, as well as Hunt in press. Such animistic interpretations of Erysichthon were still being kept alive by Henrichs 1979: 92: 'The story of Erysichthon's crime is the best illustration of the concept of the tree-nymph and of trees as animate that has come down to us from Greco-Roman antiquity. Callimachus saved it from oblivion, and Ovid revived its true spirit.' (Indeed, as an overt animist, Henrichs 1979: 95–97 also drew attention to the rich work of Tylor, Mannhardt and Frazer on 'tree-souls'.)

Arboriculture and arboreal deaths

seems to be lurking behind Lucan's description of Caesar's attack on a grove near Massilia (3.399–452).[8] Since his men were too overcome 'by the awesome majesty of the place' (*verenda maiestate loci*; 429–430), Caesar decides to lead by example, swinging the first blow and 'burying his blade in violated wood' (*merso violata in robora ferro*; 435). Reflecting Ovid's language, Caesar himself calls this violation of arboreal matter a *nefas* (outrage) which he has assumed on his men's behalf (437), although it is hard not to feel that Lucan's Caesar uses this word of his own actions with some scepticism.[9] Personified trees or girls metamorphosed into trees also reinforce this imagery of arboreal matter in pain by issuing warnings not to harm them.[10] Dryope, freshly transformed into a lotus, begs her son not to pluck flowers from trees and, in a striking assimilation of deity and material tree, urges 'let him consider all bushes to be the *body* of goddesses' (*frutices omnes corpus putet esse dearum*; Ov. *Met.* 9.381). Likewise another personified tree advises:

> δένδρεον ἱερόν εἰμι· παρερχόμενός με φυλάσσευ
> πημαίνειν· ἀλγῶ, ξεῖνε, κολουομένη. (*AG.* 9.706.1–2)
> I am a holy tree. Take care not to harm me
> as you pass by. I feel pain, stranger, when cut.[11]

Again colouring damage to sacred trees in terms of human pain, a tree violator's comeuppance is often losing a limb, mirroring the violence they first inflicted on the tree's 'limbs'.[12] Thus, Halirrhotius once attacked certain olives, only to find that the axe slipped from its handle and decapitated him (Serv. *G.* 1.18).

---

[8] Leigh 1999 offers an insightful close reading of this passage, which he frames as a classic example of 'the archetype of the impious axeman who engages in violence' against trees and groves in Greek and Latin literature; again Ovid's Erysichthon is discussed as a crucial intertext (177–178).
[9] Phillips 1968 also argues that Ovid's Erysichthon account was an important influence on Lucan 3.394–452.
[10] Conversely, preserving a tree's matter is figured as the pious preservation of a naiad or hamadryad in Statius *Silv.* 1.3.59–63.
[11] Cf. *AG.* 9.282, in which a laurel, announcing that she is in fact a maiden, encourages travellers to cut branches from the nearby arbutus or terebinth trees instead.
[12] For discussion of this motif see Mannhardt 1877: 6, Phillips 1968: 296–297 and Leigh 1999: 179–185. Cf. the irony of *AG.* 9.233, in which we learn that Mindon, having hacked at some old trees, was bitten by a venomous spider; this led to an amputated leg and his reliance on a staff cut from a wild olive tree.

Lycurgus too, being mad enough to insult Bacchus and cut down certain vines, ended up cutting off his own foot by mistaking it for a vine (Hyg. *Fab.* 132). Aware of such horror stories, in Lucan Caesar's men are reluctant to attack the grove when ordered to do so, fearing that the axes 'would rebound against their own limbs' (*in sua ... redituras membra secures*; Lucan 3.431).

Complementing by contrast this topos of the violated sacred tree was that of the unviolated wood. A phrase amounting to 'never violated' makes a frequent epithet for woods in Latin poetry: the motif is especially beloved of Ovid, who introduces us to a *silva vetus ... nulla violata securi* (an old wood violated by no axe; *Met.* 3.28) and a grove of Juno *multis incaeduus annis* (unhewn for many years; *Fast.* 2.435). In Statius too we meet a wood *aeternum intonsae frondis* (of eternally uncut foliage; *Theb.* 4.420) and the grove which Lucan's Caesar wanted destroyed was also *longo numquam violatus ab aevo* (unviolated from ancient times; 3.399).[13] To return to Ovid, we find that a wood's virgin state could encourage religious responses to it: thus a *multos incaedua silva per annos* (a wood uncut for many years; *Am.* 3.1.1) prompts Ovid to observe that it is easy to believe there's a *numen* within (*Am.* 3.1.2). Indeed, in his depiction of another unviolated wood as *Maenalio sacra relicta deo* (left as sacred to the Maenalian god; *Fast.* 4.649–650) Ovid presents being untouched and being sacred as interdependent qualities for a wood: leaving the wood alone was a way of both expressing and securing its sacrality.[14]

As they draw together all these images of trees in pain and unviolated woods, scholars extrapolate universal rules about arboreal sacrality, without stopping to acknowledge the generic focus of their chosen evidence, and the obvious risk that it paints a misleadingly

---

[13] See Seidensticker 1886: 346–349 on this motif. Parkes 2012: 220 suggests intertextual resonances for the emphasis on dense foliage ('a key feature of such grove descriptions') in the Statius passage.

[14] These images of untouched woods were also deeply bound up with Roman idealisation of their primitive, rustic and morally pure past. According to Pliny, early grafting procedures took into account that *timebant prisci truncum findere* (the first men feared to split trunks; *Nat.* 17.102), whilst Lucretius' portrait of primitive men paints them as being ignorant of how to cut off branches with a sickle (5.931–6). It was also a topos of portraits of the Golden Age that nobody felled trees to go sailing (Ov. *Met.* 1.94–95; Cat. 64.11–18). For further discussion of the role of trees and woods in Golden Age ideology see pp. 11–14.

uniform picture of what such interference might mean to Roman thinkers. Nor do they take into account, for example, the idealised romanticism of Ovid's beloved topos of untouched woods, nor the fact that the pantomime villain Erysichthon is hardly a straightforward foil to 'standard' Roman attitudes to interfering with sacred trees.[15] Moreover, this commitment to the model that arboreal sacrality equals inviolability only intensifies when scholars turn to 'groves', a word often implicitly used to indicate a sacred wooden space (and a traditional way to translate *lucus*, ἄλσος and sometimes *nemus*). Of all wooded spaces, it is groves which are often singled out as inherently or *de facto* sacred, as Scheid here illustrates:

> Les bois sacrés possèdent un caractère sacré intrinsèque. Certes, on peut envisager qu'un *nemus* soit consacré à une divinité ... Mais le *lucus* seul possède cette qualité par lui-même, sans l'intervention de l'homme; il a en quelque sorte le statut sacré sans avoir été consacré par un magistrat du peuple romain.[16]

The model of sacrality Scheid presents here is now deeply familiar: groves are 'auto-consecrated', sacred by virtue of belonging automatically to a deity.[17] Indeed Dowden presents this as *the* obvious way to think about the sacrality of groves in Roman

---

[15] Griffin 1986: 58–60 characterises Erysichthon as an exaggerated 'personification of evil' (59).
[16] Scheid 1993: 19. Cf. Ouseley 1819: 362–363, who, almost 200 years previously, also observed that 'so frequently were groves and woods dedicated to Religious purposes, that at last those very terms (in Greek *alsos*, *lucus* in Latin), implied consecration', a position then echoed by Barlow 1866: 99. Servius' compartmentalising of wooded spaces in his comment at *A*. 1.310 has exercised some influence here: *interest autem inter nemus et silvam et lucum; lucus enim est arborum multitudo cum religione, nemus vero composita multitudo arborum, silva diffusa et inculta* (there is a difference between *nemus*, *silva* and *lucus*; for a *lucus* is a group of trees with *religio*, whilst a *nemus* is an ordered group of trees and a *silva* is one which is spread out and uncultivated). Passing over the ambiguity of what *cum religione* might mean, as well as the dangers of applying rigid commentary-style definitions to lived experiences of Roman religion, Scheid 1990: 556 turns to this passage to underline the special nature of groves. For Grimal 1943: 72, however, Servius' distinction is 'trop rigoureuse' (he argues that a *nemus* can also be a 'bois sacré') and for Rüpke 2007: 275 too this distinction 'seems artificial'.
[17] Lambrinoudakis 2005: 312 paints a similar picture: 'gods created or selected groves as appropriate places for their presence on earth'. Servius may again be felt to provide support here: *ubicumque Virgilius lucum ponit, sequitur etiam consecratio* (whenever Virgil writes *lucus*, he also understands it to be consecrated; *A*. 1.441). Certainly this passage is cited by Ouseley 1819: 362 as proof that the word 'grove' implies consecration. Yet Servius' later comment – *lucum, ut supra diximus, numquam ponit sine religione* (he never writes *lucus*, as I have said above, without 'religious connotations'; *A*. 3.302) – suggests that by *consecratio* (consecration) he meant nothing more specific than that a *lucus* (grove) is always of 'religious significance' for Virgil.

culture, arguing that 'if you subscribe to a religion which is in any way anthropomorphic, then it is likely that the grove will belong to a particular god'.[18] Why are groves recognised as 'auto-consecrated'? The textbook answer leans on their divine aura, and it is no surprise to find scholarly emphasis on groves as 'numinous groups of trees or copses', 'places of *numen*' or examples of 'numinous natural resources'.[19] Indeed since Boetticher we have been told that the sacrality of groves is due to their being inhabited by figures like 'Baum-Numen', 'Baumseele' and 'Hamadryade'.[20]

Predictably enough, scholars then go on to emphasise that the inherent sacrality of the grove entails its inviolability:

As is well known, in strict usage *luci* were by definition sacred and therefore protected by sacral law against profanation of any kind.[21]

Regulations against cutting and removing wood were virtually the *sine qua non* of sacred groves in the Greco-Roman world.[22]

The underlying principle was that the groves were property of the gods and ought not to be damaged in any way.[23]

In particular these scholars jump on an archaic inscription from Spoleto, whose meaning is debated but which appears to forbid violating a grove, and perhaps also cutting it.[24]

[18] Dowden 2000: 111. Dowden also writes of a scale of 'religious intensity' applying to groves, placing at one end those where 'the grove is scarcely more than a park' and at the other those where 'it is quite simply the grove of a god or goddess', whatever this latter statement (with its characteristic 'simply') is supposed to mean (96–97).

[19] Rüpke 2007: 275; Green 2007: 89; Bodel 1985: 27. It is informative that Bodel 1985: 26, when writing about sacrifices to a 'grove's deity', instinctively and immediately adds 'or *numen*' in brackets. Isidorus, a grammarian of the sixth to seventh century CE, also once drew an etymological connection between *nemus* and *numina* (*Etym.* 17.6.6); this kind of thinking has a long history.

[20] Boetticher 1856: 187.

[21] Bodel 1985: 4.

[22] Bodel 1985: 25.

[23] Hughes 1994: 172. For further reiterations of this orthodoxy see Grimal 1943: 180 and Dowden 2000: 108. Such understanding of the sacrality of groves among scholars of Roman religion also has a wider effect on classical scholarship: Nadeau 2010, for example, is so convinced when reading *Aeneid* 3.1–8 that Aeneas felling trees on Mt. Ida must be 'sacrilege' (224), that he understands Magna Mater's abduction of Creusa (2.788) as retribution *in advance* of the crime.

[24] Pietrangeli 1939: 31 treats this inscription as an archetype of the laws applying to other sacred groves: 'le due "leggi spoletine" ... testimoniano l'esistenza di boschi nei quali vigevano le regole sancite per altri boschi sacri'. For Panciera 2006: 204 too this law is 'noto come una delle più importanti ed antiche testimonianze concernenti i *luci* nel mondo romano'. Both Bodel 1985: 24–25 and Dowden 2000: 108 foreground this law as the quintessential example of the inviolability of groves. Dillon 1997 provides an

honce loucom ne qui<i>s violatod neque exvehito neque exferto quod louci siet neque cedito nesei quo die res deina anua fiet; eod die quod rei dinai cau[s]a [f]iat, sine dolo cedre [l]icetod. (*CIL* 11.4766)

Let nobody violate this grove nor transport nor carry out what is in the grove nor cut it (?) except on the day of the annual rite; on that day what is done for the sake of the rite, let it be allowed to cut without penalty.

The meaning of *neque cedito* in this difficult inscription is debated: was it forbidden to walk in the grove, or to cut the grove? Another inscription which appears to be a copy of this regulation has *caeditod* in place of *cedito*, which might urge us to see a precursor of *caedere* here, rather than *cedere*.[25] Also cited is Festus' definition of a *lucus capitalis* as a grove whose entry earns you capital punishment (57L).[26] Despite the uncertainty of the Spoleto inscription's meaning and the obvious fact that, whatever Festus refers to in this unparalleled statement, he is describing an unusual grove and not *every* Roman grove, these two texts are taken as 'laws' providing hard proof of groves' inviolability.

Insisting, as they do, that the sacrality of both trees and groves entailed their inviolability can quickly lead scholars into some conceptually odd situations, as they try to imagine how this would play out in practical terms. Did 'careful' Romans approach felling all trees as a *potential* religious offence, considering the difficulty of knowing for certain whether a particular tree was sacred or not?[27] Did Rome's developed timber industry thus risk being a daily and noisy insult to the divine?[28] If so, how was this to be negotiated? Musing on such questions, Granger came to the bizarrely noncommittal conclusion that 'the business of the woodman was regarded *almost as an offence* against the sanctity of the forest' (my italics).[29] Frazer's observation on the issue went as follows : 'if

---

overview of a far richer body of epigraphic evidence from the Greek world which documents varied regulations against tree felling within sanctuaries.

[25] On which see Panciera 2006: 904–907.
[26] For example, Wagenvoort 1947: 148 and Dowden 2000: 108.
[27] Ovid captures the difficulty of distinguishing sacred and profane trees – with his idiosyncratic and usual lighthearted touch – when he encourages a worshipper of Pales to ask for forgiveness if they might by chance have sat down under a sacred tree (*Fast.* 4.749): how was one to tell?
[28] Meiggs 1982: 218–259 and 325–370 examines the evidence for Rome's timber supplies and trade.
[29] Granger 1895: 95.

Arboriculture and arboreal deaths

trees are animate, they are necessarily sensitive and the cutting of them down becomes a delicate surgical operation' – a position echoed more recently by Ferguson, who states that interfering with groves requires 'great religious care'.[30] Interfering with trees is implicitly acknowledged here as a practical necessity, but what could 'great religious care' mean in practical terms? How would 'delicacy' help? Scholars have not allowed such practical questions to deter them from concluding that interference with any sacred tree's matter was sacrilege. A property-centric model of sacrality, combined with a narrow generic focus on poetic images of violated sacred trees and unviolated woods, have led to this conclusion seeming inescapable.[31] Yet if we examine just a few passages with a broader generic focus, we will encounter trees which, although clearly of religious significance thanks to their association with a deity or hero (and thus in my terms considered sacred), were by no means assumed inviolable.

A certain Publius Turullius was once put to death by Augustus. After painting a picture of Augustus' political motivations in doing so (Turullius was an assassin of Caesar and a friend of Antony), Dio goes on to explain that, since this man had once felled trees in the grove of Asclepius in Cos to build a fleet, and since he was executed in Cos, it was agreed that by his death he was paying a penalty 'also to the god' (καὶ τῷ θεῷ; 51.8.3). Dio's account reveals how much the nature of tree felling in a grove depended on the wider scenario in which it was embedded. On first cutting his timber it seems that Turullius was not charged with blasphemous behaviour. Yet when required, his felling of trees in the grove could be portrayed as a divine insult, to give greater meaning to the punishment already decided for him on quite other grounds.[32] Bringing Valerius Maximus' account of Turullius' demise into

---

[30] Frazer 1911: 18; Ferguson 1980: 30. Cf. Hubert and Mauss 1899: 59, n. 6, who also note that, in the case of a sacred tree, 'on le coupe avec précautions'.

[31] Informative by way of comparison is Parker's observation (1983: 165) that inscriptions detailing regulations about Greek sanctuaries often present removing wood from them as 'an offence against property rather than a threatening sacrilege'; the idea of offences against property and of sacrilege have not been equated in the same way here.

[32] Compare the way that Cicero introduces an alleged attack on *sanctissimis lucis* (most sacred groves) into his destruction of Clodius' character in the *pro Milone* (*Mil.* 85). Bodel 1985: 26 is surely wrong in taking the story of Turullius as an illustration of the 'principle' that any violation of a sacred grove needed expiation.

the picture further reinforces this sense that the implications of tree felling in Asclepius' grove were up for debate. In his version, which forms part of a wider discussion of how gods defend outrages against their divinity, Turullius' punishment is presented not as Caesar's decision but as that of Asclepius. The god simply chooses to work through Caesar:

imperio Caesaris morti destinatum Turullium manifestis numinis sui viribus in eum locum quem violaverat traxit, effecitque ut ibi potissimum a militibus Caesarianis occisus eodem exitio et eversis iam arboribus poenas lueret et adhuc superantibus immunitatem consimilis iniuriae pareret. (1.1.19)

He [Asclepius] dragged Turullius, condemned to death on Caesar's orders, by the manifest powers of his divinity into that place which he had violated, and brought it about that, having been killed by Caesar's soldiers in exactly that spot, with the same punishment he both paid the penalty for the trees which had already been uprooted and provided immunity against a similar outrage for those still surviving.

In Dio's account Turullius' execution on Cos secured retribution for Asclepius, but this consequence was subsidiary to Caesar's main intentions. By contrast, Valerius Maximus presents Asclepius' revenge as the cause of Turullius' death, with Caesar's agency subsidiary to divine control of events.[33] Felling trees in a deity's grove could be framed as a fatal offence against the god (as in Valerius Maximus' version), or only as a potential offence, to be leaned on when the perpetrator's name has been otherwise blackened (as in Dio's version): reading these two accounts of Turullius' execution side by side reveals that what it meant to interfere with trees in a grove was far from set in stone.

This ambiguity surrounding the nature of tree felling in a grove or sanctuary is also felt more widely in the literature and inscriptions of the Roman world. Consider the following passage from Aelian, in which he muses on the superstition of the Athenians in times past:

ὅτι τοσοῦτον ἦν Ἀθηναίοις δεισιδαιμονίας, εἴ τις πρινίδιον ἐξέκοψεν ἐξ ἡρῴου, ἀπέκτειναν αὐτόν. (*VH*. 5.17)

---

[33] Augoustakis 2006: 636 notes how Valerius Maximus elides Dio's time gap between the felling and the execution: Asclepius' wrath is immediate. See Mueller 2002 on the rich religious insights to be derived from Valerius Maximus.

Arboriculture and arboreal deaths

How great was the superstition of the Athenians! If somebody cut down a little oak from a hero's shrine, they killed him.[34]

Here Aelian makes it clear that he, at least, did not view felling trees associated with a shrine as *necessarily* problematic; in fact, for him, punishing every such act (*even* violence towards little trees!) was strangely over-zealous behaviour. Accounts of people felling trees, and only afterwards seeing this as a religious mistake, also reveal the ambiguous implications of tree felling. It was from a grove of Apollo on Mt. Ida, Pausanias recounts, that certain Greeks cut down some cornels to make the fateful wooden horse. Only later learning of the god's anger over this, they began to propitiate him and from then on called him Apollo Carneius (3.13.5). Presumably these Greeks were aware from the start that the cornels stood in Apollo's grove, but this had not deterred them from felling them: it was not automatic to assume such trees were untouchable. That Apollo turned out to have a far stronger interest in these cornels than they ever expected is then reflected in the new arboreal epithet they give him. Perhaps they pleaded that, without such an epithet, it was hard for anyone to know he would have minded. It is also interesting to wonder how large a role Pausanias' insatiable appetite for divine epithets played in prompting the inclusion of this particular story: if substantial, then this suggests that in Pausanias' eyes the cutting of trees in Apollo's grove was not itself worthy of note – it was merely an incidental detail necessary to his epithet-focused story, not strikingly impious behaviour.[35]

Also loudly pleading arboreal ignorance in another part of the Roman world, namely Lydia, was a certain Stratoneikos: in an inscription dated to 194–195 CE he records how he cut down an oak belonging to Zeus of the Twin Oaks, a mistake which was, he insists, committed 'in ignorance' (διὰ τὸ ἀγνοεῖν).[36] Having almost been killed by Zeus in punishment, he goes on to urge

---

[34] Boetticher 1856: 195 ignores the nuance of Aelian's surprise when citing this passage as proof that harming trees was sacrilege.
[35] Pausanias' enthusiasm for divine epithets will come to the fore in Chapter 6: see pp. 237–244 and 249–251.
[36] See Petzl 1978: 253 for the text. Lane Fox 1986: 127–128 briefly mentions this inscription, which very rarely attracts attention; see pp. 244–249 for further discussion of this and other inscriptional attestations of the striking epithet 'of the Twin Oaks'.

nobody to fell an oak ever again! Certainly Stratoneikos claims that he was originally unaware of Zeus' interest in this oak. Yet an inscription by Menophilos, from the same location and dated a few years earlier, records another occasion on which Zeus of the Twin Oaks punished a man (in this case Menophilos' father) for selling 'sacred wood' (ἱερὰ ξύλα).[37] This hints at a broader picture of men felling trees connected to this otherwise unheard of Zeus, and trading in their timber: Zeus was lashing out against standard behaviour![38] Despite cautionary tales about these trees' sacrality which were publicly recorded on stone, it seems that interfering with them was a risk some were prepared to take: once again we see that arboreal inviolability was by no means assumed. Finally, I turn briefly to Pausanias' mention of an injunction against removing branches which fell from trees in a shrine to the heroine Hyrnetho: rather they should be left as 'sacred' (ἱερά) to Hyrnetho (2.28.7). Some scholars cite this injunction as proof of sacred trees' inviolability, but Pausanias' lingering over the ruling, the like of which he does not mention elsewhere, and his known interest in local religious peculiarities, rather suggests to me that he saw it as an exceptional case, and that removing branches from shrines was normally considered unproblematic.[39] In short, these varied snapshots have shown us that interfering with trees understood as sacred was not considered automatic sacrilege in Roman culture. Rather the potential religious implications of interference with such trees were a live and ambiguous issue, and one which could be dangerous to negotiate.

Thus, we see that poetic images of violated sacred trees and unviolated groves are by no means the only story to be told of human interference with sacred trees in the Roman world. Indeed the narrow focus of this story particularly blinds scholars to the

---

[37] See Petzl 1978: 255–256 for the text.
[38] See Rhodes and Osborne 2003: 502, who discuss the contribution of the Cyrene purification law to thinking about the status of wood in Greek sanctuaries, with its warning that you may use wood from the sanctuary for any purposes, provided you pay the god for it.
[39] Boetticher 1856: 195 cites the passage as proof that cutting down sacred trees was 'ein Sacrilegium'. Hughes 1994: 172 also uses the Hyrnetho passage as the only illustration of his sweeping claim that, as well as a universal ban on felling trees and cutting branches, 'even removal of fallen dead timber or leaves was prohibited'. For Dillon 1997: 115 it is part of his armoury of passages proving that trees in Greek sanctuaries were protected.

Approaching arboriculture

possibility of another type of interference with sacred trees, aimed not at their destruction but their benefit: namely arboriculture. It is to such interference with sacred trees that I now turn. What did it mean to offer a sacred tree arboricultural care? What did such physical interference with the tree articulate about the relationship between the human offering the care and the divine? What did it say about Roman conceptions of the way the tree's materiality intersected with its sacrality?

Approaching arboriculture

There was once a farmer, we read in a fable of Babrius, who had a tree so unfruitful he decided to cut it down. On striking it with his axe, various cicadas and sparrows begged him to desist, but ignoring them, he swung a second and a third blow. Hollowing out the tree he found inside a swarm of bees and honey, and then ...

γευσάμενος δὲ τὸν πέλεκυν ἔρριψε καὶ τὸ φυτὸν ἐτίμα ὡς ἱερὸν καὶ ἐπεμελεῖτο.

tasting it he threw down the axe and honoured the tree as something sacred and took care of it.[40]

For those committed to the belief that arboreal sacrality entailed inviolability, it might be tempting to take this fable as a model for understanding arboricultural interference with sacred trees.[41] On discovering that a tree is sacred, the old rules allowing you to do what you like with a tree (whatever the cicadas and sparrows might think) no longer apply: now you must care for its every need. Babrius' narrative, however, elides any detail about what this caring entailed in practical terms. As such it also evades the obvious conceptual difficulty that arboricultural care is often rather violent towards arboreal matter. Are we to understand that whilst the farmer now deplored his previous attack on the tree, he understood interference like pruning the tree as acceptable, or perhaps even a religious duty? If so, how was the difference between these two types of interference articulated?

---

[40] Text taken from Crusius' 1897 edition of Babrius, where it is printed as fable 187; this fable exists only in prose paraphrase.
[41] See Morgan 2007: 63–64 for a brief reading of this fable as an observation about power.

Scholars have rarely troubled themselves with this distinction. For Baddeley, for example, pruning and felling were the same offence: he notes of groves that 'Sylvanus, the Tree-spirit ... had to be propitiated if the trees were pruned or cut down'.[42] In the same spirit, Dowden has far more recently coloured the Arvals' piacular rites when pruning and thinning their grove as a more 'routine' version of the common punishments for grove violation.[43] Arboriculture is thus framed without further thought as another version of sacrilegious interference with a tree's matter. Yet arboricultural care for a sacred tree is no straightforward process, and deserves more thought than this. Certainly basic acts of arboriculture do often entail violence towards a tree, nor does the language of arboricultural instruction shy away from this.[44] Columella, to give but one example, urges those grafting a vine to 'wound it' (*vulnerato*) with a sharp knife so that liquid flows from those 'wounds' (*plagis*) rather than the graft itself (*Arb.* 8.3). If ordinary vines can thus be troped as bleeding humans, what were the ramifications of interfering with a *sacred* tree's matter? Yet violent as it may be, the well-being of trees depends on such human interference, and far more so than the well-being of non-organic sacred objects. Did this make such violent arboriculture a paradoxical religious duty towards the tree? Besides its inherent violence, another conceptually tricky feature of engaging in arboricultural care for a sacred tree is the difficulty of gauging the level of human impact in this process. If, say, you repair a broken nose on a statue of Apollo this is clearly an improvement brought about thanks to human intervention, but if you water a sickly sacred tree

---

[42] Baddeley 1904: 5.
[43] Dowden 2000: 108. Bodel 1985: 25–26 downplays the 'minimal pruning and clearing' undertaken by the Arvals by comparison with the 'systematic logging and wood-collecting' which might take place elsewhere, but still presents such pruning and clearing within a discussion of what he considers a virtual 'law' against cutting and removing wood in Greek and Roman groves.
[44] Gowers 2011 persuasively reveals how trees and tree imagery in Virgil's *Aeneid* reflect the destruction involved in Aeneas' 'pruning' of his own family, as he eliminates contenders to his position: the innate violence of arboriculture is drawn to the fore as she notes how, in Latin literature, 'standard metaphors for grafting, splicing, and pruning in the vegetable world draw on the vocabulary of human abortions, adoptions, adulteries, and child murders' (90). See also Hunt 2010: 53–54 on violent overtones in the language used to describe pruning in Latin literature, a process Thomas 1988b: 271 labelled 'chilling' in its characterisation in Virgil's *Georgics*.

and it revives, is this only, or at all, thanks to your interference? Even with 'ordinary' trees a hazy boundary separates the human contribution from the tree's agency in bringing about its restoration, but with a sacred tree the potential involvement of a divine agent concerned for the tree is also brought into play.

Human interference with sacred trees was thus far from straightforward in conceptual terms: if you chose to engage physically with a sacred tree what *kind* of process were you involved in, and what were its implications? Here we might think back to Pliny's *colitur* in his discussion of the *ficus Ruminalis*, the multivalency of the verb suggesting that religious and practical actions blurred in this human response to the famous fig. Indeed, throughout the rest of Pliny's *Natural History* we also find hints that the way you engaged in arboriculture could have religious implications. A graft should be inserted whilst the moon is waxing and using two hands, as *religio* (religious scruple) demands (*Nat.* 17.108); myrtle should be grown from cuttings rather than grafted on elm, which *religio fulgurum* (religious scruples over lightning strikes) forbids (*Nat.* 17.124); cinnamon shrubs native to Ethiopia can only be cut with the god Assabinus' permission (*Nat.* 12.89); it is *nefastum* (forbidden) to pour a libation from an unpruned vine (*Nat.* 14.119). Tantalising as these hints are, they are, however, only hints. A different kind of source is needed to push further our questions about what kind of process interfering with a sacred tree might be. It is, then, with this aim that I turn to the inscribed records of the *fratres Arvales*, in which rich insights into 'sacred arboriculture' are simply waiting to be noticed.

Alongside many other duties, the *fratres Arvales* were overseers of the grove of Dea Dia, part of a large ritual complex a few miles outside Rome.[45] These 'scrupulously self-important' priests, as they have been characterised by Henderson, filled the grove with inscriptions 'recording' their ritual activities both in and outside the grove.[46] 'Recording' I place in scare quotes because the relationship between the Arvals' ritual activity, the notes they

---

[45] Scheid 1990: 73–76 sets out the long, complicated history of the complex's excavations. Scheid 1990: 13–40 examines in detail the rather meagre literary references to the Arvals' cult.
[46] Henderson 1995: 112.

took on this in a *codex* and the final inscriptional record is very much debated.[47] Can these inscriptions be read in any way as an 'account' of the Arvals' ritual actions in the grove, or did they serve a different purpose? Beard has influentially argued that the function of these inscriptions was primarily symbolic, and certainly was not intended as a handy guide to the brotherhood's ritual actions.[48] Yet whilst these inscriptions may not give us a precise *account* of the Arvals' activities, they do show us how the Arvals conceptualised what went on in ritual terms within the grove and how they wanted to construct that on stone. For our purposes this is just as (if not more) informative, as we turn to these inscriptions to consider what it means to the Arvals to engage with the trees of their grove.

Considering the extensive nature of the inscriptions recovered from this grove and their huge chronological span – 21 BCE to 304 CE – it is surprising that they have not attracted more scholarly attention. Their convoluted Latin and lacunose state no doubt have a part to play in this, but perhaps also off-putting is the way work on these inscriptions has been dominated by one scholar. Scheid has produced the definitive edition of these inscriptions and a rich book unpacking a portrait of the cult practices they paint, and his work in making them accessible to the academic world has been invaluable, yet one drawback of his monopoly of the Arvals is that interpretation of these inscriptions may appear a closed chapter.[49] There is, however, rich work waiting to be done on these inscriptions and room for many more angles of interpretation.[50] Certainly there is one obvious element of the grove which largely escapes Scheid's interest: the trees. This may be a subconscious offshoot of Scheid's understanding of the word *lucus*, which for him is 'à proprement parler une clairière': it is the *absence* of trees which

---

[47] Scheid 1998: iii–xi discusses the evidence the inscriptions provide for the Arvals' recording practices, summing up the problem when he writes that 'si les transcriptions épigraphiques reproduisaient l'esprit et progressivement, sans doute, également la lettre des Commentaires des arvales, ils n'en étaient pas la simple copie' (vi).

[48] Beard 1985: esp. 137–144. To the contrary, Gradel 2002: 18 presents the Arval acta as a wonderful source providing 'descriptions of the actual rituals'.

[49] Scheid 1998; Scheid 1990.

[50] Gradel 2002: 20 also notes that these 'curiously ignored' inscriptions 'still have much to give'.

makes a grove.[51] Yet I am convinced that in neglecting the trees, Scheid has neglected much. By writing the trees out of his portrait of the religious significance of the Arvals' activities in their grove, Scheid misses both a layer of complexity in the Arvals' articulation of their relationship with the divine, and a stark challenge to the scholarly consensus that, in Roman culture, the sacrality of a material object entails its inviolability. Thus, for the remainder of this chapter, the trees of the Arvals' grove will take centre stage, as I push them for insights into Roman conceptions of what it means to consider sacred an object as organic and vulnerable as a tree.

Piacular pruning in the Arval grove

Twenty seven of the Arvals' inscriptions make mention of the grove's trees, and it is these which will form the backbone of our study of the Arvals' arboriculture (for ease of reference they are gathered in the Appendix (Table 1)). To begin with I will analyse fourteen of these inscriptions, all of which follow a formulaic pattern and record a sacrifice of two expiatory pigs. Eight of these two-pig sacrifices took place on 19 May, five on 29 May and one on 27 May, dates coinciding with the highlight of the Arvals' liturgical year, a three day festival in Dea Dia's honour, for which the commonest sets of dates were 17, 19 and 20 May, and 27, 29 and 30 May.[52] Thus we see that our sacrifices always took place on the second day of Dea Dia's festival (nor does the 27 May sacrifice in 90 CE disprove the rule, for in that year the festival was in fact held on 25, 27 and 28 May). The sacrifice is recorded using the following formula, or a variant of it: *ad aram immolavit porcas piaculares duas luci coinquendi et operis faciundi*. I understand this to mean 'sacrificed at the altar two expiatory pigs for pruning the grove and performing work', an understanding which it is my first task to unpack in detail.

Outside these inscriptions *coinquere* is firmly attested only once in Festus, who glosses the verb as *coercere* (to restrain), but saying no more about it. Thanks to a passage in Cato, however, we are

[51] Scheid 1990: 556.
[52] Inscriptions 7, 8, 9, 10, 15, 16, 17, 18, 19, 20, 21, 22, 23 and 24.

urged to understand the restraining *coinquere* in arboreal terms, even though he does not directly attest to the verb. He writes as follows:

> lucum conlucare Romano more sic oportet. porco piaculo facito, sic verba concipito: si deus, si dea es, quoium illud sacrum est, uti tibi ius est porco piaculo facere illiusce sacri coercendi ergo ... (*Agr.* 139)
>
> This is how to *conlucare* a grove in the Roman manner. Sacrifice a piacular pig, and declare as follows: whether you are a god or goddess, to whom that grove is sacred, as it is right to sacrifice to you a piacular pig for the sake of *coercendi* the sacred grove ...

The prayer continues, and then Cato adds:

> si fodere voles, altero piaculo eodem modo facito, hoc amplius dicito: operis faciundi causa. (*Agr.* 140)
>
> If you wish to dig, perform another piacular sacrifice in the same way, and add these further words 'for the sake of performing the work'.

The sacrificial practice which Cato here outlines mirrors closely the sacrifices which the Arvals record by means of the formula *ad aram immolavit porcas piaculares duas luci coinquendi et operis faciundi*. The Arvals' version is simply more condensed: always including Cato's optional sacrifice 'for the sake of performing the work', the Arvals conflate this with the first sacrifice, presenting their actions as a two-pig sacrifice rather than two one-pig sacrifices. On a verbal level too, the Arvals condense Cato's two clauses *illiusce sacri coercendi ergo* and *operis faciundi causa* into their formula *luci coinquendi et operis faciundi*. The almost identical phrasing thus frames the Arvals' *coinquendi* as a substitute for Cato's *coercendi*, providing strong support for Festus' testimony that the two verbs are synonyms. We are, however, still to discover what Cato's *coercendi* means in context.

Cato's prayer formulae are intended for someone who wants to *conlucare* a grove: this should provide some indication of what *coercere* means. Unfortunately, though, *conlucare* is also a very poorly attested verb. Beyond this appearance in Cato it occurs once in Columella and twice in Festus, in all cases clearly an arboricultural action.[53] Festus informatively defines *conlucare* as to cut

---

[53] Columella, listing various activities both allowed and forbidden on 'holy days' (*feriae*), places *arborem conlucare* (to *conlucare* a tree) in the latter category (2.21.4).

Piacular pruning

off 'light-impeding' branches in a wood (*conlucare dicebant, cum profanae silvae rami deciderentur officientes lumini* (people said *conlucare* when light-impeding branches in a profane wood were cut off); 33L), or to 'fill a place with light by cutting the trees' (*succisis arboribus locum inplere luce*; 474L), emphasising the verb's obvious etymological connotations of providing light.[54] So when Cato recommends the action of *coercendi* for someone wanting to *conlucare* a grove, we might well expect this to be an action which helps fill the grove with light: and given that *coercere*'s standard meaning is 'to restrain', what better meaning to ascribe to it in a grove context than 'to prune'? After all, what other arboricultural action both restrains and lets in light at the same time? From here it is an easy step also to understand *coercere*'s synonym *coinquere* as 'to prune', with Festus providing another titbit of information to strengthen this understanding. He glosses *coninquere* (a hapax which is probably a variant or textual error for *coinquere*) as *deputare*, a much better-attested verb which we are confident means 'to prune'.[55] Finally Servius, too, may testify to the verb *coinquere* when he writes:

hos lucos eadem caerimonia moreque conquiri haberique oportet. (*A.* 11.316)

These groves should be sought out and maintained with the same ceremony and custom.

As it stands, this note is nonsensical: but Salmasius suggests *coinqui* for the baffling *conquiri*, and certainly the conjunction of *coinqui* (to be pruned) and *haberi* (to be maintained) is much more meaningful. If Salmasius' conjecture is correct, then this final attestation of *coinquere* also frames the verb as an act of grove maintenance, and one moreover which is articulated ritually, accompanied as it is by a ceremony.

Having elucidated the meaning of *coinquere*, I now turn to the whole phrase *luci coinquendi et operis faciundi*. As summarised in a table in the Appendix (Table 2), the case of the component

---

[54] What Festus means by a 'profane wood' is both intriguing and elusive; his testimony sits a little uneasily with the fact that our 'parallel scenario' as recorded in Cato is clearly articulated in ritual terms; in Columella too there is no indication that the act of *conlucandi* a tree is seen in itself to be of religious significance.
[55] *OLD* ad loc.

nouns and gerundives in this clause vary, but genitives clearly dominate. Independent genitive gerunds and gerundives can indicate purpose, and the only way to render these inscriptions coherent is to understand them as such: they sacrificed *for* the pruning of the grove and *for* the performing of the work, whatever we are to imagine this to be.[56] In effect the Arvals simply omit the *ergo* or *causa* (for the sake of) of Cato's prayer formulae. These genitives of purpose then urge us to understand the two gerundives in inscriptions 10 and 18 as dative, not ablative: again the gerundives would mean *for* the pruning of the grove and *for* the performing of the work, giving uniformity of meaning, if not case, to this set of formula variations.[57] That the Arvals present their pruning and other work as motivating the sacrifice of two piacular pigs is significant: clearly religious issues were at stake for them in interfering with these trees, meaning that we are here in the presence of what I understand as sacred trees. As such, these trees now confront us with an obvious first question as we explore the nature of arboricultural interference with sacred trees: *why* did the Arvals feel the need to sacrifice these pigs for the pruning and the other work?

I begin, however, with an even more fundamental question: why did Romans offer the sacrifices they termed *piacula* at all?[58] The scholarly orthodoxy insists that the purpose of such sacrifices

[56] Sloman 1906: 255, n. 2; Allen 1903: 318, n. 1. The Arval brothers give us no indication of what this *opus* (work) might consist, as Scheid 1993: 148 acknowledges. Given the close relationship between the Arvals' formula and the Cato passage discussed, some might presume it was a form of digging. Dumézil 1975: 45–49 argues that Cato is here expressing two stages of the process of woodland clearance (via a reading of Columella 2.2.11): the first involves the cutting back of branches; the second, more radical, step involves uprooting some trees entirely. Presumably the Arvals would hardly have had time for the latter during a busy day in Dea Dia's major festival. Tromp 1921: 94, however, imaginatively argues that the Arvals' second *piaculum* was performed 'cum in luco sacro fodiendum erat, quod sive fossa erat ducenda, sive novae arbores reponendae'.

[57] Inscriptions 8, 10, 15 and 16 seem to link a genitive gerundive to a dative or ablative noun. The Arvals are not above mistakes (and besides, as Beard 1985: 115 observes, their language is far from 'rigidly standardised'), but these are puzzlingly consistent mistakes. Perhaps we can at least emphasise an underlying logic: a sense of purpose is indicated by both the genitive gerundives and the nouns, if taken as dative.

[58] For a general account of the 'Roman sacrificial process' see Scheid 2007: 264–266, Prescendi 2007: 31–51 and Gradel 2002: 15–16 (with interesting comment by Elsner 2012: 121–123 on the intellectual dangers of this 'structuralist' approach to sacrifice); Roman thinkers rarely comment on the practicalities of sacrifice, leaving us heavily dependent on Dion. Hal. 7.72.15 when constructing such an account.

Piacular pruning

'was to present excuses for past or imminent action' (to use Scheid's *Oxford Classical Dictionary* definition); or to borrow Dowden's words, 'a piaculum is an offering, typically of a pig, to restore good relations with a god'.[59] Discussion of *piacula* thus tends to ally itself with those interpretations of Greco-Roman sacrifice which frame sacrifice as an attempt to make contact with a divine being; this is by contrast with those of 'Burkert and the French scholars' who – as Naiden provocatively puts it – 'wrote the gods out of sacrifice' in their sociological emphasis on sacrifice as a reflection on hunting or a feasting ritual which articulates social cohesion.[60] Scholars who promote the 'divine contact' reading of sacrifice insist – in tandem with the ingrained consensus that to be sacred means to be a possession of the divine – that to sacrifice (literally, to make *sacer* (sacred)) transfers victims to the possession of the divine.[61] More than simple gift exchange, however, sacrifice becomes a system of representation which acts out and symbolically establishes a hierarchy between humans and gods (a distinction further reinforced by sacrifice's focus on animal victims).[62]

---

[59] Scheid 1996: 1346; Dowden 1992: 3. Cf. Tromp 1921: 29, who defines *piacula* as 'sacrificia quae fiant ob sacra quaedam sive commissa sive committenda', as well as Thome 1992: 86, Wallace-Hadrill 1982: 24–29 and Turcan 2000: 6. Tromp 1921: 26–34 also usefully insists on the multivalency of the word *piaculum*: it can, for example, refer to 'quod est piaculo dignum', a 'nefas' or 'scelus', a 'poena' or 'ultio' and a 'victima piacularis'. Cf. Rüpke 2007: 81, who emphasises that a *piaculum* is both the 'act requiring expiation' and the 'expiatory sacrifice' which sets it to rights.

[60] Naiden 2013: 4. Representing the 'divine contact' camp, Scheid 2005: 21: defines 'un sacrifice canonique' as one which does no more than offer victims to a divinity. For Gradel 2002: 23 too Roman sacrifice 'constituted the 'natural', eternal and traditional way of communicating with divine powers whose assistance the worshippers required'. Smith 1982 offers a very different interpretation of sacrifice as a reflection on the domestication of wild animals.

[61] Prescendi 2007: 25–26 reflects on the meaning of *sacer* (turning as standard to the definitions of Festus, Trebatius and Gallus (on which see pp. 3–5)), to conclude that *sacrificare* must mean 'donner aux dieux' and is a form of consecration. Cf. Scheid 1996: 1345; Faraone and Naiden 2012: 4.

[62] Scheid repeatedly argues that the point of sacrifice is to 'établir une hiérarchie entre les hommes et les dieux, au cours d'un partage alimentaire dont les hommes prennent l'initiative' (2005: 275). Cf. Scheid 1996: 1346: 'sacrifice fixed the superiority and immortality of the gods, along with the mortal condition and the pious submission of their human partners, at the expense of the animal victims'. Cf. also Scheid and Linder 1993: 53 and Scheid 2012b: 86. Gilhus 2006: 116 also understands sacrifice to articulate both the hierarchical structure gods–humans–animals and a hierarchy of human social relationships.

Within such discussions of sacrifice, when the focus turns to the nature of *piacula*, two motifs are prominent. One is to emphasise a distinction – first made much of by both Mommsen and Wissowa – between faults willingly and unwillingly committed. According to these two scholars, those guilty of wilful faults were liable to both a fine and an expiatory sacrifice.[63] Tromp, in his 1921 thesis *De Romanorum Piaculis*, supported this distinction between voluntary and involuntary faults, but from here went on to challenge the Mommsen–Wissowa consensus, emphasising that those who committed a fault willingly were technically 'inexpiable'.[64] Here a passage of Varro (*LL*. 6.30) was the key proof text, in which Varro writes that a praetor who makes a legal decision on a *nefastus* (forbidden) day can be expiated by means of an 'expiatory victim' (*piaculari hostia*) if he did it 'unknowingly' (*imprudens*); if he did it 'knowingly' (*prudens*), however, then according to Quintus Mucius he cannot be expiated.[65] Tromp emphasises that a *piaculum* could do nothing for someone who had committed a fault knowingly, but this did not mean it was to be omitted altogether. Rather a magistrate was responsible for performing the *piaculum*, which aimed to guarantee the religious well-being of the city; the city could be expiated, if the individual could not. Several decades later, Tromp was of huge influence on Scheid, who largely follows his understanding of *piacula*, but placing rather more emphasis on the way such sacrifices respond

---

[63] Mommsen 1899: 810–811; Wissowa 1912: 393–394. Wissowa 1912: 392 framed *piacula* as 'die sakralrechtliche Parallele zu der *multa* des weltlichen Strafrechts'.

[64] Tromp 1921: 38 sets out the by now classic distinction between faults committed willingly and unwillingly. Tromp 1921: 81–85 challenges the Mommsen–Wissowa view, acknowledging that his own claims about the inexpiability of certain offenders constituted a 'dura lex' (82). Bodel 1985: 27 provides a useful summary of the last century's arguments over *piacula*.

[65] Linderski 1995: 592 presents the Varronian passage as 'the principle rule governing Roman religious infractions and their expiations'. Yet caution needs to be exercised in our use of this passage. Varro is hardly presenting his observation as a universal rule – rather this is something applicable to specific actions, by a specific religious official, on specific days within the ritual calendar – nor does he himself take responsibility for the claim that a praetor who knowingly commits this fault is inexpiable. Tromp 1921: 82, alongside the Varro passage, also calls to his aid Macr. *Sat*. 1.16.10, in which similar claims are made about those who work on *feriae* (holy days); here Scaevola the *pontifex* is author of the claim that those who so acted *prudens* (knowingly) could not offer expiation, although Umbro challenges this as a hard and fast rule, proposing some exceptional situations.

to an emotional need to re-establish good relationships between the human and divine communities (whereas Tromp's approach is more legalistic).[66] Indeed the second prominent motif in today's discussion of *piacula* is, as Scheid does, to present religious faults as 'la rupture de la pax deorum', with *piacula* the sole means to repair such a rupture.[67] Very recently, Lennon has provided a valuable note of caution in drawing to our attention that the phrase *pax deorum*, loosely understood as the state of being in right relationship with the gods, is nowhere near as well attested in ancient literature as its prominence in studies of Roman religion suggests.[68] Yet in general scholars take for granted that the concept of the *pax deorum* was central to Roman thinking about their relationship with the divine and in particular their performance of *piacula*.[69]

It is certainly not my intention to add another view to this rather legalistic debate on the precise meaning of a *piaculum*: rather I want to sound a note of caution about some of the emphases and presuppositions of the secondary literature. Firstly, there is an acknowledged (but unquestioned) reliance on the evidence of the Arval acta and Cato; indeed Scheid frequently draws attention to his indebtedness to these two sources, from which he argues he can paint a broader picture of what sacrifice means in Roman culture.[70] Turcan too explicitly sets up the Cato passage as the foundation for his understanding of wood-maintenance *piacula*:

Cato (*Agr.*, 139) had the same respectful uncertainty. When a wood had to be cleared, the crime constituted by such an attempt on divine property had in some way to be expiated, by means of a *piaculum*: the sacrifice of a pig accompanied by a prayer whose recipient remained anonymous (*si deus, di dea*).[71]

[66] Scheid 1981: 128 signals his debt to Tromp in his understanding that 'l'*imprudens* est expiable, le *prudens* reste inexpiable et impie'. Cf. Scheid 1981: 137–138 and Scheid 1990: 567–569 for his reliance on Tromp. Scheid 1981: 148–151 articulates his modified understanding of Tromp's claims. It seems to me that both Bodel 1985: 27 and Linderski 1995: 594 somewhat overstate the distinction between Tromp's and Scheid's views.
[67] Scheid 1981: 130. Cf. Rüpke 2007: 81.
[68] Lennon 2014: 16.
[69] Indeed Thome 1992: 92, in her reflection on the concepts of fault and expiation in Roman culture, has argued that preserving 'an equilibrium between the human and the divine level' was the 'highest aim' of the 'sacral and legal structure' of the Roman state.
[70] Scheid 1981: 137, Scheid 2005: 17 and Scheid 2012b: 85. Running in tandem with this, at least within French scholarship, there is also a worryingly deferent reliance on Scheid: see, for example, Prescendi 2007: 17.
[71] Turcan 2000: 39.

Likewise when Bodel claims that 'Roman custom called for the ritual expiation of any conceivable infringement of a grove's sanctity', or Hughes writes that 'since cutting sacred trees involved formal violation of the groves, special sacrifices had to be held to obtain forgiveness', both signal their reliance on the Arval acta and Cato *Agr.* 139.[72] I also wish to flag up two insistent emphases in this rather legalistically minded scholarship which will prove problematic when we come to look in detail at the Arvals' piacular sacrifices in the grove: the first is the idea that *piacula* appease unwitting faults; the second that *piacula* are sacrifices aimed at appeasing a particular god or gods.[73]

Without further ado, I now return to my original question: why did the Arvals feel the need to sacrifice two piacular pigs for the pruning and the other work? The standard explanation given proposes that the Arvals used iron implements for pruning, and then leans on the 'fact' that taking iron in and out of the grove required expiation. Indeed this has been the orthodoxy since Henzen, who explained in 1874 that:

Lucus autem coercetur deputando ramos exuberantes, eamque ad rem cum ferrum in lucum inferendum esset, id quod religione prohibebatur, piacula fieri necesse erat.[74]

Some years later, Warde-Fowler put it in less than impartial terms:

These brethren had originally suffered from the taboo on iron; but in characteristic fashion they had discovered that a piacular or disinfecting sacrifice would sufficiently atone for its use whenever it was necessary to take a pruning-hook within the limits of the grove.[75]

This explanation continues to dominate in modern scholarship too: Beard, among many others, notes that 'since the iron

---

[72] Bodel 1985: 25–26; Hughes 1994: 175.
[73] Indeed discussion of Roman sacrifice in general often takes a legalistic, definition-heavy approach, and especially so when scholars are reliant on the jurists' definitions of *sacer* (sacred) in constructing what *sacrificare* (to sacrifice) means, on which see pp. 3–5. Within Tromp's seminal work on *piacula* there is also a disconcerting reliance on the evidence of scholars like Festus and Servius, with no pause for reflection on the *nature* of the evidence they provide, which surely encourages a legalistic or category-centric approach to Roman religion.
[74] Henzen 1874: 22.
[75] Warde-Fowler 1911: 35. Cf. Tromp 1921: 107: 'omnem ferri usum in luco deae Diae fuisse prohibitum'.

Piacular pruning

inscribing chisel was a taboo substance in the sacred grove, sacrifices were performed in expiation each time it was brought into the area or taken out'.[76] Nor is it only the assumption of a general 'taboo' on iron which prompts this line of thought: the 'iron prohibition' is also presumed to be confirmed by other inscriptions from the Arvals' grove, which mention *piacula* performed for the carrying in and removal of iron needed for their own engraving.[77] These self-reflexive inscriptions are understood to vocalise the motivation left tacitly assumed in our 'pruning sacrifice' formulae, with Scheid arguing that the engraving and pruning sacrifices fulfilled 'une fonction analogue'.[78] Yet this 'iron hypothesis' is far from convincing. Granted iron was a popular metal for pruning instruments, but if iron were the crucial issue at stake in the pruning sacrifices why did these obsessive recorders not mention it, as they did elsewhere?[79] Rather the unembellished formula *luci coinquendi et operis faciundi* (for pruning the grove and performing work) insists that it was something about the pruning itself, and the other work, which prompted these sacrifices.

---

[76] Beard 1985: 118. Cf. Bodel 1985: 25; Scheid 1990: 86; Hughes 1994: 175; Lennon 2014: 46.

[77] Such sacrifices were articulated using a formula like the following: *in luco deae Diae piaculum factum ob ferrum inlatum scripturae et scalpturae ... in luco deae Diae piaculum factum ob ferrum elatum scripturae et scalpturae* (in the grove of Dea Dia a piacular sacrifice was performed because of the bringing in of the iron for the writing and engraving ... in the grove of Dea Dia a piacular sacrifice was performed because of the taking out of the iron for the writing and engraving; Scheid 1998: 212 (inscription 69 (57–60))).

[78] Scheid 1990: 557. Cf. Hughes 1994: 175, who, through an unjustified conflation of various sacrificial formulae in the Arval acta, manages to present it as though sacrifices *ob ferrum illatum* (because of iron brought in) and *ob ferrum elatum* (because of iron taken out) were actually a part of the sacrifices for pruning and other tree-management work in the grove.

[79] Granger's 1895: 103 claim that 'without iron, trees could not be pruned or cut down' cannot strictly be true, but White 1967: 72 does confirm that iron was the material of choice for arboreal tools. Beard 1985: 126 points out that sacrifices for taking in and removing iron inscribing instruments are only recorded from the 80s CE onwards: this at least suggests that iron's presence in the grove was not always considered an urgent issue to address. The Arvals do in fact once mention a sacrifice for removing iron within the context of arboricultural work, when some trees were replanted and temporary altars repaired (inscription 25). Yet this one-off appearance is surely thanks to the likewise one-off mention of altar repairs in this inscription: as in the 'inscribing sacrifices', it would seem that this iron was intended for work on stone, not trees (unless Scheid 1990: 138–140 is correct in his suggestion that these temporary altars were made of turf, but there is no definitive evidence for their material).

Was it perhaps the trees' relationship with Dea Dia which problematised such work? Would she have taken offence at the harm pruning does to arboreal matter, if the trees concerned were standing in her grove? This is the obvious assumption for those who believe that the sacrality of individual trees and groves consists in belonging to a deity, with the result that the trees are considered inviolable. Indeed many have made this assumption. As Wagenvoort confidently put it: 'the expiation of the fratres Arvales was intended for the Dea Dia' (*sic*).[80] Wagenvoort's view is also implied in much recent scholarship: consider, for example, how Beard observes that 'the Arval grove was sacred to the goddess Dea Dia and ... any mishap within it required expiation'.[81] Expiating damage to Dea Dia's property seems to be a tempting way to understand the Arvals' motivations in their sacrifice of two piacular pigs: but should we be tempted into doing so? What worries me here is the circularity of the thinking. Are we not running the risk of interpreting the Arvals' piacular pruning sacrifices on the basis of an understanding of *piacula* which is constructed, to a large degree, on the evidence of the Arval acta and the 'parallel' passage in Cato?

A fresh look at the evidence is required: and the results are disconcerting. Our understanding of *piacula* frame them as sacrifices aimed at appeasing the divine for faults committed or about to be committed. In the case of the Arvals we assume the fault to be that of the violent application of iron to the trees of the grove. Yet the Arvals' inscribed formulae in no way suggest that their *piacula* were prompted by a guilty sense of the damage pruning does to Dea Dia's property: she is not foregrounded in the sacrificial formulae, with the sacrifices simply said to take place 'in the grove of Dea Dia ... at the altar'.[82] Nor do the formulae suggest that their *piacula* were prompted by a guilty sense of the damage pruning does to arboreal matter: we cannot simply say, along with Turcan,

---

[80] Wagenvoort 1947: 149. Cf. Boetticher 1856: 190.
[81] Beard 1985: 118.
[82] Inscription 15 provides an example: *in luco deae Diae M. Valerius Trebicius Decianus mag(ister) ad aram immolavit porcas piaculares* (in the grove of Dea Dia M. Valerius Trebicius Decianus the *magister* sacrificed at the altar two piacular pigs). On two occasions (inscriptions 8 and 9, although the latter is heavily reconstructed) the sacrifice is said to take place *ante lucum in aram* (in front of the grove, on the altar).

Piacular pruning

that 'the president sacrificed two young sows known as "piacular" (to expiate the pruning of trees with a knife)'.[83] Indeed, to the contrary, there are substantial hints in these sacrifices' timing that the Arvals' sacrifice-cum-pruning was not at all focused on the material well-being and integrity of the trees concerned, as I will now argue in detail.

As we have seen, these sacrifices always took place in May, on the second day of Dea Dia's festival, but there is some debate as to whether the pruning and other work took place on that day too. Henzen argued that the sacrifice established a year-long grace period for pruning and other maintenance work, but his understanding is problematised by Cato's instructions on grove maintenance which, as we have seen, closely reflects the Arvals' practice in other ways.[84]

si fodere voles, altero piaculo eodem modo facito, hoc amplius dicito: operis faciundi causa. dum opus, cotidie per partes facito. si intermiseris aut feriae publicae aut familiares intercesserint, altero piaculo facito. (*Agr.* 140)

If you wish to dig, perform another piacular sacrifice in the same way, and add these further words 'for the sake of performing the work'. During the work, do this every day throughout parts (of the land?). If you interrupt the work or public or family holidays intervene, perform another piacular sacrifice.

Cato's text is hardly crystal clear, but in depicting this ritual negotiation of grove pruning he implies that such sacrifices certainly did not set up a year-long grace period for work. Every day it was necessary to reiterate, as it were, that the sacrifice had been performed, and if work was interrupted you had to make sure to repeat the sacrifice. Indeed only a year after Henzen published his arguments, Oldenberg expressed intense unease ('vehementer dubito') about the grace-period hypothesis.[85] Certainly his unease is supported by the fact that there is no suggestion in the inscriptions themselves that the Arvals entered the grove at other times of the year to engage in general (rather than crisis-driven) arboricultural

---

[83] Turcan 2000: 71.
[84] Henzen 1874: 22. Henzen's view continues to have some influence: thus Bodel 1985: 25 claims, without supporting inscriptional evidence but simply a reference to Henzen, that 'thinning of the grove was evidently permitted throughout the year whenever necessary'.
[85] Oldenberg 1875: 11–12.

maintenance.[86] More recently, Henzen's hypothesis has come under attack from Scheid too.[87] He persuasively argues that the sacrifice allowed the Arvals to prune for the day only, leaning on the Cato passage and also the Spoleto inscription, with its suggestion that cutting trees in the grove at Spoleto was permitted only 'on the day of the annual rite' (*quo die res deina anua fiet*).[88]

Why did the Arvals choose to prune only on the middle day of Dea Dia's major festival? For Scheid, the Arvals pruned when they did because they wanted to prepare the grove for their major sacrifice to Dea Dia later that day, facilitating access to her temple which stood within the grove.[89] Thus the pruning had practical intentions, but this is not its only significance in Scheid's eyes. Indeed Scheid wavers between emphasising that this pruning would by necessity be cursory – part and parcel, as it was, of a day already packed with ritual activities – and that it was nevertheless not a 'fiction', since the Arvals did not carry out any maintenance on the grove at any other time of the year.[90] For Scheid, the Arvals' engagement in light pruning is of *some* practical import. Its real significance, however, is that in so doing the Arvals found themselves putting *lux* (light) back into the *lucus* (grove), and thus acting out its definition as a clearing: '[S]i nous considérons le sens étymologique précis du terme *lucus* ... nous pouvons difficilement nous soustraire à la conclusion que les travaux en question étaient destinés à "ouvrir, à créer la clairière".'[91] This symbolic element meant that the pruning was part of the worship of Dea Dia, not simply its preparation. Neither 'une simple opération arboricole', nor 'un élément indépendent du programme liturgique de la journée', it was a mixture of the two; or in other words, 'ces travaux d'élagage devaient être à la fois symboliques et nécessaires'.[92]

---

[86] For one *possible* exception, see discussion of inscription 27 on pp. 170–171.
[87] Scheid 1993: 149.
[88] Scheid 1990: 555–558; Scheid 1993: 148–150.
[89] For his twin accounts of the pruning's significance see Scheid 1990: 554–558 and Scheid 1993: 148–152. Beard 1985: 128 and Turcan 2000: 71–72 provide brief summaries of the festival's main events.
[90] See Scheid 1990: 558; Scheid 1993: 149–151.
[91] Scheid 1993: 151.
[92] Scheid 1993: 149–150. Cf. Scheid 1990: 558: this pruning was part of 'la représentation symbolique du statut du lucus'. We might have expected Scheid to make more here

Piacular pruning

I certainly agree with Scheid that this pruning is no straightforward practical act, but I am less than convinced that this depends on connotations of light being dominant in the Arvals' minds when they performed sacrifices *luci coinquendi* (for pruning the grove): after all, strictly speaking to prune a clearing is nonsensical. Certainly the Arvals give us no direct prompt to imagine that what matters for them in this pruning is the symbolic creation of daylight, nor can we rely on the significance Scheid attributes to the etymological connotations of *lucus* (grove). In order to support his insistent claim that 'clairière' is the 'sens premier de lucus', Scheid refers us to the *Thesaurus Linguae Latinae*, whose entry for *lucus* begins with the claim that it is 'derivatur a lucere, lux, lumen', before breaking this down into two mutually contradictory subcategories: sometimes *lucus* takes its meaning 'per absentiam lucis, sc. per antiphrasin', sometimes 'per praesentiam luminis'.[93] This distinction is inherited from a handful of ancient grammarians and etymologists (Quint. *Inst.* 1.6.34; Serv. *A.* 1.441; Isid. *Etym.* 14.8.30 and 17.6.7), who explain that some people derive the word *lucus* (grove) from the fact that a dense wood boasts very little natural light (e.g. *lucus ... dicitur quod non luceat* (it is called a grove because there is no light; Serv. *A.* 1.441)). The phrase *lucus a non lucendo* has passed into English usage to mean an illogical explanation because of this absurd etymology, and it jarred with the ancient grammarians too. This in itself should alert us to the

of the etymological connection many have drawn between Dea Dia and the phrase *sub divo* (under the open sky), leading to her being characterised as 'the Bright Goddess' by Jenkyns 2013: 196. Schilling 1969: 675–676 in particular is known for arguing that Dea Dia was a 'goddess of daylight', relying on Varro's connection of the archaic adjective *dius* (which seems to mean 'divine' or 'daylit', see *OLD* ad loc.) with the phrase *sub divo* (under the open sky; *LL.* 5.66). Multiple interpretations of the nature and personality of the elusive Dea Dia can be found in the secondary literature; for Wissowa 1912: 562 she is 'eine Indigitation der Ceres', whilst Paladino 1988: 229–231 discusses her perceived affinity with Diana and Fortuna. See Scheid 1990: 664–669 for an overview of these interpretations, with a focus on those who have chosen the 'daylight' reading. Cf. Scheid 1990: 463–464 on the significance scholars have read into the Arvals' *indictio* taking place *sub divo*. On the idea of the Arvals' pruning being part of the worship, cf. Bodel 1985: 26, who acknowledges that in the Spoleto inscription there is clearly 'intentional cutting' of wood, but justifies this by wondering whether it was 'considered an integral part of the ceremony itself and was therefore exculpable on religious grounds'.

[93] Scheid 1993: 150; Scheid 1990: 556. Dumézil 1975: 43 makes the same claim as Scheid – 'étymologiquement, *lucus* est "clairière", "Lichtung"' – but unlike Scheid, acknowledges the clash between this etymological sense and the fact that *lucus* also means a wood (as it were the opposite of a clearing).

149

dangers of pushing light-centric readings of *lucus* (grove); with the awkwardness of the derivation from *lux* (light) felt even by a grammarian – Quintilian counts this etymology among *foedissima ... ludibria* (the most awful ... absurdities; *Inst.* 1.6.34) – it is easy to see how it might have seemed artificial, or indeed irrelevant, within lived experiences of Roman religion. Moreover, when the grammarians give their alternative etymology for *lucus* (grove), connecting it with the *presence* of light, it is highly significant that they do not talk of the light produced by a clearing, but that of candles brought along for ceremonies in such a naturally dark place (Serv. *A.* 1.441; Isid. *Etym.* 14.8.30 and 17.6.7). This leaves Scheid's insistence that *lucus* (grove) is etymologically connected to the idea of a light-filled clearing on very shaky ground indeed.

In addition, I also diverge from Scheid in his emphasis on the practical intent of this pruning. For Scheid's focus on the practical benefit of the pruning to the humans who are about to sacrifice in Dea Dia's grove misses something crucial to our understanding of its significance: this pruning was of precious little benefit to the trees. Of course I hardly wish to deny that pruning is in general aimed at improving the health of a tree: the problem here is in the *timing* of the Arvals' pruning. The best time of year to prune depends on the type of tree, and sadly we know little of what trees made up the Arvals' grove (only one holm oak, some laurels and one fig make it into the limelight).[94] Yet whatever the tree, May is always a bad time to prune, when foliage is a hindrance and cut trees are likely to 'bleed'.[95] Annual pruning like the Arvals'

---

[94] Holm oak (inscription 8); laurels (inscription 14); fig (inscription 22).

[95] Coombs 1992: 15, in his pruning handbook, explains that autumn is the best time for pruning fruit trees, winter for others. This was knowledge shared by Roman thinkers too. Varro recommends winter for pruning trees, provided the bark is free from ice and rain (*RR.* 1.27); vines should be pruned between the autumnal equinox and the setting of the Pleiades, except in localities with severe early frosts, when it is best done in spring (*RR.* 1.34). Columella also discusses the pros and cons of the two times of year for pruning vines, namely autumn and spring (4.9–10, but going into further detail at 4.23). Columella also observes that pruning a mixed vineyard well (that is taking the correct approach for each type of vine) is hard because pruning is done when the vines do not have 'distinctive foliage' (*folium notabile*; 3.21.7), and that it is better for vines to receive the pruning-hook in autumn than for superfluous foliage to be cut off in summer, when new shoots will immediately reappear (4.6.5). Pliny also advises pruning vines directly after the vintage (*Nat.* 17.191); for other trees, however, he recommends much lighter treatment in spring (*Nat.* 17.257).

Piacular pruning

can also be actively harmful for mature trees, a *trucidatio inutilissima* (most futile slaughter) as Pliny melodramatically puts it (*Nat.* 17.257).[96] All in all it may have been a blessing for these trees that the Arvals restricted their pruning to one day, and a day packed with other duties, so that only a handful of trees could have received attention. The timing of the Arvals' pruning insists that their priorities in interfering with these trees were ritual, not arboreal. Pruning was for them part of the liturgical year: how many even knew when it featured in an arboriculturalist's calendar?

Another concerning feature of Scheid's understanding of the Arvals' piacular pruning sacrifices is his emphasis that these *piacula* softened ('adoucissaient') the *necessary* breaking of sacral law: 'les violations pouvaient toutefois être autorisées quand une nécessité les imposait. Dans ce cas il convenait toutefois d'offrir un piaculum operis faciendi operisque perfecti.'[97] Here Scheid refers us back to Tromp, who had argued that that there were three reasons for which you could escape being branded inexpiable for willingly committing a fault: firstly, if it was truly necessary; secondly, if you were so acting for the sake of a cult act; thirdly, if it avoided a greater *nefas* (outrage).[98] In any such situation, Tromp argued, you performed a *piaculum operis faciendi*, thus setting a trend for scholars to use the Arvals' formula *piacula operis faciundi* as though it were a recognised 'label' for a particular kind of sacrifice in Roman culture.[99] Predictably enough, the example Tromp immediately turns to is that of a grove which needs to be pruned, with discussion of Cato, the Spoleto law and the Arval acta.[100] In short, the Tromp–Scheid consensus argues that 7

---

[96] For the vast majority of trees Pliny here advises pruning at least less than every other year, noting that pruning must not be 'battering' (*plaga*; *Nat.* 17.257). Likewise Columella notes that olive groves must only be pruned at intervals of several years, citing a proverb to that effect which likens pruning to 'forcing' (*cogere*; 5.9.15).

[97] Scheid 1990: 558; Scheid 1981: 137.

[98] Tromp 1921: 90.

[99] For example, Bodel 1985: 27; Linderski 1995: 594.

[100] Tromp 1921: 90–112. Tromp's 1921: 92 emphasis when discussing the Spoleto law is to note his surprise that no *piaculum operis faciendi* is mentioned, suggesting that this was because the wood was used in the grove and not taken out. Tromp also considers the presence in the Arval acta of *piacula operis perfecti*, attributing the performance of such sacrifices to religious fear (1921: 112), a particularly serious fault (114), or the inability to appease the gods beforehand (82). Linderski 1995: 593–594 also follows the Tromp–Scheid

these piacular pruning sacrifices were intended to 'evade' or 'make good' a necessary fault, but was the pruning really necessary? Surely there was no necessity to prune these trees: hasty pruning on one busy day in May can hardly have been much advantage from a human perspective in terms of 'grove management', and it certainly was not of advantage to the trees. These *piacula* were not intended to amend a necessary 'sacrilege', since the 'sacrilege' was so easily avoidable. Thus, we are left with a picture of the Arvals *choosing* to undertake pruning on the second day of Dea Dia's major festival, and yet at the same time offering piacular sacrifices for doing so. This may be conceptually difficult for us, if we understand *piacula* to be in some way about atoning faults (even necessary ones), but we must not shy away from the evidence.[101] Perhaps a reassessment of what we understand by *piacula* is needed? One thing at least is certain. Physically engaging with these trees was clearly of deep religious significance to the Arvals, but this was not prompted by a concern for the trees' inviolability. In fact it was through their *choice* to engage in some light pruning – indeed making rather a song and dance of their cutting off some arboreal matter – that the Arvals expressed just how much their relationship with these trees mattered to them.

Conceptualising crises

I turn now to certain inscriptions which allow individual trees, and even occasional branches, to step into the limelight.[102] All are in crisis: the trees have fallen over and the branches have dropped off.[103] These arboreal crises prompt further expiatory sacrifices from the Arvals which, unlike the clockwork 'pruning sacrifices', are attested at various times throughout the year. The inscriptions recording these sacrifices follow a fairly standard format: we are

line, going so far as to claim that, since the Roman state could never acknowledge having wilfully offended the gods, all public offences were '*ex definitione* involuntary' (594).

[101] Linderski 1995: 594, in his review of Scheid, argues that *piacula operis faciundi* were not meant to serve as atonement, but rather to restore the *pax deorum*, but I am not convinced that there is a watertight distinction between these two concepts: is not acknowledging a need to restore good relationships with the divine a form of atoning and amending?

[102] Inscriptions 1, 2, 3, 4, 5, 6, 8, 9, 10, 11, 12, 13, 14, 17.

[103] The trees in inscription 14 are possibly not quite dead, for discussion of which see pp. 157–158.

Conceptualising crises

told that 'a piacular sacrifice was performed' (*piaculum factum*) 'because of a tree' (*ob arborem* or *quod arbor*), followed by the briefest of explanations of the tree's demise, with the two options being 'from old age' or 'from stormy weather' (*vetustate* or *a tempestate*). The use of *ob* and *quod* (because) means that the dead trees are explicitly presented as the issue at stake prompting the *piaculum*, an understanding which is even more strikingly expressed in the rarer inscriptions which describe the dead trees as *expiandae* (requiring expiation) or *expiatae* (having been expiated).[104] These trees thus provide a rare opportunity to examine Roman thinking about what the death of a sacred tree meant, and to ask how this affected conceptions of its matter's significance. What made a living tree different from a dead tree, if shortly before and after death they were, materially speaking, indistinguishable? Was the tree's matter to be treated differently once it died?

In the Arvals' records of these arboreal crisis sacrifices there is, as in their accounts of the pruning sacrifices, a surprising absence: whilst the sacrifices are said to take place in Dea Dia's grove, she is not obviously framed as the sacrifices' recipient. So ingrained into the way we think about sacrifice is the idea that it mediated communication between the human and divine sphere, that the idea of a recipient-less sacrifice may seem like a contradiction in terms. So what is happening here? The Arvals' inscriptions, as I emphasised earlier, should not be approached as a straightforward blow-by-blow account of their ritual activities. We cannot conclude from the inscriptions alone that no prayers were offered as part of this sacrifice, prayers for which Dea Dia would have made an obvious addressee. What is significant, however, is that in the Arvals' conceptualisation and articulation of their ritual activities, no divine recipient is made a priority: rather it is the tree which is the priority. Informative for understanding these tree-focused sacrifices is to turn to another conceptually difficult – but very prevalent – form of sacrifice in the Roman world, namely those which articulated 'imperial cult'. Price famously drew attention to ways in which Roman thinkers were deeply sensitive to the prepositions

---

[104] Inscriptions 6, 9, 10, 11, 12 and 21. Tromp 1921: 108 bizarrely wants to read the *ob* in the Arvals' formulae for their 'engraving sacrifices' as temporal.

used in sacrificial formulae when negotiating imperial cult: instead of sacrificing *to* an emperor, you might sacrifice *for* or *on behalf of* an emperor.[105] In the light of Price's arguments, it is interesting for our purposes that imperial cult also made heavy demands on the Arvals' time, and certainly has a weighty presence in their inscriptional record: trees were far from their only concern! Moreover, prepositions turn out to be significant when the Arvals articulate their acts of imperial cult too. To give just two examples, we find the Arvals sacrificing 'because of the well-being and victory' (*ob salute<m> victoriamque*) of Caracalla on 6 October 213 CE, and 'on behalf of Poppaea's safe childbirth' (*[pr]o partu et incolumitate Poppaeae*) on 21 January 63 CE.[106] Sensitive use of prepositions here allowed the Arvals to negotiate the delicate matter of sacrificing to/about/for a 'living god'; indeed the sheer difficulty of expressing what sacrifices within imperial cult *do* without using a preposition reveals just how central they were to its meaning.

That the Arvals were clearly sensitive to prepositional niceties in their acts of imperial cult should also inform the way we approach their tree-focused sacrifices. Articulating these sacrifices through an *ob* or *quod* clause, the Arvals present themselves as sacrificing *about* an arboreal crisis, rather than to a deity (even if Dea Dia was perhaps always at the back of their minds): thus they highlight the tree's death as the focus of their religious attention.[107] This dominating focus on the arboreal deaths as a religious crisis is also reinforced by the nature of some of the offerings which made up the Arvals' *piacula* in response. The most common sacrificial victims specified are a pig and a lamb, but on four occasions we also have mention of two types of sacrificial cake being offered alongside the meat offerings: the Arvals sacrifice *struibus ferctisque* (with *strues* and *fercta*; inscriptions 13, 14, 17 and 21).[108] Our evidence for sacrificial

---

[105] Price 1984: 210–220.
[106] Scheid 1998: 284 (inscription 99a (23)); Scheid 1998: 76 (inscription 29I (20)).
[107] Authors like Livy with a penchant for portents are frustratingly silent on the phraseology of the prayers used in the sacrifices responding to those portents; it is hardly surprising that on occasions *ob* and *quod* are used to describe *why* the sacrifices took place (e.g. Livy 38.36 and Livy 3.29).
[108] In inscriptions 12 and 14, where multiple trees have died, the sacrifices include multiple pigs and lambs; this was not a hard and fast rule, however, as in inscription 6 multiple tree deaths led to the sacrifice of only one pig and one lamb.

cakes in the Roman world is sparse to say the least; indeed the focus of the evidence makes it easy to forget that many sacrifices in the Roman world must have been vegetarian-friendly. In the specific case of the cakes known as *strues* and *fercta* the evidence is dominated by Cato and Festus.[109] Cato instructs those wishing to bring in the harvest to make several sacrifices first: alongside a pig for Ceres, a *strues* is to be offered to Janus and a *fertum* to Jupiter (*Agr.* 134). Clearly there is some similarity here with the combination of pig, lamb, *strues* and *fercta* offered by the Arvals. Far more interesting, however, is the fact that Festus links *strues* and *fercta* to cases of trees being struck by lightning (376L and 377L). Not only are these 'arboreal' types of cake in Festus' mind – something which suggests they could have come loaded with tree-specific significance when the Arvals chose them too – but he also connects them with a lightning strike on trees, a situation which, like any other lightning strike, could easily be understood to be of negative portentous significance.[110] Indeed Festus' testimony may illuminate the presence of these cakes in inscription 14: had its 'badly burned' (*perusta[e*) trees been victims of a lightning strike? Such a fate could also have befallen trees lashed by a *tempestas* (storm) in inscription 17, although presumably not the victims of old age in inscriptions 13 and 21. Also of interest in Festus' account is the way that he frames the offerings of *strues* and *fercta* as *sacrificia ad arbores fulguritas* (sacrifices *at* lightning-struck trees; 377L). Festus' use of *ad* – these are sacrifices *at* trees, not *to* or *for* those trees – reminds us of the prepositional sensitivity in the Arvals' formulae as they sacrifice *because of* an arboreal death.

That the Arvals colour the arboreal deaths as a religiously negative – perhaps even portentous – situation may seem rather odd: for they also show themselves perfectly capable of explaining

[109] See Turcan 2000: 40 for brief discussion.
[110] Pliny the Elder presents lightning-struck trees as religiously negative by stigmatising the use of them in certain ritual acts. Thus a type of oak frequently struck by lightning is not to be used as wood for sacrifice (*Nat.* 16.24); likewise it is forbidden to pour wine to the gods from vines which have been lightning-struck (*Nat.* 14.119). The fear of a tree being struck by lightning also prompts religiously articulated rules about arboreal cultivation: myrtle is to be grown from cuttings rather than grafted on elm, which *religio fulgurum* (religious scruples over lightning strikes) forbids (*Nat.* 17.124); nor is it right to perform grafts on a thorn thanks to the difficulty of expiating lightning bolts when they hit it (*Nat.* 15.57).

these deaths in 'natural terms', always specifying whether their demise was due to old age or a storm. These two approaches to the same event may not seem straightforwardly compatible. Yet evidence from outside the grove can shed light on this surprising attitude, revealing that arboreal portents and 'natural' arboreal ailments were rarely conceived of as wholly distinct categories in Roman culture. Thus it is, for example, that Pliny slots his discussion of arboreal portents into a far wider section on arboreal illnesses: *inter vitia arborum est et prodigiis locus* (among the illnesses of trees there is also space for portents; *Nat.* 17.241). Consider too a vicious storm of 60 BCE, which both Cassius Dio and Julius Obsequens record, and in so doing reveal Pliny's mental framework in practice. Obsequens, in the unusual and late text that is his *Liber de prodigiis*, includes uprooted trees in a list of the events which occurred in the context of this *turbo*, a whirlwind type storm.[111]

turbinis vi tecta deiecta. ponte sublapso homines in Tiberim praecipitati. in agris pleraque arbores eversae radicibus. (*Liber de prodigiis* 62)

Buildings were hurled down by the storm's force. Men were cast headlong into the Tiber when a bridge collapsed. In the fields trees were for the most part uprooted.[112]

Cassius Dio also lists uprooted trees, shattered houses and the collapse of the bridge as part of the way in which τὸ δαιμόνιον (the divine) revealed the future to those who could understand (37.58). Very little, we might object, is surprising about trees being uprooted in a storm, nor indeed the destruction of buildings or the collapse of bridges. Yet in the worldview of Dio and Obsequens these uprooted trees take on a portentous significance. Doubtless neither was stumped for a natural explanation of these trees' demise, but – in the context of this storm – they did not rule out a 'natural' phenomenon being of divine significance.

---

[111] See Rasmussen 2003: 21–22 for an overview of this text and the debates surrounding the elusive author.

[112] Cf. Obsequens' account of another vicious storm in 44 BCE: *tabulae aeneae ex aede Fidei turbine evulsae. aedis Opis valvae fractae. arbores radicitus et pleraque tecta eversa* (Bronze tablets were torn from the temple of Fides by the storm. The doors of the temple of Ops were broken. Trees were torn up by the roots and buildings for the most part overthrown; *Liber de prodigiis* 68).

Conceptualising crises

Hints in the Arvals' phrasing of their inscriptional records suggest that they too were tuned into the potential for divine involvement in 'natural' arboreal disasters. On two occasions the common explanation that a tree died from a storm is embellished as follows: one tree collapsed *tempestate vel vi maiori* (from a storm or from a greater force; 17), another *vetustate vel vi maiori* (from old age or from a greater force; 12). What did the Arvals mean by this *vis maior* (greater force)? According to Pliny, *vis maior* is a term for a particularly violent type of storm (*Nat.* 18.278) and such a technical interpretation could make *some* sense of the distinction *tempestate vel vi maiori* (from a storm or from a very strong storm); it would not, however, make much sense of *vetustate vel vi maiori* (from old age or from a very strong storm). What would be the logic in ascribing a tree's death either to old age or a very particular type of storm? Consequently it seems to me that this phrase *vel vi maiori* (or from a greater force) does not refer to a particularly vehement storm, but rather articulates the Arvals' awareness that what looked every bit like a 'natural' arboreal death might also be meaningful in divine terms; agencies of which they knew little (a vague 'greater force') might also express themselves through the trees. In short, knowledge of the 'naturalness' of arboreal deaths in the grove does not prevent the Arvals from colouring them and responding to them as crisis situations of deep significance on a divine level.

Considering this, you might expect that the Arvals would treat the matter of these dead trees with cautious respect. As it is, the Arvals rarely tell us how they dealt with their dead trees – which in itself may be informative – and when they do, their handling of the trees is surprisingly violent. On one occasion it is decided that a dead tree should be used up 'for/at a sacrifice', presumably by burning its wood for the sacrificial fire:

c(ensuerunt) [cum arbo]r vetustate in luco deae Diae cecidisset ut [in luc]o ad sacrificium consumeretur neve quid [ligni] exportaretur. (inscription 1)
They decreed that, since a tree had fallen over from old age in Dea Dia's grove, it should be used up in the grove for/at a sacrifice nor any of the [wood?] taken out.

On another occasion, consultation among the Arvals leads to certain laurels 'requiring felling' (*caedendae*; 14). Whether these latter trees were in fact entirely dead is up for debate. We know they have been 'badly burned by storms' (*tempestatibus perusta[e*) and are presumably victims of lightning; however, they seem not to have fallen over, for the standard *deciderunt* (they collapsed) is missing from this relatively complete inscription. Still standing – whether dead or nearly so – these trees must have been a liability, likely to come crashing down at any moment. This is why I would argue that in context *caedendae* must mean that the trees needed felling, the obvious action which the situation requires.[113] But what justified the Arvals in showing such violence towards their dead, or nearly dead, trees?

Let us begin with the tree which was consumed 'for/at a sacrifice'. Unusually for the inscriptions focused on an arboreal crisis, there is no mention here of a *piaculum*; rather the blander *sacrificium* (sacrifice) is used. For Henzen, it is the burning of the tree itself which explains this lack of overtly piacular sacrifice: consuming the tree in this way stands in for the need of a *piaculum*.[114] Certainly one possible Roman response to a portentous object was to burn it. Consider, for example, Livy's account of certain cows who disturbingly climbed the stairs of a house and were consequently burned (36.37.2).[115] It may be telling that Livy excludes mention of any sacrifices in conjunction with the cows' extermination; perhaps their burning was understood as a substitute sacrifice in itself, since the killing of animals is a quintessential sacrificial act. Likewise we can imagine that, in the scenario suggested by our inscription, the burning of wood – another essential element of any sacrifice – also played a double role. Burning the tree was

---

[113] To prune, another meaning of *caedere*, would be of little use in this crisis. Scheid reconstructs *ob arb[orum caeden]darum causa<m>* in inscription 17, but the unparalleled *ob causam* with a dependent genitive gerund suggests we are far from the original text here. The fact that these trees have fallen over also casts doubt on inscription 17 providing a parallel to inscription 14.

[114] Henzen 1874: 136. Cf. Bodel 1985: 26, who follows Henzen's reading. Scheid 1993: 150 extrapolates a general rule from this one inscription: 'le bois mort est enlevé, debité et brûlé au cours des sacrifices, les arbres morts ou détruits sont remplacés'.

[115] Further examples can be found in Livy, Obsequens and Diodorus Siculus: when a great storm of wasps had settled in a temple of Mars they were carefully collected and consumed by fire (Livy 35.9.4); a boy born with four feet, hands, eyes and ears was burned, with the ashes thrown into the sea (Obseq. 25); an owl whose voice was heard on the Capitol was captured and burned, the ashes then thrown into the Tiber (Obseq. 26); a hermaphrodite was burned alive on the orders of the senate (Diod. Sic. 32.12.2).

Conceptualising crises

both part of the sacrifice and at the same time also cancelled out the existence of the religiously offending object.

The response to the trees which 'need felling' (*caedendae*) in inscription 14 is somewhat different. Here the violence towards the trees is not articulated as part of the sacrificial process, but rather a *piaculum* is offered because of these trees. Yet these two glimpses of interference with dead (or nearly dead) trees share one thing in common: they leave little room for assuming that a sacred tree's matter was inviolable. Also intriguing is the fact that both these glimpsed images of violent tree elimination follow deliberation over the crisis at hand. In inscription 1, following a report by the augur to the Arval brothers of the tree's demise, an official decision is announced by means of the formal *q(uid) d(e) e(a) r(e) f(ieri) p(laceret) d(e) e(a) r(e) i(ta) c(ensuerunt)* (with regard to what it might please them to be done, thus about that thing they announced). Likewise in inscription 14, following Scheid's reconstruction, Decianus the *magister* reports the matter of the badly burned laurels to his colleagues, before a decision that they should be cut down is taken. It seems that something about these two cases prompted deliberation which was not felt necessary in other cases of arboreal demise (or at least its recording was not). In inscription 14 we can imagine that deliberation was prompted by the Arvals finding themselves in the unusual situation of being faced with trees which were not quite dead.[116] What prompted the deliberation behind inscription 1 is much more open to conjecture. However, what is informative here is that on all other occasions in which an arboreal death is recorded, the Arvals keep resolute silence over how they responded to the trees' remains. When there are no unusual circumstances, their response to dead arboreal matter was not something for which they felt a need to be religiously accountable on stone.

This apparent insouciance towards the dead trees' matter is matched by the Arvals' seeming indifference to preventing unnecessary arboreal deaths in the grove, or at least to postponing

---

[116] Certainly the recording of the type of tree here involved, namely laurel, suggests a heightened attention to detail in comparison with the other sacrifices *ob/quod* the death of a tree.

those deaths for as long as possible. For the sum total of recorded assistance which the trees receive is the limited pruning in May, when the trees stand more chance of being harmed than benefited by such interference. Otherwise, the Arvals intervene only in crisis situations (or again, at least present themselves as so doing), by which time any arboricultural assistance would be far too late.[117] In addition, a rather lax attitude to recording arboreal deaths in the grove may also be detected. Considering the fact that our tree-focused inscriptions span a 226-year period we might expect more deaths to be recorded, even taking into account the lacunose state of the inscriptional record. Did a large number of arboreal deaths in the grove simply go ignored?[118] Was M. Valerius Trebicius Decianus, who records his involvement in one pruning sacrifice (inscription 15) and two crisis sacrifices (inscriptions 14 and 17) simply a particularly conscientious *magister*, with a soft spot for trees?[119] Perhaps political circumstances also heightened the Arvals' awareness of potentially meaningful arboreal behaviour in the grove? After all, four of our eighteen arboreal crises occurred during the rule of Domitian. Exceptions like that of Decianus and the flurry of sacrifices under Domitian underline the *laissez-faire* nature of the Arvals' usual attitude towards the grove: despite signalling how theologically significant a tree's death was to them by means of their *ob arborem* sacrifices, they were hardly attentive to their

---

[117] Scheid 1993: 150, observing that the grove does not receive arboricultural attention throughout the year, but only when cult demands or trees die, immediately notes that 'on a l'impression que les prêtres s'occupent avant tout de veiller sur l'intégrité du bois sacré et d'éloigner de lui toute souillure, notamment celle qui était produite par la mort', but this is to overlook the fact that some interference would have helped to protect the grove from the 'souillure' of death.

[118] As already mentioned, we do not know what kind of trees populated the grove – which would help us to make conjectures about the frequency of arboreal deaths – bar reference to one holm oak (inscription 8), one fig (inscription 22) and some laurels (inscription 14). Figs, as discussed at p. 100, were known in the Roman world for their shortness of life; laurels, too, Pliny places in the category of trees which 'grow old quickly' (*senescunt ... velociter*; *Nat.* 16.241) but then put out new shoots quickly.

[119] Indeed the arboreal crisis sacrifices are often said to have been performed by slaves (*calatores* and *publici*), and only rarely by the *magister* or *promagister* of the priesthood: does this also suggest that these sacrifices were not always at the top of the Arvals' list of priorities? See Lennon 2014: 104, n. 74 for useful references on the role of slaves in public sacrifice, and the way this might detach the official 'sacrificers' from the killing itself.

trees' health whilst alive. It may be objected here that the Arvals sometimes sacrificed regarding individual branches (inscriptions 2 and 8), an attention to detail which belies arboreal negligence. Yet the Arvals notice these branches because they are dead: individual trees, or bits of trees, loom large in the Arvals' minds only when they are on their death-bed.

The Arvals, however, are not alone in this surprisingly lax attitude towards sacred wooden objects. Consider the care received by the wooden *casa Romuli*. Dionysius of Halicarnassus tells us that the guardians of this hut preserve it as sacred and add nothing to it to make it more impressive. Indeed, the only times when they intervene with the hut are if it is damaged by a storm or old age, 'restoring what is left' (τὸ λεῖπον ἐξακούμενοι) and returning it – to the best of their ability – to its previous state (1.79.11).[120] This kind of crisis-driven response – where only old age or a storm prompts interference – is now very familiar from the Arvals, with the striking τὸ λεῖπον (what is left) suggesting just how far the guardians of this hut are prepared to let it decline.[121] Also perhaps reminiscent of the Arvals (at least if we read an expiatory tone into the *piacula* they offer as they respond to arboreal deaths) is Dionysius' use of ἐξακούμενοι to describe the response to the decaying hut; as well as meaning 'healing completely', or 'restoring', this verb also has connotations of amending. Indeed Cassius Dio's two depictions of the *casa Romuli* make explicit Dionysius' hint that damage to the hut was seen as a religiously negative sign. For he includes among the omens of 12 BCE the fact that crows dropped burning chunks of meat on the hut and it caught fire (54.29.8), and prior to that the hapless hut had also been set alight by *pontifices* performing rites within it, adding to the omens of 38 BCE (48.43.4).

---

[120] Cf. Conon's emphasis that preservation of the hut aims to keep it looking as primitive as possible (*Narr.* 48). Edwards 1996: 30–43 discusses these (and many other) passages to examine the contested history of the *casa Romuli* in detail. Unlike Edwards 1996: 34, I would not emphasise priestly 'vigilance' in Dionysius' account of the *casa Romuli*.

[121] Balland 1984: 64 understands the 'as few repairs as possible' approach to the preservation of the *casa Romuli* as the 'traitement classique des *aedes sacrae* rebâties', and draws to his support Dionysius of Halicarnassus' depiction of the restoration of the temple of Jupiter Feretrius (2.34.4).

The wooden *pons sublicius* was also subject to similar treatment. In Dionysius' day, we are told, people still preserved this bridge, considering it sacred, and if it were in trouble the priests offered sacrifices 'at the same time as performing repair work' (ἅμα τῇ ἐπισκευῇ; Dion. Hal. 3.45.2); as with the hut, this bridge only receives attention when it is struggling. Varro – arguing his belief that the title *pontifices* comes from 'bridge' – likewise tells us that the *pons sublicius* is often restored by the *pontifices*, 'for which reason' (*ideo*) they perform rites 'with no mean ceremony' (*non mediocri ritu*; *LL.* 5.83). Plutarch, whilst dismissing as laughable the majority opinion that *pontifex* means 'bridge builder', also notes that the reason for this ridiculous belief is that the *pontifices* carry out most holy and most ancient sacrifices at a bridge (*Num.* 9.2–3). Striking here is the explicit emphasis on how such repair work was understood to be a religious issue, accompanied as it was by showy sacrifices. Varro insists that these sacrifices are on behalf of (*ideo*) the repair work (a preposition recalling the Arvals' formula *operis faciundi causa*), something which Dionysius also implies by his temporal correlation of restoration and sacrifice (ἅμα τῇ ἐπισκευῇ).

Surprising as this *laissez-faire* approach to venerable wooden objects in Roman culture may be, it shows that the Arvals were not idiosyncratically flouting the norms of care for vulnerable sacred wood in their crisis-driven responses to the trees in their grove. Nevertheless, both the Arvals' apparent indifference to preventing arboreal deaths, and their heavy-handed treatment of arboreal matter once dead, sit strangely with the way the use of prepositions in their *ob/quod arborem* sacrifices present an arboreal death as the sole focus of their religious attention. From this it seems that for the Arvals the religious significance of each tree was *not* deeply bound up with its matter: rather it was what the living tree stood for, the life which was now lost, which was the issue at stake in these sacrifices. Thus, despite question marks concerning the Arvals' understanding of their responsibility towards the grove's trees, what is clear is that their sacrifices were prompted not by the damage to arboreal matter which death by storm or old age entails, but by the loss of arboreal life: as their sacrificial formulae insist, they sacrificed because a tree had died.

Conceptualising crises (again)

On 8 February 183 CE, the Arvals were dealing with another crisis. A fig was growing in the roof of Dea Dia's temple. Going into the grove, they responded to this structural nightmare by sacrificing *suovetaurilia maiora* 'for the work to be undertaken' (*operis inchuandi causa*), namely removing the tree and repairing the temple (inscription 22). The tone of the *suovetaurilia maiora* (a sacrificial combination of pig, sheep and bull which commonly features in response to situations perceived as portentous) colours the fig's existence as a religiously negative situation which the Arvals take urgent steps to eliminate.[122] This is followed by a second sacrifice to a long list of little-heard-of deities, such as Mater Larum or Juno Deae Diae, which takes place in front of Dea Dia's temple. (Many questions surround the identity of these deities, and the pertinence of their presence here; arguably the threat to Dea Dia's temple called for a roll call of many potentially affected parties.[123]) Next there is a third sacrifice of two sheep to Adolenda Conmolenda Deferunda (Needing to be Burned, Needing to Be Chopped Up, Needing to be Taken Down), and finally a fourth to the *divi* in front of the Caesareum. These sacrifices are separated in the inscriptional record by *item* (in addition, or perhaps, likewise), which is not a stark divider but which does imply that the sacrifices were conceptually distinct, even if responding to the same crisis; this is reflected too in their different locations.[124] The

---

[122] For the standard scholarly claim that *suovetaurilia* are sacrifices of purification – often known as *lustra* – which restore the *pax deorum* see Wissowa 1912: 390–391; Ogilvie 1969: 88–89; Dowden 2000: 195; Turcan 2000: 41 and 88; Warrior 2006: 57. Lennon 2014: 100–109 himself articulates a version of the standard view, but also discusses variant views, namely Kirkpatrick's reading of *lustra* as propitiation rather than purification (12–13) and Rüpke's similar take on the *lustratio exercitus* (lustration of the army; 126–127). Whilst the frequent use of *lustra* and *suovetaurilia* as responses to situations deemed portentous (see the useful table of portents provided by Rasmussen 2003: 53–116) does, in my eyes, provide strong support for the standard interpretation, I would also emphasise, as when discussing *piacula*, how strongly scholars lean on one passage of Cato for their understanding of the *suovetaurilia*, namely *Agr.* 141 (e.g. Turcan 2000: 41 and Warrior 2006: 20–21), and their unquestioning use of the term *pax deorum*.

[123] Scheid 2003b: 168–171 discusses the 'spheres of action and influence' of these elusive deities (168).

[124] Cf. Scheid 2003b: 174, who sees *item* as articulating a hierarchy of deities within this set of sacrifices.

inscription ends by recording a mirror set of four sacrifices 'for the completion of the work' (*operis perfecti causa*). The Arvals viewed this fig very differently from those growing in the grove. It was not the tree's poor condition which constituted the religious crisis at hand, but rather the structural damage to Dea Dia's roof, and therefore, it seems, the sacrifice is focused on the removal work rather than the tree. Again Pliny provides a parallel scenario here. When another similarly invasive fig had upset a statue of Silvanus, it too was removed after sacrifices were offered by the Vestal Virgins (*Nat.* 15.77).[125] Such removals, however, were not always straightforward, as Pliny knew well. In the grove of Juno at Nocera, he reports, an elm which had been drooping onto an altar once had its crown lopped, only to spring back to its former bushy glory (*Nat.* 16.132). Pliny interprets this particular case as a positive omen, but the event illustrates just how religiously fraught it could be to interfere with a tree entangled with an altar or temple, based on assumptions about the relative importance of each. The Arvals could not have been absolutely positive that removing the fig was the right course of action: hence the sacrificial focus on the removal process, reinforced by the sacrifice to Adolenda Conmolenda Deferunda, a kind of 'divine sponsor' for the tasks of taking down, chopping up and burning demanded by the troublesome fig.[126] The one-off crisis of the fig in Dea Dia's roof called for a tailored response.

Yet, at the same time, it seems this unique set of sacrifices moulded the way future Arvals conceptualised and recorded other types of interaction with the trees of the grove, establishing a precedent then adopted out of its original context.[127] For, from this point onwards, the Arvals blended formulaic patterns previously used in the sacrifices for pruning living trees with formulae used in the sacrifices because of arboreal deaths; this conflation was, perhaps, encouraged by the application of a sacrificial model initially

---

[125] Boetticher 1856: 45 views the removing of this fig as its 'Ausweihung'. Juvenal's allusion to the threat which figs pose to tombs (10.144–146) paints the invasiveness of these trees as a well-known fact in Roman culture.
[126] The tasks are arranged in alphabetical, not logical, order.
[127] Beard 1985: 129 argues that the Arvals did not consult earlier inscriptions as a guide to action, but I believe that inscriptions 22, 25 and 27 prove that certain Arvals did pay attention to precedent.

Conceptualising crises

designed to deal with one annoyingly vivacious fig to situations of more fatal arboreal crisis. We see this conflation in inscriptions 25 and 27, when the Arvals are again involved with struggling trees, some dead and some apparently on the brink of it. Previously such crises had prompted *ob arborem* or *quod arbor* sacrifices, but now the inscriptions focalise their concern through sacrifices for the process of interference with those trees. Thus in inscription 25 the Arvals first 'sacrificed' in the grove (the bland *imm(olaverunt)* is used here) because of the trees which burned, before performing a *lustrum* with *suovetaurilia maiora* for the sake of both a variety of arboreal tasks (to which I will return) and repairing altars. This is followed by a further sacrifice of two cows in front of the temple of Dea Dia and then a variety of sacrifices at the 'temporary altars' to a list of deities almost identical to that in inscription 22. Next up is a sacrifice of two sheep to Adolenda Coinquenda (Needing to be Burned, Needing to be Pruned), before final sacrifices to the *genius* of the emperor and the *divi* take place in front of the Caesareum: the whole format is then repeated in the post-eventum set of sacrifices. Similarly in inscription 27 the Arvals record how they performed a *lustrum* with *suovetaurilia maiora* in the grove for the beginning of arboricultural work, followed by a sacrifice in front of the temple for a similar list of gods as above, and finally sacrifices in front of the Caesareum to the *genius* of the emperor: and at this point the inscription breaks off.[128] Arboreal crises, it seems, are now dealt with ritually by articulating concern for the interference with those trees, not for the dead (or dying) trees themselves.

The notorious goddess Adolenda Conmolenda Deferunda, and her lesser-known sister Adolenda Coinquenda, epitomise this change in focus. These goddesses were extremely distasteful to the first scholars of Roman religion, with Rose memorably calling the first 'three very curious little godlings'.[129] One grammatical reason lay at the heart of their instinctive recoiling from Adolenda

---

[128] Inscription 26, which *appears* to record a similar sacrificial response to 'another tree' (the phrase *aliam arborem* is one of the best preserved in the inscription), seems to me too lacunose for proper comment.
[129] Rose 1926: 49. Words such as 'curious' and 'ludicrous' also characterise Warde-Fowler's 1911: 161–162 engagement with this goddess.

Conmolenda Deferunda: gerundives require an object. Moreover, the obvious object to supply for these gerundive goddesses is *arbor* (tree), which to these Protestant-centric scholars sounded unsettlingly like 'direct and absolute-tree worship'.[130] Thus we find the scholarship full of rather convoluted attempts to 'read away' these gerundives. Wissowa, for example, reads them in an active sense to avoid having to view them as applied to a 'Baumseele', a tactic also adopted by Richter.[131] Altheim relies on a claim that the old form of the gerundive did not have a sense of obligation attached to it (despite the late dates of these inscriptions!), so as to read the deities as 'Deferunda for the felling, Commolenda for the chopping up', etc.[132] Only Wagenvoort – arguing that these gerundives function as medio-passive participles – is keen to make the tree their object (in order to emphasise just how primitive Roman 'tree worship' was):

> These epithets, applied to goddesses, are absurd, but make excellent sense if applied to ... the tree itself. There was a time when the priest addressed his prayers – or rather his conjurations – to the tree, the *arbor deferunda*, etc., as is still the case nowadays with primitive peoples.[133]

Such grammatical sidestepping seems to me to be missing the point. For the precedent of the *quod arbor* and *ob arborem* type sacrifices insists that we do not have to rethink the meaning of the gerundive in order to avoid concluding with Wagenvoort that trees in Dea Dia's grove were the 'recipients' of the Arvals' prayers or sacrifices. Just as the *ob arborem* inscriptions articulated the fact that the Arvals were sacrificing *about* a situation, so the sacrifices to these unique goddesses reveal the Arvals sacrificing *about* human interference with certain trees. By 'deifying' the process of interfering with the trees – the burning, the toppling, etc. – the Arvals assert that every step of the process was to them a matter

---

[130] Tylor 1871b: 202.
[131] Wissowa 1896: 1483; Richter 1916: 1353. The Arvals' use of gerundives is quite fluid – on occasions they seem interchangeable with perfect passive participles (e.g. inscriptions 9, 22 and 25) – but not so as to justify such a stark reinterpretation of the gerundive's meaning.
[132] Altheim 1938: 188. Indeed few scholars acknowledge the late date of our testimony to these two goddesses, although Warde-Fowler 1911: 162 argues that the Arvals have inherited the tradition of 'an earlier age' and are 'pedantically imitating the pontifices of five or six centuries earlier'.
[133] Wagenvoort 1947: 81.

of religious consideration (not that they were worshipping a tree). These sacrifices articulate human interference with certain trees in the grove as a process of the utmost religious significance. From Wagenvoort onwards, a mixture of bafflement, distaste and amusement has continued to define scholarly responses towards Adolenda Conmolenda Deferunda (sometimes treated as one, sometimes as three goddesses): for Dumézil they are 'pâles Entités', for Scheid the goddess is 'pittoresque'.[134] Echoing Rose, Jenkyns has recently observed that 'the Brothers ... concerned themselves with the cult of some curious mini-deities'.[135] Surprise at the Arvals having time for such gods is mirrored by surprise at their presence so late in the history of Roman religious culture. Thus Ogilvie framed the existence of Adolenda Conmolenda Deferunda as something strikingly primitive for 183 CE:

As late as A.D. 183 the Arval brethren were reduced to praying to Getter-down, Breaker-up and Burner (Deferunda, Conmolenda, Adolenda) in their attempts to deal with a fig tree which they had discovered surreptitiously growing on the roof of the temple of Dea Dia.[136]

Once these scholars have moved beyond their surprise, they engage with these goddesses not by offering grammatical 'solutions' to their existence, but through an emphasis on what Turcan terms the 'Roman sense of operational realism'.[137] Adolenda Conmolenda Deferunda is held up as a classic example of Usener's category of 'Sondergötter', specialist deities or, to use Ferguson's terms, 'powers, involved in or presiding over a limited but necessary operation, and having no existence apart from that operation'.[138] She is presented as one of many 'minor deities' who oversee a particular aspect of Roman life, with a healthy dose of condescension for such Roman thinking:

[134] Dumézil 1975: 53; Scheid 2005: 63. Scheid 2003b: 183 also emphasises the 'modesty' of goddesses like this who are linked to manual labour.
[135] Jenkyns 2013: 196.
[136] Ogilvie 1969: 13.
[137] Turcan 2000: 38.
[138] Ferguson 1970: 68. For scholars introducing Adolenda Conmolenda Deferunda and Adolenda Coinquenda within discussion of functional gods or Sondergötter see e.g. Warde-Fowler 1911: 161–162; Ogilvie 1969: 12–13; Ferguson 1970: 68–69; Jenkyns 2013: 200.

Gods were presumed as and when the need for them arose, but the multiplication of functional deities could be carried to ridiculous and quite unreal lengths, especially by professional priests with an urge for systematisation and a liking for lists.[139]

Scheid – who has spent more time than most thinking about Adolenda Conmolenda Deferunda and Adolenda Coinquenda – also understands them in this way, valuing them for the insights they provide into Roman 'creation of deities according to context'.[140] Indeed he diverges from the 'Usener-model' only to emphasise that such *Sondergötter* were clearly not 'fossils of the most primitive Roman piety': to the contrary, these goddesses reveal that 'priestly savoir-faire' was alive and well in the third century CE.[141] Whilst Scheid is unusual in not seeing these deities as 'primitive', a tendency to belittle them still remains, as he insistently frames them as 'servant gods'.[142] Another distinctive aspect of Scheid's engagement with these goddesses is his portrayal of them as 'the result of a desire to capture all the moments of an active process, while subordinating them to divine power and protection'.[143] His emphasis on the way the goddesses encapsulate the full process of interfering with the trees is of great value; where I disagree with Scheid, however, is in his understanding of the ritual need to articulate that process so precisely. For Scheid sees the sacrifices to Adolenda Conmolenda Deferunda and Adolenda Coinquenda as 'extended versions' of the regular *piacula* offered for the pruning of the grove.[144] The Arvals were covering their backs, making sure they had included all deities who might 'be offended by any damage inflicted on the sacred grove in the course of the repairs'.[145] For Scheid, the presence of Adolenda Conmolenda Deferunda and Adolenda Coinquenda is dictated by the Arvals' awareness that they were violating an inviolable grove.

---

[139] Ogilvie 1969: 12.
[140] Scheid 2003b: 180.
[141] Scheid 2003b: 164 and 183.
[142] Scheid 2003b: 182. Cf. Scheid 2003b: 172, 175 and 181. Scheid's understanding of these goddesses as 'servant-deities' relies on notes in Festus and Servius, as well as a (worryingly) broad gesture to 'patristic literature', without any acknowledgement of the biases of any of these sources (181).
[143] Scheid 2003b: 186.
[144] Scheid 2003b: 178.
[145] Scheid 2003b: 182.

Conceptualising crises

There is, however, no justification in the Arvals' inscriptional record for reading the significance of the goddesses in this way. For despite articulating religious concern for every step of the process of their involvement with these trees, the Arvals' interference shows precious little respect for the matter of the trees concerned; burning, toppling and pruning are all fairly violent actions. We might perhaps have expected this in inscription 22, where an offending fig needs to be removed from Dea Dia's temple. Yet in inscriptions 25 and 27, where the trees in question are struggling after a storm, the striking combination of arboreal violence and religious concern over the minutiae of that violence continues.[146] Consequently, I want to linger a little over what was happening here. Understanding what was done to the trees in inscription 25 is a challenge, not helped by our text for the 'beginning the work' sacrifices being partly dependent on a sixteenth-century manuscript by Fulvius Ursinus. He copied the inscription shortly after it was excavated in 1570, and fortunately so because it soon got broken into five pieces, circulated around various scholars and the top right-hand corner of what is now called fragment b completely lost.[147] In the post-eventum set of sacrifices we have the original inscription and not Ursinus alone, so here we stand on firmer ground. This mentions a sacrifice to Adolenda Coinquenda, indicating with some certainty that during the proceedings trees were burned and pruned.[148] So when Ursinus' text tells us that the first set of sacrifices were for trees which are *eruendar(um), ferr(o)* ⌈*f*⌉*endendar(um), adolendar(um), commolendar(um)* (needing to be dug up, needing to be split (?) with iron, needing to be burned, needing to be chopped up) his *adolendar(um)* finds confirmation in the later sacrifice to Adolenda Coinquenda. His *commolendar(um)* (needing to be chopped up) is, however, baffling: surely *coinquendarum* (needing to be pruned) would have been more pertinent, and I suggest that Ursinus misread

---

[146] In his discussion of Adolenda Conmolenda Deferunda and Adolenda Coinquenda, Scheid: 2003b does not properly distinguish the very different scenarios which led to inscription 22 and inscription 25; indeed at times he bizarrely seems to present Adolenda Coinquenda as a modified or reduced 'version' of Adolenda Conmolenda Deferunda, when surely they were perceived as different deities (178 and 180).

[147] Scheid 1998: xvi–xviii.

[148] It is not clear what arboreal scenario is being imagined here, in which some trees are beyond saving but others simply need pruning.

the text here.[149] There is no obvious reason to object to Ursinus' *eruendar(um)* (of which the first two letters are preserved on the stone), therefore adding digging up trees to the list of the Arvals' tasks.[150] Finally there is ⌈*f*⌉*endendar(um)*, understood as a scribal mistake for *findendarum*, which if correct suggests the Arvals chopped up some of these trees.[151] Little here speaks of the Arvals understanding sacred arboreal matter as inviolate! Finally, we also find in this inscription some *restituendae* trees: *restituere* is a multivalent verb, but its meaning here is clinched when the work is summed up by reference to *repositae* (replaced) trees – these trees needed replacing. When storms were particularly destructive replacements must have been needed for the grove's preservation, but again replacements speak against the Arvals understanding the sacrality of each tree to be deeply bound up with its matter.[152] Certainly the Arvals do not suggest they then carefully preserve the remains of the trees they have replaced as the Aulians did their plane (Paus. 9.19.7)!

Arboreal replacements are needed again in inscription 27, alongside some apparently widespread pruning (*luci sublucandi;* thinning the lower branches of the grove) and whatever action is required by *oblaqueandae* trees.[153] The only other attestation of this verb is in a rural calendar allocating *arborum oblaquiatio* to November (*CIL* 6.2305).[154] The TLL derives *oblaqueare* from *laqueus* (noose), suggesting the verb means to ensnare or bind, and such connotations would make sense of the Arvals' phrase in its context: *arborum oblaqueand(arum) et aliar(um) restituendarum* (trees needing to be bound and others needing to be replaced).[155]

[149] Applied to trees, *commolendar(um)* could mean needing to be chopped up, but the later reference to Coinquenda would lead us to expect a pruning counterpart at this stage in the proceedings.
[150] Although, as Scheid 2003b: 181 points out, on the basis of Ursinus' text we might expect to find a deity more like 'Adolenda Conmolenda Eruenda Fendenda' in the post-eventum set of sacrifices.
[151] See Scheid 1998: 314–315 for apparatus criticus.
[152] Nevertheless, there is no proof for Hughes' belief that the Arvals had a duty – in fact were bound by their own 'rules' – to replant *every* tree which died (1994: 175).
[153] Festus 474L provides our only testimony for this verb *sublucare*, defining it as to prune branches from the bottom, thus letting in light from beneath.
[154] In this calendar technical types of arboricultural work are intriguingly intertwined with sacrifices and religious banquets.
[155] The *OLD* defines *oblaqueare* as 'to loosen the soil round the roots'. To me it would make sense to understand *ablaqueare* in this sense, but I am unconvinced that *ablaqueare* and *oblaqueare* are interchangeable forms as the *OLD* would have it.

Conceptualising crises

After, we suppose, a serious storm, some trees needed to be bound to give them extra support, but others were too far gone for such treatment and needed to be replaced entirely. In this inscription we see a gentler arboricultural side to the Arvals, as they go about pruning and binding, actions which are nowhere else attested in the 'crisis' inscriptions. Indeed in many ways this is the most idiosyncratic of all our arboreal inscriptions, as it combines the idea of pruning the grove as a whole (familiar from the May pruning sacrifices) with the model of sacrifices dealing with an individual arboreal crisis. As such this inscription is a timely reminder of the Arvals' refusal to be pigeonholed in the way they articulate their relationship with trees in the grove; innovations and idiosyncrasies reflect the active thinking about this relationship which went on behind the inscriptional record.

Yet, fluid and innovative as this thinking may be, one motif has been persistent throughout the Arvals' presentation of their engagement with the trees of Dea Dia's grove: physically interfering with these trees was a process of deep religious significance for the Arvals, but this was not because they conceived of the trees' matter as inviolate. Their annual pruning in May took little notice of the impact this had on arboreal matter; rather the very act of cutting off bits of this matter ritually articulated the significance of the trees within the context of Dea Dia's major festival. Arboreal deaths were coloured as situations of religious crisis, but this did not discourage fairly violent treatment of the dead trees' remains. Names of deities were coined which encapsulated every step of the process of human interference with particular trees, but these trees were still burned and chopped up. Arboreal matter in the Arvals' grove was far from being treated as inviolate. Yet, at the same time, the Arvals were far from insensitive to the fact that they were here dealing with vulnerable, living material objects. The vulnerable materiality of these trees added layers of complexity to the Arvals' understanding of their relationship with the grove's trees and consequently their relationship with the divine. In particular, these trees prompted the Arvals into imagining and articulating relationships between themselves and the divine community which stretched their 'sacrificial thinking', as they relied on sensitive use of prepositions in sacrificing *ob* or *quod* (because of) an arboreal crisis situation, or made a one-off sacrifice to the newly imagined Adolenda Conmolenda Deferunda, looking up with unease at the fig in their temple's roof.

CHAPTER 5

CONFRONTING ARBOREAL AGENCY: READING THE DIVINE IN ARBOREAL BEHAVIOUR

A recent book examining the social construction of trees in modern Britain – something the authors Jones and Cloke term 'arboriculture' – urges us to cast off any anthropocentric presumptions about who or what can be agents. Trees too, they insist, need to be acknowledged as active and powerful agents, shaping the culture in which they are rooted.[1] Moreover, in so doing the authors hope to plug what they see as a serious gap in recent anthropological and sociological scholarship:

> While some conceptual approaches ... have adopted a serious approach to non-human agency, there remain some significant gaps in the types of non-human agent that have been subjected to serious study. Overall, there has been a distinct preoccupation with technological materials as non-human agents, and an underemphasis on organic non-humans whose rather more unruly agency has been neglected by comparison.[2]

Taking a leaf out of Jones and Cloke's book, it is the 'unruly agency' of trees which will now come to the fore in this book. Trees of course often make shows of their agency: they grow, change colour, lose and regain leaves, wither and die. This agency is also more obvious than that of many organic but non-animal phenomena. Flowers, for example, are so much frailer and shorter-lived than trees that any displays of agency might well go unnoticed.

---

[1] Since trees are neither human nor animal, and cannot boast intentionality, we can be reluctant to view them as agents; on our instinctive requirement that agents should have intentionality see Jones and Cloke 2002: 82. Yet Jones and Cloke 2002: 7 argue that trees *are* agents by emphasising how they are 'palpably active ... when bound up in the construction of ecological, social, economic, cultural, political and material formations'. Their book appeared amid a blossoming of academic interest in what we can meaningfully think of as agents, within (in particular) art history, anthropology and archaeology departments. Gell 1998 influentially argued that we should think of art objects as actors in a series of social networks, from which we 'abduct' the agency of the artist or commissioner, whilst Wobst 2000 urged us to think of human artefacts as 'material interferences' which mediate a kind of agency (42).
[2] Jones and Cloke 2002: 48.

173

Confronting arboreal agency

Rocks too undoubtedly change over time, but at a rate imperceptible to the human eye. Springs and rivers make far more overt shows of their agency, but arguably enjoy fewer options than trees for expressing it. By contrast, continual changes in trees' appearance and their relatively fast growth intensify and foreground their apparent agency. As well as being obvious, the agency of trees is also 'unruly', in the sense that it often feels beyond human control and prediction. And it is thanks to its unruly nature that arboreal agency makes its impact on Roman religious thinking. For, as we will soon see, the unpredictable behaviour of trees prompted questions which went straight to the heart of Roman grappling with the nature and meaning of divine interference in the human world.

Since Aristotle, Greek and Roman thinkers have attempted to account for the 'agency' of plant life, the apparently autonomous ability to change which Aristotle would call every living thing's innate ἀρχή: but this was no easy idea to grasp.[3] In the pseudo-Aristotelian *De plantis* – which Drossaart Lulofs argues derives from the lost *De plantis* by Nicolaus Damascenus, a Greek who was writing in the Augustan period – the sheer *slipperiness* of plant life is summed up:

ἡ ζωὴ ἐν τοῖς ζῴοις καὶ ἐν τοῖς φυτοῖς εὑρέθη. ἀλλ' ἐν μὲν τοῖς ζῴοις φανερὰ καὶ πρόδηλος, ἐν τοῖς φυτοῖς δὲ κεκρυμμένη καὶ οὐκ ἐμφανής. εἰς τὴν ταύτης γοῦν βεβαίωσιν πολλὴν ἀνάγκη ἐστὶ ζήτησιν προηγήσασθαι. (*Pl.* 815a)

Life is found in animals and in plants. But in animals it is visible and obvious, whilst in plants it is hidden and unclear. To prove its existence it is necessary to conduct much investigation.[4]

Indeed few observers of plants, in any time or culture, would deny that they are alive, but the way in which they are alive is felt hard to pin down. Instinctively most of us feel that plants are not alive

---

[3] See Leunissen 2010: 10–48 for an in-depth account of how Aristotle understands causation within nature. As Lehoux 2011: 48 puts it, for Aristotle 'nature just is this process of self-change'.

[4] Our Greek text under the title *De plantis* should not be conflated with Aristotle's lost Περὶ Φυτῶν. Drossaart Lulofs and Poortman 1989: xvi offer a stemma which makes a *c.* 900 CE Arabic text the precursor of a *c.* 1200 Latin translation, which in its turn spawns a *c.* 1300 Greek translation, and which provides the basis for our Greek text. Drossaart Lulofs and Poortman 1989: 9–14 further argue that the *c.* 900 Arabic text is a translation of Nicolaus Damascenus' lost *De plantis*, and that this work borrowed heavily from Aristotle's Περὶ Φυτῶν and Theophrastus' botanical works.

in the same way that animals are, as our author points out, yet there is also something about plants which means we are unhappy to lump them in the same category as objects like rocks. For our author, setting out on the path of enquiry into plant life, the most burning question to answer is whether plants have a soul, and therefore a capacity for desire, pain, pleasure and discrimination (*Pl.* 815a). Indeed for Aristotle and his successors, enquiry into plant souls equalled enquiry into the way in which plants are alive. Aristotle argued that plants *are* alive – and therefore have souls – because they evidently have a capacity and first principle through which they are able to grow and decay (*de An.* 413a). The souls of plants are distinguished from those of animals and humans by the fact that they boast only this one 'faculty' (δύναμις) of the soul, which Aristotle also refers to as the 'nutritive soul' (θρεπτικὴ ψυχή; *de An.* 415a).[5] This latter has two functions, the use of food and reproduction, central to how Aristotle fits plants into his teleological view of the whole natural world.[6] That is, plants have one τέλος (goal) which is to grow to their mature and healthy size, and another which is to reproduce; and since no plant can live for ever, in this way they gain for themselves a kind of surrogate immortality and so have a share in the divine (*de An.* 415a).

Aristotle's account of plant life paved the way for later thinkers almost automatically to approach plants as living agents, with their own innate sense of purpose and a role to play in the divine structure of the universe. In particular his influence on Stoic thought, which itself had a wide impact on intellectual life in the Roman world, is undeniable.[7] In Cicero's *De natura deorum*, for example, when Balbus gets his chance to advocate the Stoic worldview, the picture of plant life he advances is strikingly Aristotelian: plants enjoy only the faculties of nurture and growth, unlike animals, which know sensation, and humans reason too; every plant has an idea of full perfection and progresses towards

---

[5] Such thinking is echoed by Pseudo-Aristotle at *Pl.* 815b.
[6] Sedley 2007: 168 argues that whilst for Aristotle there is no divine oversight of the world, nevertheless 'throughout the natural world there are irreducibly purposive structures'.
[7] If our Greek text of the *De plantis* does most closely reflect a work by Nicolaus Damascenus, then this is certainly one prominent example of Aristotle's biological thinking living on in a first-century BCE thinker.

its goal of 'full development' (*ad ultimum pervenire* (35); *Nat. d.* 2.33–35). Similarly the Stoic Seneca the Younger reveals a strong Aristotelian vein in his biological thinking: plants are not alive in the way that animals are, but we still say they have an *anima* (soul) and understand them to live and die, whilst rocks do not make it into this category (*Ep.* 58.10). Pliny, whose thinking displays strong Stoic colourings, also reinforces this Aristotelian classification of living entities.[8] He opens Book 12 of his *Natural History*, the first in which he fully turns his attention to trees, by stating that having dealt with animals he will now look at things produced by the earth or dug up from it, since these too are not lacking in *anima* (soul), without which nothing can be alive (*Nat.* 12.1).

Aristotle's research into plant life, and the intellectual legacy it left the Roman world, is often said to have pioneered the discipline we know as biology: however, ancient enquiry into the natural world was never purely a matter of advancing what we might call 'scientific' knowledge. Just as our contemporary debates about arboreal agency are bound up with ethical issues concerning the right relationship of humans and trees – the question of whether trees have 'rights' follows hard on discussions of arboreal agency – so, in a similar way, Roman explorations of arboreal agency straddled a blurry line between natural and theological enquiry.[9] What forces were working through a tree if, for example, it unexpectedly withered? Was a 'natural' explanation in terms of cause and effect the only way to account for it, or could divine agents be at work in the tree's decline? Did a satisfactory 'natural' explanation in any way exclude divine involvement with the tree? And on a practical level, how were you to identify divine interference in arboreal behaviour and, just as pressingly, interpret what it meant? For the Romans posing these questions the underlying

---

[8] Beagon 1992: 26–33 discusses the degree of Stoic thought informing Pliny's understanding of the relationship between god and nature, concluding that he builds a 'unique' picture of the world from 'familiar' philosophical components (32). Paparazzo 2011: 90–95 provides a rather niche example of this, arguing for Stoic influence on Pliny's understanding of the regrowth of lead mines.

[9] On the debate provoked by the question of whether trees can have rights see Stone 1972 and Attfield 1994: 153–171. Lehoux 2012 offers fascinating and theoretical reflection on the nature of 'Roman science'. Of particular relevance to my discussion here is Lehoux's analysis of Cicero's *De divinatione* as a window onto Roman ideas about nature (2012: 21–46).

Numina and nymphs

concern was not, as for Jones and Cloke, whether they stood in right relationship with trees, but whether they stood in right relationship with the gods. The Romans were not eco-activists: they engaged with arboreal agency as theologians.

As I turn now to analyse how arboreal agency enriched Roman theological thinking it is important to acknowledge that in many ways my angle of enquiry is nothing new: ever since the early comparativists became interested in sacred trees, their agency was seen as central to their religious significance. These scholars argued that when primitive people observed the agency of a tree – when they saw it growing or bursting into bud – they presumed that it was inhabited by a divine spirit. With reference to Roman culture they seized in particular on the association of the word *numen* with certain trees, and to a lesser degree the idea of dryads and hamadryads, as proof that early Romans were no exceptions in this regard.[10] This weighty history of scholarly interest in arboreal agency cannot be ignored, and in what follows I will first confront past use of 'arboreal *numina*' and of (hama)dryads to bolster an animistic agenda. For our evidence for the concept of 'arboreal *numina*' resists their being understood in terms of the agency of a tree, whilst the slippery nature of (hama)dryads means that they are best seen only as part of a cultural currency *allowing* trees to be thought of as agents. Foregrounding of *numina* and (hama)dryads has also ironically distracted attention from ways in which arboreal agency *did* stand at the heart of theological questions about trees' significance in the Roman world, and in the second section of this chapter I will tackle this new area of enquiry, examining how the 'unruly agency' of trees challenged and shaped Roman conceptions of ways in which the divine and human worlds intersected.

Numina and nymphs

Numen is so important a word in the Roman religion that it is necessary to be perfectly clear as to what was meant by it.[11]

---

[10] For detailed discussion of this scholarship see pp. 43–47, 50–54 and 58–61.
[11] Warde-Fowler 1911: 118.

So Warde-Fowler decisively asserts: nor was he alone among early scholars of Roman religion in thinking this a realistic aim. To the contrary, I will show that trying to pin down the meaning of *numen* – especially when applied to trees – is a futile task. In fact it was the slippery undefinability of *numen* which gave the word its theological value. First, however, I will set out what Warde-Fowler and others have meant by *numen* and explore their insistence that, when applied to a tree, *numen* encapsulated its perceived agency or animation. As I will go on to argue, there is actually precious little evidence that ideas of agency stood at the heart of Roman understanding of an 'arboreal *numen*'.

Early scholars confidently derived *numen* either from the Indo-European root *neu-*, meaning to move, or from the Latin *nuere*, meaning to nod. Those in the first camp used their derivation to emphasise that 'the word *numen* is everywhere employed, where a divine action, an activity or function is meant'.[12] Those in the second camp emphasised that *numen* was an expression of divine will, calling to witness the famous Homeric image in which Zeus nods his head in assent to a request from Thetis (*Il.* 1.528–530).

> It must be formed from *nuere* as *flumen* from *fluere*, with a sense of activity inherent in the verb. As *flumen* is that which actively flows, so *numen* is that which actively does whatever we understand by the word *nuere*; and so far as we can determine, that was a manifestation of will.[13]

Yet, as Warde-Fowler's phrasing indicates, these two interpretations of *numen* were rarely seen as strictly incompatible. Rather both were used to confirm the consensus that primitive Romans saw the world around them as animated by various divine forces, with great emphasis placed on the significance of *numen* being a neuter noun. The Romans' *numina* were the most basic of impersonal forces, without a gender, a name or any personal characteristics at all.[14] Indeed much was made of the homophonic likeness of *numen* and *nomen* (name), it being said that obtaining a name was the first

---

[12] Altheim 1938: 192. Cf. Wagenvoort 1947: 74. Halliday 1922: 90 and Bayet 1969: 44 both emphasise the nature of *numina* as activity.
[13] Warde-Fowler 1911: 118. Cf. Rose 1926: 44; Rose 1948: 13; Bayet 1969: 109; Dumézil 1970: 29.
[14] As emphasised by Halliday 1922: 89–90.

Numina and nymphs

step for any *numen* wishing to develop into a more personal god.[15] In addition, as discussed in Chapter 2, *numen* was held up as the Roman counterpart to the Melanesian concept of *mana*, which the comparativists had already hailed as a blueprint for animistic conceptions of the world.[16] In this one word scholars of Roman religion felt they had all the ammunition they needed to back up their contention that early Roman religion was quintessentially animistic.

Only one problem presented itself. The word *numen* is hardly present in early works of Latin literature; rather its attestations flourish in the Augustan period and beyond. How was this to be explained? The answer was to construct a narrative of how *numen*'s meaning developed, the legwork for which was done by Pfister in a chronological analysis of its usage.[17] Pfister argued that in Cicero *numen* only ever had the sense of 'eine Eigenschaft einer Gottheit', but that in Augustan literature *numen* began to be used as a synonym for 'Gottheit'.[18] In addition Pfister noted that in the Augustan period we first find institutions like the senate, or individuals like Augustus or particular poets, endowed with their own personal *numen*. Thus Pfister posited a huge broadening of *numen*'s sphere of reference during this period, with the chief change being that *numen* no longer necessarily indicated divine power or will, but could also indicate a fully fledged personal deity. Taking the phrase *numen fontis* as a test case, he argued that by the Augustan period this had three potential meanings: (1) the divine power of the spring, (2) the power of the deity Fons or (3) the deity of the spring. Adopted as the new orthodoxy, Pfister's narrative was often painted as one of 'decline', with Rose so championing the significance of the 'earliest' understanding of *numen* that he presented later Roman usage of it as an aberration:

Until the time of Augustus it never is used to mean any personal or individual god, and even then it is not often so misunderstood by good writers such as Vergil or Ovid.[19]

[15] For example, Warde-Fowler 1911: 119–120, Pfister 1937: 1273 and Wagenvoort 1947: 78.
[16] See pp. 58–59.
[17] Pfister 1937.
[18] Pfister 1937: 1278.
[19] Rose 1948: 13. Wagenvoort 1947: 73 openly acknowledges Pfister's influence on his own thinking.

179

Drawing this distinction between pre- and post-Augustan usage of *numen* crucially enabled scholars to preserve the idea of a truly animistic stage within Roman religion, whilst squaring this with the prominence of *numen* in literature from a period which, they claimed, was characterised by belief in more developed anthropomorphic gods.

With his inimitable boldness, it is not hard to see how Rose quickly became the figurehead of animist scholars. Nor is it surprising that when animism finally came under attack within scholarship on Roman religion, Rose was the prime target. Weinstock began the offensive in 1949 with his review of Rose's *Ancient Roman Religion*, but it was with Dumézil's *Religion romaine archaique* (1966) that the theories of the now dead Rose were put through the mill. He argued powerfully against Rose's construction of *numen* as a divine impersonal power, claiming that *numen* was never used in Latin literature without being understood in relation to a personal god: *numen* was always, as it were, shorthand for *numen dei* (the *numen* of a god).[20] Dumézil's discrediting of Rose's arguments valuably tempered early enthusiasm for *numina* and their single-minded interpretation. Yet by demoting *numen* from its pedestal, Dumézil also succeeded in so discrediting the concept that it is noticeably absent from scholarship on Roman religion from the second half of the twentieth century. Consequently its complexities and ambiguities have to this day been roundly ignored. Some scholars act as though Dumézil has wrapped up the *numen* controversy for good:

> The once heated debate over the Latin term *numen* is now over. Nowadays nobody considers … that *numen* means 'a diffused sacredness'. Instead, *numen* is now translated, depending on the context, as the 'will or power of a deity'.[21]

Here Scheid reaffirms Dumézil's conclusion, but without re-examining the evidence: the complexity of *numen* thus gets swept under the carpet. Other scholars, by contrast, unthinkingly echo the pre-Dumézilian orthodoxy. Lomas is particularly upfront about this – 'the most ancient of all forms of religious belief attested in

---

[20] Dumézil 1970: 18–31.
[21] Scheid 2003a: 153.

Numina and nymphs

Italy is the animist tradition of *numina*' – whilst others simply give an animist colouring to their understanding of *numina*, with Turcan calling *numina* 'manifestations of the divine' and Rives linking the term to 'superhuman force'.[22] Indeed recent scholarship has paid serious attention to the word *numen* only within work on imperial cult: here a central question is to ask what it means, for example, to worship the *numen* of Domitian, rather than to worship Domitian 'himself'. Disagreement is intense, as one example will illustrate: this is Fishwick and Gradel's spat over the significance of an altar in the Italian town of Forum Clodii at which, an inscription tells us, worship was offered to the mysterious *numen Augustum*. Before jumping into the nitty gritty of their disagreement, I wish to pause for a moment on the kind of understanding of *numen* which both scholars bring to this altar and its elusive deity: it will now seem very familiar. For in defining the word *numen* Fishwick overtly references his intellectual dependence on Rose's animist orthodoxy, whilst Pfister's narrative of how *numen* changed in meaning (with the key turning point being the Augustan period) is also of evident influence:

> *Numen* is a difficult word to translate; perhaps the nearest is 'power' or, as Rose put it, 'a result of the existence of power'. As such, it seems to belong among the oldest Roman religious concepts, though the word itself is first attested in Accius. By the Augustan period *numen* can be attributed to a wide variety of things – in fact anything, inanimate as well as animate, considered to have this special property: a fountain, a tree, a boundary-stone, a place, a poet, the emperor ... [I]n Augustan literature and later *numen* began to be used not only to denote the essential property of a god but by a metonymy the god or divinity himself; that is, from meaning the impersonal property of a god *numen* can now denote a personal god or divinity.[23]

As Fishwick's opening nod to the difficulty of translating *numen* quickly yields to confident claims about the word's meaning, so Gradel too is prepared to acknowledge that *numen* is 'a very vague term, difficult to pin down in concrete terms', only immediately

---

[22] Lomas 1996: 166; Turcan 2000: 5; Rives 2007: 19. Cf. Warrior 2006: 5. Jenkyns 2013 makes varied (and baffling) use of the noun *numen* and adjective numinous, without specifying what he means by them: sacrifice did not 'change anything or bring numen into the city' (208); Roman authors may be found 'stripping the gods of their numen for humorous effect (211); a line of Lucretius has 'numinous beauty' (222).

[23] Fishwick 1991: 383-384.

to undercut this with a definition which reads almost like a dictionary entry:

> The basic meaning of the word *numen* is not in doubt. As any Latin dictionary will tell us, the word means 'divine power' or 'divinity'/'godhead'. It is impersonal (cf. its gender), but belongs to a god, and is the force or power by which the god manifests himself in the world. Alternatively, but of course very close to this meaning, it could, at least in the imperial age, denote the deity himself, or herself, and thus be a synonym for '*deus*' (or '*dea*'), like 'divinity' or 'godhead' in English.[24]

In the language of force and power which Gradel privileges, as well as his insistence on the significance of *numen* being neuter, the animist orthodoxy again reveals itself, alive and well.

This orthodoxy shapes Fishwick and Gradel's arguments over the Forum Clodii inscription as follows. In 1969 Fishwick argued that the phrase *numen Augustum* was a variant of *numen Augusti*, with this latter to be understood as a 'divinized abstraction … immanent in the emperor'; the animist influence is evident here in the word 'immanent', an instinctive falling back on the idea that *numen* means some kind of *internal* power.[25] Gradel challenged this in 2002, claiming that 'worshipping the emperor's divinity (*numen*) was simply synonymous with worshipping him directly as a god', or, to phrase it another way, '*numen* cult was merely a linguistic synonym for direct, godlike cult'.[26] A crucial strand to his argument was that *numen* is neuter, and therefore cannot be personified and receive sacrificial victims, echoing previous insistence on the significance of this noun's gender.[27] With his use of 'simply' and 'merely' Gradel also implies that the phenomenon he is describing is straightforward, revealing that modern scholars have lost none of the old tendency to treat *numen* as a concept fully within our intellectual grasp. Finally, in a coda to the disagreement – Fishwick's comeback in 2007 – another aspect of the animists' construction of *numen* makes itself felt. For this

---

[24] Gradel 2002: 235.
[25] Fishwick 1969: 385.
[26] Gradel 2002: 245 and 248. Cf. Galinsky 2011: 81, who follows Gradel: it is 'plain that worship of the emperor's divinity (*numen*) was the same as worshiping him directly as a god'.
[27] As argued at Gradel 2002: 243, on the grounds that 'in Roman sacral law the sex of the victim should correspond to that of the god receiving the sacrifice'.

time Fishwick argued that 'the recent decease of Augustus may account for the aberrant use of the impersonal adjectival form at Forum Clodii during a time of uncertain terminology', his legalistic instinct to explain away exceptions to his rules about the meaning of *numen* reminiscent of Pfister's determined attempts to make *numen* fit a narrative pattern.[28]

In short, the slippery word *numen* is left crying out for a sensitive reanalysis. Here I sketch out a few examples illustrating how far *numen* eludes our intellectual grasp, and suggest that the very 'undefinability' of *numen* – its resistance to rules – was in fact what made it of value to Roman thinkers, as they used it to push at the boundaries of what they could consider in some way 'divine', be it objects like springs or trees, institutions like the senate or individuals like poets. This is by no means to deny occasions when *numen* is best understood as 'power' or 'god', but rather to argue that we should not restrict its meaning in this way. I begin with a few non-arboreal examples, before turning to focus on the attribution of *numina* to trees, and in particular three passages championed by scholars as the ultimate proof that Roman religious responses to trees were animistic. Often this sense that *numen* is a word with which you push at conceptual boundaries is palpable in the hesitancy with which it is introduced: there are some, Ovid tells us, who think that poets have *numen* (*Am.* 3.9.18); he also introduces us to a spring which, if you are prepared to believe it, has *numen* (*Fast.* 5.674). Similarly, when Lucan calls on Rome as the *instar* (likeness) of a great *numen* (1.199–200), or describes the death of a virtuous man who has 'a quasi *numen* in his chest, which had been stabbed clean through' (*velut inclusum perfosso in pectore numen*; 6.253), the tentative tone of *velut* (quasi) and *instar* (likeness) draws out and exacerbates the inherent ambiguity of the concept of *numen*.

We also find authors using *numen* to highlight the status of things which are of more than human significance perhaps only in their *own* worldview: this is a word with which individuals push at

---

[28] Fishwick 2007: 251. Another apparent example of a *numen Augustum* from Vaga in Africa Fishwick 2007: 253 also explains away as 'an instance of confused grammar rather than of supposed creative theology'.

accepted boundaries of thinking. Thus in Cicero *numen* is applied to the senate and the Roman people (*Phil.* 3.32; *Post red.* 18), whilst in Ovid, predictably enough, beauty has *numen* (*Am.* 3.3.12), the *numen* of his harsh mistress prevents him from writing tragedy (*Am.* 2.18.17) and a lover's body is apostrophised as *mea numina* (my *numen*; *Her.* 13.159). Context is everything: in the *Heroides*, Cydippe suggests that even a letter might have *numen* (*Her.* 21.150). Similarly, in funereal inscriptions we also find *numen* attributed to deceased loved ones (e.g. *CIL* 6.37965; *AE* 1976.243), suggesting that – as with Cicero's *numen*-filled senate, or Ovid's numinous mistress – *numen* is something which rests in the eye of the beholder. In short, these uses of *numen* appear to help Roman thinkers imagine how something in their world (or recently departed from it) might be of 'more than human' significance. Giving the word a precise definition here would, I suggest, often elude them as much as it does us. For its vagueness is part of what makes the word 'good to think with', as we see when one author goes beyond attributing *numen* to a person or object or institution, and instead paints a richer picture of the relationship between a *numen* and a particular phenomenon. Horace is bewailing his chilly fate as an uninterested woman bars him from her house: does she hear, he moans, 'how Jupiter freezes the lying snow with an unclouded *numen*' (*positas ut glaciet nives puro numine Iuppiter*; *C.* 3.10.7–8). Rose once commented on these lines that 'in plain prose, it is a clear, frosty night', but there is in fact nothing 'plain' going on here.[29] Rather Horace's difficult lines *suggest* that the weather can somehow intersect with Jupiter's self-expression, and that it is something called a *numen* – which itself displays weather-like properties – which enables this intersection.

Numen is no less slippery and complex a concept when associated with trees. However, this has not stopped scholars from the nineteenth century onwards highlighting three passages of Latin literature as though they straightforwardly define an 'arboreal *numen*'. First is Ovid, *Fasti* 3.295–296, lauded by Rose as 'one of the most perfect expressions of the oldest recoverable stratum of Italian, or even Mediterranean, religious sentiment':

[29] Rose 1948: 13.

Numina and nymphs

> lucus Aventino suberat niger ilicis umbra
> quo posses viso dicere numen inest.
>
> There was a grove under the Aventine, black with shady holm oaks,
> On seeing which you might say 'there is a *numen* within!'[30]

Bailey also singles out these lines as proof that *numen* is the word which most evokes 'the spirit of the earliest animism', but is this really what *numen* does here?[31] At the risk of pedantry, it is worth noting that Ovid does not say there *is* a *numen* in the Aventine grove, only that you *might think* there is. This is no confident theological pronouncement. It is also significant that the description of the grove comes within a mythological narrative of how Numa tied up the drunken Picus and Faunus to obtain advice on expiations. In part this comic, rustic narrative creates a sense of distance between Ovid's urban readership and the idea of saying '*numen inest*' (despite Ovid's address to the reader at this point). More important, however, is the fact that Picus and Faunus are three times described in this narrative as *numina* (292, 303 and 314), as well as *di nemorum* (gods of the woods; 309) and *di ... agrestes* (rustic gods; 315). This use of *numina* in reference to personal divine agents, who may frequent the grove but are physically independent of it, makes it hard – in context – to interpret *numen inest* as referring to some impersonal spirit animating the grove. The use of *numina* in this passage is confusingly fluid, but one thing we can take away from Ovid's *numen inest* is that, since the possibility of perceiving a *numen* in the grove follows hard on Ovid's description of its foreboding appearance, being aware of a *numen* seems to mean responding to a certain quality about the grove. Likewise in *Amores* 3.13.7–8 (a passage occasionally cited alongside the omnipresent *Fasti* passage) it is the gloomy quality of a grove which might prompt you to say *numen inest*:

> stat vetus et densa praenubilus arbore lucus;
> adspice, concedas numen inesse loco.

---

[30] Rose 1935: 237.
[31] Bailey 1932: 133. The passage is also cited by Granger 1895: 95; Bailey 1932: 43; Pfister 1937: 1279; Wagenvoort 1947: 79; Rose 1948: 15; Ogilvie 1969: 13; Glay 1971: 18; Hughes 1994: 170; Dowden 2000: 111.

A grove stands there, old and extremely gloomy with its dense trees;
Look at it, you might concede that there is a *numen* within the place.[32]

Ovid's use of the subjunctive *concedas* again frames this as a potential response, and again it is one strongly linked to perceptions of the wood's appearance.

The second passage commonly adduced as proof that Romans saw trees as 'charged with the presence of the divine', to use the words of Rives, comes from a letter by Seneca the Younger.[33] Again Seneca talks of perceiving a *numen* in a wood, emphasising how the wood's appearance – its ancient and huge trees, its darkness and seclusion – will psychologically work on you to 'make you believe in its *numen*' (*fidem tibi numinis faciet*; *Ep.* 41.3). Seneca's language paints this belief as one constructed by the grove's appearance, something rather different from saying that such woods *are* animated by *numina*, which is how it is always interpreted.[34] This phrase also needs to be read within the context of the letter as a whole, the didactic thrust of which is to persuade Lucilius that god is 'with you and within you' (*tecum est, intus est*; 41.1). Standard forms of worship such as lifting our hands to the sky or approaching statues can be dispensed with, Seneca insists, if we acknowledge that 'a sacred spirit dwells within us' (*sacer inter nos spiritus sedet*; 41.2). Indeed within every good man, he continues, 'a god dwells, but we do not know which god' (*quis deus incertum est, habitat deus*; 41.2). Here Seneca lifts the famous Virgilian line in which Evander describes his people's religious dread of a local grove (*Aen.* 8.352) and in the crafted rhetoric of this letter it is this Virgilian line which leads us immediately into the reflection on Roman responses to groves and the temptation to believe in a grove's *numen*. Relying on the Virgilian tag to reinforce and give a layer of literary sophistication to his claims about the 'god within us', Seneca's statement about the perceived *numen*

---

[32] The passage is mentioned by Pfister 1937: 1279 and Wagenvoort 1947: 79. Cf. Ovid's observation on another ancient, unhewn wood that it is 'easy to believe' (*credibile*) has a *numen* within (*Am.* 3.1.2); surprisingly this passage does not attract scholarly comment.
[33] Rives 2007: 89.
[34] This particular passage was not popular with Rose and co., but makes its presence felt in recent scholarship, being cited by Hughes 1994: 170; Dowden 2000: 94–95; Turcan 2000: 39; Warrior 2006: 5; Rives 2007: 90.

Numina and nymphs

within a grove is deeply coloured by the image of Evander's grove and its Golden Age tinge.[35] This contributes to an ironised sense of distance between us, the readers of this sophisticated text, and such thinking about a grove's *numen*, a sense of distance which is yet further widened by the stark contrast between the religious panic felt by the inhabitants of Pallanteum and the urbane philosopher's insistence that we can dispense with 'traditional' religion. Seneca's claim about the temptation to perceive a *numen* in a grove must be read within this highly constructed didactic stance; one thing he is not expecting his readers to do is to take his claim at face value.

A sense of urban idealisation of the countryside and Rome's rustic past is also present in the third and final piece of evidence brought to bear on arboreal *numina*:

> haec fuere numinum templa, priscoque ritu simplicia rura etiam nunc deo praecellentem arborem dicant; nec magis auro fulgentia atque ebore simulacra quam lucos et in iis silentia ipsa adoramus. arborum genera numinibus suis dicata perpetuo servantur, ut Iovi aesculus, Apollini laurus, Minervae olea, Veneri myrtus, Herculi populus; quin et Silvanos Faunosque et dearum genera silvis ac sua numina tamquam e caelo attributa credimus. (Pliny *Nat.* 12.3)

> These [trees] were the temples of *numina*, and with primitive rites even now simple rustics dedicate an exceptionally tall tree to a god; nor do we adore statues gleaming with gold and ivory more than groves and the very silences within them. Types of trees are kept perpetually dedicated to their own *numina*, for example the oak to Jupiter, the laurel to Apollo, the olive to Minerva, the myrtle to Venus, the poplar to Hercules; indeed we even believe that Silvani and Fauni and types of goddesses and their own *numina* are assigned to the woods as if from heaven.[36]

Pliny's assertion that Romans worship the silences in groves as much as they do lavish statues reflects the suggestion in both Ovid and Seneca that it is a particular *quality* about wooded spaces which might prompt religious responses to them. Also present here is a typical anti-*luxuries* (luxury) strand in the moralising discourse of Pliny's *Natural History*.[37] It is, however, the repeated

---

[35] For discussion of which see p. 13.
[36] This passage is cited by Granger 1895: 96; Pfister 1937: 1280; Wagenvoort 1947: 79; Ogilvie 1969: 14; Ferguson 1970: 66; Glay 1971: 18; Hughes 1994: 170; Dowden 2000: 94; Rives 2007: 91.
[37] For a classic account of this discourse see Wallace-Hadrill 1990: esp. 85–96, as well as Beagon 1992: 190–194.

use of *numen* which draws scholars to this passage as proof of a 'primal attitude' in which 'the presence of deity was recognized in the quality of the environment itself', making it vital to ask what the word means for Pliny in this context.[38] Pliny's assertion that in Rome's early days trees were imagined as the temples of *numina* is the real focus of all the excitement: yet claiming that something is a temple of a deity does not entail that the deity was understood to live in it, pervade it or 'animate' it. Indeed Pliny goes on to present this idea as a parallel phenomenon to today's country bumpkins dedicating huge trees to a god, thereby suggesting a less concrete relationship between *numen* and tree than one of habitation. He also pulls the rug from under the animists' feet by appearing to use *numen* as a rough synonym for *deus* (god) here, not to indicate a vague impersonal power. Indeed, when it appears for a second time *numen* again seems to equate to a god, for Pliny exemplifies the *numina* to which trees are dedicated with Jupiter, Apollo, Minerva, Venus and Hercules. Finally, Pliny tells us that Silvani, Fauni, 'types of goddesses' and *sua numina* (their own *numina*) are believed to be 'assigned to woods'. Whilst it is unclear whether he intends to link the *numina* to the woods or to the goddesses (whose *numina* are they?), once again we find *numina* in the frame along with figures personal enough to be called goddesses. Surely, then, this passage provides next to no grist for the animists' mill. Moreover, for all its idealisation of the simplicity of Rome's rustic past and rural present, Pliny in fact presents here a complex variety of ways in which a tree might be in relationship with a *numen*, be it dedication, attribution or its role as a 'temple'.[39]

Yet to date, scholars championing arboreal *numina* as proof of Roman animism have not only ignored the nuances of these three favoured passages, but also turned a blind eye to other passages which connect a *numen* with a tree, many of which again present

---

[38] Hughes 1994: 170.
[39] Alongside these passages, Cato's prayer to a *sive deus sive dea* (god or goddess) in a wood was also cited as proof that early Romans saw woods as pervaded by an impersonal, genderless power (*Agr.* 139). See, for example, Baddeley 1905: 100–101, who romantically imagines the leaves of sacred trees whispering *sive deus sive dea*, Bailey 1932: 44 and Gall 1975: 133–134. Scheid 2003a: 153–154 emphasises the need to move on from this interpretation of the passage.

Numina and nymphs

an arboreal *numen* as something dependent on a particular *quality* of the tree in question. In Statius, for example, we read that a wood *stat sacra senectae numine* (stands sacred by the *numen* of its old age; *Theb.* 6.93–94): this translation-resistant phrase suggests that it is something about the age of this oak which gives it its religious power, and to such a degree that the *numen* is actually attributed to the oak's age, rather than the tree itself. On another occasion too Statius pushes the boundaries of how existing scholarship has led us to expect the word *numen* to be used; describing an oak which Atalanta 'had consecrated' (*desacraverat*), he adds that 'by reverencing it she had made its *numen*' (*numenque colendo fecerat*; *Theb.* 9.586–588).[40] Thus Statius paints an arboreal *numen* as a quality of the tree which exists firmly in the eye of the beholder. This is the force of an arboreal *numen* which appears in Calpurnius Siculus too, when the shepherd Thyrsis vows that if a god brings his lover Crocale to him then he will declare *sub arbore numen hac erit; ite procul (sacer est locus) ite profani* (under this tree there will be a *numen*; depart far off, profane people, the place is sacred; 2.54–55). The potential presence of a *numen* under (not pervading!) this particular tree is pinned to Thyrsis' conception of its significance as a place where he might dally with his lover.[41] Finally I turn to a line from Silius Italicus' description of Jupiter Ammon's grove, discussed in Chapter 3: *arbor numen habet coliturque tepentibus aris* (the trees have 'religious power' and are worshipped on glowing altars; 3.691).[42] What did Silius mean by this? The enigmatic phrasing of the line leaves much about its interpretation open, but again this arboreal *numen* follows immediately on a description of the grove's appearance, thus loosely framing it as a quality which the trees possess and which prompts religious responses to them. (Here it seems that connotations of

---

[40] This overlooked oak did long ago attract the attention of Ouseley 1819: 368, who sees what is going on here in characteristically bold and straightforward terms: the oak is 'adored as a Divinity'.

[41] Clearly its significance for Thyrsis is essentially romantic, but his desires are articulated in strongly religious terms: this may well be part of the gentle mockery of shepherds common in pastoral.

[42] See pp. 85–86 for previous discussion of this passage. In many ways it is strange that the animists did not jump on this line, which it is easy to imagine them reading as proof of trees housing a 'spirit'.

worship must be uppermost in Silius' *colitur*, unlike when Pliny plays with this multivalent verb in his depiction of the *ficus Ruminalis*.)[43]

Arboreal *numina*, in short, are not the animist trump-card they were once held to be: but what of the dryads and hamadryads, whom early scholars of Roman religion presented as a 'sister phenomenon' to these *numina*?[44] Are these arboreal 'spirits' or 'nymphs' not clear proof that Roman thinkers entertained something approximating to animistic conceptions of trees?[45] Certainly in 1897 Philpot could confidently state that 'the idea of an actual tree-soul' is most clearly exemplified in hamadryads specifically; today, however, such thinking tends merely to colour the language with which hamadryads are depicted, as when Leigh writes of them that the 'divine is *immanent* in the landscape in the form of the nymph' (my italics).[46] One supposed fact lies behind such assumptions: that a 'Hamadryad's life was bound up with her tree'.[47] Yet although the idea of trees and hamadryads being coeval certainly has an impressively early pedigree, it is in fact attested less often than secondary literature would lead us to believe. The story starts with the Homeric Hymn to Aphrodite, in which the lifespan of the mountain nymphs who bring up Aeneas is paralleled with

---

[43] For discussion of which see pp. 116–118.

[44] Pfister 1937: 1280, for example, refers to an arboreal *numen* as 'etwa einer Hamadryade'. As we will soon see, dryads and hamadryads are distinguished in Roman *definitions* of their nature, but there is no strong differentiation between the two 'types' in their literary depictions; consequently I will analyse them side by side, and make use of the shorthand (hama)dryads. They leave few epigraphic or visual traces.

[45] In Greek literature of the Roman world hamadryads are often explicitly called nymphs, e.g. Athenaeus *Deip.* 78b; Antonius Liberalis 30; *AG.* 9.823; Nonnus 16.35. As Larson 2001: viii has pointed out, we rarely ask what a nymph is because the answer is assumed 'self-evident', but in fact nymphs are a rather 'elastic concept': not heroines, but not goddesses either, they enjoy – to borrow Sourvinou-Inwood's words – an 'ambiguous type of immortality' (2005: 104). Moreover, when it comes to (hama)dryads, the already elastic concept of nymph is further stretched by the presence in Latin literature of (hama)dryads who are explicitly *not* called nymphs: Catullus introduces us to *hamadryades deae* (hamadryad goddesses; 61.23); Ovid calls dryads *semideae* (half-goddesses; *Her.* 4.49) and in Virgil they are *puellae* (girls; *Ecl.* 5.59; *G.* 1.11). Thus the divine status of (hama)dryads stubbornly resists categorisation.

[46] Philpot 1897: 58; Leigh 1999: 179. Larson 2001: 8–11 also discusses the close association of nymphs with various aspects of landscape.

[47] Baddeley 1905: 101–102. This orthodoxy was being phrased in these terms as early as Grimm 1835: 480 and Jennings 1890: 80, and its presence is still strong today, e.g. Athanassakis 1977: 130, Larson 2001: 73–78 and Lambrinoudakis 2005: 311.

that of certain trees: at their birth pines or oaks spring up from the earth, whilst the decline of each tree signals that of the nymph, before the souls of the nymph and tree leave the light of the sun together (264–272). (Interesting to note here is the surprising *lack* of justification for scholarly framing of hamadryads as a 'treesoul': for whilst the lives of nymph and tree parallel each other, they have *separate* souls.) Several centuries later Apollonius Rhodius described a hamadryad as ἧλιξ (coeval) with a tree (2.479), with the scholiast on this passage leaning on the etymology of hamadryad to emphasise that these beings are born and die ἅμα ταῖς δρυσί (with their trees; ad loc.). This scholiast also cites Pindar's description of hamadryads as ἰσοδένδρου τέκμαρ αἰῶνος λαχοῖσαι (having a lifespan equal to a tree; fragment 165) – a passage also twice mentioned by Plutarch (*De def. or.* 415D; *Amat.* 757E) – whilst the scholiast on Theocritus similarly glosses a hamadryad as ἡλικιῶτις (coeval) with a tree (3.13).[48] The idea of hamadryads sharing a lifespan with trees was still influential by the time of Nonnus, who three times describes a hamadryad as ἧλιξ (coeval) with her tree (2.93, 22.117, 48.519–520) and once σύγχρονος (coeval; 2.95) with it. In short a handful of Greek passages – with a heavy element of re-citation and scholiastic comment – emphasise that hamadryads are born and die with their trees.

Within Latin literature, evidence for the idea of hamadryads being coeval with their trees is even more sparse. Praising Manilius Vopiscus for having allowed an old tree to stand unharmed at the centre of his house, Statius suggests that perhaps a 'slippery' (*lubrica*) naiad or hamadryad now owes him her uninterrupted years (*Silv.* 1.3.62–63).[49] Here, then, is one romanticised image confirming the idea that a tree's death entails that of its hamadryad: yet strangely this slippery hamadryad is ignored by scholarship on Roman religion. Instead it is Erysichthon's victim in Ovid's *Metamorphoses* who is the image of choice here. For as Erysichthon swings his final blows at the oak, a dying nymph

---

[48] Whilst Theophrastus appears to use the rare adjective ἰσόδενδρος to mean 'the same size as a tree' (*HP.* 3.1.1), Plutarch clearly sets the term within discussion of nymphs' lifespans.

[49] Cf. a similar motif in Martial 6.47 in which a nymph is welcomed as a guest to Stella's house, as she glides with her spring through his halls.

points out that she is physically present 'under this wood' (*sub hoc ... ligno*; 771): she is part of the tree, and the tree's death unambiguously entails hers. As early as Servius this image was cited as quintessential proof that a hamadryad was born *with* and died *with* her tree:

> hamadryades nymphae, quae cum arboribus et nascuntur et pereunt. qualis fuit illa, quam Erysichthon occidit: qui cum arborem incideret, et vox inde erupit et sanguis, sicut docet Ovidius. dryades vero sunt quae inter arbores habitant. (*Ecl.* 10.62)
>
> Hamadryads are nymphs which are born with trees and die with them. Such was she whom Erysichthon killed: he who when he was cutting down the tree both a voice and blood burst forth from it, as Ovid teaches us. The dryads, however, are those nymphs which live among trees.[50]
>
> amadryades namque cum arboribus et nascuntur et pereunt, unde plerumque caesa arbore sanguis emanat. nam, <ut> Ovidius ait, cum Erysichthon arborem incideret, primo sanguis effluxit, post ululatus secutus est. (*A*. 3.34)
>
> For hamadryads are born and die with trees, for which reason blood often flows from a cut tree. Indeed, as Ovid says, when Erysichthon was chopping the tree, first blood flowed, followed by a scream.[51]

Servius had – and openly acknowledges that he had – one Ovidian narrative in mind when producing these definitions: it is therefore unnerving, to say the least, when later scholars reproduce Servius' definitions as though they were of general validity.[52] Moreover, the fact that all our evidence for hamadryads being coeval with trees is so dominated by scholiasts and commentators should

---

[50] In defining dryads as nymphs who *inter arbores habitant*, strongly connected with trees but not assimilated with them, Servius was surely still thinking of the Ovidian passage. For a few lines earlier Ovid had painted a picture of the oak's happier past when dryads used to dance around the tree (746–748), suggesting for them an existence far more independent of trees than that of the dying nymph.

[51] Elsewhere, without reference to Ovid, Servius offers a similar definition: hamadryads are nymphs *quae cum silvis nascuntur* (who are born with woods; *A* 1.500).

[52] For example, Kennedy 1982: 378. Servius' clear distinction between nymphs' spheres of interest can be blurry in practice, with naiads and (hama)dryads in particular seeming to invade the space Servius allocates to each. Thus, Ovid calls Syrinx both naiad and hamadryad (*Met*. 1.690–691), and elsewhere paints a wounded naiad dying when a tree is cut down (*Fast*. 4.231–232): naiads, it seems, could have strongly arboreal identities too. Vice versa, in Orphic Hymn 51 hamadryads are called ὑγροκέλευθοι (those who leave a wet train; 14) and are asked to provide rain, thus sounding much more like our traditional view of naiads! Statius too, as we have just seen, chose not to commit as to whether it was a naiad or a hamadryad who found a home with Vopiscus (*Silv*. 1.3.62–63).

prompt a niggling worry that we are witnessing here the commentator's reflex to create tidy categories and ignore the muddiness of the waters. The fact that hamadryads so frequently prompted glosses and attempts at clarification should speak to us of a general ambiguity shrouding their nature and divine status, rather than encouraging us to take as gospel that hamadryads are born and die with their trees.

With the idea of trees and hamadryads being coeval cut down to its proper size, I now wish to consider other ways in which the relationship between (hama)dryads and trees was imagined. I start with one of Antonius Liberalis' miniature metamorphosis narratives. Certain hamadryads, we are told, once transformed Dryope from a mortal into a nymph – presumably also a hamadryad – and in her new form she becomes somehow 'conflated' with a poplar.

ἀντὶ δ' ἐκείνης αἴγειρον ἀνέφηναν ἐκ τῆς γῆς καὶ παρὰ τὴν αἴγειρον ὕδωρ ἀνέρρηξαν, Δρυόπη δὲ μετέβαλε καὶ ἀντὶ θνητῆς ἐγένετο νύμφη. (*Met.* 32)

In her place they made a poplar burst forth from the ground and by the poplar they made a spring gush forth, and Dryope changed and became a nymph instead of a mortal.

I have translated ἀντί in two ways, but the repetition of the preposition is pointed, and parallels the growth of the new poplar with Dryope's transformation into a nymph. The hamadryads made a poplar burst forth in Dryope's place, or if you like *instead of* her (ἀντί), and she became a nymph *instead of* a mortal (ἀντί). Liberalis thus implies that both the poplar and the nymph somehow take over from the previous mortal Dryope, but leaves obscure what relationship that establishes between the new nymph and poplar. Trees and (hama)dryads are also to some degree conflated when Ovid depicts trees which respond to Orpheus' death by shedding their leaves in grief; at the same time naiads and hamadryads dishevelled their hair, an image which lightly aligns the actions of the trees and those of the naiads and hamadryads (*Met.* 11.46–49). Nonnus too employs a similar motif when he parallels an image of whispering trees and rejoicing woods with that of singing dryads, suggesting that the agency shown by the trees could also be expressed in terms of the dryads' actions (3.68–70). He also repeatedly presents dryads, hamadryads and the far rarer (but seemingly similar) hadryads as tree-like in appearance, either with leafy bodies or half emerging from trees (2.94–97; 12.231–232; 22.84–85 and 96; 44.11–12; 48.519–520; 48.641).[53] In these Ovidian and Nonnian examples (hama)dryads mirror trees in their agency, actions and appearance.

On other occasions, we often meet (hama)dryads who act as though they are deeply implicated with, but nevertheless independent of, trees. In Seneca's *Hercules Oetaeus* dryads are among the crowd rushing to hear Orpheus sing, each 'fleeing her oak' (*quercum fugiens suam*; 1052–1053); significant is their ability to act independently of their tree, even if the rhetoric relies on the idea that only music like Orpheus' would normally induce them to do so.[54] Other hamadryads enjoy a far looser relationship with trees, perhaps best described as emotional or personal: Catullus, for example, has hamadryads nurturing the Asian myrtle as their plaything (61.21–25), whilst the hamadryad Pomona was an arboricultural specialist (*Met.* 14.623–625).[55] In Athenaeus, meanwhile, the relationship between hamadryad and tree becomes not just personal but familial, as he recounts how a certain Oxylos (Mr Thick-Wooded) married his sister Hamadryas to produce several hamadryad children – namely Nut, Acorn, Cornel, Mulberry, Black Poplar, Elm, Vine and

---

[53] However, the leafy hamadryad mentioned in Nonnus 22.84–85 soon changes her shape to that of a bird (115–116), revealing that she is not inextricably bound up with arboreal form. By contrast with Nonnus' leafy hamadryads, Ovid depicts much more anthropomorphic (hama)dryads, with loose flowing hair or clad in mourning dress (*Met.* 8.778 and 11.48–49), thus increasing the perceived gap between their existence and that of the tree. Hadryads only occur once in Latin literature (Prop. 1.20.12) but are more frequent in Greek, e.g. *AG.* 9.664.

[54] Consider too how Pausanias, telling us that the town Tithorea was so called after a nymph of that name, mentions in an aside that he is thinking of the kind of nymph 'who in older times the poets say grew out of trees and especially oaks' (οἶαι τὸ ἀρχαῖον λόγῳ τῷ ποιητῶν ἐφύοντο ἀπό τε ἄλλων δένδρων καὶ μάλιστα ἀπὸ τῶν δρυῶν; 10.32.9). These nymphs are intimately connected with trees at birth, but Pausanias does not necessarily imply that they continue being part of the tree for the rest of their lives: the preposition ἀπό (out of) might well suggest otherwise. Nonnus also suggests that hadryads are capable of existing without trees; when an irate Dionysus causes havoc in a wood, uprooting its trees, the hadryads are chased out, but they do not die (32.144). Likewise dryads in Ovid's Erysichthon narrative are messengers who report the damaged oak to Ceres (*Met.* 8.777–779).

[55] Cf. Columella's chorus of dryads who 'tend' (*colitis*) a grove (10.264–265) or the mourning hamadryads in Nonnus who inscribe an epitaph onto a tree trunk, an act which arguably shows their close allegiance with trees, but is also weirdly one of arboreal vandalism (17.311–314).

Numina and nymphs

Fig – from whom many trees derive their names (*Deip.* 78b). Here, rather than imagining the relationship between a hamadryad and a particular tree, we are encouraged to think of trees themselves as derivative of one 'proto-hamadryad'. For other (hama)dryads the strongest correlation between themselves and trees is simply that they exist in a woodland setting, as ironically seen in the passage of Virgil's *Eclogues* which prompted Servius' definition of a hamadryad as a being who lives and dies with her tree (*Ecl.* 10.62–63).[56] On other occasions (hama)dryads appear without any *overt* arboreal association at all, with a woodland setting perhaps alluded to at most: Philostratus, for example, refers to Palaestra's scorn for dryads who keep themselves white in the shade (*Im.* 2.32.3).[57] Finally, some hamadryads do not seem to have anything arboreal about them at all: when Liberalis tells us how the distressed Byblis, ready to throw herself off a cliff, metamorphosed into a hamadryad, we might be surprised to find that it is a local stream which gets named after her, and not a tree (*Met.* 30).[58]

In short, Roman thinkers imagined (hama)dryads as enjoying a variety of relationships with trees, ranging from a shared leafy appearance to a liking for shade; we have also seen no reason to

---

[56] Cf. the dryads in Ovid who simply 'stroll' (*incedere*) in woods (*Met.* 6.453), whilst a dryad whom we meet in Martial enjoys a relationship with a tree which is more utilitarian than anything else: our one sight of her is when she hides underneath the tree, which seems to be prompted less by an affinity with it than a desire to escape Pan's advances (9.61.13–14).

[57] On dryads liking shade Cf. Stat. *Theb.* 2.521. On many other occasions in depictions of (hama)dryads a woodland setting is only to be inferred from the bucolic scenario, or from traditional details about Orpheus' death, Diana's hunting habits or the wooded slopes of Mt. Ida: thus dryads listen to a song competition (Calp. *Ecl.* 2.14) and praise a poet's songs (Prop. 2.34.76); a chorus of dryads add to Orpheus' mourners (*G.* 4.460–461); Diana is attended by a hamadryad chorus (*Fast.* 2.155–156); a crowd of hamadryads saw Venus and Anchises *in flagrante* on Mt. Ida (Prop. 2.32.35–38). See Thanos 2003: 4–11 on ancient evidence for Mt. Ida being wooded.

[58] Propertius' version of the Hylas myth also undermines the idea of a particularly strong connection between (hama)dryads and trees (1.20). Most versions of this myth have naiads pulling Hylas into the pool, but in Propertius they are sometimes hamadryads, sometimes hadryads. Yet Propertius' account is no more overtly arboreal than others: a few apple trees feature but no effort is made to link them with the hamadryads. So why so many hamadryads in this poem? Kennedy 1982: 377–381 offers one answer: they are rural equivalents of the muses. This poem also – as Petrain 2000: esp. 409–416 has argued – exploits to metapoetic purpose the play in Hylas' name with the Greek word ὕλη, meaning both wood and subject matter, and although Petrain himself does not take this line, we might well see these hamadryads as reinforcing the literary play on 'wood'. On either of these readings, the hamadryads' presence in Propertius' poem is driven by a metapoetic agenda, not reflection on the significance of trees to this myth.

interpret these slippery figures as illustrations of 'the idea of an actual tree-soul'.[59] Interestingly, the (hama)dryads we have met have also rarely prompted theological comment. Erysichthon's disregard for the nymph in the tree was clearly an impious act; conversely the continued existence of a naiad or hamadryad in Statius *Silvae* 1.3 is thanks to the house owner's piety. Yet in general, any theological questions at stake in constructing the varied relationships between (hama)dryad and tree are all but elided in our evidence. In one way, however, (hama)dryads *do* make an important contribution to Roman religious thinking about trees. For the relationships which these often human-like figures shared with trees helped to 'personalise' trees in Roman culture. As such (hama)dryads form a crucial part of the cultural backdrop which ensured that, when Roman thinkers came to pose theological questions about the behaviour of trees, they found themselves predisposed to think of them as agents.

The religious significance of (hama)dryads is thus best understood alongside other elements in Roman culture which built up a picture of trees as human-like entities. Chief of these is the common motif of a girl (or sometimes boy) who turns into a tree. Ovid's *Metamorphoses* and mythological 'handbooks' circulating in the Roman world are packed with trees who were once people: Daphne the one-time laurel, Myrrha the myrrh tree, Cyparissus the cypress, Baucis and Philemon embracing as oak and linden, Phaethon's sisters the weeping poplars.[60] Much ink has been spilt over what these metamorphoses tell us about gender and sexual politics in the Roman world, but my own concern with them is what they tell us about trees.[61] Such metamorphosis stories encourage readers to think of trees and humans as fairly interchangeable species. Ovid in particular loves to linger over this blurring of human and tree in the metamorphoses he depicts, slowing down the pace

---

[59] Philpot 1897: 58.
[60] The possibility of arboreal metamorphosis is a frequently played-with trope: the exiled Ovid claims that he would be happy to be transformed into wood (*Pont.* 1.2.31–33); Apollonius of Tyana is challenged to turn into a tree (Philost. *VA.* 7.34); the nervy Lucius, being in Thessaly and therefore suspecting enchantment, presumes that all the trees he can see were formerly humans (Apul. *Met.* 2.1).
[61] See e.g. Richlin 1992: 158–179 and Salzman-Mitchell 2005: esp. 22–31.

of the transformation by mapping the vanishing human body parts onto their new arboreal counterparts (see, in particular, the graphic fates of Myrrha (*Met.* 10.489–502) and Daphne (*Met.* 1.548–552)). Another nightmaresque aspect of metamorphosis which Ovid manipulates to full pathetic potential is the loss of human voice on transition to arboreal (or animal) form, and the impact of Ovid's voiceless trees must have been heightened by the fact that, in other literary genres within the Roman world, trees are humanised precisely by being given a voice. Trees in fables are often vocal, with Babrius, Phaedrus and Avianus all programmatically drawing attention to this feature in their prologues.[62] In Greek epigram too, trees frequently speak and sometimes reveal that they were women in a former life, like Ovid's unfortunate 'heroines'.[63]

Concern with the 'permeability' of arboreal and human forms was also shared by Roman art, the popularity of such themes revealed when Lucian casually refers to our pictures of Daphne 'turning into a tree' (ἀποδενδρουμένην; *VH.* 1.8). Such pictures no doubt revelled in the artistic challenge of conveying the process of transition. Philostratus certainly has one such painting in mind when he recreates for us how an image of the sisters of Phaethon gives them roots at the extremities of their toes, with some all tree up to the waist, whilst others have had their arms too replaced by branches. By picturing for us two different stages of the metamorphosis, Philostratus (and the image he describes) encourages us to imagine the transformation in process, as he draws our gaze upwards from toe to head, finally directing our attention to their poplar-leaf hair (*Im.* 1.11.4).[64] This mirroring of human and arboreal body parts is also felt outside of depictions of metamorphoses.

---

[62] For Babrius, including talking trees in his fables is a throw back to the Golden Age, a time into which the genre of fable provides entry (*Prol.* 5–11), whilst for Avianus, making trees and animals talk helps him to convey a moral message (*Prol.*). Phaedrus is more defensive, anticipating critics of his work who will smirk at talking trees, by reminding them that he is speaking in jest through fictional tales (*Prol.* 1.5–7).

[63] For example, *AG.* 9.3, 9.30, 9.31, 9.33, 9.34, 9.75, 9.78, 9.79, 9.99, 9.131, 9.231, 9.247, 9.256, 9.282, 9.706. For speaking, sentient trees see also Avianus 16 and 19.

[64] Woodford 2003: 165–168 discusses how visual images tackle the challenge of capturing the 'delicacy' of metamorphosis (165). See Levi 1947: plate 47 and Bijovsky 2003: plates 4–5 for visual attempts to depict Daphne in this active process.

For poetic language used to describe trees often blurs them with the human form, as Nisbet observed:

> Trees are like people. They have a head (*vertex*), a trunk (*truncus*), arms (*bracchia*) ... Their life moves in human rhythms, which in their case may be repeated: sap rises and falls, hair (*coma*) luxuriates, withers, drops off.[65]

Arboricultural prose texts and philosophical accounts of the nature of plant life also strongly humanise the appearance and physical make-up of trees. There is a 'juice' (*umor*) in the body of trees which we must understand as their blood (Pliny *Nat.* 16.181); the pith of a tree is called by some the womb, some the entrails, others the heart (Ps. Arist. *Pl.* 819a); more predictably, the root, twigs, stem and branches of trees are just like the limbs of men (Ps. Arist. *Pl.* 819a).[66] The life experiences of humans and trees are also paralleled. The propagation of figs is figured in terms of pregnancy and childbirth (Pliny *Nat.* 17.155); trees and crops, like women, have a fixed number of days before they give birth (Varro *Agr.* 1.44.4); some plants lose their leaves just as hair and nails drop off from humans (Ps. Arist. *Pl.* 818b).[67]

Reversing the analogy, Gellius describes how the human foetus, when growing in the correct way with its head at the lower end of the womb, is remarkably tree-like in appearance: *non ut hominis natura est, sed ut arboris* (its nature is not as that of a man, but that of a tree; *NA.* 16.16). Interestingly, again it is babies who prompt the imagination of humans as tree-like in nature in a couple of colourful portents involving trees, both of which draw strong visual parallels between the existence of certain humans and trees. On opening Donatus' *Life of Virgil* we read how the mother of the future poet once dreamt that she gave birth not to a child but a laurel branch, which on contact with the earth grew up into a mature tree laden with fruit and flowers (Don. *Vita* 3). Moreover, shortly after Virgil's

---

[65] Nisbet 1987: 243. See Gowers 2005: 334–336 for a development of this position.

[66] Cf. Ps. Arist. *Pl.* 818a in which the author claims that all the parts of plants have a parallel part in animals, matching up, for example, a plant's bark with an animal's skin.

[67] Corbeill 2015: 32 and 68 offers fascinating discussion of a passage in Priscian (*Gramm.* 2.154.7–14) in which a perceived female quality to trees is made to account for the word *arbor* (tree), as well as most tree names having masculine morphology but feminine gender (e.g. *cupressus* (cypress), *ulmus* (elm), *pinus* (pine), *fagus* (beech), etc.).

birth, when a branch was planted in accordance with local postnatal customs, it shot up into a massive tree, mirroring the miraculous growth of the dream tree. Virgil's life as a literary superstar and that of the miraculous tree paralleled too neatly for the one not to be seen as reflective of the other, a metaphorical extension of the surreal dream in which laurel branch and baby become interchangeable objects. Continuing the theme of expectant mothers and trees pregnant with meaning, Suetonius also recounts how an oak sacred to Mars produced a new branch every time the mother of Vespasian gave birth, with the size and health of each branch reflecting the future fortune of the new baby (Suet. *Vesp.* 5.2). Whilst the first sickly girl had a matching thin and withered branch, Vespasian's, predictably enough, was more of a tree than a branch.

Trees and humans were often held up as mirror images of each other in Roman society, and it is this humanising of trees, as well as arborealising of humans, which forms the backdrop against which (hama)dryads are of significance to the study of Roman religion. These slippery beings made an important contribution to the Roman instinct to view trees in personal, human-like terms, and it was from this conceptual bedrock that Roman thinkers went on to grapple theologically with surprising displays of arboreal agency.

Arboreal portents

For the modern theorist of religion J. Z. Smith, the defining quality of ritual is an insistent questioning of what does and does not have meaning:

> If everything signifies, the result will be either insanity or banality. Understood from such a perspective, ritual is an exercise in the strategy of choice. What to include? What to hear as a message? What to see as a sign? What to perceive as having double meaning? What to exclude? What to allow to remain as background noise? What to understand as simply 'happening'?[68]

Roman thinkers, faced with a tree behaving unexpectedly, felt all of these questions acutely. How to decide what arboreal behaviour was meaningful, and what was not? And if a tree's behaviour was

---

[68] Smith 1982: 56.

to be considered a 'sign', against what criteria should you interpret its 'message'? Trees took the initiative in confronting Roman thinkers with unexpected displays of their 'unruly agency', leaving them on the back foot as they struggled to interpret what, if anything, it meant. Indeed, more time was spent contemplating such behaviour in trees than we might imagine: thanks to Pliny we know that the specialists Aristander and Gaius Epidius dedicated whole works solely to the subject of arboreal portents (*Nat.* 17.243). Pliny, having discussed a few arboreal portents himself, directs his readers' attention to these, the real experts, pulling himself up short with the reminder that he should not launch 'into a boundless topic' (*in infinitum*; *Nat.* 17.243). Ignoring Pliny's advice, I now dive into the topic which afforded such food for thought in Roman culture, on the look-out for ways in which the unruly agency of trees prompted thinkers to question how the divine world intersected with their own. But first a caveat is necessary. Whilst my enquiry pivots around Roman discussion of portents, I will not be restricting this to portents in the technical sense of events which took place on *ager Romanus* (Roman soil) and which were officially recognised as *prodigia* (portents) by the senate, although some such *prodigia* will certainly make an appearance.[69] For the technical sense of *prodigia* also bleeds into a more general sense of events understood as portents or communication from the divine, and it is this broader category of Roman portents in which I am interested.

[69] Rosenberger 2011: 293–294 confidently sums up the senatorial procedure for recognising a *prodigium* (portent) in the technical sense, but Beard 2012: 24–25 has recently raised several questions revealing how little we know of this process. MacBain 1982: 25–33 discusses the *ager Romanus* (Roman soil) qualification. I have chosen not to approach arboreal portents from this angle, but Roman senators did sometimes distinguish arboreal *prodigia* (portents) in their technical sense from other arboreal portents. Thus, Livy tells us that when a palm had sprung up in the precinct of the temple of Fortuna Primigeneia, this was taken to be a *prodigium* (portent), but when a palm sprang up in the *impluvium* of T. Marcius Figulus it was not, because this was a private space (43.13.5). MacBain 1982: 30 analyses the politics behind this particular case. The oak at Dodona in Greece, a tree famed for giving messages from the gods, was of course well known in the Roman world, yet this oak will stand in the background of my discussion. For an oak understood to confirm oracular requests by its *fatidico ... murmure* (prophetic murmur; Sil. 3.680) does not raise the same questions as trees whose unsolicited behaviour was to be interrogated for potential divine meaning, although the sense of agency inherent in trees may well have contributed to the Dodonian oak's rise to prominence as an oracular medium.

Arboreal portents

The most pressing question facing a Roman thinker when a tree did something unexpected, be it to suddenly collapse, spring up through a pavement or change the colour of its leaves, was this: was its behaviour meaningful or not? We may be tempted to phrase this question by asking whether the tree's behaviour was seen to be 'natural' or 'portentous', but this, I believe, would be a drastic oversimplification of Roman thinking about divine involvement in the natural world. We often describe Roman portents as phenomena which were seen as 'inexplicables, contre nature', to borrow Bloch's words, or as 'some kind of violation of nature', to borrow Davies'.[70] There are, however, many ways in which this obscures our understanding of Roman thinking about portents, and especially portentous behaviour in trees. Firstly we have to ask ourselves what we mean by 'natural' and 'unnatural' behaviour in a tree; it is important to note too that these are not the terms Roman thinkers choose to articulate what makes arboreal behaviour portentous or not.[71] Often we may use the word 'natural' of a tree's behaviour in relation to the power or agency which seems to be inherent in a tree, that which makes it alive; the actions of a tree are natural, in this sense, in opposition to the actions of a machine. But we also use the word 'natural' as a synonym, effectively, for 'normal'; something natural is something that we would expect to happen. Often we allow these two uses of the word natural to blur, and when it comes to trees, this obscures a lot. If a tree does something unexpected, but seemingly of its own accord, are we still to think of this as natural behaviour? Further complicating matters here is the difficulty of knowing what we can expect from trees. We are soon to meet some self-resurrecting trees in Pliny's *Natural History*. We may be convinced that this is impossible, or unnatural, behaviour in a tree (Pliny is less sure), but is not the occurrence of a graft between two wild trees – something which *we* happen to *know* occurs naturally – just as astounding

---

[70] Bloch 1963: 118; Davies 2004: 29. Alternatively we have a tendency to explain away supposed portents as behaviour the Romans did not realise was natural; Beard, North and Price 1998: 37 note that Roman portents 'were for the most part what we would call natural events'.

[71] Natural and unnatural are very much loaded terms, something which often goes ignored in scholarship on portents, although Davies 2004 shows his awareness of it when discussing portents in Livy, by frequently putting the word natural in scare quotes.

and unexpected, just as seemingly 'unnatural'? The virtuosic possibilities of a tree's behaviour make it particularly hard to know at what point a tree's behaviour has stepped outside the realm of what is 'natural', in the sense of expected. Nor is this the end of why it is an unhelpful simplification to think of arboreal portents as 'unnatural' behaviour in a tree. For it also seems that, in the Roman world, a theological account of an event's significance did not have to be incompatible with a 'natural' account of that event, in the sense of one which focuses on the tree's own agency. Arboreal behaviour, as I will argue, had the potential to be understood as both natural and portentous at the same time in Roman culture. Indeed we will soon see awareness of this potential in action as Roman thinkers grappled to understand and interpret arboreal behaviour, but first I wish to sketch out an important intellectual context which shaped this way of thinking.

At the heart of Stoic thinking lies the idea, put simply, that the universe is god, a bold claim here boldly put forward by Cicero's Balbus:

deum esse mundum omnemque vim mundi natura divina contineri. (*Nat. d.* 2.30)
The world is god and all the world's forces are held together by the divine nature.

Through the doctrine of κρᾶσις (total blending) Stoics argued that god and the matter of the world were mutually coextended; god did not fill the world as a water soaks into a sponge, filling up the available gaps, but rather occupied exactly the same space as matter. God, however, is qualitatively different from that matter, characterised perhaps as the *animus* (mind) of the world (e.g. Sen. *Ep.* 65.24) or a pervading πῦρ τεχνικόν (creative fire; translated into Latin as *ignis artificiosus*, e.g. *Nat. d.* 2.57). The relationship of *deus* (god) to *mundus* (world) in Stoic thought was every bit up for debate, and subject to numerous modifications: indeed Seneca advocated using your leisure time to ponder questions such as whether god directs or merely watches his creation, and whether he encircles it from outside or is completely blended with it (*De otio* 4.2). Differences aside, however, Stoic understanding of the *mundus* (world) as to some degree assimilated with *deus* (god) ensured that the behaviour of natural entities like animals, rivers or trees was never conceptually straightforward, or without theological implications. It is hardly surprising, then, that portents and signs played a crucial role in Stoic theology and cosmology, with Cicero's Balbus even claiming the widespread practice of divination as *proof* of the existence of the gods (*Nat. d.* 2.12). For the behaviour of any element of the world in which a Stoic lived was at once both natural and divine, and could always be viewed as divine communication; the meaninglessness of trying to distinguish the two is illustrated by the Stoic tendency to refer to god simply as *natura* (nature).[72]

Such thinking was widely influential, and had a particularly marked effect on the cosmology of Pliny. He opens his *Natural History* with the grand claim that the world is rightly believed to be an eternal *numen* (2.1), and a little later puts forward his own version of the Stoic custom of naming god *natura* (nature). Pointing out that there are several things it *seems* that god cannot do – like commit suicide, change the past and make ten times two not equal twenty – he argues that such facts forcibly demonstrate the *naturae potentia* (power of nature) and thereby prove that it is this power of nature 'which we mean by god' (*idque esse quod deum vocemus*; 2.27).[73] Considering Pliny's Stoic leanings and fascination with the natural world he is a predictably key source of information on arboreal portents in Roman culture. Yet engaging with arboreal behaviour as having portentous potential was certainly not restricted to those who held views as consciously Stoic as Pliny. As we turn now from theory to real-life examples, we will find that constructions of how divine and natural causation might overlap – albeit far weaker than those of many Stoics – always made themselves felt in Roman grappling with the potential religious significance of arboreal behaviour.[74] In that

[72] For example, Sen. *Nat.* 2.45.2.
[73] Beagon 1992: 26–54 analyses how Pliny's view of *natura* (nature) mirrors and differs from various Stoic conceptions of *natura* (nature).
[74] I strongly disagree with Ogilvie 1969: 10 and his condescending picture of Roman thinking about causation in plant growth. He claims that Romans saw the growth of a plant as 'something supernatural', on the grounds that it was out of their control; to assume that all action was the result of divine agency was, he argues, the easiest and most pragmatic option, for Romans found that 'life worked better for them if they did not look too hard for the causes'.

sense Stoic ideas were an extreme manifestation of a common concern running through Roman theological engagement with trees: to what degree might seemingly natural behaviour be 'contaminated' with the divine? I begin with a phenomenon which is not an 'arboreal portent' in the sense of a tree doing something seen to have divine meaning, but rather a portent involving trees. Objects unexpectedly turning into a tree were not an uncommon feature of mythological traditions circulating throughout the Roman world. Pausanias reports a local story of how the gods cut off the penis of Agdistis, and from it grew up an almond tree (7.17.10–11), whilst at Corinth he comes across a bay tree which sprang from the objects used for cleansing Orestes (2.31.8). He expresses more scepticism, however, for the story that Hercules' club, once casually left leaning against a statue of Hermes, replanted itself and returned to its original form as a wild olive (2.31.10). Perhaps the most famous of such transformations was the story of how Romulus hurled his spear into the ground of the Aventine hill, where it took root and turned into a cornel tree (Plu. *Rom.* 20.5; *Met.* 15.560–564; Serv. A. 3.46); indeed Silius Italicus plays on the renown of this event when he makes Scipio hurl a spear which then sprouts into a tree (16.586–591), in a meaning-laden mirroring of Romulus' action. In such accounts of arboreal growth Roman thinkers were confronted with something a long way from the realm of the biologically explicable, a clear indication that the divine might here be interfering in the human world, and this is surely what prompted the Romans in Plutarch's account of the Romulean cornel to wall it in, 'preserving it and honouring it as one of their most sacred objects' (ὡς ὄν τι τῶν ἁγιωτάτων ἱερῶν φυλάττοντες καὶ σεβόμενοι; *Rom.* 20.5).[75] Italicus' tree too is confidently interpreted as a 'portent' (*praesagium*; 590) and 'sign' (*signum*; 591) of Scipio's future success, a 'message from the gods' (*id monstrare deos*; 591). The sudden appearance of these new trees unambiguously embodied the intrusion of the divine into the human world.

---

[75] Hercules' club was once a tree, and the two spears were presumably carved from trees, but at the moment of transformation all would have been presumed dead wood; these metamorphoses thus reinforce the agency of trees by suggesting that it can, as it were, survive beyond the grave.

Arboreal portents

By contrast most other changes in trees were far less attention-grabbing and less self-evidently portentous; after all, we are more than used to seeing trees change on a regular basis. Indeed when Pliny attempts to draw up a kind of 'handbook' to arboreal portents, the difficulty of laying down any solid rules as to which changes in the behaviour and appearance of trees were and were not religiously significant emerges clearly. Pliny first approaches arboreal portents as a subset of arboreal illnesses: *inter vitia arborum est et prodigiis locus* (among the illnesses of trees there is also space for portents; 17.241). Thus he frames them as something to be understood within a spectrum of expected changes to arboreal health.[76] Yet after this confident start, Pliny quickly becomes hesitant about the ease of diagnosis.

> inter vitia arborum est et prodigiis locus. invenimus ficos sub foliis natas, vitem et malum punicam stirpe fructum tulisse, non palmite aut ramis, vitem uvas sine foliis, oleas quoque amisisse folia bacis haerentibus. sunt et miracula fortuita. nam et oliva in totum ambusta revixit et in Boeotia derosae locustis fici regerminavere. mutantur arbores et colore fiuntque ex nigris candidae, non semper prodigio, sed eae maxime, quae ex semine nascuntur. et populus alba in nigram transit. quidam et sorbum, si in calidiora loca venerit, sterilescere putant. prodigio autem fiunt ex dulcibus acerba poma aut dulcia ex acerbis, e caprifico fici aut contra, gravi ostento, cum in deteriora mutantur, ex olea in oleastrum, ex candida uva et fico in nigras aut, ut Laodiceae Xerxis adventu, platano in oleam mutata. qualibus ostentis Aristandri apud Graecos volumen scatet, ne in infinitum abeamus, apud nos vero C. Epidii commentarii, in quibus arbores locutae quoque reperiuntur. subsedit in Cumano arbor gravi ostento paulo ante Pompei Magni bella civilia paucis ramis eminentibus; inventum Sibyllinis libris internicionem hominum fore, tantoque eam maiorem, quanto propius ab urbe portentum factum esset. sunt prodigia et cum alienis locis enascuntur, ut in capitibus statuarum vel aris, et cum in arboribus ipsis alienae. ficus in lauro nata est Cyzici ante obsidionem. simili modo Trallibus palma in basi Caesaris dictatoris circa bella civilia eius. nec non et Romae in Capitolio in ara Iovis bello Persei enata palma victoriam triumphosque portendit. hac tempestatibus prostrata eodem loco ficus enata est M. Messalae C. Cassii censorum lustro, a quo tempore pudicitiam subversam Piso gravis auctor prodidit. super omnia, quae umquam audita sunt, erit prodigium in nostro aevo Neronis principis ruina factum in agro Marrucino, Vettii Marcelli e primis equestris ordinis oliveto universo viam publicam transgresso arvisque inde e contrario in locum oliveti profectis. (17.241–245)

[76] Roman thinkers of course expected trees to behave, to some degree at least, according to predictable patterns; Lehoux 2012: 47–76 offers intriguing reflection on the idea of 'laws of nature' within Roman intellectual culture.

Confronting arboreal agency

Among the illnesses of trees there is also space for portents. We find figs born under leaves, a vine and a pomegranate which have produced fruit on their trunks, not on a shoot or branch, a vine which has produced grapes without any leaves, and olives also which have lost their leaves whilst their fruit remained. There are also 'fortuitous' miracles. For even a completely burnt olive has come back to life and in Boeotia figs gnawed by locusts have rebudded. Trees even change in colour and turn from black to white, not always portentous, but chiefly those which grow from seed. The white poplar also turns into a black one. Certain people also think that the sorb becomes barren if it moves into a warmer climate. But it is a portent when sharp fruits appear on sweet-fruit trees or sweet on sharp, figs on a wild fig tree or vice versa, and it is a serious portent when trees change into a worse kind of tree, changed from an olive into a wild olive, from a white grape or fig into a black variety, or, as happened at Laodicea on the arrival of Xerxes, from a plane into an olive. Lest we enter into a boundless subject, the volume of Aristander teems with such portents among the Greeks, and also in our own country the commentaries of Gaius Epidius, in which trees are even found which have talked. In the territory of Cumae a tree sank, with only a few branches still protruding – an alarming portent – a little before the civil wars of Pompey the Great; it was discovered in the Sibylline books that there would be a slaughter of humans, and the nearer the portent was to the city the greater the slaughter would be. It is also a portent when trees grow in the wrong places, as on the heads of statues or on altars, and when different kinds of trees grow on other trees themselves. A fig grew on a laurel at Cyzicus before the siege; likewise at Tralles a palm grew up on the pedestal of a statue of Caesar the dictator around the time of his civil wars. Also at Rome on the Capitol a palm which grew up on the altar of Jupiter in the Persian war foretold victory and triumphs; when this tree was laid low by storms in the censorship of Marcus Messala and Gaius Cassius a fig was born in the same place, from which moment the respected authority Piso asserted that shame was overthrown. A portent which will surpass all those which have ever been heard took place in our own time at the fall of the emperor Nero, in the territory of the Marrucini; a whole olive grove, belonging to Vettius Marcellus, a leading equestrian, crossed the public road and the crops in that place set out from the opposite side for the site of the olive grove.

To many Pliny may seem uncharacteristically credulous concerning the portents he reports in this passage – Rackham, for one, feels it necessary to explain that the talking trees were presumably no more than 'noisy flocks of starlings roosting in trees' – but we should not miss the deep-seated hesitancy of this passage as well.[77] Pliny focuses on tell-tale signs and hints in arboreal behaviour which guide us to what *might* be a *prodigium* (portent), packing out the theory with examples. Fruit growing in an unusual

---

[77] Rackham 1950: 168.

place on a tree, trees coming back to life, a change in the colour of the tree or the sweetness of its fruit, trees growing out of altars or on the heads of statues, or even talking trees; all these *could* be signs of divine interference in the human world. Crucially, however, Pliny is not offering a foolproof checklist. He tells us, for example, that when trees change from black to white this is *non semper prodigio* (not always a portent; 17.242). How to be confident when it is or is not? The only further guidance Pliny offers is that this change seems to happen most often in trees which are grown from seed, suggesting some degree of correlation between natural factors and religious meaning in arboreal behaviour.[78]

Elsewhere in this passage we may also feel that Pliny rather frustratingly obfuscates any distinctions between natural and religious factors prompting arboreal behaviour. When gesturing to those who think that a sorb becomes barren on moving to a warmer climate, is he suggesting that this is a natural explanation, by force of contrast with the following case of sweet-fruited trees becoming bitter (but it is a portent when ...; *prodigio autem fiunt* ...)?[79] Or when he follows his claim that trees turning from black to white is not always a portent with the bland statement 'the white poplar also turns into a black one', is this meant (by contrast) as a description of natural behaviour, or an example of a change which might or might not be portentous? What, moreover, is the difference implied between the type of arboreal portents with which Pliny opens, such as figs born under leaves, and the *miracula fortuita* ('fortuitous' miracles) which follow? If we take *fortuitus* to mean something like 'determined by chance', might Pliny be suggesting that the *miracula fortuita* are 'less standard' or 'less expected', or even if you like 'less natural', than the other

[78] In the following discussion I use 'natural' with primary emphasis on the sense of behaviour caused by the tree's own agency, unless noted otherwise.
[79] Contrast the more sceptical approach of Theophrastus when he discusses spontaneous changes in the fruit of trees, such as an acid pomegranate producing sweet fruit, or in the whole tree itself, such as a white fig changing into a black one (*HP.* 2.3.1–3). Concerning the latter he notes that soothsayers call these 'portents' (σημεῖα), but himself seems sceptical of their assumption that these things are 'miraculous' (τέρατα) and 'contrary to nature' (παρὰ φύσιν), because the soothsayers do not express any surprise at ordinary changes, as when the smoky vine produces white grapes instead of black. He concludes that some changes which may seem 'abnormal' (παρὰ λόγον) are actually just 'due to other causes' (δι' ἄλλας αἰτίας).

portents previously mentioned, which did not have this element of chance?[80] (Certainly we might instinctively feel that trees growing fruit on their stems is more probable than burnt-up olives coming back to life.) Frustrating as Pliny's elusive jumps of logic may be, I would suggest that they are indicative of a mindset in which natural causes and portentous meaning in arboreal behaviour are not as distinct as we might expect. Indeed at another point in the *Natural History*, when Pliny perhaps felt less restricted by a 'handbook-style' format, he expresses this lack of distinction in a much more reflective and nuanced way. Here, as Pliny allows himself the space to discuss in detail cases of trees which collapse only to stand up again, we see that the rather disorienting experience of reading Pliny's 'official guide to arboreal portents' is not simply to be blamed on rushed and jumpy logic: the blurry lines were deliberate.

Pliny is deeply imbued in a Theophrastean tradition of identifying and distinguishing causes in plant life, and it is to Theophrastus I now briefly turn, and specifically his account of collapsed trees standing up again, in order to illuminate Pliny's own approach to the phenomenon.

εἰ δέ ποτε δένδρον ἐκπεσὸν ὑπὸ χειμῶνος ἀνέστη πάλιν αὐτόματον ὥσπερ ἐν Φιλίπποις μὲν ἰτέα ... καὶ τῆς μὲν οὐδὲν ἀφῃρέθη πλὴν ὅσοι τῶν ἀκρεμόνων κατεκλάσθησαν ἐν τῇ πτώσει ... τὴν δ' αἰτίαν <τις ἄν> ὑπελάμβανεν ὅτι πεσοῦσα ἐπὶ θάτερον μέρος ἀνέσπασε πολλὴν γῆν, ἐπιγενομένου δ' εἰς νύκτα τότε πνεύματος ἐναντίου καὶ μεγάλου, κινήσαντος αὐτὸ διὰ τὸ ἐμπίπτειν τοῖς ἀκρεμόσιν ῥοπὴν ἐποίησεν ἐγκείμενον τὸ βάρος καὶ κατασπάσαν ὤρθωσεν· οὕτω γὰρ συνέβη τῷ ἐν Φιλίπποις· ... ἀλλὰ γὰρ ταῦτα μὲν ἴσως ἔξω φυσικῆς αἰτίας ἐστίν. (*CP.* 5.4.7)

---

[80] *OLD* §1. It is helpful to compare here Pliny's description of a fig, a vine and an olive which stand in the Roman *forum* at the spot where the legendary Curtius is said to have thrown himself into an ominous chasm which had appeared (*Nat.* 15.78). The fig, he tells us, stands there 'by fortuitous planting' (*fortuito satu*) and the vine and olive are 'equally fortuitous' (*aeque fortuita*). Rackham 1945: 343 privileges the meaning 'spontaneous' in the adjective *fortuitus* when translating *fortuito satu* as 'self-sown', but this seems a perverse reading, since we are next told that the 'equally fortuitous' vine and olive were planted by the plebs, for the sake of the shade they provided. Surely the adjective *fortuitus* is used in this passage to emphasise that some kind of *fors* (a difficult word to translate, but perhaps 'divine chance') has contributed to the trees growing at such a symbolic location. After all, at the time the plebs could hardly have guessed at the future significance of the spot; they were motivated only by considerations of shade.

Arboreal portents

If ever a tree fell over in a storm and automatically stood up again like a willow did at Philippi ... and none of it was taken away except the branches which were broken off in the fall ... one would suppose the cause to be that falling to one side it pulled up much earth, and then a great wind arose during the night from the opposite direction and, having moved the tree through blowing on its branches, the weight [sc. of the soil] pressing down turned the scale and by pulling the tree down righted it. For thus it happened to the tree in Philippi ... but nevertheless these things are perhaps outside of natural causation.

Theophrastus' scientific account of the phenomenon, in which wind and soil are the main agents, is at the end seemingly undercut by his recognition that there was the possibility of an explanation 'outside of natural causation' (ἔξω φυσικῆς αἰτίας).[81] This openness to both natural and supernatural causation is also very much visible when Pliny discusses the resurrection of trees in detail (*Nat.* 16.131–133). Pliny begins by noting that it is common for fallen trees to 'be set back on their feet' (*restitui*) and as such to 'come back to life' (*revivescere*), thanks to the earth forming a sort of scar (16.131). He also notes that plane trees, which trap a lot of wind in their branches, are particularly liable to collapse and are then 'replanted' (*reponuntur*; 16.131). Here soil and wind are again identified as key agents, although Pliny's no-nonsense approach appears to go one step further in scientific rationalism than Theophrastus in (tacitly) recognising the involvement of humans: presumably the trees which are 'replanted' (*reponuntur*) are done so by human hands, since just before that he also mentions lopping. However, Pliny then continues that:

est in exemplis et sine tempestate ullave causa alia quam prodigii cecidisse multas ac sua sponte resurrexisse. (*Nat.* 16.132)

There are also examples of trees falling and of their own accord getting up again without a storm or any other cause than that of a portent.[82]

Pliny even mentions Theophrastus' Philippian willow as one such example, noting that this was an occurrence 'of good omen' (*fausti ominis*; *Nat.* 16.133). Pliny may thus disagree with Theophrastus

---

[81] This use of the term 'natural' by Theophrastus is not copied by Roman thinkers engaging with arboreal portents.

[82] Cf. Obsequens 103 in which an elm knocked over by the wind righted itself again. As usual, Obsequens does not elaborate on this portent's causation or meaning.

over the explanation and meaning to be attributed to this particular willow's behaviour, but he mirrors the way his predecessor foregrounds natural causation with regard to the resurrection of trees, only to temper this with the possibility of alternative explanations. For Theophrastus the alternative is something 'outside of natural causation' (ἔξω φυσικῆς αἰτίας). Tellingly though, for Pliny, the alternative explanation – that of a *prodigium* – is not an 'overriding' of causation, but is in itself a *causa*. Moreover, this cause is closely linked to the agency of the tree itself, as it stood up *sua sponte*: divine intervention in the form of the *prodigium* works causally through the tree's own agency.[83] Pliny has shown himself to be sensitive, on one level, to differences between *kinds* of causation in arboreal behaviour, but in the case of these resurrecting trees divine and natural causation have in effect become one and the same thing.[84]

Another example of arboreal collapse and resurrection – this time of a cypress on Vespasian's estate – illustrates further the nuances of attempting to account causally for such behaviour. According to Tacitus, this cypress's revival on the day after its collapse was taken as an unambiguously positive omen of Vespasian's future power,

---

[83] It is interesting to wonder whether Pliny's *sua sponte* may have been felt to have a technical sense, echoing the use Theophrastus (and before him Aristotle) made of the term 'spontaneous' to distinguish types of plant growth; growth from seed is contrasted with 'spontaneous growth', which occurs in particular wet conditions (*HP*. 2.1; *CP*. 1.1–2). (See Balme 1962 on the theory of spontaneous generation.) If using the phrase *sua sponte* in connection with plant growth does evoke a specialist term for a type of 'natural' growth, then its presence here would reinforce the way that divine and natural agency blur in Pliny's presentation of the self-resurrecting trees.

[84] As Davies 2004 has argued in his exploration of Livy's thinking about portents, trying to distinguish between divine and human agency was 'a question of different perspectives rather than ontologically different categories' (96). I find this formulation of Davies' reading of Livy particularly insightful when thinking about this passage of Pliny. For Pliny too, the distinction between divine and natural causation has become so minute that the language of perspective is particularly apt; what we are dealing with is the same process, but looked at in different lights. Confusingly, though, Davies' formulation here sits uneasily with his characterisation of Livy's thinking in the rest of the chapter. Davies 2004: 86–96 encourages us to bring to Livy's portent narratives the idea of 'double motivation'; most frequently invoked when commenting on the Homeric epics, we use this term to capture the way Greco-Roman thinkers may seem to understand a particular event as determined both by a human and a god. He then suggests a development of this idea – calling it 'multiple over-determination' – as a way of approaching Livy's portents. Livy, he argues, instead of thinking in terms of 'divine and human forces at play simultaneously', presents to the reader '*multiple* levels of explanation: the human and several distinct categories of the divine' (88). Davies' emphasis on distinct categories of explanation seems to me at odds with his emphasis a few pages later, which dispenses with the idea of 'ontologically different categories' (96).

'with the *haruspices* all in agreement' (*consensu haruspicum*; *Hist.* 2.78); Dio and Suetonius too report the same interpretation (65.1; *Vesp.* 5.4). Yet despite apparent unanimity regarding the portent's meaning, there were differing emphases in accounts of its causation. Tacitus simply tells us that the cypress suddenly collapsed and then rose up again, but Dio and Suetonius scrutinise these actions more closely. According to Dio the tree's collapse was due to violent wind, but it got back up 'by its own power' (ὑφ' ἑαυτῆς; 65.1.3). Suetonius insists that the cypress fell 'without the agency of any storm' (*sine ulla vi tempestatis*; *Vesp.* 5.4) before it 'stood up' (*resurrexit*) the following day, greener and stronger than before. For Suetonius, with his emphatic *sine ulla vi tempestatis* (without the agency of any storm), the absence of natural forces contributing to the tree's fall seems to reinforce this event's portentous meaning; here it is an overriding of 'the natural', particularly in the sense of the expected, which makes this behaviour portentous. Yet for Dio the tree falling over was nothing to write home about, the only surprise for him being the agency of the tree itself as it got up ὑφ' ἑαυτῆς (by its own power). This tree is clearly doing something very unexpected, and its behaviour can also be read in terms of an overriding of 'the natural'. Yet the use of the phrase ὑφ' ἑαυτῆς also brings to the fore the natural agency of the tree (as, to a lesser extent, does Suetonius' *resurrexit*); Dio's choice of phrasing subtly implies that the actions of the tree itself could be seen as permeated with divine meaning. In short, be it Vespasian's invincible cypress or a tree changing from the black to the white variety, there was no simple (or correct) way to read the delicate balance of the natural and the divine when accounting for unexpected arboreal behaviour. What's more, even behaviour understood as natural – that is something explicable in arboreal terms – still had the potential to be contaminated with the divine; Roman thinkers did not rule out the possibility that 'natural' behaviour might be articulating divine meaning.

Of course, to perceive divine meaning in a tree was only half the battle. How to establish *what* meaning was being communicated? Tacitus may have been confident in the consensus regarding the meaning of Vespasian's self-resurrecting cypress, but unusual behaviour in a tree tended to leave plenty of leeway for interpretation, even if it was agreed that the behaviour was portentous. An olive grove said to have crossed the road at the end of Nero's reign screamed the intervention of the divine, but what did it *mean*? Pliny is coy over this, just as he is over the meaning of most portents which make it into his 'official guide' (*Nat.* 17.241–245). We learn that a tree changing from a good tree to a 'worse kind' (*deteriora*; 17.242), such as an olive to a wild olive, was a 'negative portent' (*gravi ostento*; 17.242), but Pliny does not flesh out the interpretation further. Nor is he alone in this hesitancy to move beyond positive and negative readings of arboreal portents: Julius Capitolinus, for example, records barley sprouting from tree tops in Moesia simply as an example of *adversa* (negative signs; *Ant. Pius* 9.1–4). Hesitancy also made itself felt over the question of whether an arboreal portent could be read as communication from a *particular* deity. This we see in the case of the fabled olive which Athena produced when competing with Poseidon over Athens; one day burned to the ground by the Persians, this resilient olive then sprang back to vigorous life. Unusually, the possibilities for interpretation are rather restricted here, thanks to this tree already having such symbolic significance, and when Dionysius of Halicarnassus recounts the tale it is hardly surprising that he saw it as a sign from the gods that the city would soon recover and send up 'new shoots' (βλαστοὺς ... νέους; 14.2.1). Yet Dionysius' vague assertion that 'the gods' were communicating through the tree is more surprising, considering the close ties of this olive to Athena: could the message not be assumed to be from her?[85] Perhaps Dionysius was convinced that all the gods supported Athens' recovery, and communicated through this portent? Or perhaps his interpretation speaks of his awareness of the 'blankness' of the arboreal medium: when observing behaviour in a tree, how could you ever *know* who was communicating through it?[86] Indeed, as we continue to engage

---

[85] Cf. Silius' interpretation of Scipio's spear morphing into a tree as an anonymous 'message from the gods' (*id monstrare deos*; 16.591); for further discussion of this spear-tree see p. 204. Herodotus (8.55) and Pausanias (1.27.2) also tell the story of this miraculous olive, but neither give an opinion on whether particular divine agents were responsible for its regrowth. It is interesting, however, that Sourvinou-Inwood 2000: 23–24 instinctively reads the olive as a guarantee of Athena's support for Athens.

[86] We might compare here Horace's varying takes on the significance of his near escape from a falling tree, which he once attributes to the intervention of Faunus

Arboreal portents

with examples of Roman grappling with arboreal portents, more often than not we will see them read in terms of an anonymous 'divine' expressing itself in the human world.[87] Arboreal portents did not have to be conceived as *personal* communications.

When a tree did not have the symbolic force of the olive at Athens, how were you to interpret what looked like portentous arboreal behaviour? Pliny suggests one way in by noting that location could be crucial: *sunt prodigia et cum alienis locis enascuntur* (it is also a portent when trees grow in the wrong places; *Nat.* 17.244). A notorious palm which sprang up through the paving stones right next to a statue of Caesar, itself standing in a temple of Victory at Tralles (Caes. *Civ.* 3.105; Val. 1.6.12; Obsequens 65a; Plu. *Caes.* 47.1–2; Pliny *Nat.* 17.244), provides a nice illustration of this. Caesar, Valerius Maximus and Obsequens all mention the *coagmenta lapidum* (pavement joints) through which this palm had to burst, whilst Plutarch spells out his surprise at the tree's force:

καὶ τὸ περὶ αὐτῷ χωρίον αὐτό τε στερεὸν φύσει καὶ λίθῳ σκληρῷ κατεστρωμένον ἦν ἄνωθεν· ἐκ τούτου λέγουσιν ἀνατεῖλαι φοίνικα παρὰ τὴν βάσιν τοῦ ἀνδριάντος. (*Caes.* 47.1)

And the ground around it was naturally firm and was laid over with hard stone, but from this they say that the palm sprang up by the pedestal of the man's statue.[88]

Timing also intersected with the palm's clear commitment to emerging in this particular spot, thus securing the meaning of its appearance. Pliny locates the portent 'around the time of Caesar's

---

(*C.* 2.17.27–29), once Liber (*C.* 3.8.6–8) and once the Camenae (*C.* 3.4.21–28). All of these figures are influential in Horace's self-constructed poetic persona, but his fluctuation is not only interesting in metapoetic terms, it also reflects an ambivalence about the ability to attribute divinely meaningful behaviour in trees to particular gods, and an openness to multiple interpretations of arboreal agency.

[87] Davies 2004: 133–134 points out a similar phenomenon in Livy's presentation of portents: 'typically it is "the gods" in a generic and virtually anonymous plural who are thanked and acknowledged for their support' (133). Tellingly, the example he chooses to illustrate this also involves surprising behaviour from a living entity, namely a raven, which suddenly alights on the helmet of the tribune Marcus Valerius (7.26.2–4). Hard to know if any one particular god prompted this raven's actions (Valerius prays to 'whichever god or goddess' (*si divus si diva*) has sent the bird), whereas a statue of Apollo sweating blood, say, may have been felt easier to read as one god's intervention in the human world.

[88] Pliny is less emphatic in this regard, simply noting that the tree grew on the statue's base.

civil wars' (*circa bella civilia eius*; *Nat.* 17.244), but Caesar himself is more precise, arguing from retrospective calculations that this palm emerged on the very day of his 'victory', with Obsequens too assigning the palm's growth to the day of Pompey's death in Egypt. All this ensures that the palm is, in Plutarch's words, one of 'the most notable of many signs of victory' (σημείων δὲ πολλῶν γενομένων τῆς νίκης ἐπιφανέστατον; 47.1), with Valerius Maximus also driving home that thanks to the palm:

> apparet caelestium numen et Caesaris gloriae favisse et Pompei errorem inhibere voluisse. (1.6.12)
>
> It is clear that 'divine powers' both favoured Caesar's glory and wanted to put a check to Pompey's error.

In Valerius' account it is interesting to see again how an arboreal portent is imagined as an impersonal communication from unspecified 'divine powers', but the main point to be drawn from the multiple depictions of this portent is that together the location and timing of the palm's emergence unambiguously ensured that its growth had to be meaningful. Combined with the palm's victory associations in Roman culture, this palm easily became an indisputable sign of divine support for Caesar. The symbolism read into the conditions of this palm's emergence then led, in retrospect, to a rhetorical emphasis on the feat of a palm growing through pavement joints, a 'feat' which in other contexts would surely have been no more than an annoyance.

In the case of this pavement-wrecking palm, the victory associations of the tree-type only reinforced the obvious significance of the palm emerging in a temple of Victory, but on other occasions the type of tree involved in a portent offered a far more crucial hook into its meaning. Thus the so-called Aelius Lampridius, in his life of Severus Alexander, tells how a laurel once sprang up in the emperor's house close to a peach tree, and within a year had outgrown the peach (13.7). This was a clear prompt for the soothsayers, no doubt also a little motivated by the opportunity for sycophancy, to interpret the event as a prophecy of Alexander's defeat of the Persians. Lampridius does not explain the interpretation, but the fact that the peach was believed to have been introduced from Persia (hence its name *malus Persica*), and that the laurel had long been used for

Arboreal portents

Roman victory wreaths, must have been the key clues.[89] Consider also Pliny's confident interpretation of a palm which had sprung up on an altar of Jupiter on the Capitol during the Persian war: 'it portended victory and triumphs' (*victoriam triumphosque portendit*; *Nat.* 17.244).[90] The palm's location and its victory connotations made its meaning, in the context of the war at hand, loud and clear: again timing, location and tree-type work together to secure meaning. But this is not the end of this particular portent. Pliny continues the story of how, one day, during the censorship of Messala and Cassius, this palm came crashing down in a storm, only to be replaced by a fig which shot up in its place. You might think this a positive sign, a reaffirmation of Roman strength in the face of the destructive storm, but the continuity of *a* tree growing on the altar of Jupiter was not enough to please everyone. In the eyes of Piso, Pliny tells us, the appearance of this fig signalled the moment in Rome's history when 'shame was overthrown' (*pudicitiam subversam*; *Nat.* 17.244).[91] Moral objection to a proposal from the censors to build a stone theatre seems to have lurked behind his interpretation of this portent, a righteous indignation which the appearance of the fig helped him to bring out into the open. For the renown of fig trees as a 'manifest symbol of sensuality' urged (or allowed) Piso to view this fig as divine moral comment on the censors' shameless building proposals.[92] Reading the tree in context, for Piso a fig simply did not mean what a palm did.

The temporal and political context – be it war with Persia or a particular censorship – not only made all the difference to the interpretation of arboreal portents, but also heightened sensitivity to them. Thus, Gowers has recently shown a striking clustering of arboreal

---

[89] However, the type of tree was by no means a fixed guarantee of its behaviour's meaning. Livy cites a report from Macedonia of a laurel growing from a warship's stern as a negative portent (32.1.12), but it is easy to conceive how, in another situation, a laurel so located might have been read as a sign of forthcoming victory.

[90] Interestingly this portent is not, as you might expect, taken as a message from Jupiter; again the agency behind it is presented as impersonal.

[91] Fragment T6 in Cornell 2013: 290.

[92] Mehl 2011: 57 suggests that we see objections to the censors' plans as the context of the portent. Beck and Walter 2001: 324 cite evidence for opposition to the theatre building, also noting the fig's connotations of 'Zügellosigkeit'. The *ficus* (fig) has strong sexual connotations partly due to its alternative meaning of anal wart: Buchheit 1960 discusses *ficus* as 'Geschlechtssymbole' in detail (200).

portents in 68 CE, the year in which Nero would die.[93] Nor was it only during this momentous year that trees gave the impression of being in tune with the political climate. Two myrtle trees in front of the shrine of Quirinus were renowned for a *fatidico ... et memorabili augurio* (prophetic and remarkable augury; Pliny *Nat.* 15.120–121). One, called the patrician myrtle, flourished up until the Marsian war; but when the political tide turned in favour of the plebs, this myrtle yellowed, whilst the myrtle known as plebeian came into its own. Another politically minded tree grew in the grove of Juno at Nocera. This elm, having been lopped because it was drooping onto an altar, was suddenly restored to its previous state, a rebirth which also signalled the start of the renewal of Roman fortunes during the Cimbrian wars (Pliny *Nat.* 16.132). Of course the significance of these trees' actions was only visible in retrospect, once, for example, Nero actually *had* died; their meaning may have seemed quite different at the time, if indeed they were considered meaningful at all. Take, for example, the recovery of the *ficus Ruminalis* towards the end of Nero's reign, which, according to Tacitus, was viewed as a positive omen (*Ann.* 13.58). With Nero dead it is easy to see how the fig's new life could have been taken to suggest better times just around the corner, but at the time of its revival could it not also have been a worrying indication that Nero would last for a while longer yet?[94] Suetonius in fact provides us with a precious glimpse of arboreal behaviour being read differently over time when he tells the story (as previously discussed) of the oak which grew new branches every time Vespasia gave birth.[95] Suetonius describes each branch as *haud dubia signa futuri cuiusque fati* (a clear sign of the fate of each; *Vesp.* 5.2.), but this reading of the branches was only clear with hindsight. At the time, Suetonius tells us, Vespasia's father felt it necessary to consult the gods by means of a *haruspicum*, and on then informing Vespasia that she had given birth to a Caesar, found himself met only with her derision.[96] Sceptics will point out that you

---

[93] Gowers 2011: 88.
[94] Gowers 2011: 88 notes the irony of 'a tree that perversely chose Nero's decline as the moment to take on a new lease of life'.
[95] See p. 199.
[96] Vespasian's grandfather's instinct to seek out a professional interpretation may remind us of the sinking tree in Pliny's summary of arboreal portents, whose meaning was only elucidated on consultation of the Sibylline books (*Nat.* 17.243). Granger 1895: 99 once

Arboreal portents

would only notice something different about Vespasia's tree with the hindsight afforded by Vespasian's rise to power, but the sycophancy – not to mention the healthy dose of invention – no doubt inherent in narratives like Suetonius' is not what interests me here; rather it is the tacit acknowledgement of how hard it was to identify meaningful behaviour in a tree, so much so that you might easily overlook it when it was actually happening.

As well as reassessing arboreal actions with the benefit of hindsight, there were also times when Roman thinkers took the initiative and tried to control how arboreal behaviour would be read in the future. An anecdote in Suetonius tells how Augustus, on spotting a palm tree growing up through the pavement in front of his house, had it transplanted to the *conpluvium* to stand among his *penates*, taking great care that it should flourish (*Aug.* 92.1). No chances should be taken with such a potential sign of your destined success! Like father, like son, Suetonius also depicts Julius Caesar trying to take control of an arboreal sign. Leading the felling of a wood at Munda, he came across a palm and 'ordered it to be spared as an omen of victory' (*conservari ut omen victoriae iussit*; *Aug.* 94.11); apparently he hoped to turn this tree into a Caesarian spokesman. Yet Caesar was not expecting what happened next. A shoot sprang up from the palm, quickly overshadowed the parent tree and became filled with nesting doves: this itself was clearly a 'sign' (*ostentum*), and one which convinced Caesar that he should adopt Octavian as his successor.[97] Caesar may have thought that he was in control of this tree's meaning, but this story illustrates just how much the agency of trees evades human control; it is the tree which is producing the omens here.

The citizens of Tarraco also learned the hard way that they were not in control of arboreal portents, when they tried to determine the meaning of another unruly palm, which sprang up one day on their altar of Augustus.[98] Only this time it was not the actions

commented on a 'strange fellow feeling of the Italian trees for Vespasian', and it is certainly true that this emperor seems to attract arboreal portents.
[97] Vigourt 2001: 359 sees the doves as a gesture to Venus, and thus an indication to Caesar to choose a successor from within the Julian family.
[98] Quintilian *Inst.* 6.77 elliptically refers to *ara eius* (his altar), of great frustration to those interested in understanding the kind of divine honours Augustus received

Confronting arboreal agency

of the palm itself which made controlling its meaning difficult, but the intellectual consequences of the Tarraconians' interpretation, and their proclamation of this interpretation to the world. Of course they did not have to see the palm's growth as significant. A 'purely natural' explanation for its emergence would have been perfectly possible: seeds wedged in stone do sprout into saplings. Yet the emergence of a palm, imbued with victory connotations, on an altar of Augustus, made reading it as a message of divine support for the emperor hard to resist. No doubt this was especially true for the citizens of a city which Augustus had chosen as his headquarters for the early Cantabrian campaigns.[99] Their initial response, as we know from Quintilian (*Inst.* 6.77), was to report the portent to Augustus.[100] Frustratingly, Quintilian skimps on the nature of the communication, so we do not know whether they leant heavily on the palm's victory associations, or left the meaning of the growth to be inferred. If the Tarraconians had wondered whether a particular deity, rather than an anonymous divine source, was behind the palm's emergence, presumably they kept tactfully silent over this. For the involvement of Augustus, with his debated divine status, raises another rather unnerving possibility here. Had Augustus himself had an affect on the palm? Certainly an anecdote about a visit Augustus made to Capri would complement the understanding that Augustus' physical presence in Tarraco was influencing its flora; a withered holm oak, we are told, revived as soon as he set foot on the island

---

during his lifetime. Quintilian's genitive could seemingly imply anything from an altar dedicated by Augustus, to one dedicated to Augustus, to one devoted to worship of Augustus, although this latter would sit uneasily with our wider picture of deep-seated hesitancy regarding Augustus' divine status during his lifetime. Price 1984: 218 helpfully notes that many altars are dedicated to Augustus, but that this does not entail that the sacrifices burned on it were made 'to' Augustus, and to take this kind of 'middle reading' of Quintilian's genitive seems most plausible to me. Fishwick 1987: 171–174 discusses evidence for the date and location of this altar.

[99] Perhaps the portent took place during his residency there, in the early 20s BCE, but it cannot be dated with certainty. Fishwick 1987: 176 naively wonders 'whether the palm took root of its own accord or was not deliberately put there as a symbol of loyalty and sympathy with imperial aims'. Debating the historicity of the palm's sudden growth is hardly a fruitful path of investigation; what is of interest is how the event (contrived or not) is interpreted and manipulated.

[100] Quintilian's brief account does not allow us to know whether this was a report by delegation or letter, nor whether it was taken to Augustus in Rome, or whether he was present in Tarraco.

(Suet. *Aug.* 92).[101] Vigourt places weight on this tree being an oak, and thus a sign which reinforces Augustus' favoured relationship with Jupiter, but an equally valid interpretation might emphasise Augustus' effect on the tree to the exclusion of Jupiter.[102] An emperor who is to some degree a god can only complicate understanding of how the divine interferes in the arboreal community.

Whatever the precise wording of the Tarraconians' message, unfortunately for them, Augustus did not seem impressed. Quintilian reports his witty response: *et Augustus, nuntiantibus Tarraconensibus palmam in ara eius enatam, apparet, inquit, quam saepe accendatis* (and Augustus, when the Tarraconians announced that a palm had sprung up on his altar, said 'it's obvious how often you light fires on it'; *Inst.* 6.77). Quintilian is only interested in the joke, but there is more than a joke going on here. Certainly, as Gradel points out, the Tarraconians cannot have found being slapped down in this way very funny.

> Witty as the remark was, the delegation from Tarraco can hardly have found it very amusing. As this story can be quoted to show, there is little doubt that Augustus appreciated such honours.[103]

I am unconvinced, however, by Gradel's claim that this palm illustrates how much Augustus 'appreciated' the Tarraconians' move. To the contrary, the Tarraconians' sycophancy would have put him in an awkward theological (and political) position. Accepting the portent could easily smack of religious arrogance, and taking a stance which is – at least on the surface – sceptical, is characteristic of a generally hesitant attitude to divine honours which emerges from our sources.[104] Yet in adopting this stance Augustus also finds himself asserting his own religious authority over that of

---

[101] Likewise the powerful Xerxes turned a plane into an olive merely by arriving at Laodicea (Pliny *Nat.* 17.242). This anecdote about Augustus reviving the holm oak on Capri has been little discussed, but a century ago did prompt Granger 1895: 97 to suggest that Romans were sensitive to 'a secret sympathy between the life of trees and of human beings'.

[102] Vigourt 2001: 300.

[103] Gradel 2002: 98.

[104] Suetonius, to give but one example, has Augustus vehemently refuse temples to himself, unless they are also jointly dedicated to Roma (*Aug.* 52). See Gradel 2002: 109–139 for detailed exploration of the kind of divine honours which were offered to a man who 'consistently avoided direct deification' (112).

the Tarraconians, undercutting their reading of the palm's growth. For Augustus, choosing to call into question the significance of the palm also meant making a positive statement about *his* authority to decide whether arboreal behaviour on his altar did or did not have divine meaning. Yet at the same time, Augustus' quip is carefully designed so as not to *rule out* the Tarraconians' implications: whilst he comes across as sceptical and dismissive, there is still room for the palm to have divine significance. For Augustus implies his scepticism by making a dig about the regularity of the Tarraconians' religious observance, rather than commenting specifically on the palm. His comment has the tone of someone deflecting a compliment with a joke, in order to avoid confirming or denying the compliment.

Given Augustus' response, we might expect this to be the last we hear of the Tarraconians' palm. Weirdly, it is not. For as soon as Augustus was dead, the Tarraconians began to mint coins with an image of the altar and its protruding tree; our first attested version of this type dates to 15 CE (for an example see Figure 1). For Zanker, the point of this coinage was simple: the new coins were produced and disseminated 'in order to boast of the miracle to other cities'.[105] Yet boasting about this palm was hardly straightforward, considering its history. So what prompted the Tarraconians, once Augustus had died, to parade their public image as persistent believers in the divine significance of the palm? No doubt they saw the first imperial succession as an important moment to advertise their city's special relationship with Augustus, and perhaps they hoped that Augustus' original response to the palm might now be forgotten, and that the coins would speak only of divine favour for Augustus *and* Tarraco. Alternatively, perhaps the coinage was intended to enshrine their persistent piety towards Augustus, in that they saw divine significance where others, Augustus included, had allowed natural factors (namely the lack of fires on the altar) to come to the fore. Or were they even hoping to suggest, with the timing of the coins' release, that it was Augustus' deification itself which had retrospectively proved them right about the palm's divine meaning?

---

[105] Zanker 1988: 305. Fishwick 1987: 175 bizarrely understands the coins to prove that the event had 'some basis in fact': 'were it not for the numismatic evidence, the incident might have been consigned to the realm of anecdotal "history"'.

Arboreal portents

FIGURE 1 Reverse of Tiberian sestertius from Tarraco, depicting an altar with protruding palm tree.
Copyright: The Trustees of the British Museum.

If we read the coins along these lines, it is hard not to wonder how theologically unsettling it was for the Tarraconians to privilege their reading of the palm over Augustus' implied position about its lack of significance, especially now that he was deified. For minting these coins suggests that Augustus had been mistaken in adopting a sceptical stance: perhaps this could be softened by gesturing to Augustus' *humilitas* (humility) whilst on earth, but the implication is hard to avoid entirely. Another troubling question also raises its head. What would Augustus himself now think of the palm's emergence? Would (or could) Augustus as *divus* have changed his mind? For the Tarraconians, advertising their belief in the divine significance of the palm's behaviour may have had sycophantic motivations, but this was hardly 'easy' sycophancy. Not only did their insistence on their understanding of the palm advertise their awkward exchange with Augustus, it also opened a can of theological worms concerning the nature of Augustus' status and self-knowledge, both pre- and post-deification.

As they minted their new coins, no doubt the Tarraconians hoped to have the final word on the palm; but even this is not the end of its story. An epigram by Philippus of Thessalonica also celebrates the famed tree's growth, only in his version the palm has become a laurel, a substitution which again foregrounds how important the type of tree was to a portent's meaning (*AG.* 9.307).[106] If the palm's associations with victory helped secure its significance for the Tarraconians, what did the choice of laurel mean for Philippus? Was it purely to pull off a sycophantic joke? For the thrust of his poem is that Daphne, who once refused the advances of Apollo and metamorphosed into a laurel as a result, had not refused to rise up on Caesar's altar, having found in him a 'better god' (θεὸν ... ἀμείνονα; 3). Sycophancy is one easy way to dismiss this, but Philippus' focalising of this anecdote through the myth of Daphne also had theological weight. Firstly, by humanising the tree, Philippus expressed the sheer force of agency felt in its unexpected appearance. The details of the mythological parallel also allowed him to emphasise that, whereas Daphne had put down roots in soil, this tree had done so in rock, which seemingly undermines a reading of the event purely in 'natural' terms. In addition, by overlapping images of Augustus and Apollo, the latter responsible for Daphne's metamorphosis, Philippus could subtly toy with the question of what influence, if any, Augustus had on the new tree's emergence. In Philippus' engagement with this tree, questions of Augustus' self knowledge have moved to the background, but his divine status is once again the focus of attention. This laurel's surprising show of agency allows Philippus to bring under the spotlight the difference between Augustus and other gods, playfully

---

[106] Fishwick 1987: 171 is being unnecessarily pedantic in seeing this as a different event, because we are now dealing with a laurel not a palm: the details of such stories were hardly set in stone.

suggesting that the physical presence of this temporarily 'earthbound' god might have 'infected' arboreal behaviour.

As this palm (or laurel) came bursting onto the Augustan scene, its unruly agency posed politically urgent forms of the fundamental questions which any unexpected display of arboreal agency might prompt. Does it mean anything? And if so, what? Recognising and interpreting arboreal portents was not, as we might have expected, about separating out natural and unnatural behaviour in trees. Rather the trees met in this chapter have shown us a Roman way of thinking about their environment in which natural and divine causation blur, or, in other words, in which natural behaviour always has the potential to be infected with divine meaning. Consequently, deciding when the divine was expressing itself in the natural world, let alone what it meant, was a subtle and demanding task. This was a question of tuning in to the behaviour of the natural environment in all its detail, being sensitive to the fact that a black tree changing to the white variety is not always a portent, or that a fig growing on an altar of Jupiter might mean something quite different to a palm. Nor were the stakes here small. Trying to interpret arboreal behaviour constituted no less than a continual reshaping of Roman knowledge of the divine, as it communicated itself through the natural world.

CHAPTER 6

IMAGINING THE GODS: HOW TREES FLESH OUT THE IDENTITY OF THE DIVINE

When divine agents expressed themselves through arboreal behaviour, the human world and the world of the divine temporarily overlapped. The startling and unsettling nature of these arboreal portents made getting to grips with their meaning pressingly urgent: as such it is hardly surprising that these portents have quite a noisy presence in the literature of the Roman world. Yet to focus purely on such attention-grabbing moments in the life of a tree is only to scratch the surface of how Romans understood trees, rooted in the human world, to intersect with the world of the divine. Turning now to the more mundane existence of trees, we will find that Roman thinkers envisaged a diverse spectrum of ways in which a tree might stand in relation to a particular deity, as a point of contact between the human world and the world of the divine. Continuing the theme of Chapter 5 – how the divine is articulated and read in the arboreal world – in this chapter I explore how trees fleshed out Roman imagination of the identity of the deities they worshipped.

A striking fresco from the east wall of the *calidarium* in the villa at Oplontis gives us an idiosyncratic preview of the kind of thinking about trees which will dominate this chapter. Here we find Hercules hugging a tree, around which is tied a large yellow ribbon (Figure 2).[1] Standardly this image is said to be of Hercules in the garden of the Hesperides, but I see no reason to accept this.[2] The one gold shape which some might have seen as a cluster of

---

[1] A badly damaged fresco from the north wall of the *calidarium* appears to depict an ensemble of tree and column, also decorated with a yellow ribbon; Clarke 1991: 128–129 describes both east and north wall frescoes. This suggests that, in the *calidarium*, Hercules took his place within a wider scheme of mural decoration, but the state of the evidence does not allow us to explore this further.

[2] For example, Cazanove 1993: 119 and Guzzo and Fergola 2000: 22. Coralini 2001: 243 also questions this interpretation.

FIGURE 2 Fresco from the *calidarium* (east wall) of the *villa di Poppaea*, Oplontis, depicting Hercules hugging a tree.
Copyright: Andrew Hasson / Alamy Stock Photo.

golden apples is, on close examination, in fact a bird flying close to the tree. Without any apples on the tree, or a snake twisting round it, why see this as the Hesperides' garden? Odd as it may be to us, we should not ignore the fact that what we see here is Hercules embracing a tree. As such this image makes a tantalising contribution to our thinking about the relationships Roman

Imagining the gods

thinkers constructed between trees and deities. Matters are made particularly complicated by Hercules' own ambiguous divine status: are we to imagine this as Hercules the temporarily earth-bound hero, Hercules the deity, or something in between? Suppose we read this image as a snapshot of the hero during his lifetime. Are we to imagine that Hercules was responsible for the yellow ribbon? Is he 'worshipping' this tree? Or does his warm embrace of the tree emphasise his 'arboreal interests', as suggested also in stories testifying to Hercules' involvement with trees during his time on earth, be it planting two oaks at Heraclea (Pliny *Nat.* 16.239), or introducing certain trees to Greece, namely the white poplar from Thesprotia and the wild olive from the Hyperboreans (Paus. 5.14.2 and 5.7.7)? Interestingly Hercules is also wreathed in the image, recalling Pliny's mention of a wild olive at Olympia from which Hercules was first crowned, although the tree in the fresco seems far too tall to represent an olive (*Nat.* 16.240). Read as an image of the hero Hercules, perhaps his strikingly physical relationship with the tree also foreshadows, and helps us to imagine, the concern he is said to have for the genus of poplar once deified, although this tree does not have the poplar's distinctive conical shape; Coralini's suggestion of a pine is more convincing.[3] Another possibility is that we see Hercules as god here, his interest in a particular tree in the human world boldly depicted by having him bodily present in that world and embracing it. This image confronts us with a seemingly basic question: why is Hercules hugging a tree? The various answers I have suggested have all gone some way towards filling in an image of Hercules as a deity or hero with a deep-seated interest in trees. Thus the seemingly basic question leads us into a more nuanced one: how did the presence of the tree in this image shape the identity of this particular Hercules, as imagined by the users of the *calidarium* at Oplontis? This beautiful and intriguing image gives no confident answers, but invites us to play with the questions.

---

[3] See Phaedrus 3.17 and Pliny *Nat.* 12.3 on Hercules' relationship with the poplar, which will soon be discussed in detail. Coralini 2001: 243. As Peters 1963: 186 acknowledges, however, identifying tree types in Roman painting is a hard task.

Gods and tree types

Only one kind of relationship between tree and deity has a real presence in past and current scholarship on sacred trees: this is the idea, in Hersey's words, that 'each god and goddess had a special tree'.[4] Indeed the idea that the oak is sacred to Jupiter, or the laurel to Apollo, or the olive to Minerva, are treated as 'facts'. As early as 1819 Ouseley thought not to tire his reader with unnecessary pleading for this position:

> That various trees were consecrated, each to a particular divinity, we know from numerous passages so familiar to every classical reader, that I scarcely need quote on this subject Virgil and Pliny.[5]

Leaving aside for now whether these relationships really were so embedded into Roman religious thought as Ouseley implies, we should first question why scholars have so foregrounded this one idea. In large part this seems due to their insistence, as previously discussed, that material objects only achieved sacred status in Roman culture by undergoing a formal process of consecration, which set them aside as the property of the gods.[6] Notions of property or belonging have dominated our understanding of the possible relationships between objects in the human world and the world of the divine. Thus, whilst there is in fact extremely little evidence for the consecration of trees (especially compared with inorganic objects like statues, altars or temples), the idea that a genus of trees was 'consecrated to' or 'belonged to' a certain deity (the two phrases used interchangeably) has reassuringly allowed trees to slot into this property-centric mode of thinking about sacrality.

It is important to pause for a moment here and consider just how rarely we do glimpse trees in the Roman world which are presented as having been consecrated or 'made sacred'. As will soon be discussed in detail, Pliny does use language of dedication for thinking about the relationship of tree species and certain deities (*Nat.* 12.3);

---

[4] Hersey 1988: 11. See Boetticher 1856: 9–10, Seidensticker 1886: 137, Thiselton-Dyer 1889: 32, Hughes 1975: 50, Forbes Irving 1990: 131 and Dorcey 1992: 19 for iterations of the same position.
[5] Ouseley 1819: 354–365.
[6] See pp. 3–8.

Imagining the gods

Fronto too makes a vague reference to *arbores sacratas* (consecrated trees) as though this were nothing out of the ordinary (*Ver*. 2.6). As for specific cases of arboreal dedication, we have seen Titus Pomponius Victor promise to dedicate a thousand tall trees to Silvanus (*CIL* 12.103) and in a fragment of Catullus the poet announces that he is dedicating and consecrating a grove to Priapus (frg. 2). An epigram of Thyillus also foregrounds certain elms, palms and one holy plane tree as 'dedicated' (ἄγκειται) to Pan (*AG*. 6.170). A few lone dedicated trees also come to our attention: Virgil tells us that long ago Latinus dedicated a laurel tree to Apollo (*Aen*. 7.59–63), and we catch Horace posing in the process of dedicating a pine tree to Diana, declaring 'may the pine shadowing my house be yours' (*imminens villae tua pinus esto*; *C*. 3.22.5).[7] Downscaling yet further, in the *Anthologia Graeca* we encounter a beech branch dedicated to Hercules (6.351) and another to Pan (6.37). These tantalising brief examples – which, to the best of my knowledge, constitute the whole body of evidence for arboreal dedication – show that dedication could be a live concept in thinking about the sacrality of a tree, and one which foregrounds the tree's sacrality almost purely in terms of its relationship with a particular deity. Interestingly, though, only Horace explicitly articulates this as a relationship of belonging (*tua pinus esto*; may the pine be yours). Moreover, the minimal amount of evidence for the idea of arboreal dedication shows that the concept hardly formed the bedrock of Roman thinking about what it meant for a tree to be sacred.[8]

I now return to Ouseley's rhetorical claim that there is no need to cite any proof to state that 'various trees were consecrated, each to a particular divinity'. In light of this it is sobering to reflect just how rarely Roman authors comment on or theorise this famed relationship between certain deities and their tree species. But claims like Ouseley's not only insist far too loudly on

---

[7] Nisbet and Rudd 2004: 260 emphasise how Horace's language diverges from standard dedicatory language here. See also Henderson 1995 for an idiosyncratic take on the idiosyncrasy of this dedication.

[8] Sulpicius Severus, urging certain pagans to come to terms with the fact that their pine is 'dedicated to a demon' (*daemoni dedicata*; *VSM*. 13.2), also seems to work from the flawed assumption that pagans commonly conceptualised the sacrality of their trees in terms of dedication: for further discussion of this passage see pp. 72–73.

Gods and tree types

the importance of one mode of Roman thinking about what constitutes a tree's sacrality, they also greatly over-simplify Roman thinking about the relationship of a particular deity to a genus of trees. One of the most straightforward formulations of this relationship we find in a fable of Phaedrus (3.17): long ago the gods chose the trees they wanted to be 'under their patronage' (*in tutela sua*), Jupiter picking the oak, Venus the myrtle, Apollo the laurel, Cybele the pine, Hercules the poplar and Minerva the olive.[9] Only Lucian writes as boldly and simply as this about the relationship between a god and a tree species, inverting Phaedrus' narrative in his picture of how humans first categorised and made sense of the divine community:

καὶ πρῶτον μὲν ὕλας ἀπετέμοντο καὶ ὄρη ἀνέθεσαν καὶ ὄρνεα καθιέρωσαν καὶ φυτὰ ἐπεφήμισαν ἑκάστῳ θεῷ. (*Sacr.* 10)

First men fenced off woods and dedicated mountains and consecrated birds and assigned plants to each god.

Since this account sits within a tirade against human construction of the nature of deities, it is little surprise to find that in Lucian's eyes the links between plant types and specific deities were initiated by humans.[10] Indeed, considering Lucian's invariably scathing approach to religious norms, it might be tempting to interpret this passage as straightforward mockery of standard thinking about plant or arboreal sacrality, as represented by Phaedrus, say. Yet I believe it would be a mistake to take Lucian's ideas simply as a foil to Phaedrus' basic picture of divine patronage of trees. Lucian's view may be an extreme position, but it is not entirely idiosyncratic.

---

[9] Fronto, echoing Phaedrus' choice of terminology here, places the vine 'under the patronage of one god' (*in unius tutela dei*; *Eloq.* 1.13). Originary stories, similar to Phaedrus' picture of the gods making their tree choices, tell how certain gods first gave a tree species to humankind or to individuals. Phytalus welcomed Demeter into his house, for which she gave him the fig which they now call ἱερά (sacred; Paus. 1.37.2). Namatianus calls Minerva the *inventrix oleae* (discoverer of the olive; 73): this species came into existence, as it were, as an invention of Minerva. Humans who are responsible for the plantlife of communities are also revered for this benefaction: in early Rome, Virgil tells us, stood a cedarwood statue of *pater Sabinus vitisator* (father Sabinus the vine planter; *Aen.* 7.178–179).

[10] Lucian turns next to ridicule human confidence in their production of statues which supposedly reproduce the appearance of the gods.

Imagining the gods

In fact the idea that the relationships between tree types and gods were somehow humanly constructed also lurks behind Pliny's discussion of the five arboreal species he connects with specific deities, omitting from Phaedrus' list only the pine:

arborum genera numinibus suis dicata perpetuo servantur, ut Iovi aesculus, Apollini laurus, Minervae olea, Veneri myrtus, Herculi populus. (*Nat.* 12.3)

Types of trees are 'kept' perpetually dedicated to their *numina*, as the oak to Jupiter, the laurel to Apollo, the olive to Minerva, the myrtle to Venus, the poplar to Hercules.

In addition to the slipperiness of the word *numina* – which, as previously discussed, in the context of this passage seems to equate roughly to gods like Jupiter and Apollo – the word *servantur* (are 'kept') makes this a baffling sentence: how should we understand it?[11] Considering that Pliny is talking about all the oaks, laurels, olives, myrtles and poplars in the world, it is hardly likely that *servantur* describes a uniform response of practical care for these trees. No, surely Pliny means that it is *knowledge* of the trees' various dedications which is preserved: the trees are mentally 'kept' or 'set aside' as dedicated to their particular *numina*.[12] This interpretation finds strong support in the fact that *servantur* is paralleled by *credimus* (we believe) as the sentence continues, confirming that Pliny is thinking here in terms of human *conceptions* of trees:

quin et Silvanos Faunosque et dearum genera silvis ac sua numina tamquam e caelo attributa credimus. (*Nat.* 12.3)

Indeed we even believe that Silvani and Fauni and types of goddesses and their own *numina* are assigned to the woods as if from heaven.

Yet beyond this it is hard to say anything with confidence about Pliny's conception of the relationship between Minerva and the olive, or Hercules and the poplar. Pliny sheds no light on how the tree types came to be *dicata* (dedicated) to various gods in the first place. Unlike in Phaedrus, no gods are active agents in this account, nor does Pliny follow Lucian in explicitly asserting that humans consecrated tree types to the gods. In fact this passage

---

[11] For discussion of the use of *numina* in this passage see pp. 187–188.
[12] See *OLD* §§4 and 8 for such usages of *servare*.

Gods and tree types

might provide the most support of any ancient text for the idea that trees, to use Bodel's term, were 'auto-consecrated': Pliny is frustratingly silent on what led to their dedicated status.[13] All he does tell us is that this status is dependent on human conceptions of the tree types: they are 'mentally preserved' as 'dedicated'. In short, whilst Pliny confirms the idea, so prominently featured in our secondary literature, that tree types were divided up among, or dedicated to, several Olympians, he certainly does not encourage us to see this relationship in terms of property or belonging. To say that the genus of oak is 'kept as dedicated to its own *numen* Jupiter' is far more nuanced and theologically hesitant than this.

Finally, I turn to a passage from Servius' commentary on the *Georgics*, which might seem to provide a 'blanket rule' about the relationship of the *genus* of oaks and Jupiter. The passage of the *Georgics* in question urges us to allow flocks to seek out shade in the midday heat, anywhere where the 'oak of Jupiter' (*Iovis ... quercus*) stretches its huge branches or where there 'lies a grove, dark with crowded holm oaks and sacred shade' (*nigrum ilicibus crebris sacra nemus accubet umbra*; G. 3.333–334). Servius then comments on what Virgil says as follows:

quia omnis quercus Iovi est consecrata. quod autem dicit 'Iovis quercus' et 'ilicibus crebris sacra nemus accubet umbra', non re vera consecratos lucos nos dicit petere debere, sed ita densos, quales sunt illi, quos religio defendit: unde apparet Iovis quercum et sacram umbram generalia esse, non specialia epitheta; nam ut diximus, et omnis quercus Iovi est consecrata, et omnis lucus Dianae. (*G.* 3.332–334)

[He says this] since every oak is consecrated to Jupiter. Yet because he says 'oak of Jupiter' and 'the grove lies with clustered holm oaks and sacred shade', he is not telling us that we ought to imagine 'properly consecrated groves', but groves so dense such as those which religious scruple protects: from here it is clear that the oak of Jupiter and the sacred shade are general, not specialised epithets; for as I have said, every oak is consecrated to Jupiter, and every grove to Diana.

Servius mentions two levels on which an oak or a grove can be sacred: in this case he is not talking about 'properly consecrated groves' (*re vera consecratos lucos*) but rather the level at which *every* oak is consecrated to Jupiter, and *every* grove to Diana. Dowden, for one, takes this passage at face value as proof that

---
[13] Bodel 2009: 24.

every grove and every oak in the Roman world was sacred, and indeed on one level that *is* what Servius is saying.[14] Yet he also makes it clear that to say this is not to say much. He ascribes such a general, non-controvertible level of sacrality to all oaks and groves that to say an oak is an oak of Jupiter, or that a grove has 'sacred shade', are merely 'general epithets': in Servius' eyes the qualifying phrases are almost superfluous. Servius then goes on to articulate this general level of arboreal sacrality in terms of consecration, but contrasting this with groves which are 'properly consecrated' (something clearly different, but on which he frustratingly does not elaborate). The contrast starkly undermines the significance of saying that 'every oak is consecrated to Jupiter', colouring the language of consecration here as essentially metaphorical. Interesting too is the fact that Servius does not articulate such consecration in terms of property, but rather strongly connects it, in the case of the grove at least, with the trees' appearance: the density of a grove leads to its being 'protected' by *religio* (religious scruple).[15] Certainly Servius gives us no reason to believe that 'belonging to a deity' is at the heart of what he means when he writes that every oak is consecrated to Jupiter, every grove to Diana. Moreover, it is important to bear in mind that Servius displays a noticeably strong interest in divine names and epithets, observations on which constitute a recurrent feature of the rather idiosyncratic construction of Roman religion which emerges from his commentaries.[16] The style and tone of a commentary help to present Servius' ideas as a rule, but there is no reason to assume that other inhabitants of the Roman world thought in exactly these terms about Jupiter's relationship with oaks.

In short, in these few passages in which ancient authors *do* actively engage with or theorise the idea of a relationship between tree species and certain deities, we have not come across a single unambiguous or unqualified assertion that each tree type was

[14] Dowden 2000: 111.
[15] Servius' ideas here parallel my earlier discussion of the way that an arboreal *numen* was often something closely associated with the *quality* of a wooded space: see pp. 185–187.
[16] This I will argue more fully in a forthcoming article, which will set out the extent of the intellectual damage done by modern scholars of Roman religion over-relying on Servius' vision of Roman religion.

consecrated to, or belonged to, a particular deity.[17] Theory aside, we find that in practice too there was no uniform way of envisaging relationships between a tree species and a deity in the Roman world, nor were these relationships uncontested. It is authors writing in Greek who favour language of consecration in constructing these relationships: Diodorus Siculus notes that the Egyptians 'consecrate' (καθιεροῦσιν) ivy to Osiris, just as the Greeks do to Dionysus (1.17.4). For Plutarch too 'the ancients' (οἱ παλαιοί) 'consecrate' (καθιεροῦσιν) the laurel to Apollo, because both tree and god have a fiery nature (frg. 194); he also reports a discussion as to why the ancients 'consecrated' (καθωσίωσαν) the pine to Poseidon and Dionysus (*Quaest. conv.* 675E). Others are far more imaginative in articulating such relationships. In Virgil we find that the oak 'is especially luxuriant in foliage for Jupiter' (*Iovi ... maxima frondet aesculus*; *G.* 2.15–16), whilst for Pliny Venus 'presides over' the myrtle and marital union (*praeest*; *Nat.* 15.120). Propertius, calling as witnesses of his love for Cynthia certain trees on which he has carved her name, gestures to the genus of pine as 'the girlfriend of the Arcadian god' (*Arcadio pinus amica deo*; 1.18.20). In similar vein, Ovid's frustrated Apollo exclaims to Daphne, metamorphosed into a laurel, 'since you cannot be my wife, you will certainly be my tree' (*quoniam coniunx mea non potes esse arbor eris certe ... mea*; *Met.* 1.557–558).[18] This possessive phrase *arbor mea* (my tree) might seem to play into the hands of those assuming that tree types *belonged* to a deity, an aetiological story replicating in miniature Apollo's relationship

---

[17] Besides enjoying species-specific relationships with certain deities, trees could also find themselves split into the categories of *felices* (lucky) and *infelices* (unlucky). This division Macrobius understands to work in tandem with a division of trees among deities: he quotes from Tarquitius Priscus both a list of unlucky tree species and Priscus' explanation that such trees are *inferum deorum avertentiumque in tutela sunt* (under the protection of gods of the underworld and apotropaic powers; 3.20.3), echoing Phaedrus' concept of 'arboreal patronage'. Yet, for Fronto, this is not what it means for a tree to be lucky. When he notes laws against cutting down a lucky tree and wonders of what the *felicitas* (good luck) of a tree consists, he concludes that it is simply being fruitful (*Amic.* 2.7.6). Gellius' note that the *flamen Dialis* should bury his nail and hair cuttings under a *felix arbor* (lucky tree) does not help us to get to grips with what this label means in his eyes (*NA.* 10.15.15).

[18] A similarly passionate relationship between Apollo and the laurel is imagined in a Greek epigram, whose date and author are unknown, in which Apollo is strikingly described as δαφνογηθής (rejoicing in laurel; *AG.* 9.525.5).

with the whole genus of laurel.[19] Yet Apollo is here expressing his affection for one particular tree, not the whole genus, just as he might have called Daphne in human form *mea vita* (my darling). It is also vital that we do not deprive this passage of its sense of fun. Its humour relies on the awkward substitution of 'tree' for 'wife': 'you will be my tree' is not meant to sound natural to a Roman audience.

Not only were there multiple ways of imagining relationships between tree types and deities in Roman culture, but these relationships were also hardly set in stone, as the pine nicely illustrates. Whilst Phaedrus set the pine aside as Cybele's favoured tree (3.17), for Plutarch it was of significance to Dionysus and Poseidon (*Quaest. conv.* 675E), and for Propertius Pan (1.18.20). Nor was there anything to prevent a tree of one genus being in relationship with a deity who never takes on a role of 'patronage' for that genus.[20] Both Phaedrus and Pliny inform us that it is Hercules who enjoys a special relationship with the genus of poplar, but a sacred poplar in an epigram by Antipater of Thessalonica warns us not to touch her because Helios cares for her (*AG.* 9.706). The back-story to this epigram is that of the Heliades, who wept for their deceased brother Phaethon until they were turned into poplars; we might think of this as a filial bond overriding Hercules' tie with the poplar. In addition to this 'competition' over tree species, Plutarch in particular gives us further reason to dismiss any simple understanding that 'each god and goddess had a special tree'.[21] For he reveals how relationships between a deity and a tree species might be questioned and pulled apart behind closed doors, with layers of reasons constructed to explain their existence.

First of all, I turn to the tantalising fragment in which Plutarch tells us that the ancients consecrated the laurel to Apollo, noting that this was because the plant is 'full of fire' (πυρὸς πλῆρες), whilst Apollo simply is fire (frg. 194).[22] For Plutarch, to say the

---

[19] See Forbes Irving 1990: 131–138 on the role of metamorphosis in arboreal aetiologies.
[20] There is no need, for example, for Keary's 1882: 172 concerned attempts to explain away the existence of a Jupiter Fagutalis by making *fagus* (beech) originally mean oak!
[21] Hersey 1988: 11.
[22] The laurel was known for its fiery properties in the Roman world: Pliny places it, along with the lime, mulberry and ivy, in the category of 'hot' (*calidae*) trees, which provide kindling (*Nat.* 16.207).

Gods and tree types

laurel is 'consecrated' to Apollo means to talk in terms of an overlap in their identities. A much fuller discussion staged in the *Quaestiones conviviales* fleshes out this kind of thinking. Many guests, we are told, were pointing out that the crown of pine was ἴδιόν (personal) to Poseidon, when Lucanius interjected that it was also dedicated to Dionysus (*Quaest. conv.* 675E–676B). The conclusion to this disagreement? Plutarch notes that there seemed to them 'nothing illogical' (μηδὲν ... παράλογον) in this, seeing as both gods have 'power over the moist and the generative' (τῆς ὑγρᾶς καὶ γονίμου κύριοι). There was, then, no contradiction after all! Plutarch's surprising comment not only shows us that one tree type may enjoy a relationship with more than one deity. He also presents aspects of Dionysus' and Poseidon's characters (namely the wet and the generative) as that which made them suitable to be in close relation with the pine. As with his presentation of Apollo's love affair with the fiery laurel, when Plutarch thinks about a god's relationship with a tree species, it is the characteristics or interests of that god which come to the fore.[23] At this point you might think the diners' debate now resolved, the discussion closed, but in fact Plutarch goes on to nuance his original implication that both Dionysus and Poseidon are equally suited for a relationship with the pine. You could say, he ventures, that the pine is '*especially* suited' (κατ' ἰδίαν ... προσήκειν) to Poseidon: this is not, as Apollodorus believes, because it grows by the sea, but because it loves the wind – or so at least some argue – and above all because pine is the most suitable wood for shipbuilding. But on the other hand, he adds, the pine has been dedicated to Dionysus because it is thought to sweeten wine ... and at this point Plutarch's train of thought gets sidetracked. This rather rambling coda to the discussion reveals the level of debate that could be provoked by saying, for example, that the genus of pine enjoyed a relationship with Poseidon, even if we ought to temper this observation by acknowledging Plutarch's uncommon interest in niche academic detail. Moreover, Plutarch also shows us that such relationships were

---

[23] Unlike with the fiery laurel, however, the pine is not known for its 'wetness' in the Roman world (whilst arguably all trees have 'generative' qualities); perhaps Plutarch's later reference to the tendency of the pine to grow by the sea lies behind this kind of thinking.

Imagining the gods

constructed on a wide variety of criteria: characteristics of the deity (concern for the wet and the generative), common location of the trees (Apollodorus' seashore argument), characteristics of the trees (loves wind) and practical uses of the trees (shipbuilding and wine sweetening). All of these connections between tree type and deity built up the meaning of deceptively simple phrases such as 'consecrated to Dionysus' (τῷ Διονύσῳ καθωσιωμένον; 675E).

Hercules and Helios might 'compete' over the poplar, as might Poseidon and Dionysus over the pine; but even when one deity's special interest in a tree type was so well known as to seem unassailable – as with Jupiter and his oak – this did not prevent authors from pushing and pulling this relationship as far as it would go conceptually. What were the implications for an understanding of Jupiter's character to say that oaks were sacred to him, or, perhaps, that the oak is especially luxuriant for him? That he felt *concern* for oaks? The idea of Jupiter as a god who cares deeply for oaks is certainly rather hard to square with the storm damage for which Jupiter was typically held responsible. This potential clash between Jupiter's investment in both oaks and storms colours a passage of Silius Italicus, in which we feel the conceptual difficulties of positing a unique relationship between Jupiter and the genus of oak (10.164–169). Silius compares the demise of the warrior Crista to the moment when a lofty oak topples, 'struck by Jupiter's lightning bolt' (*fulmine ... percussa Iovi*; 164–166); it brings down with it 'boughs sacred through the ages' (*sacros per aevum ... ramos*; 166–167) and then crashes to the ground, 'conquered by the god' (*victa deo*; 168). To see the stricken oak 'struck by the bolt of Jupiter' is disturbing enough within a cultural world in which Jupiter might be thought to have a natural affinity with the oak. Yet Silius pushes this unease further when describing the oak as *victa deo* (conquered by the god), bluntly driving home the paradox of an oak being victim of the deity known for his interest in oaks.[24] Babrius too plays around with the idea that Jupiter can be selective about 'observing' his relationship with oaks. One of his fables recounts how certain oaks come to Zeus, addressing

---

[24] For other lightning attacks on woods by Jupiter see *Dirae* 35–36, Ov. *Am.* 3.3.35–36 and Hor. *C.* 1.12.59–60.

him as their 'first ancestor and father of all plants' (γενάρχα καὶ πατὴρ φυτῶν πάντων; 142.3). 'Why', they moan, 'did you beget us, if we are only to be chopped down?' (εἰ κοπτόμεσθα, πρὸς τί κἀξέφυς ἡμας;; 142.4). In reply, Zeus unfeelingly turns the tables on the oaks: if they had not themselves provided handles, farmers would not have axes. This joke relies on the *expectation* that Zeus might have concern for oaks, but plays off his nonchalance in ignoring this very expectation.

The purpose of this section has been largely deconstructive, unsettling the idea that Roman thinkers understood there to be a fixed set of relationships between particular deities and tree types. We have seen that it is clearly an injustice to Roman thinking simply to say, as Hersey did, that 'each god and goddess had a special tree'. Relationships between deities and tree species were articulated in imaginative ways; nor were these pairings unthinkingly accepted, but were questioned, pushed to their conceptual limits and, on occasion, laughed at. Moreover, whilst most of the examples considered here have been too fleeting to say much about the *nature* of the relationship imagined between a deity and a tree type, Plutarch's interest in Apollo and his fiery laurel, as well as Poseidon's and Dionysus' competition over the pine, showed us how the characteristics, uses and common location of the tree type could be felt to reflect or embody something about the identity of the god who enjoyed a relationship with it.

Arboreal epithets

Jupiter's preference for oaks is common knowledge, but how many know that in the town of Lepreum in Elis his 'counterpart' Zeus enjoyed a relationship with the white poplar?[25] It is thanks to a brief mention in Pausanias alone that we know of a temple there of Zeus of the White Poplar (Λευκαῖος Ζεύς; 5.5.5). But the tiny footprint which Zeus of the White Poplar leaves does not prevent us from asking questions about how he was imagined. What *kind*

---

[25] Much work needs to be done on Greco-Roman understanding of the relationship between Zeus and Jupiter, Hera and Juno, etc., putting under pressure the widespread and deceptively simple idea that these deities can be thought of as 'counterparts' or 'equivalents': see further pp. 250–251.

Imagining the gods

of relationship was thought to exist between Zeus and the white poplar? How is Zeus of the White Poplar different from Zeus? We ask such questions in something of a theoretical void; Versnel has recently observed that epithets are a 'curiously neglected chapter in the study of Greek religion' and this holds just as true for Roman religion, if not more so.[26] Scholarly thinking about epithets lacks acknowledgement of our agnosticism concerning the role and value of epithets in Roman culture; Rives is happy simply to term epithets 'supplementary names', explaining that Lucina and Sospita, for example, help 'to specify which version of Juno a worshipper had in mind'.[27] But what does it mean to talk of a 'version' of a god?

An exploration of arboreal epithets will inevitably be indebted to Pausanias, whose imagination was strongly captured by deities such as Zeus of the White Poplar. Thanks to him we also know of a temple of Apollo of the Plane (Ἀπόλλων Πλατανίστιος; 2.34.6) on the road from Troezen, a statue of Artemis of the Nut Tree at Caryae in Laconia (Ἄρτεμις Καρυᾶτις; 3.10.7), a sanctuary of Athena of the Cypress at Asopus in Laconia (Ἀθήνη Κυπαρισσία; 3.22.9) and perhaps another at Cyparissia (4.36.7), a sanctuary of Asclepius of the Agnus Castus (Ἀσκληπιός Ἀγνίτας; 3.14.7) in Sparta, a sanctuary of Helen of the Tree (Ἑλένη Δενδρῖτις) on Rhodes (3.19.10), a statue of Athena of the Ivy (Ἀθήνη Κισσαῖα; 2.29.1) at Epidauros, a sanctuary of Artemis of the Laurel at Hypsoi in Laconia (Ἄρτεμις Δαφναῖα; 3.24.9) and a statue of Artemis of the Cedar (Ἄρτεμις Κεδρεᾶτις) at Orchomenus in Arcadia (8.13.2).[28] Pausanias also introduces us to Dionysus of the Ivy (Διόνυσος Κισσός; 1.31.6), whom the people of Acharnae used to call on, and again it is through Pausanias that we learn of an alternative arboreal derivation for Apollo's epithet Καρνεῖος, believed by many to commemorate a murdered seer of Apollo,

---

[26] Versnel 2011: 60.
[27] Rives 2007: 15.
[28] The reason for my hesitancy over the second sanctuary of Athena of the Cypress is that it stands at a place called Cyparissia, leaving it unclear whether the epithet refers to Athena's location, or a connection with cypresses; perhaps the first would secure the latter meaning too. Cf. Craik 1980: 158, who discusses the difficulty of knowing whether Apollo Ixios on Rhodes was an Apollo worshipped at Ixos, or whether he had a connection with mistletoe (ἰξός).

Arboreal epithets

whose name was Carnus. Pausanias records another tradition that certain Greeks, having cut down cornel trees in a grove of Apollo in order to make the wooden horse, then experienced the god's wrath and so sacrificed to a god they named Apollo of the Cornels: the necessary transposition of 'ρ' and 'α' to allow Καρνεῖος to be derived from κράνεια (cornel tree) was, Pausanias adds, common in ancient times (3.13.4–5).[29] Certainly Pausanias is unusually interested in arboreal epithets, but he is not our sole witness to them. Athenaeus mentions a Dionysus of the Fig (Διόνυσος Συκίτης; *Deip.* 3.78c) and Strabo an Artemis of the Laurel (Ἄρτεμις Δάφνια; 8.3.12), whilst Pliny tells us of an altar to Venus of the Myrtle near the shrine of Quirinus in Rome (*Venus Myrtea*; *Nat.* 15.121). A Jupiter of the Beech is also known: one inscription refers to the district of this Jupiter (*vici Iovis Fagutal[is]*; *CIL* 6.452), and Pliny mentions him in the context of various parts of Rome which are named after trees (*Nat.* 16.37). Pliny's testimony is also supported by Varro's reference to an area of Rome known as the *fagutal*, where the shrine of this Jupiter Fagutalis stood (*LL.* 5.152); Varro also mentions a similar-sounding *lucus Facutalis* at *LL.* 5.49. Festus, taking a slightly different approach, defines the *fagutal as* a 'shrine of Jupiter' (*sacellum Iovis*; 77L). It is Varro again who provides our sole testimony to a shrine of the intriguing *Lares Querquetulanae* (oakwood lares?; *LL.* 5.49), whilst four inscriptions from Lugdunum Convenarum in Southern Gaul testify to another otherwise unknown god, simply called *fagus deus* (beech god; *CIL* 13.33, 13.223, 13.224, 13.225).[30] Finally, some inscriptions from Lydia, to be discussed in detail shortly, witness to another one-off deity, Zeus of the Twin Oaks (Ζεὺς ἐκ Διδύμων Δρυῶν).

The elliptical evidence for these intriguing epithets provokes many questions, and allows for no confident answers. Clearly they establish some kind of relationship between a deity and a tree or trees, but which trees, and what kind of relationship? Take Zeus

---

[29] Farnell 1909: 11 discusses whether, linguistically speaking, this epithet *could* refer to cornels.

[30] In a rare scholarly comment on this god, Cook 1925: 402 notes that 'the beech-tree seems to have retained something of its sanctity in this district', which does little to illuminate the nature of this intriguing deity.

Imagining the gods

of the White Poplar as our first example. Did this epithet celebrate Zeus' relationship with a particular white poplar or group of poplars, or did it rather paint Zeus as being in relationship with the whole genus of white poplar?[31] In either case, another question soon raises its head: how did the tie between Zeus and the white poplar/s play out with his well-known relationship with the genus of oaks, and was it ever problematic?[32] Note that most of the relationships between trees and deities conjured up by these epithets disregard the neat marrying up of tree species and deities found in Phaedrus (3.17) or Pliny (*Nat.* 12.3), with the only exceptions being Pliny's mention of an altar to Venus of the Myrtle and the inscriptions to Zeus of the Twin Oaks. All this raises the question of just how *unusual* these epithets were in the Roman world. Without Pausanias we would not know of Zeus of the White Poplar, but what does this actually tell us? Pausanias certainly had an unusually intense interest in divine epithets – after all, if it were not for him we would not know of Dusty Zeus (Ζεύς Κόνιος; 1.40.6) or Zeus Averter of Flies (Ζεύς Ἀπόμυιος; 5.14.1) either – so perhaps we should not read too much into the arboreal epithets he mentions being unattested elsewhere. What does seem significant about the Pausanian evidence, however, is that the arboreal deities he mentions are also all 'one-offs' in Pausanias' world.[33] It

---

[31] There is no reason, as Farnell 1896: 429 does, to see these arboreal epithets as evidence that the deity in question was originally a 'tree-goddess'.

[32] Moreover, even in Elis it seems that Zeus was not the only deity to enjoy a relationship with the white poplar. For elsewhere we learn from Pausanias that the Eleans used white poplar for their sacrifices to Zeus, a custom he strangely explains not by reference to Zeus' affinity with this tree; rather he states that they do so 'for no other reason' (κατ' ἄλλο μὲν οὐδέν) than that Hercules introduced this tree from Thesprotia (5.14.2).

[33] An *apparent* exception to this rule is Apollo Carneius, who received cult across a number of geographical locations. Pausanias states that all the Dorians worshipped Apollo Carneius, but it is also clear from his account that by no means all the Dorians believed that in so doing they were worshipping Apollo of the Cornels (3.13.4–5). For Pausanias' explanation of the epithet in arboreal terms – as the coinage of the Greeks who felled cornels on Mt. Ida – comes second to an explanation based on the murder of Carnus, a seer of Apollo. It is therefore dangerous to assume arboreal connotations whenever we encounter cult of Apollo Carneius. Indeed on the four other occasions when Pausanias mentions this god he makes no hint of any cornel-tree connection (4.31.1; 4.33.4–5; 2.10.2; 2.11.2), unless we count the fact that on the first two of these occasions the deity is linked with a grove. Could this be a suggestion that the cornel tree explanation of the epithet was active in the minds of those worshippers of Apollo Carneius? The first instance is really too brief to be informative: 'a little distance from Pharae is a grove of Apollo Carneius and a spring of water in it' (4.31.1). The second tells us of a grove in

is obviously dangerous to draw conclusions from the absence of evidence, but I do believe that we could expect the conscientious Pausanias to mention if he had, for example, encountered the cult of Apollo of the Plane beyond the environs of Troezen. That he does not suggest to me that when Pausanias gives us a glimpse of this Apollo we are here in the presence of a deity of very local significance. This understanding is strengthened by the nature of the non-Pausanian evidence too. Only Athenaeus tells us of Dionysus of the Fig, whilst *fagus deus* appears only in one area of Gaul, and our testimonies to Jupiter of the Beech all closely tie him to a particular area of Rome: these arboreal epithets were embedded in local religious landscapes.[34]

A logical next step from here might be to assume that the epithets linked the deity in question to a specific tree or group of trees in the physical landscape, that Athena became Athena of the Cypress because of a significant cypress or cypresses near her sanctuary. Pausanias does frequently site groves or other groups of trees in relation to temples or sanctuaries in his bricolage image of Greece, and the Rhodians' sanctuary of Helen of the Tree (Ἑλένη Δενδρῖτις) he explicitly ties to the belief that Helen was hanged on a tree in Rhodes (3.19.10). It is, therefore, all the more surprising that he makes no mention of any grove, or even a single tree, in connection with the cult buildings of Apollo of the Plane, Zeus of the White Poplar, Athena of the Cypress (either of them) or Artemis of the Laurel; nor does he paint an arboreal environment for the statue of Athena of the Ivy. The statue of Artemis of the Nut Tree, moreover, he explicitly distances from any trees by telling us that it stands 'in

---

Messenai known as the Carnasian grove where there stands a statue of Apollo Carneius, as well as one of Hermes carrying a ram (4.33.4–5). Yet far from being a cornel-tree grove given over to worship of Apollo Carneius, Pausanias tells us that this grove was thick with cypresses and was the home of the mysteries of the great goddesses. There is no suggestion in all of this that cornel associations were widely felt to be of significance when approaching Apollo Carneius, even when he was linked with a grove. As such Pausanias' wider engagement with this particular epithet cannot give us insight into its meaning in arboreal terms. Both Pindar and Plutarch also mention a festival of Carneian Apollo without acknowledging any arboreal connection (*Pyth.* 5.79–80; Plu. *Sympos.* 717D).

[34] Pausanias (3.24.9) and Strabo (8.3.12) both refer to an Artemis of the Laurel (although they spell the epithet differently). Pausanias' goddess is worshipped in Hypsoi in Laconia, Strabo's at Olympia: *if* she is to be understood as 'the same goddess' then this would be one 'exception which proves the rule'.

241

the open' (ἐν ὑπαίθρῳ; 3.10.7). It seems, then, that Cole was jumping to conclusions when she wrote of Artemis that:

> The epithets of the goddess describe the environment of her sanctuary: Agrotera, Limnatis, Heleia (of the marsh), Koryphaia (of the peak), Kedreatis (of the cedar trees), Karyatis (of the walnut trees), and Kyparissia (of the cypress trees).[35]

In fact, of all the deities in Pausanias who enjoy arboreal epithets, only Artemis of the Cedar and Asclepius of the Agnus Castus are depicted as having some kind of 'arboreal environment'; Artemis' epithet is derived from a wooden image of the goddess which sits in a cedar tree, and Asclepius' epithet is tied to the fact that his statue is made from *agnus castus*. To both of these I will soon return once our focus shifts to 'arboreal statues'.[36] For now, however, let us consider arboreal epithets outside of Pausanias. Pliny's reference to the altar to Venus Myrtea is simply too vague about its location for us to know whether it was accompanied by a myrtle tree or two; likewise Strabo's gesture to Artemis of the Laurel. However, at the *fagutal* of Jupiter we learn from Pliny that there was *once* a 'beech grove' there (*lucus fageus*; *Nat.* 16.37), an idea strengthened by Varro, firstly by his mentioning of the *fagutal* in the context of areas of Rome named after the trees in which they once abounded (*LL.* 5.152), and secondly by his reference to a *lucus Facutalis* ('Fagutalian' grove; *LL.* 5.49). Festus, meanwhile, in a departure from the grove line of thinking, confidently notes that the *fagutal* boasted *a* beech 'considered sacred to Jupiter' (*quae Iovis sacra habebatur*; 77L). We may not be able to conclude much about Jupiter Fagutalis from these brief references, but we can say that his identity was strongly coloured by the beech tree/s once so closely associated with his shrine. Thus the evidence for this god suggests one way of understanding the surprising lack of trees connected to other deities with arboreal epithets. This is to imagine that a tree or grove once connected with the temple or sanctuary, and now no more, had given the deity its epithet.[37] Nevertheless, if stories to this effect existed, say, about Artemis

[35] Cole 2004: 181.
[36] See pp. 260–261.
[37] Such a reading might be tempting, say, for the Zeus of the White Poplar at Lepreus, where we are told that the temple itself had disappeared by Pausanias' day (5.5.5).

Arboreal epithets

of the Nut Tree we might expect Pausanias – of all people – to record them. The absence of trees in connection with Pausanias' 'arboreal deities' is still puzzling.

Perhaps, then, we are coming to these arboreal epithets with the wrong expectations. Could we instead understand them in non-locational ways?[38] Could Athena of the Cypress' epithet indicate her *general* concern for cypresses, not just a few which happened to be on her doorstep? Certainly Pausanias mentions the Acharnians' prayers to Dionysus of the Ivy in the company of deities like Dionysus Singer and Athena Horse-Goddess, whose epithets might seem to encapsulate a wide ranging interest of the deity rather than a relationship with a specific place or object (1.31.6).[39] Ultimately, though, whilst we can justifiably assume that deities like Zeus of the White Poplar formed part of *local* religious conceptions, Pausanias frustrates us in knowing whether those conceptions themselves had a local or a cosmic scope: for the citizens of Lepreum, was Zeus in relationship with certain poplars at Lepreum alone, or poplars the world over? If the latter, how did this understanding sit with Zeus' well-known relationship with the genus of oaks? Pausanias may frustrate us here, but Athenaeus, who provides us with our testimony for Dionysus of the Fig, is far more forthcoming as to why the Spartans worship this deity: it was to prove that the fig tree was a discovery of Dionysus (*Deip.* 3.78c). In this precious and perhaps surprising

---

[38] Perhaps we should be giving more weight to the striking passage which leads into Pausanias' depiction of the statue of Artemis of the Nut Tree (3.10.6). Here he explains that the name of the district, Σκοτίτας (Dark), is not due to the surrounding woods but to Ζεύς Σκοτίτας, who had a sanctuary nearby. Here Pausanias suggests a surprising *disjunct* between divine epithets and the environment of the sanctuary of the deity concerned.

[39] Plutarch's mention of a Διόνυσος Δενδρίτης (Dionysus of the Tree) whom all Greeks worship (*Quaest. conv.* 675F) offers another tantalising glimpse of an arboreal epithet with a non-location-specific meaning, sadly too brief for us to say more about the nature of the relationship imagined between this god and the trees his epithet conjures up. At an extensively excavated sanctuary of a god with a similarly broad sounding arboreal remit, namely the sanctuary of Apollo Hylates, or 'Woodland Apollo', at Kourion on Cyprus, attempts have been made to draw a close link between the deity and specific trees understood as sacred to the god. Soren 1987: 35 and 42 claims that the Round Building, with pits cut into bedrock for planting, would have been filled with sacred trees, but such arguments are far from convincing. Planting holes alone can only ever be taken as evidence for trees, not trees considered sacred. See Scranton 1967: 74–76 on Roman period activity at the site.

piece of evidence we see that arboreal epithets *could* be about far more than location: in the eyes of the Spartans, Athenaeus claims, this epithet reinforces an important aspect of Dionysus' identity and personal history (not just a relationship of local scope). This is surely also the one thing we can take away from our meagre evidence for the god known as *fagus deus* in Gaul: for those paying vows to this god, his identity was so overwhelmingly 'beech-like' that the word *fagus* (beech) alone summed up what was really significant about him.

I now turn to consider an arboreal divine epithet attested in six of the so-called 'confession inscriptions', representatives of an epigraphic habit from a far flung corner of the Roman empire, namely rural areas of Lydia, Phrygia and Mysia, which flourished during the second and third centuries CE. As witnesses to local religious conceptions these inscriptions thus nicely complement our focus so far on Pausanian evidence. The inscriptions follow a fairly standard format: address to a god; confession of a sin; acknowledgement of how the god punished it; statement of a stele being erected in gratitude (often demanded by the god); proclamation of the power of the god in question.[40] In recent years they have attracted quite a lot of scholarly attention, but to my knowledge nobody has yet analysed in full the evidence for an otherwise unattested deity who appears in six of these inscriptions: this is Ζεὺς ἐκ Διδύμων Δρυῶν (Zeus of the Twin Oaks, or perhaps 'from the Twin Oaks'; the significance of this dilemma regarding translation I will discuss shortly).[41]

The first two known inscriptions which mention this god were published by Petzl in 1978. They come from Börtlüce, a village near Saittai in Lydia, the first (which I shall call inscription A) dating to 191–192 CE and the second (inscription B) to 194–195 CE.[42]

---

[40] See Schnabel 2003: 160–162 for a more expansive summary of the key components of these inscriptions. Mitchell 1993: 189–195 also provides a useful introduction.

[41] Much debate has centred on attempts to explain why our surviving 'confession inscriptions' are restricted to such a small geographical and temporal window. For a summary of the arguments see Schnabel 2003: 179–182; in the rest of the article he puts forward his hypothesis that the spread of Christianity in Anatolia contributed to the popularity of this genre of inscribed texts. See Mitchell 1993: 190 for a map locating the 'confession inscription' finds.

[42] Petzl 1978: 249–258. These inscriptions are also printed as *TAM* 5.1 197a and 197b.

Inscription A begins by addressing the god as follows: μέγας Ζεὺς ἐκ Διδύμων Δρυῶν κατεκτισμένος καὶ αἱ δυνάμις αὐτοῦ (great is Zeus 'made' of the Twin Oaks and his powers). Since, the inscription continues, Menophilos sold 'sacred wood' (ἱερὰ ξύλα), he was punished by the god and suffered greatly. Menophilos concludes by announcing to all men that they must not despise the god. Inscription B also opens with an announcement: μέγας Ζεὺς ἐγ Διδύμων Δρυῶν (great is Zeus of the Twin Oaks). Stratoneikos son of Euangelos then recounts how through ignorance he cut down an oak of 'Twin Zeus' (Διὸς Διδυμείτου) and that in response the god almost killed him. Having been saved from great danger he set this inscription up in thanks, which he finishes on a note of warning: παρανγέλλω δέ, αὐτοῦ τὰς δυνάμις μή τίς ποτε κατευτελήσι καὶ κόψει δρῦν (I exhort no one ever to scorn his powers and cut down an oak).[43] Next, in 1983, Robert published another two inscriptions attesting to this god, again both found at Börtlüce. The first (inscription C) dates from 262 CE–263 CE, the second (inscription D) from 252 CE–253 CE.[44] Inscription C begins just as Stratoneikos' did: μέγας Ζεὺς ἐ(γ) Δεδύμων Δρυῶν (great is Zeus of the Twin Oaks). The author then introduces himself as Athenaios and explains that, having been punished by the god for a mistake committed in ignorance and chastised in a dream, a stele was demanded from him. Inscription D was set up by a certain Bassa and is addressed to Διὶ ἐγ Διδύμων Δρυῶν (Zeus of the Twin Oaks). Bassa then explains that, having been punished for several years and 'not believing in the god' (μὴ πιστεύουσα τῷ θεῷ), he then discovered why he was suffering and in gratitude set up this stele. In 2004 Malay and Sayar published another testimony to Zeus of the Twin Oaks (inscription E) which came to light at the village of Kalburcu, south west of Silandos and just a few miles from Saittai, and which dates from 203 CE–204 CE.[45] It also is addressed to Διεὶ ἐγ Διδύμων Δρυῶν. We then learn that Menophila, daughter of Asclepiades, had been punished by the god and vowed a votive tablet. Only she had wasted time and so

---

[43] Lane Fox 1986: 127–128 briefly discusses this inscription.
[44] Robert 1983: 515–523.
[45] Malay and Sayar 2004.

Imagining the gods

her sister Julia, who had made the vow with her, found the god demanding a stele from her too, a demand which she here fulfils. Finally (or at least for now), in 2007 Herrmann and Malay published one more inscription testifying to this Zeus, which dates from 209 CE–210 CE (inscription F).[46] In this we simply learn that μέγας Ζεὺς ἐγ Διδύμων Δρυῶν appeared to Poplianus and demanded a stele, which Poplianus is now providing.

The Zeus of these six inscriptions is addressed in three different ways. By far the most frequently he is Ζεὺς ἐγ Διδύμων Δρυῶν (Zeus of the Twin Oaks), but in inscription A he is also referred to as Ζεὺς ἐκ Διδύμων Δρυῶν κατεκτισμένος (Zeus 'made' of the Twin Oaks), and in inscription B Ζεὺς Διδυμείτης ('Twin Zeus') makes an appearance. Petzl, who was the first to introduce this deity to the world, argues that the title ἐγ Διδύμων Δρυῶν indicated the cult location for this 'Lokalgott Zeus'.[47] An impressive 'double oak' – probably two oaks growing out of the same stem, Petzl suggests – accounted for the name of the area; presumably the phrase 'double oak' could also have referred to two lone oaks standing side by side.[48] As Petzl acknowledges, however, this locational reading of the epithet is complicated by the other reference to this god as Ζεὺς ἐκ Διδύμων Δρυῶν κατεκτισμένος.[49] How to translate κατεκτισμένος? Petzl believes the best way to take this (otherwise unattested) verb is as a synonym for κτίζειν, which can mean, as well as to found, to build or make.[50] Petzl then suggests that we understand the Zeus in question as represented by a wooden cult statue, and one specifically made out of the 'double oak'. Is μέγας Ζεὺς ἐγ Διδύμων Δρυῶν a shorthand for μέγας Ζεὺς ἐκ Διδύμων Δρυῶν κατεκτισμένος, Petzl ponders.[51] Here we see some of what is at stake in translating ἐκ as either 'from' or 'of' in

[46] Herrmann and Malay 2007: 99–100.
[47] Petzl 1978: 251.
[48] Petzl 1978: 251. Schnabel 2003: 173 also assumes that Twin Oaks is a place name, and in this thinking both are supported by Lane's testimony that gods in Anatolia commonly took epithets derived from place names (1989: 41). For the idea of two trees growing from one stem see Paus. 8.37.10, where a holm oak and olive growing from the same root are a major attraction of a grove.
[49] Petzl 1978: 252. Indeed, twenty years after the original publication, Petzl 1998: 9 revealed increasing hesitancy in observing that Zeus of Twin Oaks was *probably* a place name.
[50] Petzl 1978: 252.
[51] Petzl 1978: 252.

Arboreal epithets

this phrase. The former suggests a locational reading, whilst the latter could indicate the 'twin oaks' as the constituent material of this Zeus. Nor do the two readings make comfortable bedfellows, as any statue made of this 'double oak' would have destroyed the reason for the place to be known as Twin Oaks.

There is also another factor, not properly acknowledged by Petzl, which problematises any understanding of μέγας Ζεὺς ἐγ Διδύμων Δρυῶν which insists that this deity was closely connected with an area famed for a double oak, or set of twin oaks. For in inscriptions A and B this Zeus seems to enjoy a relationship with far more than one or two oaks. After all, for Stratoneikos' excuse that he cut down an oak of Ζεὺς Διδυμείτης *by mistake* to be plausible, we would expect there to be more than two oaks which enjoy a connection with the god, unless Stratoneikos was simply denying all knowledge of the existence of Ζεὺς Διδυμείτης (inscription B). That Menophilus 'bought sacred wood', and thereby angered μέγας Ζεὺς ἐκ Διδύμων Δρυῶν κατεκτισμένος, suggests even more strongly that there were more than just two trees closely connected with this deity, again unless Menophilus had been so brazen as to buy into the destruction of the sole two trees associated with the god (inscription A). Perhaps, then, ἐγ Διδύμων Δρυῶν should not be taken as a locational restricter of the god's identity but rather as an insight into something more personal about the nature and interests of this god. Indeed his other epithet Διδυμείτης (an adjective elsewhere unattested) suggests a close relationship between his identity and that of the 'double oaks': both share this quality of 'doubleness'.[52] Perhaps δίδυμος is a technical arboricultural term (meaning now lost to us) for a particular type of oak with which Zeus enjoyed a relationship, just as we saw him linked only to the *white* poplar at Lepreus? This idea of an overlap of qualities between god and tree reminds us of Plutarch's pairing up of Apollo and the laurel, on the grounds that both are fiery in nature.[53]

---

[52] Petzl 1978: 252 informs us that είτης is a common Lydian adjective ending.
[53] See pp. 234–235. It is intriguing to compare an inscription from Praeneste, addressed to *Deo Magno Silvano Marti Hercule Iovi Zabasio* (Great God Silvanus Mars Hercules Jupiter Sabazius) in which the words *Iovi Zabasio* (Jupiter Sabazius) are apparently

One way to push this interpretation – that ἐγ Διδύμων Δρυῶν tells us about this Zeus' identity and interests rather than his location – would be to ask how invested in oaks Zeus ἐγ Διδύμων Δρυῶν appears to be. Certainly in inscription B he is angered at Stratoneikos' cutting down of an oak, and in retrospect Stratoneikos calls this 'an oak of Double Zeus', suggesting that he now understands a strong relationship to exist between Zeus and the tree he cut down. The 'sacred wood' of inscription A also seems to refer to trees enjoying a relationship with Zeus ἐγ Διδύμων Δρυῶν, with his anger prompted by interference with them. It might be tempting to assume that these were trees close to the cult place of Zeus ἐγ Διδύμων Δρυῶν, perhaps forming a grove. An inscription from Sandal dated to 235–236 CE would seem to provide a useful parallel here, with its picture of how a Stratoneikos (again!) got in trouble for having cut down trees in the grove of Zeus Sabazius and Artemis Anaeitis (*TAM* 5.1 592).[54] Since this took place only a few miles away from the location of our inscriptions, could we assume from this that Zeus ἐγ Διδύμων Δρυῶν was also protecting his own grove? This is quite possible, but it is interesting that the moral Stratoneikos draws from his experiences is a blanket warning never to cut down *any* oak ever again, rather than a warning about a specific grove; nor is any sacred complex or grove connected with Zeus ἐγ Διδύμων Δρυῶν mentioned in either inscription A or B. Rhetorically exaggerated as Stratoneikos' new proclamation of piety towards the god might well be, he does seem to present the god as having a non-local sphere of arboreal influence, with an interest in every oak you might consider harming. With this in mind, it is also intriguing to ask what we should make of the fact that in the later inscriptions C–F Ζεὺς ἐγ Διδύμων Δρυῶν does not obviously appear as a god with an explicit interest in arboreal crimes. Frustratingly, none of the penitents in C–F confess what their crimes actually were, but what does this mean?

encircled with an oak wreath (*CIL* 14.2894). Could we not see this wreath as a visual equivalent to an epithet like ἐγ Διδύμων Δρυῶν, with both capturing something arboreal about the god's identity? Sadly I have not been able to view an image of this inscription, and according to Lane 1985: 33 its whereabouts are unknown.

[54] Lane 1989: 28 relies on this inscription to interpret an image of Jupiter Sabazius (Lane 1985: plate 35) in the corner of which stands a small man with an axe; he must be another 'opponent of the god'.

Arboreal epithets

Was Zeus ἐγ Διδύμων Δρυῶν a deity with more than one string to his bow, quite capable of being angered by non-arboreal sins, or does the surprising lack of specificity in these four inscriptions actually insist to the contrary that it was so obvious that Zeus ἐγ Διδύμων Δρυῶν only steps in to deal with arboreal matters that it was not worth stating? Due to our elliptical evidence, it is easier to ask than answer questions about the nature of the relationships envisaged between a deity and a tree, or trees, when those deities boast an arboreal epithet. Yet our conclusions from these encounters with such rarely heard of deities as Dionysus of the Fig or Zeus of the Twin Oaks should not only be to acknowledge a position of agnosticism. Firstly this foray into the world of arboreal epithets has, when the evidence suffices, shown us again how trees articulated something about the divine for those communities, enriching human understanding of the nature of the deities concerned by shading in an arboreal side to their identities. There is Zeus of the Twin Oaks, so like these oaks in the imagination of Stratoneikos that he can be thought of as 'double' Zeus. And there is Dionysus of the Fig, so called because he was the first to discover it, the epithet helping to preserve the god's past exploits in cultural memory. The second point to take home from our exploration of arboreal epithets builds on our thinking about gods and tree types. As Phaedrus and Pliny illustrated, some ancient thinkers attempted to tidy the world of deity–tree relationships with an authoritative list of which deities had concern for which trees. By contrast, these arboreal epithets show us that on the ground religious conceptions of deity–tree relationships were much messier than this. A far remove from Phaedrus' image of six canonical deity–tree relationships, these epithets reveal how a multitude of such relationships were constructed, and had their meaning, at the micro level of individual communities.

In particular, it is individual communities across Greece which we have seen imagining the world of deity–tree relationships quite differently from the way it is painted by more Roman-centric authors. Of course, the way Pausanias dominates our evidence for arboreal epithets is of clear influence here, and this may raise concerns about the applicability of his evidence.

Imagining the gods

We might worry that Pausanias represents a way of thinking about the world which should be considered more 'purely Greek' than 'multiculturally Roman' and that consequently his snapshots of deities like Artemis of the Cedar should not have much weight in an exploration of arboreal epithets within the Roman world.[55] Yet I do not think this would be a logical way to respond to the evidence. There is no reason to believe that constructing relationships between the arboreal world and the divine world through epithets like 'of the white poplar' was something peculiarly Greek: it just so happens that Pausanias waxes lyrical on a phenomenon which was clearly also important – to give but one example – to those inhabitants of Rome who called Venus 'of the Myrtle'. We are not here confronted by a distinctively Greek way of thinking, but rather by a uniquely Pausanian sense of priorities when it comes to ordering his world of information, in which the minutiae of local cult differences are of paramount importance. Our inevitable viewing of arboreal epithets through Pausanian eyes is something we have to think our way around, but it is not only a problem, it is also the reason that we get to see that messy variety of deity–tree relationships, of significance at a local level, which more Rome-centric sources may obscure.

Finally, in light of the lack of current scholarly sophistication when it comes to thinking about divine epithets, we should value the *unanswered* questions which these trees have raised for having brought them to our attention at all. Pliny and others understood Jupiter to be especially interested in oaks, yet in one part of Rome it seems he was so closely associated with a beech grove as to be called Jupiter Fagutalis. Was this Jupiter 'the same' as the one who was interested in oaks? Did Jupiters worshipped elsewhere in the empire have interests in beeches, if not the epithet? Whether we suppose ourselves here in the presence of 'different Jupiters', or different 'versions' of Jupiters, or different ways of fleshing out Jupiter's identity, with his multifaceted interest in trees, the situation gets yet more complicated when we turn to Lepreum, and wonder about the relationship of Zeus of the White

---

[55] On the temptation to see Pausanias as an idiosyncratic and 'purely Greek' voice, uncomfortably out of place in the world of the Roman empire, see pp. 24–25.

Arboreal epithets

Poplar to Jupiter Fagutalis. These seemingly conflicting arboreal epithets bring to the fore questions which must have underlain wider Roman thinking about the meaning and purpose of giving a god an epithet. In addition, they prompt us to consider the nature of the relationship between 'Greek gods' and 'Roman gods' in the Roman world, and to start to explore the huge theological questions underpinning the idea, so easily bandied around in textbook-style, that Minerva *was* the Roman Athena, or the Roman 'equivalent' of Athena.

From gods who take arboreal epithets, I turn now to one whose first name, as it were, is arboreal: this of course is Silvanus, whose name screams a connection with trees. Dorcey, who has devoted a book to this god, repeatedly emphasises this: 'as forest god, Silvanus embodied trees, tree branches and shrubs'; 'Silvanus' role as overseer of the woods (*silvae*) obviously is implicit in his name'; 'the tree was of prime importance in the worship of Silvanus'.[56] Thinking etymologically, we would indeed expect Silvanus to be the kind of god Dorcey paints, but the reason for his almost complete absence from my discussion so far is that evidence for this god, lightly attested in Latin literature but enjoying a strong inscriptional presence, does not often confront us with questions about his relationship with trees.[57] An Alpine inscription already discussed in detail, which invokes Silvanus as *semicluse* (half shut up) in a sacred ash (*CIL* 12.103) is the obvious exception; my discussion of the complex ways in which Silvanus was imagined to be materially associated with this tree will not be repeated here.[58] Certainly it is true that on many other occasions Silvanus is *associated* with woods.[59] Nemesianus addresses Silvanus as *nemorum ... potens* (ruler of groves; 2.56), whilst Plautus and Virgil mention a grove of Silvanus (*Aul.* 674; *Aen.* 8.600–601). Both Livy and Valerius Maximus report how an ominous voice emitting from

---
[56] Dorcey 1992: 18, 18 and 31.
[57] Dorcey 1992: 1 also notes the centrality of inscriptional evidence; hundreds of dedications survive.
[58] See pp. 87–89.
[59] See Dorcey 1992: 153 for a list of all literary references to Silvanus. Dorcey 1992: 17 notes with surprise that 'literary sources do not make clear which tree or plant was holy to Silvanus', but why would we expect this, especially with a god whose name evokes generic woods?

certain woods was understood to come from Silvanus (2.7.2; 1.8.5); Propertius calls a wood the *Silvani ramosa domus* (branchy home of Silvanus; 4.4.5) and Cato describes a sacrifice to Mars Silvanus which takes place in a wood (*Agr.* 83). Woods could be seen as a significant location to meet with Silvanus. Silvanus is also given arboreal interests, behaviour and qualities: Grattius has Silvanus rejoicing in uncultivated branches (20); in Virgil he pulls up a cypress by its roots (*G.* 1.20); both Horace and Martial describe him as *horridus* (bristling; *C.* 3.29.22; 10.92.6). None of this, however, really theorises the relationship between Silvanus and *silvae* (woods), or helps us to get to beyond bland comments like Servius' observation that Silvanus is a 'woodland god' (*deus est silvarum*; *G.* 1.20).

Moreover, in the inscriptional record, where Silvanus makes his presence most strongly felt, arboreal concerns very rarely seem at the forefront of the minds of those engaging with him. The best example of a dedicant engaging with him in consciously arboreal terms comes from Lugdunum, where Tiberius Claudius Chrestus records setting up an altar and statue for Silvanus *inter duos arbores* (between two trees; *CIL* 13.1780). By giving the god's 'representation' in Lugdunum this arboreal context, Chrestus articulates his understanding of trees' crucial contribution to Silvanus' identity. Two expansive verse inscriptions also contribute to an arboreal image of Silvanus. One (broken) inscription from Africa refers to Silvanus as *falciten(ens)* (sickle-holding), whilst something missing from the inscription, but clearly associated with him, is described as *pinifera* (pine-bearing); there is also talk of 'a grove springing from rock' (*gignitur e saxo lucus* (5); *CIL* 8.27764). An Italian inscription addresses Silvanus as having oversight of a grove and invokes him using a Virgilian citation, *teneram ab radice ferens Silvane cupressum adsis* (be present Silvanus, carrying the tender cypress by its roots; *CIL* 9.3375).[60] These inscribed poems display some imaginative ways of articulating Silvanus' association with trees, as he lugs around a cypress or stands

---

[60] The Virgilian line in question is *G.* 1.20. The rather baffling behaviour depicted here is hardly clarified by Servius' testimony (ad loc.) that Silvanus once loved a boy called Cyparissus, who metamorphosed into a cypress. Indeed this simply takes the image from the realm of the baffling to the surreal: Silvanus is carrying around his dead boyfriend?

Arboreal epithets

holding a sickle, perhaps poised to engage in some arboricultural work. Yet such depictions of Silvanus acting out an arboreal role are swamped by the vast number of (far briefer) inscriptions in which no arboreal connection is drawn out. Indeed, the fact that Silvanus is fairly often given the epithet *silvestris* (woodland) could be taken to suggest that his name alone, ironically, would not conjure up particularly strong arboreal connotations.[61] Even more surprisingly, on all the occasions when he is addressed as Silvanus Silvestris even then these inscriptions do not show us people approaching him with an overtly 'arboreal agenda'. At most we can point to a certain G. Titius Platanus (Mr Plane Tree) who made a vow to Silvanus Silvestris (*AE* 1962.120) and an estate slave, whose line of work might conceivably have given him a vested interest in woods, who did the same (*AE* 1938.168): but clearly these examples are scraping the barrel! It is also clear that people approached this god with quite other than arboreal concerns, as did M. Rubrius Felix and C. Iulius Ianuarius when they made a vow to an 'augmented' Silvanus Silvestris Augustus for the emperor's well-being (*CIL* 8.8248).

Silvestris is not, however, the only arboreal epithet which Silvanus ever adopts. One Manius Poblicius Hilarus, a dealer in pearls, once made a dedication to Silvanus Dendrophorus (*CIL* 6.641). This one-off title must remind us of Virgil's image of Silvanus carrying his cypress (as later copied in the Italian inscription), but the epithet also conjures up an image of a god taking part in a cult act, aping the *dendrophori* whose role it was to carry trees in the processions of Cybele. The Virgilian image and this 'matching' epithet suggest that one way to think about Silvanus was to imagine him as the 'prototype' tree carrier, a woody god who shared the interests and concerns of Cybele's tree-carrying attendants.[62] Indeed, that worshippers of Cybele might find themselves drawn to Silvanus is illustrated in a couple of inscriptions from Ostia, which introduce us to devotees of Cybele who also cultivated an active interest in Silvanus: the tombstone of Lucius Calpurnius Chius records his involvement in the *collegia* both of

---

[61] Dorcey 1992: 18 also discusses this epithet.
[62] Taylor 1912: 40 long ago cautiously suggested as much.

Silvanus and the *dendrophori* (*CIL* 14.309), whilst an *apparator* of Magna Deum Mater is proud to have set up a statue of Silvanus (*CIL* 14.53). This god called Woody was, perhaps, an obvious candidate for the tree carriers to appropriate as their own, although Attis too takes on a similar role when he is invoked as *genius dendroforum* (*genius* of the *dendrophori*) by a *dendrophorus* called Exuperans (*CIL* 8.7956).[63]

Many surviving inscriptions record dedications to Silvanus, but the evidence is hardly discursive; whatever thinking about the nature of Silvanus' relationship with trees lay behind these dedications goes unsaid. In general, our evidence for Silvanus makes him a surprisingly uninformative god for thinking about deities with arboreal identities. Yet on the rare occasions when the evidence is more giving, we get a glimpse of the varied and vibrant ways in which Roman thinkers imagined how a god called Woody stood in relationship to trees in the human world. Invoked as half shut up in a sacred ash, Silvanus forces us to imagine him enjoying a conceptually awkward relationship with a material tree. Given the epithet *dendrophorus*, he stands as a divine 'mirror image' of those whose tree-carrying enacts and commemorates the arboreal interests of another deity, visually articulating Cybele's own 'arboreal side'.

---

[63] Cybele, Attis and the *dendrophori* do not enjoy a large role in this book, which may occasion surprise. The reason for this absence is partly because the activities of the *dendrophori* are almost entirely known to us from hostile Christian sources. Evidence for a procession on 22 March in which the *dendrophori* carry pines – the day labelled *arbor intrat* (the tree enters) in the *Fasti* of Philocalus (produced in 354 CE) – comes from Firmicus Maternus (*Err.* 27.1) and Arnobius (*Ad. nat.* 5.16). (Vermaseren 1977a: 113–115 sets out what would have happened on this day, with no acknowledgement of the Christian bias of our sources.) Only occasional epigraphic glimpses offer pagan evidence of what this 'tree carrying' meant to those involved, like an Ostian inscription in which a man chooses to remember his brother, a late priest of Cybele, by noting that he *induxit arbores* (carried in trees; *AE* 1914.158). (Östenberg 2009: 187–188 briefly discusses the practice of carrying trees in triumphal processions.) Consequently, given the nature of the evidence, it is hard to say anything with confidence about what it is that the *dendrophori*'s tree carrying articulates about the nature of Cybele, or Attis. Perhaps at best we could point out that this ritual act reinforces the mythical associations of Cybele with the pine under which Attis died, or perhaps metamorphosed into (according to Ov. *Met.* 10.103–105). The *dendrophori* are well attested epigraphically but, predictably enough perhaps, these inscriptions do not tend to toy with theological thinking about the relationship of Cybele or Attis with the pine, or what it is that the act of tree carrying expresses about these two deities.

Arboreal statues

What is the difference between a statue and a tree? One Roman answer to this question would have been 'not much'. Indeed we often encounter Roman trees posing as though to all intents and purposes they were statues. In the *Anaglypha Traiani*, for example, we come face-to-face with what is either a statue of a fig tree, or a fig imagined as growing out of a pedestal and thus framed in 'statue-like' terms (Figure 3). The other monuments surrounding this fig invariably prompt scholars to identify it as the *ficus Ruminalis*, so in this case it is usually assumed that we are looking at a tree rather than a statue, but bizarrely the fact that this 'tree' appears to be 'growing out of' a pedestal has not occasioned any scholarly comment.[64] The fig also stands adjacent to an anthropomorphic statue (often identified as Marsyas) on its own pedestal, a visual parallel which should further draw attention to the statue-like role this tree is being made to play. Nor is this fig on a pedestal in the *Anaglypha Traiani* a completely freak phenomenon.[65]

[64] That the top of the block or pedestal is depicted as solid rules out the possibility that this is a tree planted in a tub. See Kleiner 1992: 248–250 for an overview of the intense scholarly debate concerning both the date of these reliefs (some call them the *Anaglypha Hadriani*) and the identification of the monuments depicted. Torelli 1982: 95–96 provides a summary of his reconstruction of the monuments depicted on the reliefs.

[65] In the background of a painting from *casa* VII.2.18 in Pompeii another tree appears to sprout from a pedestal; for a drawing of the fresco (which is in a damaged state) see Blanckenhagen and Alexander 1990: plate 61. I also want to consider briefly here an artistic motif found on many votives and funerary monuments from Thrace and Macedonia during Roman rule: a young male figure on horseback takes up several different poses in these reliefs, but a common one has him facing a tree, with a snake looping itself round the trunk. The identity of this figure is very much up for debate: a hero, Asclepius, Sabazios, an underworld god? (See Dimitrova 2002: 210 for an overview of the many interpretations put forward.) Mitropoulou 1996: 42 represents one standard approach to this elusive figure by giving him the vague label of 'mounted god or hero'. The tree – which is of course the focus of my interest in these images – sometimes appears to stand behind or to the side of a small cube-shaped block (e.g. Dimitrova 2002: fig. 6), sometimes on top of it (e.g. Dimitrova 2002: figs. 1 and 2). It is standard to assume that this is an altar for a sacred tree (on which see Dimitrova 2002: 214), but in images such as Dimitrova's figures 1 and 2 we may well wonder whether it is the limitations of working in stone which result in a tree which looks as if it is sprouting out of the 'block', or whether the tree was being thought about in statue-like terms. Of particular interest here is a relief from Tomis in which Cybele appears alongside the Thracian horseman and his tree: due to our hazy understanding of the Thracian horseman it is hard to say why he and Cybele would choose to spend time in each other's company, but we may hypothesise that his close visual association with a tree was part of his allure to the pine-loving Cybele (for the image see Vermaseren 1977a: image 77). Mitropoulou 1996: 142 is confident that what we see here is a rectangular altar and behind it a tree,

Imagining the gods

FIGURE 3 Detail from the *Anaglypha Traiani*, Rome, depicting a forum scene and fig tree identified as the *ficus Ruminalis*.
Copyright: su concessione del Ministero dei beni e delle attività culturali e del turismo – Soprintendenza Speciale per il Colosseo, il Museo Nazionale Romano e l'Area archaeologica di Roma.

Viewers of a Pompeian fresco from *casa* VII.9.47 are also encouraged to imagine a tree in statue-like terms (Figure 4).[66] The tree, however, is not the immediate visual focus of attention. Instead we are drawn to a female figure, with crown and sceptre, who stands proud and tall inside a four-columned temple, flanked by two smaller figures. On the steps of this temple stands Hercules (with tell-tale club and lion skin), offering his hand to a woman. On the left-hand side of the image a procession moves away from the temple; on the right hand side a procession approaches: the members carry various objects, the larger ones resting on four-legged

but the presence of Cybele with her known arboreal interests – and about whom we know so much more than the 'rider god' – could encourage us to read the visual monumentalisation of the tree by means of its 'block base' as a comment on the significance of the tree to both divine figures.

[66] This house is given various names; the most common are *casa delle nozze di Ercole* and *casa di Marte e Venere*. The fresco in question is now in an extremely damaged state, and we rely on drawings and archived photographs taken by S. A. Jashemski in 1961.

Arboreal statues

FIGURE 4 Fresco from the *oecus* (north wall) of *casa* VII.9.47, Pompeii, depicting a cult procession.
Copyright: Soprintendenza Archeologica di Pompei. Upon authorisation for the Ministry of Cultural Heritage and Environment. Reproduction or duplication by any means is forbidden.
Photo credits: Kenneth Walton.

fercula (frames/stretchers used in processions). This image has been variously interpreted: Ryberg sees it as a wedding procession, 'lifted to the realm of allegory or cult significance' by depicting the bride and groom as Hercules and Iuventas; in similar vein, Della Corte reads the image as a ritual acting out of Hercules and Iuventas' wedding during the Iuvenalia.[67] Perhaps by extension of such readings, the goddess in the temple is commonly seen as Venus, but her identification seems most strongly secured by the likelihood that Venus, 'patron deity' of Pompeii, would feature prominently in a Pompeian wall painting.[68] Herbig also sees the goddess as Venus, but reads the image not in nuptial terms but as an *exauguratio* of Venus (conducted by Hercules) in favour of Isis, the new goddess whose cult – he argues – symbolically arrives with the procession in the right-hand side of the picture, led by a woman who appears to be holding a *sistrum* (rattle), used in Isis' noisy worship.[69]

---

[67] Ryberg 1955: 169; Della Corte 1924: 94–95.
[68] Tran Tam Tinh 1964: 132 confidently refers to her as 'Venus Pompeiana', as does Della Corte 1924: 92. And once we see this figure as Venus, we then notice that Priapus can be made out to one side of her, whilst a more shadowy figure on her other side is often read as an Amor, as, for example, do Tran Tam Tinh 1964: 132 and Herbig 1939: 54.
[69] Herbig 1939: 54. Östenberg 2009: 188 also confidently sees an Isiaic procession here; Tran Tam Tinh 1964: 132 is more hesitant. As Hackworth Petersen 2006: 36–37 notes, an association between Venus and Isis was felt particularly strongly at Pompeii, which could encourage such interpretations. Yet bar the *sistrum*, I see no other or more compelling iconographic reasons for following an Isiaic line of thought.

Imagining the gods

For me, the identification of the figures on the steps as Hercules and Iuventas is iconographically convincing, but there is not such overwhelming support for seeing the goddess as Venus: perhaps this image also invites us to see her as Cybele. According to Coralini, the crown and sceptre identify Venus in her role as patroness of Pompeii, but Cybele also often wears a crown, encouraging the viewer to play with other possibilities.[70] And then there is the yet to be discussed tree: one of the *fercula* carried in the procession supports a tree, with a snake curling round its trunk. Della Corte interprets this tree as a wedding present for Hercules, a statue representing his labour against the snake who guarded the golden-apple tree in the garden of the Hesperides.[71] Yet, as we watch two men walking along with what looks like a tree on a table, we might also see in this striking detail an engagement with the tree-carrying ritual of Cybele's *dendrophori*.[72] The snake twisting around the tree trunk would suggest that we understand this as a statue of a tree, rather than the more fantastical scenario of a live tree (with live snake) being carried on a *ferculum*, but this does not rule out the possibility that the tree-statue in this fresco conjures up Cybele and her *dendrophori* in the viewers' imaginations: we know so little of what her tree-carrying ceremony entailed, and 'know' what we do know only from Christian apologists, that we cannot confidently discount the possibility that it was arboreal statues which were carried.[73] This iconographically dense image draws its viewers down multiple avenues of interpretation, and has much left to give, but for my current purposes the conclusion I wish to draw is simple: if the tree we see carried on a *ferculum* is not a statue of a tree, it is certainly posing hard as one.

---

[70] Coralini 2001: 204. Tran Tam Tinh 1964: 132 notes the crown as well, simply seeing the goddess as a crowned Venus.

[71] Della Corte 1924: 93. Coralini 2001: 204 also reads the tree as a representation of Hercules' labour.

[72] On our evidence for the dendrophori see n. 63, above. Whilst the idea of Hercules and Iuventas getting married on the steps of Cybele's temple may at first seem rather odd, this becomes less so when we realise that temples of Cybele and Iuventas were associated by virtue of their being dedicated in the same year, 191 BCE (Liv. 36.36). De Vos 1980: 20 briefly describes this tree bound with a snake, as does Tran Tam Tinh 1964: 133. De Vos 1980: 20 interprets the tree as an Egyptianising, and possibly Isiaic-coloured, motif.

[73] Östenberg 2009: 188, by contrast, sees here not a statue of a tree, but 'a sacred tree carried upright on a *ferculum*'.

Arboreal statues

A few literary texts also undeniably show us statues of trees: a golden olive statue, the work of Pygmalion, was kept in a temple of Heracles and famed for the verisimilitude of its branches and its fruit, covered as it was in emeralds (Philost. *VA*. 5.5). Athenaeus describes a lavish procession in which were carried seven gilded palm trees (*Deip*. 5.202c); did they, we might wonder, come on individual four-legged bases as the tree being carried along in the Pompeian fresco? Plutarch tells us how Nicias dedicated a bronze palm tree as an offering at Delos (*Nic*. 3.6), and at Delphi too there stood another bronze palm in the treasure house of the Corinthians, with frogs and water snakes around the base (*De Pyth. or*. 399F). Besides, statues, columns and trees are also blurred in Roman art, hardly surprising perhaps in a culture in which architectural legend has it that the Corinthian column was modelled on an acanthus plant (Vitr. 4.1.9–10). In a fresco from the *casa di Livia*, for example, a column is embraced by a tree, and on occasion these biform tree-columns are also seen emerging from pedestals, as in a painting from *casa* V.2.10 in Pompeii and also from the *Aula Isiaca* in Rome, thus further blurring the forms of tree, column and statue.[74]

Complementing these artistic blurrings, literary texts also frame trees in statue-like terms. Horace uses the verb *statuere*, commonly used for erecting a statue (*OLD* §4), to describe the planting of a tree (*C*. 2.13.10). Pan too, frustrated in love by an unwilling nymph, plants a tree as a 'memorial' (*pignus memorabile*) of the event, using the verb *deponere* (Stat. *Silv*. 2.3.43).[75] The standard meaning of this verb is simply to put down, but Statius' use of it seems to combine two rarer meanings: firstly to plant (*OLD* §5a), and secondly to set up a monument (*OLD* §5b). Pan is obviously planting a tree, but his emphasis on its memorial function works to draw out the monumental connotations of *deponere*. Statius' unusual choice

---

[74] See Blanckenhagen and Alexander 1990: plate 52 for the *casa di Livia* image. For a drawing of the Pompeian fresco, which is no longer extant, see Dawson 1965: image 23a. Peters 1963: image 38 reproduces the fresco from the *Aula Isiaca*.

[75] The only other glimpse of a Roman deity actively involved in planting which I have encountered is the possible 'Planter god' mentioned by Varro, if that is how the address to Cozevi, which he quotes from the hymn of the Salians, should be interpreted (*LL*. 7.26). On this reading Cozevi is taken to be a vocative of Consivius. In Stoic thought planting is used as an analogy for understanding the nature of god (e.g. Cic. *Nat. d*. 2.86). Similar ideas are found in Dio Chrysostom 12.29 and Philo *Plant*. 2.

of verb thus paints Pan's act as a kind of planting-cum-dedication. Planting aside, an ancient holm oak on the Vatican hill in Rome is also pushed towards the category of statue when Pliny describes a bronze tablet with an Etruscan inscription which is attached to it. With its inscribed plaque, this tree starts to look very much like a dedicated statue or votive object: indeed it is thanks to the inscription, Pliny states, that we know the tree is 'worthy of religious honour' (*religione ... dignam*; *Nat.* 16.237).[76] Trees are also framed as statue-like objects in two poems which put a tree at the heart of their idealised images of domestic religion, as each tree takes up a place among the *penates*. Statius roots his tree among statues of the household gods in the villa of Manilius Vopiscus, with which it is visually entangled on the page, *mediis servata penatibus arbor* (a tree preserved in the midst of the *penates*; *Silv.* 1.3.59). Martial also depicts a plane, planted by Caesar in the middle of a house at Cordoba, as being entangled with these statues, *totos amplexa penates* (embracing all the *penates*; 9.61.5). We might well be reminded here of Augustus' desire to transport a palm sapling from the pavement outside his house to be in the *conpluvium* alongside his *penates* (Suet. *Aug.* 92.1).[77]

So far we have met trees which stand in statue-like poses, as well as occasional statues of trees: this Roman tendency to think of trees and statues as similar or overlapping forms constitutes the intellectual background against which I wish to discuss various blurrings of trees and statues in the Roman world, which work to articulate something about the identity of a god. Firstly I briefly return to two deities previously singled out for their arboreal epithets – namely Artemis of the Cedar and Asclepius of the Agnus Castus – to think about how these epithets were articulated artistically. Pausanias' portrait of the statue of Asclepius of the Agnus Castus is brief: we are simply told that it was made out of *agnus castus* (3.14.7). Here is one straightforward way of visually reinforcing the relationship between Asclepius and the *agnus castus*, as drawn by his epithet.[78]

---

[76] See Kruschwitz 2010 on the literary evidence for the Greco-Roman practice of inscribing tree trunks, which again frames trees as 'monuments'.
[77] For previous discussion of which see p. 217.
[78] Platt 2011: 99 notes of this Asclepius statue that the *agnus castus* was 'well known for its healing properties', although with no further references.

Arboreal statues

The statue of Artemis of the Cedar at Orchomenos in Arcadia is, however, conceptually more complicated. As Pausanias points out, this statue stands on no ordinary pedestal (8.13.2).[79] In fact it 'is set up' (the verb used, ἵδρυται, is standard for erecting a statue) in a large cedar tree, and for this reason they call it Artemis of the Cedar. Intriguingly, Pausanias ascribes the deity's epithet to the statue's location, rather than the epithet prompting such an unusual choice of home for a statue. The epithet articulates an understanding of a relationship between a deity and a tree which is of very much local significance, with no suggestion of Artemis and the cedar's connection outside of Orchomenos. When he writes τὴν θεὸν ὀνομάζουσιν ἀπὸ τῆς κέδρου Κεδρεᾶτιν (they call the goddess 'of the cedar' from the cedar tree), he is referring to this one specific tree in Orchomenos. This particular Artemis worshipped in Orchomenos enjoys such a close physical relationship with this particular cedar that it was only fitting for her to take the tree's name.

This Artemis' identity is deeply bound up with the cedar in which she stands, but there is still *some* distance between her and the tree, both physical and conceptual. Pausanias gives no reason to believe that this Artemis' statue is not anthropomorphic, but on other occasions trees blur so strongly with statues of the gods in Roman thought as to result in forms which hesitate between that of 'god' and that of tree. Depictions of these ambiguous tree-statue forms can be part and parcel of the characterisation of 'primitive' religion, whether this means the religious practices of foreigners or the early, rustic days of Rome's own religious

---

[79] Pausanias uses ξόανον of this statue, which *may* mean it is made of wood. Donohue 1988 has argued against a common assumption that the term ξόανα refers to archaic wooden statues, showing that the assumption stems from a relatively late construction (both polemic and antiquarian) of early Greek art and religion, channeled largely through Plutarch, Pausanias and Clement. Indeed Donohue believes that ξόανα are always wooden in Pausanias' worldview (140–147), pointing to his 'peculiarity' (145) and explaining this as part of 'the sober antiquarian purpose of his project' (147). This is rather an oddly dogmatic stance, given her emphasis on widening the meaning of ξόανον throughout her extensive examination of the term (9–174), and seems driven at least in part by her acknowledged debt to Bennett 1917, who believes we have evidence for at least sixty wooden statues in Pausanias. I do not find Donohue's conviction convincing: certainly Pausanias' claim at 8.17.1 does not have to mean that, in his eyes, *all* ξόανα were made of wood, only that in early times wood was used (pace Donohue 1988: 140–141).

traditions. Representing the former, Lucan depicts the divine statues of the locals at Massilia as crudely carved images which barely extrude from the tree trunks of which they were made: *arte carent caesisque extant informia truncis* (shapeless and artless they jut out from the hewn trunks; 3.413). Dio Chrysostom also attributes the fact that barbarians call δένδρα ἀργά (unworked trees) gods to their πενίᾳ τε καὶ ἀπορίᾳ τέχνης (lack of means and artistic ability; *Or.* 12.61).[80] Representing the latter, Pliny insists that in the good old days Rome's 'statues of the gods were made of trees' (*arborea et simulacra numinum fuere*; *Nat.* 12.5): by not simply labelling them 'wooden', he suggests that the statues he is imagining are noticeably tree-like in form.[81] Apuleius too includes in his list of objects which would delay a pious old-fashioned traveller in the countryside a 'tree trunk shaped into an image by carving' (*truncus dolamine effigiatus*; *Fl.* 1).[82] Yet thinkers in the Roman world did not only engage with tree-statue forms when passing art-historical and religious comment on other times and cultures. Theological issues much closer to home concerning the relationship between deities and trees were also at stake in their imagining of how trees and statues of the divine might morph.

Since Gordon's seminal analysis of Greco-Roman thinking about the representational status of statues of the gods, it has been hard to ignore the theological issues bound up with the omnipresence

---

[80] On this simple equation of tree and god when characterising the religion of 'the other' cf. Maximus of Tyre's comments on Celtic arboreal statues: 'the Celts' statue of Zeus *is* a lofty oak' (ἄγαλμα δὲ Διὸς Κελτικὸν ὑψηλὴ δρῦς; 2.8).

[81] In the context of a passage about the *uses* of trees, 'made of trees' seems the best translation of *arborea*. Since Boetticher 1856: 11 trees have been viewed as primitive precursors of statues in Greco-Roman culture, as argued by Freedberg 1989: 70–74, whilst Stackelberg 2009: 35 similarly sees trees as the original inspiration for columns. This evolutionary model of statue development has, however, more recently been challenged, for example by Donohue 1988: 191–194 and *passim* and Steiner 2001: 81–85. Steiner does argue for a blurring of tree and statue in Greek thought, but one which is present throughout the history of archaic and classical Greece, not just its early stages; this she does by examining visual images which 'imagine gods and goddesses barely differentiated from the tree trunk used for the modeling' (85).

[82] This, it seems, was not an unusual way to think about 'rustic' statues. As I have argued in Hunt 2011, statues of the deity Priapus, in his role as garden-guardian, are also blurred with trees in Roman literature and art. A Greek epigram which depicts a figwood statue of Pan (a god with strong countryside 'associations') is also described as having 'the bark left on' (αὐτόφλοιον; *AG.* 6.99.1).

Arboreal statues

of statues of the gods in the Greco-Roman world.[83] Was a statue of Apollo in fact Apollo himself? Or was it a 'mere' representation of Apollo? In practice Greco-Roman thinkers often found themselves somewhere between these two extremes: the nature of individual statues of a god – and their relationship to the god in question – was deeply contested. Imagine, then, how much more contested this became when the 'statues' in question were part anthropomorphic, part arboreal! Before we can ask where such a statue sat on this scale between 'being' and 'representing', we have to face a more fundamental question: what was it a statue *of*? Unsurprisingly it is Pausanias, known for his interest in the ambiguous status of statues of gods, who provides us with an insight into one such conceptually complex 'arboreal statue' of the divine.[84] In Temnos, Pausanias writes, there stands 'an image of Aphrodite made of a flourishing myrtle', dedicated by Pelops when he was asking the goddess for Hippodamia as wife (Ἀφροδίτης ἄγαλμα ... πεποιημένον ἐκ μυρσίνης τεθηλυίας; 5.13.7). For Philpot this ἄγαλμα (image) was 'wrought out of a fresh verdant myrtle-tree'; for Hersey 'Pelops carved a statue of the goddess *from* a myrtle'; for Dowden the statue was 'made from "a flourishing myrtle"', prompting him to note that any 'substantial wooden statue inevitably must be made from a tree trunk'.[85] Yet Pausanias' odd emphasis that the myrtle is 'flourishing' (τεθηλυίας) complicates reading this passage, as Philpot, Hersey and Dowden do, as a description of a statue made from a tree. The adjective τεθηλυίας (flourishing) suggests that the statue was understood still to be alive; this was essentially a tree which had undergone a little carving, and thus was as conceptually close to a tree as a statue.[86] I would not, however, go as far as Boetticher, who denies any artistic interference with the tree whatsoever, summing up the passage as follows: 'ein Myrtenbaum von ihm [Pelops] gepflanzt und geweiht

---

[83] Gordon 1979. See discussion on pp. 80–81.
[84] As previously mentioned on p. 80, Elsner 2007: 44 holds up Pausanias for presenting to us 'a much more dynamic interpenetration of image and referent, representation and prototype, than we usually allow for' when thinking about statues of the divine.
[85] Philpot 1897: 32; Hersey 1988: 11; Dowden 2000: 69. Bennett 1917: 83 also makes the same assumption.
[86] I now recognise that my attempt in Hunt 2011: 42, n. 33 to negotiate this awkwardness by seeing τεθηλυίας as metaphorical was to take the wrong angle of approach.

vertrat das Bild der Aphrodite', a position now echoed by Platt.[87] Rather Pausanias' bizarre phrase 'flourishing statue' shows us that this was not a myrtle-wood statue, nor a myrtle tree, but something in between the two. As we know from Phaedrus' allocation of the myrtle to Aphrodite's patronage (3.17), and Pliny's mention of an altar to *Venus Myrtea* (Venus of the Myrtle; *Nat.* 15.121), it was common for Aphrodite to be imagined in relationship with this genus. This liminal tree-statue visually captured Aphrodite's close relationship with the myrtle, an earthly embodiment of this arboreal side to her identity.

An omen involving destructive crows ensures we have three testimonies to another striking arboreal statue, dedicated by the Athenians at Delphi after victories against the Persians (Paus. 10.15.4; Plut. *Nic.* 13.3; Plut. *De Pyth. or.* 397F); considering the significance of these victories for Athenian cultural identity it is of little surprise that all three testimonies are in Greek. The statue in question is a bronze palm attached to which is a gold image of Athena. Pausanias personally blames thieves, not ominous crows, for the damage done to the gold, but notes that according to Cleitodemus the crows broke off the spear, owls and imitation fruit.[88] Plutarch also draws our attention to the fruit, although his accounts of its fate are contradictory: on one occasion we are told that ravens bit off its gold fruit (*Nic.* 13.3), on another that the fruit – this time specified as dates – dropped off the palm tree, whilst the ravens were only responsible for pecking the shield (*De Pyth. or.* 397F). Details of the attack aside, we have here an image of a bronze palm tree, complete with dates, attached to which is a gold image of Athena, complete with spear, shield and owls. This happens to be the third bronze palm we have met through Plutarch, and it is not hard to imagine that the palm's associations with victory prompted the dedication of such statues, in this case in gratitude for successes against the Persians. That Plutarch dates the crow attack to the time of the disastrous Sicilian expedition also supports thinking of the palm as a representation of Athenian military power, which at this moment was reeling from a heavy

---

[87] Boetticher 1856: 448; Platt 2011: 99.
[88] Cameron 2004: 236 briefly discusses Pausanias' potential sources for this anecdote.

blow (*De Pyth. or.* 397F). Yet this is no straightforward statue of a palm tree. Rather it adopts an uneasy position between arboreal and anthropomorphic form, with its attached gold image of Athena. On the one hand the meaning of this hybrid statue seems obvious: victory for the Athenians, as represented by the palm, is closely linked to their protecting goddess Athena. Yet the striking form which emerges is also conceptually challenging.[89] With statues of the divine we are used to being able to ask questions (if not to give confident answers) about ways in which it was understood to 'represent' the deity concerned. Statues like this hybrid Athena-palm certainly complicate such questions. Helpful here, I find, is Steiner's analysis of how aniconic images of deities communicate their meaning: these images, she argues, can 'promote contacts between men and gods not by resembling the immortals, but by being directly associated with one facet or characteristic of the divinity whom they represent'.[90] This statue at Delphi is hardly aniconic: to the contrary it is doubly iconic, a hybrid form which is loaded with the 'additional extras' of owl, shield and spear. Yet in a similar way this statue communicates to us something about the identity of the Athena imagined by the Athenians who dedicated it and by subsequent visitors to Delphi. Palms mean victory: this statue communicates to the viewer that victory is so ingrained a part of who Athena is that her statue hesitates between anthropomorphic and arboreal form.

Be it an Athena-cum-palm, a flourishing myrtle-cum-Aphrodite or an Artemis who takes her name from her seat in a tree, we have seen how trees can add a layer of complexity to the way in which statues communicate divine identities to a human audience. From the expression of local ideas about the nature of Artemis at Orchomenos, to Athenian presentation of their understanding of Athena on the world stage at Delphi, these goddesses have been given fresh colour and definition by the blurring of their statues with trees.

---

[89] Striking, certainly, to us: yet it is interesting that neither Plutarch nor Pausanias expresses any surprise at the hybrid nature of the statue – their attention is reserved for the crows – suggesting perhaps that such tree-deity statue combinations were more common than we might think.

[90] Steiner 2001: 85.

Trees in cult space

When Tiberius Claudius Chrestus dedicated a statue of Silvanus *inter duos arbores* (between two trees; *CIL* 13.1780) he consciously created an arboreal context for the focus of his cult actions. For him, worshipping this woody god required an arboreal environment. Chrestus' dedication thus provides a miniature *exemplum* to lead us into this final section, in which I examine how trees contributed to cult spaces, fleshing out the imagined identity of the deities worshipped within them. In a relief from the arch of Constantine, for example, we encounter a more formal version of Chrestus' homely dedication. Behind an altar stands a large base, topped with a statue of Apollo and tripod, and behind that a tree which provides Apollo with a leafy backdrop; the leaves, moreover, look very much like laurel (Figure 5).[91] The presence of this tree in an imagined space for cult consolidates Apollo's well-known interest in the laurel, reminding the viewer of his arboreal side. Nothing about this is particularly subtle or surprising, but in the paintings, reliefs and texts which provide the material for the following discussion, we meet trees which contribute in far more complex and imaginative ways to the meaning of cult spaces. Archaeological evidence, however, will not feature in this discussion, which may come as a surprise considering my focus on cult sites: to clear the ground, I start by explaining why.

Over a century ago Spano excitedly excavated an altar in the peristyle of *casa* VII.6.28 in Pompeii.[92] With no remains of a cult statue or *lararium* nearby, but only the root cavity of a once impressive tree, he concluded that here was a precious glimpse of Roman tree worship: 'vediamo con evidenza, che questo era un albero sacro e quella un'ara costruita espressamente presso l'albero, per sacrificare dinanzi alla stesso'.[93] This conclusion is clearly methodologically suspect, based as it is on absence of evidence and hampered by the fact that Pompeian gardens tend to be small, meaning that proximity in such a space is not necessarily meaningful. No doubt Spano would have been disappointed to

---

[91] See Brilliant 1974: 125–128 for a general introduction to the iconography of the arch.
[92] For his account of the excavation see Spano 1910: 466–467.
[93] Spano 1910: 467.

FIGURE 5 Detail from the Arch of Constantine, Rome, depicting a statue of Apollo with laurel tree behind.
Copyright: PRISMA ARCHIVO / Alamy Stock Photo.

learn of Jashemski's later extensive excavations of urban gardens at Pompeii in which she identified several lone altars, but no tree-root cavities accompanying them.[94] In recent years, however, with techniques for excavating tree roots developing, the momentum for identifying sacred trees on the basis of tree-root cavities has picked up. Excavations of the sanctuary of Juno at Gabii, that of Hercules at Tivoli and the temple of Venus at Pompeii have all led to the positing of 'sacred groves' within these cult sites.[95] Of course, on my loose definition of a sacred tree – as one which intersects with Roman religious practices or thinking about the divine – it is more than possible that some, or even all, of the trees

[94] On which see Jashemski 1979: 133–134.
[95] See Coarelli 1993: 48–51 on Gabii; Coarelli 1987: 89–90 and Reggiani 1998: 36 on Tivoli; Carroll: 2010 on Pompeii.

Imagining the gods

which stood within a temple's grounds were sacred. Yet for me, these excavations have yet to unearth any evidence which *urges* us to understand the trees in question as sacred; the working assumption – inadequate in my eyes – seems to be that trees within temples and sanctuaries were sacred simply by virtue of their location. Were such trees understood to be of religious significance, part of the way in which you express your worship of a deity at a particular site? Or was their integration into the cult site more utilitarian than that? Is their shady presence to be explained away by a gesture to the Mediterranean climate, or, as Boetticher would have argued, was it the usefulness of arboreal products in various rituals that guaranteed their presence on site?[96] The nature of the archaeological evidence does not allow us to push such questions, and consequently is not given space in the following discussion.[97] What these tree-root excavations have contributed here, however, is to open up a theoretical question which underpins the following discussion: was the presence of a tree within cult space meaningful or not?

Before we dive into this discussion, however, further reflection on the type of evidence privileged here is necessary: my heavy reliance on sacro-idyllic landscapes means that we must start on a note of warning. This genre, which emerged in the Augustan period, presents to us highly idealised images of rural landscapes, punctuated by shrines, altars, votive offerings and attendant worshippers. Distinctive in style, these images have been characterised as a 'nexus of contradictions' and have a dream-like quality to them, as Zanker's attempt at a 'summary' of the style illustrates:

> The little landscapes are remarkably constructed. The individual elements do not compose a unified pictorial space, but are simply set beside one another, as in Chinese landscape painting. As a result, the views have a peculiar, floating quality, and the lack of a frame gives them the character of a vision or epiphany. Artists were more concerned with communicating a certain atmosphere than with rendering specific details. But these new idylls are full of contradictions. In this highly sophisticated society, sated in luxury, painters could only imagine the simple

---

[96] For example, Boetticher 1856: 13–14. In Boetticher's eyes this role as provider of 'ritual products' also guaranteed their sacrality.
[97] For a *possible* exception regarding the archaeological evidence for one tree at Tivoli, see the arguments of Coarelli 1993.

Trees in cult space

pastoral life against a background of elegant parks and villas. The simple stone altar stands in front of extravagant and exotic religious architecture and lavish votive offerings ... We are presented with nostalgic visions combining the very real urge for a quiet weekend in the country villa with the imagined longing for a simpler and harmonious way of life. Rustic piety and the pastoral idyll are the poetic metaphors for this life.[98]

For Zanker these paintings construct images of rural religion by means of an unreal mish-mash of architectural elements and impossible contrasts (the simple stone altar versus exotic religious architecture), all saturated with a sense of Golden Age nostalgia for the rural life. Drawn to the language of 'poetic metaphor' when thinking about these images – which he elsewhere terms 'bucolic fantasies' – Zanker does not inspire confidence in those who might wish to use these landscapes as an insight into Roman theological thinking.[99]

Indeed, concern as to whether these images are a valid source for the student of Roman religion has made itself widely felt. For Dowden 'such religion as might be found in painted landscapes' is hollow and fake; it 'scarcely rises above the kitsch'.[100] Leach has also emphasised that 'religion' in these landscapes is heavily constructed, and that what we see in them is sophisticated urban commentary rather than rural religious practice. Like Zanker she also turns to an analogy with poetry to suggest how these images distort 'real religion':

> Existing at a midpoint between design and reality, these precincts are to be equated with religious sentiment only in the qualified sense that the Fons Bandusiae ode capitalizes upon the sacrificial occasion conventionalized within the traditions of its subject and form.[101]

Certainly these images hardly provide 'photographs' of cult sites and practices, but what they do show us is how Roman thinkers (both the artist and the viewers) might imagine the role and significance of trees within cult sites. That Zanker was drawn to describe these images' effect in terms of a religious experience, as having

---

[98] Evans 2008: 22; Zanker 1988: 287.
[99] Zanker 1988: 285.
[100] Dowden 2000: 99.
[101] Leach 1988: 230.

'the character of a vision or epiphany', offers a valuable insight into their power to shape Roman thinking about the intersection of trees and the world of the divine.[102] As such these sacro-idyllic landscapes are of vital importance for my purposes, with the crucial caveat that they show us theological thinking about trees, not religious practice in action.

This caveat is crucial because those scholars who have turned their attention specifically to the depiction of trees in sacro-idyllic landscapes have been far less cautious about what these might contribute to our understanding of Roman religion than have Zanker, Leach and Dowden, as Peters here illustrates:

> On the paintings discussed in the preceding we saw trees which were found to have a special significance. This was apparent from their standing within a more or less elaborate enclosure, or from their being depicted in combination with a porta sacra, a column with the statue of a deity, or with an altar ... It also seems obvious that both in Italy and elsewhere the sacred trees were protected by an enclosure and that the scholae we here see on the paintings were inspired by real examples encountered by the painter in his immediate surroundings.[103]

Ferguson is only slightly more cautious: these images must have 'some basis in fact', rather than being 'inspired by real examples'.

> In general the frescoes portraying country scenes show us an aspect of the countryside which is sometimes forgotten. Nearly always there is a shrine, or a sacred tree; often there is a procession of worshippers ... When all allowance has been made for a standardized 'sacral-idyllic' style of painting, there must be some basis in fact; the countryside was littered with holy places ... One could hardly have taken a step outdoors without meeting a little shrine, a sacred enclosure, an image, a sacred stone, or a sacred tree.[104]

Both Peters and Ferguson were writing around two decades before Zanker, yet thinking about trees in sacro-idyllic constructions of sacred space did not noticeably change even with the advent of scepticism like Zanker's, as Farrar here illustrates:

> A gnarled old tree often completes this romantic setting, and is usually found to the side of the building where its canopy would shade the building and worshippers who had ventured this distance. Sometimes the tree appears actually to be

---

[102] Zanker 1988: 287.
[103] Peters 1963: 44–45.
[104] Ferguson 1970: 67.

Trees in cult space

growing inside the building or a small walled enclosure, implying that the tree itself was sacred.[105]

That these landscapes show us 'sacred trees' is simply taken for granted, with both Peters and Farrar confident that there are telltale signs of a sacred tree: it will be 'depicted in combination with a porta sacra, a column with the statue of a deity, or with an altar' or appear 'actually to be growing inside the building or a small walled enclosure'.

Trees in such positions are indeed omnipresent in sacro-idyllic wall paintings and reliefs. Trees stand within stone enclosures, either alone or 'in combination with' small shrines, statues and columns. Others burst out of a tetrastylon or find themselves entangled with a structure known as a *porta sacra* (consisting of two columns topped by an architrave), their branches stretching up through the spaces between columns.[106] Peters, Ferguson and Farrar would doubtless assume all these trees to be sacred in Roman eyes, but we are not in a position to read these images so confidently.[107] Certainly in some such images trees are foregrounded so as to become the focal point of the landscape. In a fresco from the House of Apollo in Pompeii, for example, the way the tree is encased in its stone circular wall suggests that, within the imagined world of the landscape, it is treated as something of significance in its own right (Figure 6). Yet to assume that it must be of religious significance is to take a step further than the nature of the image allows. Even when the tree forms part of a landscape where religious 'motifs' (such as altars and offerings) are prominent, the role of the tree is invariably hard to discern. I illustrate by means of one famous image from the villa at Boscotrecase. Here a cluster of objects form the centrepiece of the landscape: a column topped with an amphora, a seated (bronze?) statue and

---

[105] Farrar 1998: 60.
[106] For examples see Blanckenhagen and Alexander 1990: plates 13 and 61, Peters 1963: images 9, 56, 57, 141, 175 and 176 and Dawson 1965: images 7, 17 and 43.
[107] Dall'Olio 1989: 516 assumes that all trees twisting through *portae sacrae* are sacred, thanks to their close involvement with this architectural feature. Yet the term *porta sacra* is itself misleading. How do we *know* these structures were of religious significance, especially considering that they are unattested outside visual sources, leaving it to us to coin for them this Latin name?

FIGURE 6 Fresco from the garden of *casa* VI.7.23, Pompeii; sacro-idyllic landscape depicting a tree in a semi-circular enclosure.
Copyright: Soprintendenza Archeologica di Pompei. Upon authorisation for the Ministry of Cultural Heritage and Environment. Reproduction or duplication by any means is forbidden.
Photo credits: Kenneth Walton.

a large tree (Figure 7).[108] People approaching – the leader with raised arms – look very much like worshippers. Arguably, then, we could read this tree as being central to the meaning of worshipping the deity whose statue shelters under it, just as the cedar was central to worshipping Artemis at Orchomenos.[109] Arguably again, neither painter nor viewer would ever have questioned that

---

[108] For similar images of trees within sacro-idyllic landscapes at Boscotrecase see the west and east walls of the Red Room (Blanckenhagen and Alexander 1990: plates 30 and 31).
[109] On which see pp. 260–261.

FIGURE 7 Fresco from the Red Room (north wall), Villa at Boscotrecase; sacro-idyllic landscape depicting a cult scene. Museo Archeologico Nazionale di Napoli inv. 147501.
Copyright: Heritage Image Partnership Ltd / Alamy Stock Photo.

this tree was only of significance in so far as it provided shade for an exposed cult site. Such images tend to leave this interpretative dilemma very much open.

On a few occasions, however, the nature of the image allows us to push through this dilemma. In sacro-idyllic style frescoes from the temple of Isis in Pompeii, where the introduction of 'Egyptianising' features like ibis birds only adds to the surreal quality of the landscapes, trees often take centre stage. In a painting from the *ekklesiasterion* seemingly casual drapery hanging down from a tree presents it as a focus of attention, both for

FIGURE 8 Fresco from the *ekklesiasterion*, Temple of Isis, Pompeii; sacro-idyllic landscape depicting an ensemble of tree, *porta sacra* and drapery. Museo Archeologico Nazionale di Napoli inv. 8558.
Copyright: Erich Lessing – www.lessingimages.com.

us as viewers, and for the people we imagine to populate such landscapes, who are presumably also to be held responsible for the drapery (Figure 8).[110] With the presence of an altar in the left-hand corner, and a statue in the background, the encouragement is there for us to view this as a site for cult. Moreover, the visual clash between the gnarled, lumpy tree and the straight and slender columns of the *porta sacra* through which it is twisting draws attention to the way a feature of the natural world has been

[110] Hackworth Petersen 2006: 22–38 offers a useful account of the colourful excavation history of the temple of Isis and an overview of its decorative schemes; she includes a diagram of the temple which indicates the location of the impressive *ekklesiasterion*.

Trees in cult space

FIGURE 9 Fresco from the *ekklesiasterion*, Temple of Isis, Pompeii; sacro-idyllic landscape depicting a round temple and tree flanked by sphinxes on plinths. Museo Archeologico Nazionale di Napoli inv. 1265.
Copyright: Sites & Photos / Capture Ltd / Alamy Stock Photo.

incorporated into a man-made site, strongly implying that it was the tree which came first, with the site built around the tree. This tree, it would seem, is so important to the meaning of this particular cult 'cluster' that it prompted its construction. Likewise, in another image from the *ekklesiasterion* we find a huge old tree monumentalised by two flanking plinths adorned with sphinxes (Figure 9). In architectural terms these plinths with sphinxes do nothing other than provide an impressive base for the tree. This tree too has clearly been singled out for attention, with structures built around it; there is no room to argue here that the tree's presence was accidental, or that it played a supporting role within the site, such as providing shade for an altar with its attendant worshippers. Dominant in the foreground of the painting, the tree also leans backwards into the image over the head of a statue to

275

Imagining the gods

FIGURE 10 Fresco from the *ekklesiasterion*, Temple of Isis, Pompeii; sacro-idyllic landscape depicting a cult scene. Museo Archeologico Nazionale di Napoli inv. 8570.
Copyright: Sites & Photos / Capture Ltd / Alamy Stock Photo.

twine a branch through the columns of a small circular temple, visually announcing its centrality to the meaning of worshipping in the whole site depicted here.[111]

So far our observations about these sacro-idyllic images have of necessity been rather hesitant, but on examination of more images – which closely integrate a tree with what appear to be statues of the divine – we can say a little more about how trees 'colour' cult sites. Consider another image from Isis' temple in which a large tree, sheltered in its own stone enclosure, gestures towards a neighbouring *porta sacra*; the *porta sacra* likewise shelters some kind of statue within its columns, at the foot of which an Egyptian figure is sacrificing at a small altar (Figure 10). This is an odd-looking statue: an oval body, with a ribbon tied round its middle, is topped by what looks like a bird of prey with a headpiece (perhaps an Isiaic *sistrum* (rattle)?). Some have interpreted it as the sarcophagus of Harpocrates – the name by which the hawk-headed Egyptian god Horus, son of

---

[111] For other prominent trees in the paintings decorating this temple see Coarelli 2002: 95 (Museo Archeologico Nazionale di Napoli inv. 8575) and Panetta 2004: 116 (Museo Archeologico Nazionale di Napoli inv. 8574).

Isis, was known in the Roman world – but for me, more agnosticism needs to be acknowledged in front of this strange-looking composite 'statue'.[112] Yet one thing we can say about the experience of worshipping whichever deity is called to mind here is that the adjacent tree must have played a dominant role. Without this tree the cult site simply would not have been the same, its stand-alone significance represented by its enjoyment of a personal enclosure. At the same time, the way that the statue and tree visually parallel each other in their adjacent enclosures, with the tree reaching out towards the statue, might suggest that, for the worshipper at the altar, this tree helped to colour in the identity of the deity he was worshipping. An image from the villa Arianna at Stabiae could be read in a similar way (Figure 11). Here a worshipper makes an offering at an altar in front of a column topped by a statue. Incongruously 'sprouting out' of the column's base is a tree, far taller than the column itself. In contrast with many sacro-idyllic landscapes, which are often rather busy, this image is starkly simple, indeed almost abstract in its depiction of the column and statue with its arboreal growth. The schematic nature of the image encourages us to look at this not so much as a 'countryside scene', but more as a symbolic representation of what mattered when worshipping this particular deity.

An even closer relationship between a tree and statue is depicted in an image from a Pompeian bedroom; for this image we now rely on a sketch, but much about its style and content is similar to the sacro-idyllic landscapes. Here a tree and statue – a bearded herm – rise side by side out of a small enclosure, in front of which stands an altar (Figure 12). At their base tree and statue are almost identical, and are possibly to be imagined as conjoined; the statue also wears a crown which is clearly woven from the tree's leaves.[113] The clean lines of the statue's rectangular body are

---

[112] For example, Panetta 2004: 114–115. That Harpocrates was Isis' son would naturally encourage us to see him present in her temple, although matters are complicated by the fact that, in the Roman world, Harpocrates seems better known as a 'god of silence', holding his finger to his lips (e.g. Ov. *Met.* 9.692). Tran Tam Tinh 1964: 86 discusses statuettes and frescoes from Pompeii which depict Harpocrates as a curly-haired youth, with his finger to his lips in a characteristic pose. Tran Tam Tinh 1964: 142 does not connect this particular image (fig. 10) with Harpocrates, but rather reads it as the 'adoration de la momie d'Osiris'.

[113] Pugliese Carratelli 1999: 8 identifies these as ivy.

277

Imagining the gods

FIGURE 11 Fresco from the *Villa Arianna*, Stabiae (precise provenance unknown); detail in sacro-idyllic style, depicting an ensemble of column, statue and tree. Museo Archeologico Nazionale di Napoli inv. 9396. Photo credits: author

contrasted with the twisted trunk of the tree, emphasising the gift which the organic tree has bestowed upon such a clearly manufactured image. Indeed some may wish to argue that the tree's significance within the image consisted solely in this practical contribution; certainly if Boetticher were looking at this image, he would have taken it as yet further proof that trees were involved in cult sites for the fruit, leaves and branches they provided, useful for so many ritual activities. Yet for me, the tree's close shadowing of the deity's statue and the way that tree and statue alone are tightly encircled by a low-standing enclosure, suggest that we need to take the two together to understand this god. In tandem, the statue's sporting of a wreath made of the tree's leaves paints the tree as an important influence on the god's identity, as imagined by those who – within the imagined world of the image – approached the altar before him. It is easy to imagine this god taking an arboreal epithet: Hermes (perhaps?) of the wild olive?

Trees in cult space

FIGURE 12 Drawing of fresco from *cubiculum* b, *casa* IX.2.16, Pompeii, depicting a wreathed cult statue and tree within a small enclosure. Copyright: Deutsches Archäologisches Institut, Abteilung Rom, Archiv. Serie VII: Stiche, Handzeichnungen, Gemälde, Pläne. Inv. A-VII-33-014.

I have previously argued that certain Priapus statues, with their distinctive ithyphallic shape, were mirrored by boldly branched trees in sacro-idyllic landscapes.[114] Since such statues were invariably said to be wooden and were known for their rough 'tree-like' appearance, I read these images as playful blurrings of the statue and its previous form as tree. Without recapping my previous arguments in full, I do wish at this point to return briefly to the image from Boscotrecase already discussed (Figure 7), to illustrate how trees could flesh out the identity of Priapus also. With our attention distracted by the ensemble of statue, column and tree in the centre of the image, we ignored a statue of Priapus in the bottom right-hand corner. This statue also closely interacts with a tree: the tree's sole branch shadows the precise angle formed by Priapus' prominent penis jutting out from the trunk of his body, reminding the viewer of the statue's likely arboreal origins. Trees like this colour Roman imagination of Priapus, this common-as-muck garden deity, by working to bring out the rough, tree-like nature of his

[114] Hunt 2011.

279

Imagining the gods

statues, which in turn encapsulate *his* nature as a god with a wild streak, a god who belongs in the great outdoors.

The sacro-idyllic landscape paintings here explored have confronted us with a surreal composite of architectural elements and natural features, all coloured with a strong wash of the idealising nostalgia for countryside life which characterises Roman thinking about their past and the rural present. A large number of the images discussed have come from the decorative scheme of the temple of Isis, and the inclusion of 'Egyptianising' elements in these landscapes, such as the sphinxes flanking a tree, only heighten the sense that these images are presenting us with 'the other'.[115] Idealised, surreal and 'other' these paintings may be, but nevertheless they still have much to say about the way Romans *thought* about trees. The unhesitating identification of sacred trees in sacro-idyllic paintings which has so far characterised the scholarly attention paid to trees in these landscapes – based on their position within enclosures, or their 'combination' with architectural features – is an unjustifiably confident reading of these landscapes. It is also a damagingly reductive reading of the nuanced ways in which these images do articulate Roman thinking about the sacrality of trees. For it is only by paying attention to the *detail* of the way certain trees interact with surrounding architectural elements and statues of the divine – like the subtle stretch of a tree towards a statue, or its shadowing of a statue's shape – that these images open up for us how trees could inform Roman understanding of the gods they worshipped.

Outside of the sacro-idyllic corpus, too, we find highly schematic images suggesting what the integration of trees into cult sites might tell us about the worship which took place there. I begin with a relief from the amphitheatre at Capua, which formed part of a decorated barrier in the open-air seating area.[116] Here we view a cult site, bounded off by a portico, and within which stands a very large

---

[115] A similar association of 'the other' with trees dominating a cult space is met in a painting from the *casa dei Pigmei*, Pompeii; here a caricatured pygmy woman sacrifices at an altar at the base of a huge tree. For the image see Peters 1963: image 169.

[116] Bomgardner 2000: 95–104 discusses the sculptural decoration of the amphitheatre. The reliefs are of uncertain date, and the chronology of the amphitheatre disputed. It seems that a first-century BCE amphitheatre later underwent several reconstruction phases, with one led by Hadrian (*CIL* 10.3832); see Bomgardner 2000: 104–105 and Welch 2007: 202.

Trees in cult space

FIGURE 13 Detail of relief from the amphitheatre at Capua, depicting a portico and cult space with altars, trees and statue; uncertain date. Museo Archeologico Nazionale di Napoli, inv. 6759.
Copyright: Soprintendenza Archeologica di Pompei. Upon authorisation for the Ministry of Cultural Heritage and Environment. Reproduction or duplication by any means is forbidden.
Photo credits: Kenneth Walton.

figure wearing military dress under his cloak and holding a spear; near him are two small altars, behind each of which stands a small tree (Figure 13). These elements seem almost scattered in the space and it would be hard to see them as representing the physical layout of any actual site; but since so few elements have been chosen to represent it, the inclusion of these two trees must be significant. The way each shadows an altar also suggests that the trees were felt to inform or colour the worship which would have taken place here, even though we cannot be confident in defining the nature of that worship further. Zanker suggests the statue is of a military victor; Bomgardner wonders about a local hero cult; and in one niche of the portico there seems to be a statue of Athena.[117] Consider also

[117] Zanker 1988: 22–23; Bomgardner 2000: 101, who also confidently identifies two 'sacred trees'.

281

Imagining the gods

FIGURE 14 Marble relief depicting the Temple of Vesta, with oak tree; uncertain date and provenance. Galleria degli Uffizi, inv. 336.
Copyright: Soprintendenza Speciale per il Patrimonio Storico, Artistico ed Etnoantropologico e per il Polo Museale della città di Firenze.

a striking marble relief of the temple of Vesta, from behind which emerges a sturdy branch of oak (Figure 14).[118] The image itself is quite surreal (the branch seems far too large for any supporting tree to be fully hidden behind the temple) and as such presses for it to be understood in symbolic terms: perhaps the combining of the oak, often associated with Jupiter, and the Vestals' temple aimed to

---

[118] See Lugli 1946: 203 for the identification of the temple.

FIGURE 15 Marble relief depicting a sacrificial procession for Cybele from Cyzicus, Asia Minor, 46 BCE.
Copyright: RMN-Grand Palais (musée du Louvre) / Hervé Lewandowski.

articulate in arboreal terms how worship of Vesta stood at the heart of Rome's divinely favoured strength and supremacy?[119]

From an image beautiful in its simplicity, reflecting the serenity of the goddess it evokes, I turn now to a relief which calls to mind a much noisier deity, from Cyzicus in Asia Minor (Figure 15).

---

[119] Zanker 1988: 207 also briefly observes that this oak 'protrudes quite meaningfully from behind the temple'.

283

Cyzicus formed something of a cult centre for Cybele, and it is no surprise to find her worship depicted here, with a sacrificial procession heading towards an altar, and an accompanying dedication by the *gallus* Soterides; his gratitude for a friend rescued after getting into trouble during Julius Caesar's campaign in Libya allows us to date this relief to 46 BCE.[120] Over this altar looms a large tree, which we could of course read as no more than a useful provider of shade: but a pair of cymbals hanging off the tree make its presence more loaded, reminding us that we are in the presence of a deity with known arboreal interests.[121] Whilst this tree does not look like a specimen of Cybele's favoured pine – indeed its leaves look more like oak – we could still read the tree's dominant position in the image, and its interaction with an instrument symbolic of Cybele's worship, as a reflection of what your own priorities have to be when worshipping a deity with such deep-seated arboreal interests.[122]

Cybele has also had an influence on the imagery of some extraordinary fragments of wooden furniture with ivory relief decorations, recently discovered at the *villa dei Papiri* in Herculaneum (Figures 16 and 17).[123] First thought to be part of the legs of a 'throne', it is now considered more likely that these fragments formed the legs of several different pieces of furniture, most probably tripods.[124] Understanding how these fragments fitted together is no easy task. It is also not known whether the items of furniture would have been intended to work as an 'ensemble' (Guidobaldi raises the possibility that they were dragged to their find-spot by the force of the surge), although similarities in the style of the images and recurrent motifs encourage us to read the images in relation to each other.[125] Here I focus on two images (one from 'leg 6' and one from 'leg 8') which

[120] See Vermaseren 1977b: 91–96 on Cyzicus and Cybele cult, esp. 94 on our relief, which is also discussed by Ridgway 2002: 220–221.
[121] Cymbals were said to be a common feature in Cybele's noisy processions, e.g. Ov. *Fast.* 4.213.
[122] A marble relief from Pompeii has also been associated with worship of Cybele in its depiction of a tree shadowing an altar, piled high with objects which might be castanets and tambourines: for this image and discussion see Jashemski 1979: 134.
[123] My thanks go to Andrew Wallace-Hadrill for introducing me to these pieces.
[124] See Guidobaldi 2010a: 51–55 and Guidobaldi 2010b for the story of the fragments' discovery, conservation and interpretation.
[125] Guidobaldi 2010a: 51.

Trees in cult space

FIGURE 16 Detail from wooden furniture ('leg no. 6'), *villa dei Papiri*, Herculaneum, depicting winged boys gathering pine cones.
Copyright: Soprintendenza Archeologica di Pompei. Upon authorisation for the Ministry of Cultural Heritage and Environment. Reproduction or duplication by any means is forbidden.
Photo credits: Kenneth Walton.

Guidobaldi attributes to two different pieces of furniture. A large pine tree frames the fragment of 'leg 6', underneath which stands a young winged boy in pointed Phrygian hat, whilst a similar figure climbs a ladder resting in the tree's branches (Figure 16). No doubt these 'boys', in combination with the pine tree, drew to mind for the viewer the myth of Cybele and her Phrygian lover Attis.[126] The two seem to be gathering pinecones, of which a

---

[126] Guidobaldi 2010a: 54 views the winged figure under the tree as a Cupid dressed up as Attis.

285

Imagining the gods

large pile sits at the bottom of the ladder; both wear baskets with shoulder straps, that of the boy heading up the ladder seemingly empty, the other's full and ready to unload. Cybele is the dominant 'divine presence' felt in this image of pinecone collection, with the pine and its cones evoking her identity as lover of Attis.

Yet Cybele is by no means the only deity whose relationship with the pine colours the images decorating these furniture fragments. Another pine tree dominates a fragment from 'leg 8', with stylistic similarities in the depiction of both trees prompting us to see the separate pieces of furniture as designed to comment on each other (Figure 17). A set of pipes hang from a branch of this pine, reminding us that Pan too was known for his interest in the tree (Prop. 1.18.20). Yet the pine shadows an altar and statue (the apparent recipient of the altar's offerings) which is not of Pan, but Priapus. His tell-tale penis, here semi-erect and kept under his garment, is mirrored by the first stub of a branch on the pine's trunk, which stands directly behind him. As in the image from Boscotrecase, the shadowing tree instantiates Priapus' arboreal side, a part of his identity which is reinforced by the fact that the offering of choice in this image is pinecones, with a wreathed man approaching the altar adding at least one more to those already on it (as well as what looks like an apple).[127] Priapus too, this image tells us, has every right to enjoy a relationship with the pine.[128] These images are nothing if not fun, and – if we are to approach them as pieces to be viewed together – they seem to revel in the multiple iconographic signals they give out; several

[127] The motif of pinecone and apple offerings runs throughout these wooden fragments, with two further images from 'leg 5', believed to be part of yet another piece of furniture, showing pinecones and apples left at the foot of two herms (see Guidobaldi 2010b: 91 for the images). One of the herms has a semi-erect penis; Guidobaldi 2010b: 90 refers to this as an ithyphallic Dionysus, but it could also call to mind Priapus. The presence of a set of cymbals above the other herm might bring Cybele and Attis to the forefront of the viewers' mind. Whilst the common motif of the pinecone and apple offerings encourages us to view these images together, a variety of deities are evoked and imagined.

[128] A statue of Priapus features again in the fragments of this leg, this time naked, and in the presence of a different kind of tree (perhaps a pear); here the tree and statue do not work so closely together, but rather the tree overshadows the whole scene (see Guidobaldi 2010b: 97 for the image). Once again, however, the offerings on the altar before Priapus are of apples and a few pinecones, the image as a whole reinforcing Priapus' arboreal interests.

Trees in cult space

FIGURE 17 Detail from wooden furniture ('leg no. 8'), *villa dei Papiri*, Herculaneum, depicting a statue of Priapus receiving offerings from a worshipper.
Copyright: Soprintendenza Archeologica di Pompei. Upon authorisation for the Ministry of Cultural Heritage and Environment. Reproduction or duplication by any means is forbidden.
Photo credits: Kenneth Walton.

deities express an interest in the pine, depending on the signals each viewer prioritises. Yet one thing remains constant: to worship in the cult spaces imagined here is to think about the divine 'in arboreal terms', with the pine fleshing out the identity of the various gods who – in a variety of iconographic ways – colour these images with their presence.

From visual representations of cult space, I turn now to textual depictions. We have seen how sacro-idyllic artists juxtapose and intertwine elements of a cult site so that the images have, in Zanker's words, a 'peculiar, floating quality', and in a similar way authors depicting cult space are often frustratingly

Imagining the gods

vague as to the nature of the relationships they understand to exist between its components.[129] Pliny may tell us of a vine 'at' (*apud*) the temple of Cybele at Smyrna (*Nat.* 16.115), whilst Valerius Maximus locates a palm and myrtle in the vestibule of the temple of Aesclapius (1.8.2), but neither comment on what the vine means to Cybele or her worshippers, or the palm and myrtle to Aesclapius and his, if indeed they mean anything at all. Even Pliny's choice of preposition is vague (*apud* can be translated 'at', 'near', 'by' ...), whilst his reason for giving space to this vine is that it produces fruit three times a year, citing as his authority Varro (and meaning here the *De agricultura*, not the *Antiquities*).[130] In Pliny's eyes at least, the attraction of the vine in the temple at Smyrna is that of natural curiosity. Valerius' locating of two trees (the palm, of extraordinary height, towers over the myrtle) in the vestibule of Aesclepius' temple might suggest they formed an 'initiatory' part of the experience of worshipping at this cult site, but Valerius' interest in them is occasioned by an ominous snake wrapping itself around the palm, rather than anything to do with the trees themselves.[131] For the purposes of Valerius' story, these trees are part of the background.

On rare occasions, however, we do get precious glimpses of what the location of trees within cult sites might mean. Consider Pliny's portrait of a lotus tree in the precinct of Lucina at Rome, founded in 375 BCE. Although the lotus is of uncertain age it must, Pliny explains, be even older than the precinct, *cum ab eo luco Lucina nominetur* (since Lucina is named after that grove; *Nat.* 16.235). The introduction of the grove at this point is thoroughly unexpected, and never properly explained.[132] Does it refer back to the lotus, the only tree mentioned in connection with the precinct? Are we to understand that there was once a whole grove of lotus trees in the precinct, but only one survived? Whatever the explanation, Pliny's account of the relative ages of the precinct

---

[129] Zanker 1988: 287.
[130] Pliny has, in fact, not remembered his Varro with complete accuracy; Varro's fig produces fruit twice a year and he locates it by the sea in Smyrna, not at a temple (*Agr.* 1.7).
[131] Valerius' lack of comment about the location of the trees may indicate that trees in the vestibules of temples were not an unusual sight.
[132] Murphy 2004: 30 observes how Pliny's 'broad hypotactic architecture' can 'bring on a referential dizziness', on which cf. Jacob 1993: 36.

Trees in cult space

and the lotus tree/s means that the precinct must have been built around the tree/s in question. Pliny's subtext paints these trees as the reason behind the cult site's location and a crux not only for the identity of the site, but also the identity of the goddess worshipped there, since he derives her name from her relationship with 'the grove'.[133] Pliny may be frustratingly elliptical over some details, but trees are both physically and conceptually at the heart of the worship of Lucina in this precinct.

Nor is Pliny the only one to hint at how divine names could reflect the significance of trees in cult space. Pausanias tells us of a wild olive which the Eleans call the 'olive of the Beautiful Crown' (ἐλαία Καλλιστέφανος), from whose leaves are made the crowns given to winners of Olympic contests (5.15.3). Near this olive, he continues, stands an altar of the 'Nymphs of the Beautiful Crowns'. The relationship between the wild olive and the altar of the nymphs could be purely locational, but their shared epithet suggests that the two were seen to have an influence on each other's identity. These nymphs and olive, drawn together by their shared interest in 'beautiful crowns', remind me of the bearded herm whose close relationship with the tree at his back was articulated by his wearing of a crown woven from that tree's leaves (Figure 12). However, Pausanias' skating account allows us to say no more with confidence about these nymphs, so from here I turn to Varro's description of the shrine of the goddess Rumina, introduced via an explanation of the fact that 'milk' can be extracted from figs.[134] Varro then explains his belief that this is the reason why certain shepherds planted a fig tree at the shrine (*aput* is again the preposition used), adding that they are accustomed to make offerings with milk instead of wine there (*RR*. 2.11.5). The surface logic of Varro's argument might seem to be that the shepherds planted the fig for practical use, providing a milky substance they could use in their sacrifices. But could the milky sap of a fig really be used as a substitute for milk, and would one tree alone have provided sufficient liquid? It seems likely that the planting of the fig was more of a symbolic than a practical gesture. Rumina is,

---

[133] More commonly Lucina is derived from *lux*, e.g. Cic. *Nat. d.* 2.68, Varro *LL*. 5.69. Ovid typically toys with both options at *Fast.* 2.449–450.
[134] Ps. Arist. *Pl.* 818b also comments on the milky sap of figs.

Imagining the gods

after all, the goddess of breastfeeding (explaining her preference for milk over wine). Planting a milky fig by her shrine would have complemented and reinforced her milky nature, embodying her qualities in arboreal form for all the world to see.

Finally, I turn to a sanctuary in a suburb of Antioch the Great where a tree makes a rather different, but crucial, contribution to the meaning of the cult site. This suburb is called Daphne, the sanctuary one of Apollo, and it is here, according to local legends, that Daphne fled from the god and turned into a laurel: what's more, they have the laurel to prove it. According to Philostratus the locals 'honour' (τιμᾶται) this laurel 'as a substitute for the girl' (ἀντὶ τῆς παρθένου; *VA.* 1.16.1); in Eustathius' words the story goes that the laurel grew up 'over the girl' (ἐπὶ τῇ Δάφνῃ; *ad Dion.* 916). Libanius is more expansive concerning the site's history: Seleucus Nicator, we are told, 'established' (κατέστησεν) the area for Apollo when the truth of the local legend was memorably impressed on him whilst out on a hunt.[135] For coming unawares on the tree which had once been Daphne, his horse shied up and a golden arrow with Phoebus' name inscribed on it appeared from the earth. Consequently Seleucus marked off the area and 'chose trees and temples for it' (φυτὰ καὶ νεὼς ἐδέχετο): 'soon the grove was flourishing' (ταχὺ τὸ ἄλσος ἔθαλλε; *Or.* 11.94–98). Without this particular tree, and Seleucus' pious response when he realised its significance, clearly (in Libanius' eyes) there would have been no cult site. Yet the arboreal world and the divine world meet on more levels than this in this unique grove. Here is a tree whose conspicuous material overlap with the nymph Daphne (expressed by Philostratus and Eustathius in their differing ways) means that an element of the divine is always physically rooted in this grove. This tree also intensifies the presence of Apollo in the grove, with Philostratus informing us that he was known to take dips in the sanctuary's springs (1.16.1).

Of few other trees in the Roman world could it be boasted that they attracted deities to the human world, but on one level every

---

[135] That Antioch the Great (otherwise known as Antioch on the Orontes) was a Greek city must be one reason behind the fact that our surviving evidence for this tree is all in Greek, although the myth of Daphne's transformation was of course hardly of interest only to Greek authors.

tree stood as a potential point of contact between the human world and the world of the divine. For the various trees met in this chapter have all, in their own way, articulated something about the identity of particular deities, be it the fiery laurel consecrated to Apollo, a milky fig integrated into a shrine of Rumina, a cedar tree in which a statue of Artemis sat, the white poplars which prompted Zeus' epithet at Lepreum or an oak peeping out behind the temple of Vesta. Through their involvement in representations of the divine and in cult space, through their influence on divine names and through the relationships imagined between a genus of tree and a deity, any tree could help to colour in Roman imagination of the identity of their gods. Indeed Seleucus Nicator showed his insight in this regard. For when he realised that the laurel at Daphne was so important to Apollo's identity that the whole area should be given over to him, his priorities in so doing were appropriately arboreal: plant more trees.

CHAPTER 7

BRANCHING OUT: WHAT SACRED TREES MEAN FOR ROMAN RELIGION

Contrary to appearances, this book is not *all* about trees. For the significance of the trees we have met, and the theological questions they raise, spill out into our wider understanding of Roman religion. Trees have plenty to say, for example, about Roman understandings of sacrifice. Sensitivity to prepositions displayed by the *fratres Arvales* as they sacrificed *because* a tree had died has shown us that Roman thinkers might sacrifice about a situation, rather than to a deity; their pruning sacrifices too have challenged our understanding of *piacula* as atonement for unwitting faults. Trees have also enriched our knowledge of Roman thinking about statues of the divine: at Corinth, making statues of Dionysus from a tree was a way of worshipping that tree, along with the god; at Delphi a hybrid Athena-cum-palm articulated something essential about Athena's identity. To throw out a few more examples, the fig which prompted the coining of Adolenda Conmolenda Deferunda has shown us that there is nothing simplistic about Sondergötter. An oak beloved of Atalanta (among other trees) has urged us to rethink our understanding of the word *numen*. A palm which sprang up on an altar at Tarraco has revealed how engaging in imperial cult can raise challenging questions about an emperor's self-knowledge. Trees have long stood at the edge of the field in scholarship on Roman religion, but their ability to prompt Roman thinking about multiple aspects of their religious practices and the nature of the divine demands that they be rooted in the centre.

Moreover, as soon as trees are allowed to take a centre-stage position within our portraits of Roman religion, they urge us to revive those portraits in two major ways. Firstly, trees urge us to discard the inflexible legalistic definitions of 'sacrality as consecration' so dominant in current scholarship. The trees encountered in this book have insisted that their sacrality is far too diverse and multi-layered to be forced into such a model. Rather we have seen that Roman thinkers engaged with trees as sacred by placing a palm shoot among their *penates*, by sacrificing to Adolenda Coinquenda, preserving the remains of a plane in a temple, calling Jupiter 'Fagutalis' or commissioning an image of Hercules hugging a tree. Memories made the *ficus Ruminalis* sacred, as well as contagious proximity to some lightning-struck objects; Latinus' laurel was especially sacred in its foliage; a sacred laurel at Antioch was in some way Daphne. The limits to arboreal sacrality were, in short, the limits to Roman imagination of ways in which the divine might make itself known in the human world. A central tenet of scholarly thinking about sacrality in Roman culture, namely that sacred objects were considered inviolable, is also thrown out of the window when we observe how arboriculture – with all its violent interference with arboreal matter – can be a mode for articulating the sacrality of trees. Trees have a simple message for us here: Roman sacrality needs rethinking.

Trees also shake up our portraits of Roman religion by dragging 'the environment' out of the corner into which we have pushed it; framed as a 'country bumpkin subject', we presume that the environment rarely crossed the radar of Roman thinkers who turned their minds to matters of theology. To the contrary, trees have let us in on imaginative and complex Roman thinking about how the divine might express itself in their natural environment. Be it Silvanus who is half shut up in a sacred ash tree, Artemis who sits in a cedar at Orchomenos, Apollo who has a penchant for the fiery laurel, or Priapus who finds his statues shadowed by trees in painted landscapes, all these deities have aspects of their identities articulated through the arboreal world. A focus on arboreal portents has also revealed knotty Roman attempts to read the divine through the behaviour of their arboreal environment. No simple rules applied when trying to interpret trees' behaviour: a black poplar turning into a white one was not always meaningful; a fig bursting through an altar could mean something very different to a palm. Nor was there much value in trying to distinguish the 'natural' and 'unnatural' in arboreal behaviour, for what was explicable in natural terms still had the potential to mediate the divine. In short, engaging with the environment was, for Roman thinkers, an inescapable and complex part of trying to make sense of their existence in the world vis-à-vis the divine.

As scholarship on Roman religion burst onto the academic world stage in the late nineteenth century, an intellectual vogue for sacred trees was reaching its height. The new scholars of Roman religion took up the cause with uncritical delight, to the embarrassment of today's representatives of the discipline. Consequently, most of us are more than happy to relegate sacred trees to the 'Funny Old World' section of our portraits of Roman religion. This book has worked to show that choosing to do so will leave our understanding of Roman religion stunted. If, on the other hand, we choose to root trees into our portraits of Roman religion, reviving these in the process, then fruitful growth will follow close behind.

APPENDIX

TABLE 1 *Inscriptions from the Arval grove which shine a spotlight on the grove's trees. The Latin text is taken from Scheid 1998.*

[] = restored text
() = expanded abbreviation
{ } = letters to be deleted
<> = letters omitted, and added by editor
⌈ ⌉ = text corrected by editor
ạḅc̣ = letters damaged or unclear
abc = text preserved only in a manuscript edition

No.	No. in Scheid	Date (CE)	Text of inscription
1	2 (1–6)	14	[Cn. Corneliu]s Cn. f(ilius) Lentulus augur mag(ister) in locum [---] [factus ad] fratres arvales rettulit arborem [in luco d]e⌈ae⌉ Diae vetustate cecidisse q(uid) d(e) e(a) r(e) f(ieri) p(laceret) d(e) e(a) r(e) i(ta) c(ensuerunt) [cum arbo]r vetustate in luco deae Diae cecidisset ut [in luc]o ad sacrificium consumeretur neve quid [ligni] exportaretur
2	12c (22–23)	38 (18 April)	Taur{ur}us Statilius Corvinus promagister ob ramum vetus[tate delaps]um in luco dea[e] Diae sacrificium piaculare fecit ramumqu[e consumi iu]ssit
3	30 I cd (21–22)	66	[piaculum factum o]b arborem quae ceci[derat]
4	42 (14–15)	72	[piaculu]m factum [in luc]ọ deae Diae ob arborem qua[e a] ṭempestate d[eciderat] per calatorem et publicos
5	48 (18–19)	81 (15 Jan.)	in luco deae Diae piaculum factum per calatorem et publicos eius sacerdoti quod arbor a vetustate decidit expiandum porcam et agnam opimam

295

Appendix

No.	No. in Scheid	Date (CE)	Text of inscription
6	49 (5–7)	81 (29 March)	in luco deae Diae piaculum factum per kalatorem et publicos eius sacerdoti ob arbores quae a tempestate nivis deciderant exp[i]andas porcam et agnam opimam
7	53 I (3)	84 (29 May)	[po]rcas piaculares duas luco <co>in[quiendi et operis faciundi Ti. Tutin]ius Severus
8	55 II (18–20)	87 (19 May)	C. Salvius Liberalis qui vice magistri fungebatur C. Iuli Silani ante lucum in aram porcas piaculares duas luco coinquendi et operis faciendi immolavit
	(55–57)	(10 Sep.)	in luco deae Diae quod ramus ex arbore ilicina ob [v]etustatem deciderit piaculum factum est per calatorem et [p]ublicos
9	57 (48–49)	89 (12 April)	[piaculum] factum ob a[rbor]em expiata<m> cui prae [-----] per publicos [et ca]latorem
	(55–56)	(19 May)	[ante lucum in] aram por[cas pia]cul[ares] [duas lu]co coin[quendi et operis fa]ciendi [immolavit]
10	58 (45)	90 (23 April)	[porc]am et agnam expiatam arborem ob vetustatem quod decidit
	(50)	(27 May)	porcas piaculares duas luco coinquendi et operi faciundo immolavit P. Sallustius [Blaesus]
11	59 II (28)	91 (5 Nov.)	expiata arbor quod vetustat̞[e decidit]
12	62a (74–75)	101 (26 April)	in luco deae Diae arbores expiatae quod vetustate vel vi maiori deciderant porcis et [agnis]
13	62b frg. 1 (2–4)	101	[piaculum factu]m quod arbor vetusta[te deciderat porcam et agnam struibu]s fertisq[ue per calatorem] et publicos eor̞[um]
14	64 I (29–33)	105	in aedem Conco[rdiae fratres arvales convenerunt] ibique referent̞[e M. Valerio Trebicio Deciano mag(istro) ad] collegas de arbor[ibus lauribus in luco deae Diae quod] a tempestatibus per[ustae essent placuit piaculo fac]to caedi
	(38–41)		in luco deae Diae piaculum factum̞ [ob arbores lau]rus caedendas quod tempestatibus perusta[e erant] porcis et agnis struibus fertisque per M. Valeri[um] Trebicium Decianum̞ [mag(istrum)] ministrantibus public[is]

Appendix

TABLE 1 (cont.)

No.	No. in Scheid	Date (CE)	Text of inscription
15	64 II (7–9)	105 (19 May)	in luco deae Diae M. Valerius Trebicius Decianus mag(ister) ad aram inmolavit porcas piaculares duas luco <co>inquendi operis faciundi
16	67a (18)	117 (19 May)	[porcas piacula]res duas luco coinquendi et operis faciundi
17	68 I (41–44)	118 (6 March)	[i]n luco deae Diae piaculum ob arb[orum caeden]darum causa<m> quae tempestate vel vi maiori decide[rant] porcis et agnis [s]truibus fertisque per M. Valeriu[m] Trebicium Deci[an]um mag(istrum) (iterum) et publicos arva[lium]
	(59–61)	(29 May)	in luco de[ae Di]ae M. Valerius Trebicius Dec[ia]nus magister [a]d aram immolavit porcas piaculares [d]uas luci coinquendi et operis faciundi
18	69 (36–37)	120 (29 May)	in luco deae Diae C. Vitorius Hosidius Geta mag(ister) ad aram immolavit porcas piaculares duas luco coinquiendo et operis faciundi
19	74 (4–5)	133 (29 May)	in luco deae Diae Ti. Iulius Iulianus Alexander promag(ister) [ad aram immolavit porcas piaculares duas] luci coinquiendi et operis faciundi
20	78 (31–32)	145 (19 May)	in luco deae Diae Ti. Licinius Cassius Cassianus promag(ister) ad aram immolavit porcas pia[culares duas luci coinquiendi] et operis faciundi
21	80 (31–32)	155 (19 May)	in luco deae D[iae] M. Fulvius Apronianus prom [ag(ister) ad] aram immolavit p[orcas piaculares] duas luci coin[quien]di et operis faciundi
	(58–60)	(30 May)	in luco [deae Diae piaculum fact]um ob arborem expiandam quae ve[tustate deciderat porca]m et agnam struibus ferctisq(ue) per M. Fulvi[um Apronianum pro]magist(rum) et pu[b]licos fratrum arvalium
22	94 I-II (21–6)	183 (8 Feb.)	in luco deae Diae Q. Licinius Nepos mag(ister) operis inchuandi causa quod in fastigio aedis deae Diae ficus innata esset eruendam et aedem reficiendam immolavit suovetaurilibus maioribus item ad aedem deae Diae boves feminas

297

Appendix

No.	No. in Scheid	Date (CE)	Text of inscription
	94 II (7–14)	183 (13 May)	(duas) Iano patri arietes (duos) Iovi berbeces (duos) altilaneos Marti arietes altilaneos (duos) Iunoni deae Diae oves (duas) sive deo sive deae oves (duas) Virginibus divis oves (duas) Famulis divis verbeces (duos) Laribus verbeces duos Matri Larum oves duas sive deo sive d⌈e⌉ae in cuius tutela hic lucus locusve est oves (duas) Fonti verbeces (duos) Florae oves (duas) Vestae oves (duas) Vestae matri oves (duas) ite[m] Adolendae Conmolandae Deferundae oves (duas) item ante Caesareum Divis n(umero) (sedecim) verbec(es) immolavit n(umero) (sedecim) in luco deae Diae Q. Licinius Nepos mag(ister) operis perfecti causa quod arboris eruendae et aedis refectae immolavit suovetaurilibus maioribus item ad aedem deae Diae boves feminas (duas) Iano patri arietes (duos) Iovi verbeces (duos) altilaneos Marti ariet(es) altilan(eos) (duos) Iunoni deae Diae oves (duas) sive deo sive deae oves (duas) Virginibus divis oves (duas) Famulis divis verbeces (duos) Laribus verbeces (duos) Matri Larum oves (duas) sive deo sive d⌈e⌉ae in cuius tutela hic lucus locusve est oves (duas) Fonti verbeces (duos) Florae oves (duas) Vestae oves (duas) Vestae matri oves (duas) item Adolendae Conmolendae Deferundae oves (duas) item ante Caesareum Divis n(umero) (sedecim) verbeces immolavit (sedecim)
	(21–22)	(19 May)	in luco deae Diae Q. Licinius Nepos mag(ister) ad aram immolav(it) porcilias piaculares (duas) luci coinchuendi et operis faciendi
23	99a (1)	213 (19 May)	[piaculares] n(umero) (duas) luci coinquiendi et operis faciundi
24	100a (17–18)	218 (29 May)	in luco deae Diae Alfen⌈i⌉us Avitianus promag(ister) ad aram immol(avit) porcil(ias) piacul(ares) II luci coinq(uiendi) et ope⌈r⌉is faciund(i)

298

Appendix

TABLE I (cont.)

No.	No. in Scheid	Date (CE)	Text of inscription
25	105b (3–13)	224 (7 Nov.)	fratr(es) arval(es) in luc(o) d(eae) D(iae) via Camp(ana) apud lap(idem) (quintum) conv(enerunt) per C. Porc(ium) Priscum mag(istrum) et ibi imm(olaverunt) quod vi tempestat(is) ictu fulmin(is) arbor(es) sacr(i) l(uci) d(eae) D(iae) attact(ae) ar⌈d⌉uer(int) ear(um)q(ue) arbor(um) eruẹndar(um) ferr(o) ⌈f⌉endendar(um) adolendar(um) commolendar(um) item aliar(um) restituendar(um) causa operisq(ue) inc⌈h⌉oandi ara⌈s⌉ temporal(es) sacr(as) d(eae) D(iae) reficiend(i) eius rei causạ lụṣṭr(um) miss(um) suovetaurilib(us) maior(ibus) item ante aed(em) d(eae) D(iae) b(oves) f(eminas) a(uro) i(unctas) n(umero) (duas) item ad ar(as) tempor(ales) ḍịṣ inf(ra) s(ub)s(criptis) Ian(o) patr(i) ariet(es) (duos) Iovi verbec(es) (duos) Marti patri ult(ori) ar(ietes) n(umero) (duos) sive deo siv(e) ḍẹạe verb(eces) (duos) Iun(oni) d(eae) D(iae) ov(es) n(umero) (duas) Virginib(us) div(is) ov(es) n(umero) (duas) Fam(ulis) div(is) verb(eces) n(umero) (duos) Larib(us) verb(eces) n(umero) (duos) Ṃatri Lar(um) ọv(es) n(umero) (duas) Font(i) verb(eces) n(umero) (duos) Flor(ae) ov(es) n(umero) (duas) Summa(no) pat(ri) verb(eces) atros (duos) Vestae matri ov(es) II Vestae deor(um) dear(um)q(ue) ov(es) (duas) item Adolend(ae) Coinq(uendae) ov(es) (duas) et ante Caesar(eum) Genio d(omini) n(ostri) Severi Alexandri Aug(usti) t(aurum) a(uratum) item Divis n(umero) (viginti) verbec(es) viginti
	(14–19)	(10 Dec.)	fratres arval(es) in luco deae Diae via Campana apud lap(idem) (quintum) convener(unt) per C. Porc(ium) Priscum mag(istrum) et ibi immolav(erunt) quod ab ictu fulminis arbores luci sacri d(eae)

299

Appendix

No.	No. in Scheid	Date (CE)	Text of inscription
26	107 II (2–3)	237?	D(iae) attactae arduerint earumq(ue) arborum adolefactarum et coinquendarum et <quod> in eo luco sacro aliae sint repositae et arae temporal(es) refectae ferri effer(endi) huius oper(is) perfe[c]ti causa lustrum missum suovetaurilib(us) maioribus et cetera q(uae) s(upra) aliam arborem s[ubstituendam? --- huius rei] lustr(um) miss(um) suovę[taurilibus maioribus]
27	114 I (8–16)	240 (31 March)	[fr]a[t]res arva<l>es in luco deae Diae via ⌈C⌉amp(ana) apud lap(idem) (quintum) conv(enerunt) per Fab(ium) For⌈t⌉unatum Victorinum promag(istrum) vice Fl(avi) ⌈L⌉uciliani mag(istri) op(eris) inchoandi causa luci sublucandi et a⌈r⌉borum oblaqueand(arum) et aliar(um) restituendarum huius rei lustrum missum suovetaur(ilibus) maiorib(us) et ante aed(em) deae Diae b(oves) {e} f(eminas) au(ro) iunctas alb(as) n(umero) (duas) Iano patr(i) ar(ietes) n(umero) (duos) Iovi verb(eces) n(umero) (duos) sive deo sive deae verb(eces) n(umero) (duos) Virg(inibus) ov(es) n(umero) (duas) Famul(is) dis verb(eces) n(umero) (duos) Lari(bus) verb(eces) n(umero) (duos) Matri Lar(um) ov(es) n(umero) (duos) Flor(ae) ov(es) n(umero) (duos) Vest(ae) m(atri) ov(es) n(umero) (duas) ⌈i⌉tem ante Caes(areum) Gen(io) d(omini) n(ostri) Imp(eratoris) M. Antoni Go⌈r⌉diani p(ii) f(elicis) A(ugusti) t(aurum) a(uratum)

TABLE 2 *Case and spelling variations in preserved instances of the Arvals' formula luci coinquendi et operis faciundi.*

G = genitive
D = dative
A = ablative

? = uncertainty over the case ending, due to reliance on restored text or expanded abbreviation

Inscription	Text			Summary of cases		
7	luco	<co>in[quiendi]	[operis]	[faciundi]	D/A	?	?
8	luco	coinquendi	operis	faciendi	D/A	G	G
9	lu[co]	coin[quendi]	[operis]	[fa]ciendi	D/A	?	G
10	luco	coinquendi	operi	faciundo	D/A	G	D/A
15	luco	<co>inquendi	operis	faciundi	D/A	G	G
16	luco	coinquendi	operis	faciundi	D/A	G	G
17	luci	coinquendi	operis	faciundi	G	G	G
18	luco	coinquiendo	operis	faciundi	D/A	D/A	G
19	luci	coinquiendi	operis	faciundi	G	G	G
20	[luci]	[coinquiendi]	operis	faciundi	?	?	G
21	luci	coin[quien]di	operis	faciundi	G	G	G
22	luci	coinchuendi	operis	faciendi	G	G	G
23	luci	coinquiendi	operis	faciundi	G	G	G
24	luci	coinq(uiendi)	operis	faciundi(i)	G	?	?

BIBLIOGRAPHY

Ackerman, R. (1987) *J. G. Frazer: His Life and Work*. Cambridge.
  (2002) *The Myth and Ritual School: J. G. Frazer and the Cambridge Ritualists*. New York.
Alcock, S. E. (1993) *Graecia Capta: The Landscapes of Roman Greece*. Cambridge.
  (1996) 'Landscapes of memory and the authority of Pausanias' in *Pausanias historien: huit exposés suivis de discussions*, eds D. Musti and J. Bingen. Geneva: 241–276.
  (2002) *Archaeologies of the Greek Past: Landscapes, Monuments, and Memories*. Cambridge.
Alcock, S. E., Cherry, J. F. and Elsner, J. eds (2001) *Pausanias: Travel and Memory in Roman Greece*. Oxford.
Algra, K. (2003) 'Stoic theology' in *The Cambridge Companion to the Stoics*, ed. B. Inwood. Cambridge: 153–178.
  (2009) 'Stoic philosophical theology and Graeco-Roman religion' in *God and Cosmos in Stoicism*, ed. R. Salles. Oxford: 224–252.
Allen, G. (1892) *The Attis of Caius Valerius Catullus translated into English verse, with dissertations on the myth of Attis, on the origin of tree-worship and on the Galliambic metre*. London.
  (1897) *The Evolution of the Idea of God: An Inquiry into the Origins of Religions*. London.
Allen, J. H. (1903) *Allen and Greenough's New Latin Grammar for Schools and Colleges, Founded on Comparative Grammar*, eds J. B. Greenough *et al.* Boston.
Allison, D. C., Jr (2003) 'Abraham's oracular tree (*T. Abr.* 3:1–4)' *JJS* 54: 51–61.
Altheim, F. (1938) *A History of Roman Religion*, trans. H. Mattingly. London.
Ammerman, A. (2006) 'Adding time to Rome's imago' in *Imaging Ancient Rome: Documentation, Visualization, Imagination*, eds L. Haselberger and J. Humphrey. Portsmouth, RI: 297–308.
Ando, C. (2000) *Imperial Ideology and Provincial Loyalty in the Roman Empire*. London.
  (2003a) *Roman Religion*. Edinburgh.
  (2003b) 'A religion for the empire' in *Flavian Rome: Culture, Image, Text*, eds A. J. Boyle and W. J. Dominik. Leiden: 323–344.
  (2008) *The Matter of the Gods: Religion and the Roman Empire*. London.

Bibliography

(2009) 'Evidence and orthopraxy' [review of Scheid, J. *Quand faire, c'est croire. Les rites sacrificiels des Romains*] *JRS* 99: 171–181.
Ando, C. and Rüpke, J. eds (2006) *Religion and Law in Classical and Christian Rome*. Stuttgart.
Arafat, K. W. (1996) *Pausanias' Greece: Ancient Artists and Roman Rulers*. Cambridge.
Athanassakis, A. N. (1977) *The Orphic Hymns: Text, Translation and Notes*. Missoula, MT.
Athanassiadi, P. and Frede, M. (1999) *Pagan Monotheism in Late Antiquity*. Oxford.
Attfield, R. (1994) *Environmental Philosophy: Principles and Prospects*. Aldershot.
Auger, D. and Delattre, C. eds (2010) *Mythe et fiction*. Nanterre.
Augoustakis, A. (2006) 'Cutting down the grove in Lucan, Valerius Maximus and Dio Cassius' *CQ* 56.2: 634–638.
Baal, J. van. (1976) 'Offering, sacrifice and gift' *Numen* 23: 161–178.
Baddeley, W. St. C. (1904) *Rome and its Story*. London.
— (1905) 'The sacred trees of Rome' *Nineteenth Century and After* 58.19–20: 100–115.
Bagnall, R. S. and Rathbone, D. W. eds (2004) *Egypt from Alexander to the Early Christians: An Archaeological and Historical Guide*. London.
Bailey, C. (1907) *The Religion of Ancient Rome*. London.
— (1932) *Phases in the Religion of Ancient Rome*. London.
— (1935) *Religion in Virgil*. Oxford.
Bakker, J. T. (1994) *Living and Working with the Gods*. Amsterdam.
Balland, A. (1984) 'La Casa Romuli au Palatin et au Capitole' *REL* 62: 57–80.
Balme, D. M. (1962) 'Development of biology in Aristotle and Theophrastus: theory of spontaneous generation' *Phronesis* 7: 91–104.
Barasch, M. (1992) *Icon: Studies in the History of an Idea*. New York.
Barlow, H. C. (1866) *Essays on Symbolism*. London.
Bayet, J. (1969) *Histoire politique et psychologique de la religion romaine*. Paris.
— (1971) *Croyances et rites dans la Rome antique*. Paris.
Beagon, M. (1992) *Roman Nature: The Thought of Pliny the Elder*. Oxford.
— (1996) 'Nature and views of her landscapes in Pliny the Elder' in *Human Landscapes in Classical Antiquity: Environment and Culture*, eds G. Shipley and J. Salmon. London: 284–329.
Beard, M. (1985) 'Writing and ritual: a study of diversity and expansion in the Arval *acta*' *PBSR* 53: 114–162.
— (1987) 'A complex of times: no more sheep on Romulus' birthday' *PCPhS* 33: 1–15.
— (1989) 'Acca Larentia gains a son: myths and priesthood at Rome' in *Images of Authority: Papers Presented to Joyce Reynolds on the Occasion of her Seventieth Birthday*, eds M. M. MacKenzie and C. Roueché. Cambridge: 41–61.

303

Bibliography

(1992) 'Frazer, Leach, and Virgil: the popularity (and unpopularity) of the *Golden Bough*' *Comparative Studies in Society and History* 34: 203–224.

(1993) 'Looking (harder) for Roman myth: Dumézil, declamation and the problems of definition' in *Mythos in mythenloser Gesellschaft: das Paradigma Roms*, ed. F. Graf. Stuttgart: 44–64.

(1994) 'The Roman and the foreign: the cult of the Great Mother in Imperial Rome' in *Shamanism, History and the State*, eds N. Thomas and C. Humphrey. Ann Arbor, MI: 164–190.

(1998) 'Documenting Roman religion' in *La mémoire perdue: recherches sur l'administration romaine*, ed. C. Moatti. Rome: 75–101.

(2012) 'Cicero's 'Response of the *haruspices*' and the voice of the gods' *JRS* 102: 20–39.

Beard, M. and Crawford, M. (1985) *Rome in the Late Republic: Problems and Interpretations*. London.

Beard, M. and North, J. eds (1990) *Pagan Priests: Religion and Power in the Ancient World*. London.

Beard, M., North, J. and Price, S. (1998) *Religions of Rome*. Cambridge.

Beaujeu, J. (1955) *La religion romaine à l'apogée de l'Empire*. Paris.

(1964) *'Octavius': Minucius Felix*. Paris.

Beck, H. and Walter, U. eds (2001) *Die Frühen Römischen Historiker 1: von Fabius Pictor bis Cn. Gellius*. Darmstadt.

Beek, L. ter. (2012) 'Divine law and the penalty of Sacer Esto in early Rome' in *Law and Religion in the Roman Republic*, ed. O. Tellegen-Couperus. Leiden: 11–29.

Beer, G. (1983) *Darwin's Plots: Evolutionary Narrative in Darwin, George Eliot and Nineteenth-Century Fiction*. London.

Bell, C. (1992) *Ritual Theory, Ritual Practice*. Oxford.

(1997) *Ritual: Perspectives and Dimensions*. Oxford.

Bendlin, A. (1997) 'Peripheral centres – central peripheries: religious communication in the Roman empire' in *Römische Reichsreligion and Provinzialreligion*, eds H. Cancik and J. Rüpke. Tübingen: 35–68.

Bennett, F. M. (1917) 'Wooden statues which Pausanias saw in Greece' *CW* 10: 82–86.

Bettini, M. (2012) 'Vertumnus ou les aphormai de l'anthropologue classique: approches comparatives et religion romaine' in *Comparer en histoire des religions antiques: controverses et propositions*, eds C. Calame and B. Lincoln. Liège: 13–33.

Bijovsky, G. (2003) 'The myth of Daphne on a coin minted at Damascus' *AJN* 15: 53–59.

Birge, D. (1982) 'Sacred groves in the ancient Greek world', PhD thesis, University of California, Berkeley.

(1986) 'Pausanias and tree-worship in Corinth' in *Corinthiaca: Studies in Honor of Darrell A. Amyx*, ed. M. A. del Chiaro. Columbia, MO: 25–28.

(1994) 'Trees in the landscape of Pausanias' *Periegesis*' in *Placing the Gods: Sanctuaries and Sacred Space in Ancient Greece*, eds S. E. Alcock and R. Osborne. Oxford: 231–246.

Bibliography

Bispham, E. and Smith, C. J. (2000) *Religion in Archaic and Republican Rome and Italy*. Edinburgh.
Blanckenhagen, P. H. von and Alexander, C. (1990) *The Augustan Villa at Boscotrecase*. Mainz am Rhein.
Bloch, M. (1998) 'Why trees, too, are good to think with: towards an anthropology of the meaning of life' in *The Social Life of Trees: Anthropological Perspectives on Tree Symbolism*, ed. L. Rival. Oxford: 39–55.
Bloch, R. (1963) *Les prodiges dans l'Antiquité classique (Grèce, Étrurie, Rome)*. Paris.
Block, E. (1981) *The Effects of Divine Manifestation on the Reader's Perspective in Vergil's 'Aeneid'*. New York.
Bodel, J. (1985) 'Graveyards and groves: a study of the Lex Lucerina' *AJAH* 11: 1–133.
(2008) 'Cicero's Minerva, Penates, and the Mother of the Lares: an outline of Roman domestic religion' in *Household and Family Religion in Antiquity*, eds J. Bodel and S. M. Olyan. Oxford: 248–275.
(2009) ' "Sacred dedications": a problem of definitions' in *Dediche sacre nel mondo greco-romano: diffusione, funzioni, tipologie*, eds J. Bodel and M. Kajava. Rome: 17–30.
Boetticher, C. G. W. (1856) *Der Baumkultus der Hellenen nach den gottesdienstlichen Gebräuchen und den überlieferten Bildwerken dargestellt*. Berlin.
Boissier, G. (1900) *La religion romaine d'Auguste aux Antonins*. Paris.
Bomgardner, D. L. (2000) *The Story of the Roman Amphitheatre*. London.
Bommas, M., Harrisson, J. and Roy, P. eds (2012) *Memory and Urban Religion in the Ancient World*. London.
Bonnet, C. (2007) 'L'histoire séculière et profane des religions' in *Rites et croyances dans les religions du monde romain: huit exposés suivis de discussions: Vandoevres–Genève, 21–25 août 2006*, ed. C. Bonnet. Geneva: 1–37.
Borlik, T. A. (2011) *Ecocriticism and Early Modern English Literature: Green Pastures*. London.
Boyancé, P. (1972) *Études sur la religion romaine*. Rome.
Brand, J. (1777) *Observations on Popular Antiquities: including the whole of Mr Bourne's 'Antiquitates Vulgares', with addenda to every chapter of that work, as also, an appendix containing such articles on the subject, as have been omitted by that author*. Newcastle.
Bremmer, J. N. (1998) '"Religion", "ritual" and the opposition "sacred vs. profane": notes towards a terminological "genealogy"' in *Ansichten griechischer Rituale*, ed. F. Graf. Stuttgart: 9–32.
Brennan, A. and Lo, Y. S. eds (2010) *Understanding Environmental Philosophy*. Durham.
Bretschneider, G. ed. (1998) *I culti della campania antica*. Naples.
Brilliant, R. (1974) *Roman Art from the Republic to Constantine*. London.
Brock, M. D. (1911) *Studies in Fronto and his Age*. Cambridge.
Broise, H. and Scheid, J. (1993) 'Étude d'un cas: le lucus deae Diae à Rome' in *Les bois sacrés. Actes du colloque international organisé par le Centre Jean*

Bibliography

Bérard et l'École Pratique des Hauts Études (Ve section), Naples, 23–25 novembre 1989, eds O. de Cazanove and J. Scheid. Naples: 145–157.

Bruère, R. T. (1958) ' "Color Ovidianus" in Silius "Punica" 1–7' in *Ovidiana*, ed. N. I. Herescu. Paris: 475–499.

Bruggisser, P. (1987) *Romulus Servianus: la légende de Romulus dans les Commentaires à Virgile de Servius: mythographie et idéologie à l'époque de la dynastie théodosienne.* Bonn.

Brunt, P. A. (1989) 'Philosophy and religion in the late Republic' in *Philosophia Togata: Essays on Philosophy and Roman Society*, eds M. Griffin and J. Barnes. Oxford: 174–198.

Buchheit, V. (1960) 'Feigensymbolik im antiken Epigramm' *RhM* 103: 200–229.

Buckland, W. W. (1921) *A Text-Book of Roman Law from Augustus to Justinian*. Cambridge.

Bulbulia, J., Sosis, R., Harris, E., Genet, R., Genet, C. and Wyman, K. eds (2008) *The Evolution of Religion: Studies, Theories and Critiques*. Santa Margarita, CA.

Caird, E. (1893) *The Evolution of Religion*. Glasgow.

Calame, C. and Lincoln, B. (2012) 'Les approches comparatives en histoire des religions antiques: controverses récurrentes et propositions nouvelles' in *Comparer en histoire des religions antiques: controverses et propositions*, eds C. Calame and B. Lincoln. Liège: 7–12.

Cameron, A. (2004) *Greek Mythography in the Roman World*. Oxford.

Campbell, G. L. (2003) *Lucretius on Creation and Evolution: A Commentary on 'De Rerum Natura', Book 5, Lines 772–1104*. Oxford.

Camps, W. A. (1969) *An Introduction to Virgil's 'Aeneid'*. Oxford.

Carandini, A. (2011) *Rome: Day One*, trans. S. Sartarelli. Princeton.

Carey, S. (2003) *Pliny's Catalogue of Culture: Art and Empire in the 'Natural History'*. Oxford.

Caro, S. de. ed. (1992) *Alla ricerca di Iside: analisi, studi e restauri dell' Iseo Pompeiano nel Museo di Napoli*. Rome.

Carroll, M. (2003) *Earthly Paradises: Ancient Gardens in History and Archaeology*. London.

(2008) 'Nemus et templum. Exploring the sacred grove at the temple of Venus in Pompeii' in *Nuove ricerche archaeologiche nell'area Vesuviana: scavi 2003–2006*, eds P. G. Guzzo and M. P. Guidobaldi. Rome: 37–45.

(2010) 'Exploring the sanctuary of Venus and its sacred grove: politics, cult and identity in Roman Pompeii' *PBSR* 78: 63–106.

(in press) 'Temple gardens and sacred groves' in *Gardens of the Roman Empire*, ed. W. F. Jashemski. New York.

Carter, J. B. (1906) *The Religion of Numa: and Other Essays on the Religion of Ancient Rome*. London.

Cazanove, O. de. (1993) 'Suspension d'ex-voto dans les bois sacrés' in *Les bois sacrés. Actes du colloque international organisé par le Centre Jean Bérard et l'École Pratique des Hauts Études (Ve section), Naples, 23–25 novembre 1989*, eds O. de Cazanove and J. Scheid. Naples: 111–126.

Bibliography

(2000) 'Les lieux de culte italiques: approches romaines, désignation indigènes' in *Lieux sacrés, lieux de culte, sanctuaires: approches terminologiques, méthodologiques, historiques et monographiques*, ed. A. Vauchez. Rome: 31–41.

Chadwick, N. K. (1966) *The Druids*. Cardiff.

Champlin, E. (1980) *Fronto and Antonine Rome*. Cambridge, MA.

Chaniotis, A. (2004) 'Under the watchful eyes of the gods: divine justice in Hellenistic and Roman Asia Minor' in *The Greco-Roman East: Politics, Culture, Society*, ed. S. Colvin. Cambridge: 1–43.

Chapot, F. and Laurot, B. (2001) *Corpus de prières grecques et romaines*. Turnhout.

Cheney, J. (2005) 'The neo-Stoicism of radical environmentalism' in *Environmental Philosophy: Critical Concepts in the Environment*, vol. V, eds J. B. Callicott and C. Palmer. London: 181–215.

Chevalier, R. (1986) 'Le bois, l'arbre et la forêt chez Pline' *Helmantica* 37: 147–172.

Clark, A. (2007) *Divine Qualities: Cult and Community in Republican Rome*. Oxford.

Clark, G. (1996) 'Cosmic sympathies: nature as the expression of divine purpose' in *Human Landscapes in Classical Antiquity: Environment and Culture*, eds G. Shipley and J. Salmon. London: 310–329.

Clarke, J. R. (1991) *The Houses of Roman Italy, 100 B.C.–A.D. 250: Ritual, Space, and Decoration*. Berkeley, CA.

Coarelli, F. (1983–1985) *Il foro romano* (2 vols.). Rome.

(1987) *I santuari del Lazio in età repubblicana*. Rome.

(1993) 'I luci del Lazio: la documentazione archaeologica' in *Les bois sacrés. Actes du colloque international organisé par le Centre Jean Bérard et l'École Pratique des Hauts Études (Ve section), Naples, 23–25 novembre 1989*, eds O. de Cazanove and J. Scheid. Naples: 45–52.

ed. (2002) *Pompeii*. New York.

Codrington, R. H. (1891) *The Melanesians: Studies in their Anthropology and Folk-Lore*. Oxford.

Cole, S. G. (2004) *Landscapes, Gender, and Ritual Space: The Ancient Greek Experience*. London.

Connors, C. (1992) 'Seeing cypresses in Virgil' *CJ* 88: 1–17.

Conway, R. S. (1933) *Ancient Italy and Modern Religion*. Cambridge.

Cook, A. B. (1903) 'Zeus, Jupiter and the Oak' *CR* 17: 174–186, 268–278 and 403–421.

(1925) *Zeus: A Study in Ancient Religion*, vol. II.i. Cambridge.

Coombs, D. ed. (1992) *The Complete Book of Pruning*. London.

Coralini, A. (2001) *Hercules domesticus: immagini di Ercole nelle case della regione vesuviana*. Naples.

Corbeill, A. (2015) *Sexing the World: Grammatical Gender and Biological Sex in Ancient Rome*. Princeton.

Cornell, T. J. ed. (2013) *The Fragments of the Roman Historians*. Oxford.

Bibliography

Coupe, L. ed. (2000) *The Green Studies Reader: From Romanticism to Ecocriticism*. London.
Craik, E. M. (1980) *The Dorian Aegean*. London.
Crusius, O. (1897) *Babrii fabulae Aesopeae*. Leipzig.
Cumont, F. (1909) *Les religions orientales dans le paganisme romaine: conférences faites au Collège de France*. Paris.
Curchin, L. A. (1991) *Roman Spain: Conquest and Assimilation*. London.
Dall'Olio, L. (1989) 'Il motivo della "porta sacra" nella pittura romana di paesaggio' *Latomus* 48: 513–531.
Dalyell, J. G. (1834) *Darker Superstitions of Scotland: Illustrated from History and Practice*. Edinburgh.
Davies, J. P. (2004) *Rome's Religious History: Livy, Tacitus and Ammianus on Their Gods*. Cambridge.
Dawson, C. M. (1965) *Romano-Campanian Mythological Landscape Painting*. Rome.
Day, J. W. (2010) *Archaic Greek Epigram and Dedication: Representation and Reperformance*. Cambridge.
De Brosses, C. (1760) *Du culte des dieux fétiches: ou, parallèle de l'ancienne religion de l'Egypte avec la religion actuelle de Nigritte*. Paris.
De Vos, M. (1980) *L'egittomania in pitture e mosaici romano-campani della prima età imperiale*. Leiden.
Della Corte, M. (1924) *Iuventus: un nuovo aspetto della vita pubblica di Pompei finora inesplorita, studiato e ricostruito con la scorta dei relativi documenti epigrafici, topografici, demografici, artistici e religiosi*. Arpino.
Dennett, D. C. (1995) *Darwin's Dangerous Idea: Evolution and the Meanings of Life*. London.
Detienne, M. (2000) *Comparer l'incomparable*. Paris.
Dewar, M. (1991) *Statius 'Thebaid' IX: Edited with an English Translation and Commentary*. Oxford.
Dignas, B. (2002) *Economy of the Sacred in Hellenistic and Roman Asia Minor*. Oxford.
Dillon, M. P. J. (1997) 'The ecology of the Greek sanctuary' *ZPE* 118: 113–127.
Dimitrova, N. (2002) 'Inscriptions and iconography in the monuments of the Thracian rider' *Hesperia* 71.2: 209–229.
Dolganov, A. (2008) 'Constructing author and authority: generic discourse in Cicero's *De Legibus*' *G&R* 55: 23–38.
Donohue, A. A. (1988) *Xoana and the Origins of Greek Sculpture*. Atlanta, GA.
Dorcey, P. F. (1992) *The Cult of Silvanus: A Study in Roman Folk Religion*. Leiden.
Dorson, R. M. (1968) *The British Folklorists: A History*. London.
Dowden, K. (1992) *Religion and the Romans*. London.
  (2000) *European Paganism: The Realities of Cult from Antiquity to the Middle Ages*. London.
Drossaart Lulofs, H. J. and Poortman, E. L. J. (1989) *Nicolaus Damascenus 'De Plantis': Five Translations*. Amsterdam.

Bibliography

Dubourdieu, A. and Scheid, J. (2000) 'Lieux de culte, lieux sacrés: les usages de la langue, l'Italie romaine' in *Lieux sacrés, lieux de culte, sanctuaires: approches terminologiques, méthodologiques, historiques et monographiques* ed. A. Vauchez. Rome: 59–80.

Duff, J. D. (1934) *Silius Italicus 'Punica' I–VIII*. Cambridge, MA.

Dulière, C. (1979) *Lupa Romana: recherches d'iconographie et essai d'interprétation*. Brussels.

Dumézil, G. (1970) *Archaic Roman Religion: With an Appendix on the Religion of the Etruscans*, trans. P. Krapp. Chicago.

(1975) *Fêtes romaines d'été et d'automne suivi de dix questions romaines*. Paris.

Dupont, F. (1993) *Daily Life in Ancient Rome*. Oxford

Durkheim, É. (1912/2001) *The Elementary Forms of the Religious Life*, trans. C. Cosman. Oxford.

Dyson, J. T. (2001) *King of the Wood: The Sacrificial Victor in Virgil's 'Aeneid'*. Norman, OK.

Dyson, S. (1970) 'Caepio, Tacitus, and Lucan's sacred grove' *CPh* 65: 36–38.

Edlund-Berry, I. (2006) 'Hot, cold, or smelly: the power of sacred water in Roman religion, 400–100 BCE' in *Religion in Republican Italy*, eds C. Schultz and P. B. Harvey. Cambridge: 162–180.

Edwards, C. (1996) *Writing Rome: Textual Approaches to the City*. Cambridge.

Edwards, M. (1999) 'The flowering of Latin apologetic: Lactantius and Arnobius' in *Apologetics in the Roman Empire: Pagans, Jews and Christians*, eds M. Edwards, M. Goodman and S. Price. Oxford: 197–221.

Egan, G. (2006) *Green Shakespeare: From Ecopolitics to Ecocriticism*. London.

Egelhaaf-Gaiser, U. (2011) 'Roman cult sites: a pragmatic approach' in *A Companion to Roman Religion*, ed. J. Rüpke. Oxford: 205–221.

Eidinow, E., Kindt, J. and Osborne, R. eds (in press) *Theologies of Ancient Greek Religion*. Cambridge.

Eliade, M. (1949) *Traité d'histoire des religions*. Paris.

(1956/1959) *The Sacred and the Profane: The Nature of Religion*, trans. W. R. Trask. New York.

Elsner, J. (1992) 'Pausanias: a Greek pilgrim in the Roman world' *P&P* 135: 3–29.

(1996) 'Image and ritual: reflections on the religious appreciation of classical art' *CQ* 46: 515–531.

(1997) 'The origins of the icon: pilgrimage, religion and visual culture in the Roman East as "resistance" to the centre' in *The Early Roman Empire in the East*, ed. S. E. Alcock. Oxford: 178–199.

(2007) *Roman Eyes: Visuality and Subjectivity in Art and Text*. Princeton.

(2012) 'Sacrifice in late Roman art' in *Greek and Roman Animal Sacrifice: Ancient Victims, Modern Observers*, eds C. A. Faraone and F. S. Naiden. Cambridge: 120–166.

Engel, A. J. (1983) *From Clergyman to Don: The Rise of the Academic Profession in Nineteenth-Century Oxford*. Oxford.

Engels, D. (1999) *Classical Cats: The Rise and Fall of the Sacred Cat*. London.

Bibliography

(2007) *Das römische Vorzeichenwesen. (753–27 v. Chr.): Quellen, Terminologie, Kommentar, historische Entwicklung.* Stuttgart.
Evans, J. de. R. (1992) *The Art of Persuasion: Political Propaganda from Aeneas to Brutus.* Ann Arbor, MI.
Evans, R. (2008) *Utopia Antiqua: Readings of the Golden Age and Decline at Rome.* London.
Faraone, C. A. and Naiden, F. S. eds (2012) 'Introduction' in *Greek and Roman Animal Sacrifice: Ancient Victims, Modern Observers*, eds C. A. Faraone and F. S. Naiden. Cambridge: 1–12.
Farnell, L. R. (1896–1909) *The Cults of the Greek States* (5 vols.). Oxford.
(1905) *Evolution of Religion: An Anthropological Study.* London.
Farrar, L. (1998) *Ancient Roman Gardens.* Stroud.
Farrell, J. (1997) 'The phenomenology of memory in Roman culture' *CJ* 92: 373–383.
Feeney, D. (1988) *Literature and Religion at Rome.* Cambridge.
(2007) *Caesar's Calendar: Ancient Time and the Beginnings of History.* Berkeley, CA.
(2011) 'The history of Roman religion in Roman historiography and epic' in *A Companion to Roman Religion*, ed. J. Rüpke. Oxford: 129–142.
Ferguson, J. (1970) *The Religions of the Roman Empire.* London.
(1980) *Greek and Roman Religion: A Source Book.* Park Ridge, N.J.
Fergusson, J. (1868) *Tree and Serpent Worship: or, Illustrations of mythology and art in India in the first and fourth centuries after Christ, from the sculptures of the Buddhist topes at Sanchi and Amravati.* London.
Fishwick, D. (1969) 'Genius and numen' *HThR* 62: 356–367, repr. and revised in Fishwick, D. (1991) *The Imperial Cult in the Latin West II.1.* Leiden: 375–387.
(1987) *The Imperial Cult in the Latin West I.1.* Leiden.
(1991) *The Imperial Cult in the Latin West II.1.* Leiden.
(2007) 'Numen Augustum' *ZPE* 160: 247–255.
Fontaine, J. (1967) *Sulpice Sévère 'Vie de Saint Martin': commentaire.* Paris.
Forbes Irving, P. M. C. (1990) *Metamorphosis in Greek Myths.* Oxford.
Fordyce, C. J. (1977) *P. Vergili Maronis 'Aeneidos' Libri VII–VIII: With a Commentary.* Oxford.
Fox, M. (1995) *Roman Historical Myths: The Regal Period in Augustan Literature.* Oxford.
Frazer, J. G. (1911) *The Golden Bough: A Study in Magic and Religion: Part I, The Magic Art and the Evolution of Kings*, vol. I. London.
(1926) *The Worship of Nature.* London.
Freedberg, D. (1989) *The Power of Images: Studies in the History and Theory of Response.* Chicago.
Freisenbruch, A. (2007) 'Back to Fronto: doctor and patient in his correspondence with an emperor' in *Ancient Letters: Classical and Late Antique Epistolography*, eds R. Morello and A. Morrison. Oxford: 235–255.

Bibliography

Fröhlich, T. (1991) *Lararien- und Fassadenbilder in den Vesuvstädten: Untersuchungen zur 'volkstümlichen' pompejanischen Malerei*. Mainz.

Fugier, H. (1963) *Recherches sur l'expression du sacré dans la langue latine*. Paris.

Gaifman, M. (2008) 'The aniconic image of the Roman Near East' in *The Variety of Local Religious Life in the Near East in the Hellenistic and Roman Periods*, ed. T. Kaizer. Leiden: 37–72.

Galinksy, K. (2011) 'Continuity and change: religion in the Augustan semi-century' in *A Companion to Roman Religion*, ed. J. Rüpke. Oxford: 71–82.

Gall, J. le. (1975) *La religion romaine de l'époque de Caton l'Ancien au règne de l'empereur Commode*. Paris.

Galvao-Sobrinho, C. (2009) 'Claiming places: sacred dedications and public space in Rome in the principate' in *Dediche sacre nel mondo greco-romano: diffusione, funzioni, tipologie*, eds J. Bodel and M. Kajava. Rome: 127–159.

Gargola, D. J. (1995) *Lands, Laws and Gods: Magistrates and Ceremony in the Regulation of Public Lands in Republican Rome*. Chapel Hill, NC.

Garrard, G. (2004) *Ecocriticism*. London.

Geertz, C. (1973) *The Interpretation of Cultures*. New York.

(1976) *The Religion of Java*. Chicago.

Gell, A. (1998) *Art and Agency: An Anthropological Theory*. Oxford.

Gellner, D. N. (1999) 'Anthropological approaches' in *Approaches to the Study of Religion*, ed. P. Connolly. London: 10–41.

George, M. (1998) 'Elements of the peristyle in Campanian *atria*' *JRA* 11: 82–100.

Gibson, R. K. and Morello, R. eds (2011) *Pliny the Elder: Themes and Contexts*. Leiden.

Gilhus, I. S. (2006) *Animals, Gods and Humans: Changing Attitudes to Animals in Greek, Roman, and Early Christian Ideas*. London.

Girard, R. (1977) *Violence and the Sacred*. London.

Glay, M. le. (1971) *La religion romaine*. Paris.

Glinister, F. (2000) 'Sacred rubbish' in *Religion in Archaic and Republican Rome and Italy: Evidence and Experience*, eds E. Bispham and C. Smith. Edinburgh: 157–161.

Glinister, F. and Woods, C. eds (2007) *Verrius, Festus and Paul: Lexicography, Scholarship and Society*. London.

Glover, T. R. (1901) *Life and Letters in the Fourth Century*. Cambridge.

(1909) *The Conflict of Religions in the Early Roman Empire*. London.

Goldhill, S. ed. (2001) *Being Greek under Rome: Cultural Identity, the Second Sophistic and the Development of Empire*. Cambridge.

Goodhue, N. (1975) *The lucus furrinae and the Syrian Sanctuary on the Janiculum*. Amsterdam.

Goodyear, F. R. D. (1982) 'Technical writing' in *The Cambridge History of Classical Literature*, vol. II, *Latin Literature*, ed. E. J. Kenney. Cambridge: 667–673.

Bibliography

Gordon, R. (1979) 'The real and the imaginary: production and religion in the Graeco-Roman world' *Art History* 2: 5–34.
Gowers, E. (2000) 'Vegetable love: Virgil, Columella and garden poetry' *Ramus* 29: 127–148.
— (2005) 'Talking trees: Philemon and Baucis revisited' *Arethusa* 38: 331–365.
— (2011) 'Trees and family trees in the *Aeneid*' *ClAnt* 30: 87–118.
Gowing, A. M. (2005) *Empire and Memory: The Representation of the Roman Republic in Imperial Culture*. Cambridge.
Gradel, I. (2002) *Emperor Worship and Roman Religion*. Oxford.
Graillot, H. (1912) *Le culte de Cybèle, mère des dieux, à Rome et dans l'empire romain*. Paris.
Granger, F. S. (1895) *The Worship of the Romans*. London.
Green, C. M. C. (2007) *Roman Religion and the Cult of Diana at Aricia*. Cambridge.
Green, M. (1986) *The Gods of the Celts*. Gloucester.
Griffin, A. H. (1986) 'Erysichthon: Ovid's giant?' *G&R* 33: 55–63.
Grimal, P. (1943) *Les jardins romains à la fin de la république et aux deux premiers siècles de l'empire: essai sur le naturalisme romaine*. Paris.
Grimm, J. (1835/1883) *Teutonic Mythology*, vol. II, trans. S. Stallybrass. London.
Groton, A. H. (1990) 'Planting trees for Antipho in Caecilius Statius' *Synephebi*" *Dioniso* 60: 58–63.
Guidobaldi, M. P. (2010a) 'New archaeological research at the villa of the Papyri' in *The Villa of the Papyri at Herculaneum*, ed. M. Zarmakoupi. Berlin and New York: 21–62.
— (2010b) 'Arredi di lusso in legno e avorio da Ercolano: le nuove scoperte della Villa dei Papiri' *LANX* 6: 63–99.
Guzzo, P. G. and Fergola, L. eds (2000) *Oplontis: la villa di Poppaea*. Milan.
Habicht, C. (1985) *Pausanias' Guide to Ancient Greece*. London.
Habinek, T. N. (1998) *The Politics of Latin Literature: Writing, Identity, and Empire in Ancient Rome*. Princeton.
Hackworth-Petersen, L. (2006) *The Freedman in Roman Art and Art History*. Cambridge.
Hadzsits, G. D. (1936) 'The *vera historia* of the Palatine *ficus Ruminalis*' *CPh* 31: 305–319.
Hahn, D. E. (1977) *The Origins of Stoic Cosmology*. Columbus, OH.
Hales, S. (2003) *The Roman House and Social Identity*. Cambridge.
Halliday, W. R. (1922) *Lectures on the History of Roman Religion from Numa to Augustus*. Liverpool.
Hardie, P. (2006) 'Ovidian trees and birds: *Silvae* 2.3 and 2.4' in *Flavian Poetry*, eds R. R. Nauta, H.-J. van Dam and J. L. Smolenaars. Leiden: 207–221.
Harmon, D. P. (1986) 'Religion in the Latin elegists' *ANRW* 2.16: 1909–1973.
Harris, M. (1968) *The Rise of Anthropological Theory*. London.
Harrison, J. E. (1885) *Introductory Studies in Greek Art*. London.
— (1927) *Themis: A Study of the Social Origins of Greek Religion*. Cambridge.

Bibliography

Harrison, S. (1998) 'The sword-belt of Pallas. (*Aeneid* X.495-506): symbolism and ideology' in *Vergil's 'Aeneid': Augustan Epic and Political Context*, ed. H.-P. Stahl. London: 223-242.

(2005) 'Decline and nostalgia' in *A Companion to Latin Literature*, ed. S. Harrison. Oxford: 287-299.

Harrison, T. (2007) 'Greek religion and literature' in *A Companion to Greek Religion*, ed. D. Ogden. Oxford: 373-384.

Hartland, E. S. (1891) *The Science of Fairytales: An Enquiry into Fairy Mythology*. London.

Harvey, G. (1997) *Contemporary Paganism: Listening People, Speaking Earth*. New York.

(2009) 'Animist paganism' in *Handbook of Contemporary Paganism*, ed. J. R. Lewis and M. Pizza. Leiden: 393-411.

Harvey, P. B. (2006) 'Religion and memory at Pisaurum' in *Religion in Republican Italy*, eds C. E. Schultz and P. B. Harvey. Cambridge: 117-136.

Healy, J. F. (1999) *Pliny the Elder on Science and Technology*. Oxford.

Heerink, M. (2007) 'Going a step further: Valerius Flaccus' metapoetical reading of Propertius' Hylas' *CQ* 57: 606-620.

Henderson, J. (1995) 'Horace *Odes* 3.22 and the life of meaning: stumbling and stampeding out of the woods, blinking and screaming into the light, snorting and gorging at the trough, slashing and gouging at the death', *Ramus* 24: 103-151.

(1997) 'The name of the tree: recounting *Odyssey* XXIV.340-2', *JHS* 117: 87-116.

(2011) 'The nature of man: Pliny, *Historia Naturalis* as cosmogram' *MD* 66: 139-171.

Henrichs, A. (1979) '"Thou shalt not kill a tree": Greek, Manichean and Indian tales' *BASP* 16: 35-108.

Henzen, W. (1874) *Acta fratrum Arvalium quae supersunt*. Berlin.

Herbig, R. ed. (1939) *Denkmäler der Malerei des Altertums: Serie II - Text*. Munich.

Herrmann, P. and Malay, H. (2007) *New Documents from Lydia*. Vienna.

Hersey, G. (1988) *The Lost Meaning of Classical Architecture: Speculations on Ornament from Vitruvius to Venturi*. London.

Hickson, F. V. (1993) *Roman Prayer Language: Livy and the 'Aeneid' of Vergil*. Stuttgart.

Hingley, R. (1996) 'The 'legacy' of Rome: the rise, decline, and fall of the theory of Romanization' in *Roman Imperialism: Post-Colonial Perspectives*, eds J. Webster and N. Cooper. Leicester: 35-48.

(2005) *Globalizing Roman Culture: Unity, Diversity and Empire*. London.

Holland, L. A. (1961) *Janus and the Bridge*. Rome.

Hollis, A. S. (1970) *Ovid 'Metamorphoses' Book VIII*. Oxford.

Horden, P. and Purcell, N. (2000) *The Corrupting Sea: A Study of Mediterranean History*. Oxford.

Bibliography

Horsfall, N. M. (1987) 'Myth and mythography at Rome' in *Roman Myth and Mythography*, eds J. N. Bremmer and N. M. Horsfall. London: 1–11.
Howgego, C. (2005) 'Coinage and identity in the Roman Provinces' in *Coinage and Identity in the Roman Provinces*, eds C. Howgego, V. Heuchert and A. Burnett. Oxford: 1–19.
Hubert, H. and Mauss, M. (1899) 'Essai sur la nature et la fonction du sacrifice' *L'Année Sociologique* 2: 29–138.
Hughes, J. D. (1975) *Ecology in Ancient Civilizations*. Albuquerque, N.M.
  (1994) *Pan's Travail: Environmental Problems of the Ancient Greeks and Romans*. London.
Hunt, A. (2010) 'Elegiac grafting in Pomona's orchard: Ovid, *Metamorphoses* 14.623–771' *MD* 65: 43–58.
  (2011) 'Priapus as wooden god: confronting manufacture and destruction' *CCJ* 57: 29–54.
  (2012) 'Keeping the memory alive: the physical continuity of the *ficus Ruminalis*' in *Memory and Urban Religion in the Ancient World*, ed. M. Bommas, J. Harrisson and P. Roy. London: 111–128.
  (in press) 'Arboreal animists: the (ab)use of Roman sacred trees in early anthropology' in *The Classics and Early Anthropology*, ed. E. Varto. Leiden.
Hunt, E. D. (1982) *Holy Land Pilgrimage in the Later Roman Empire AD 312–460*. Oxford.
Hutton, W. (2005) *Describing Greece: Landscape and Literature in the 'Periegesis' of Pausanias*. Cambridge.
Irby-Massie, G. L. (1999) *Military Religion in Roman Britain*. Leiden.
Jacob, C. (1993) 'Paysage et bois sacré: ἄλσος dans la *Périègèse de la Grèce* de Pausanias' in *Les bois sacrés. Actes du colloque international organisé par le Centre Jean Bérard et l'École Pratique des Hauts Études (Ve section), Naples, 23–25 novembre 1989*, eds O. de Cazanove and J. Scheid. Naples: 31–44.
James, W. (1902/1982) *The Varieties of Religious Experience: A Study in Human Nature*. Harmondsworth.
Jashemski, W. F. (1979) *The Gardens of Pompeii*. New York.
Jashemski, W. F. and Meyer, F. G. (2002) *The Natural History of Pompeii*. Cambridge.
Jenkyns, R. (2013) *God, Space and City in the Roman Imagination*. Oxford.
Jennings, H. (1890) *Cultus arborum: a descriptive account of phallic tree worship, with illustrative legends, superstitions, usages, etc., exhibiting its origin and development amongst the eastern and western nations of the world, from the earliest to modern times; with a bibliography of works upon and referring to the phallic cultus*. London.
Jones, O. and Cloke, P. (2002) *Tree Cultures: The Place of Trees and Trees in Their Place*. Oxford.
  (2008) 'Non-human agencies: trees in place and time' in *Material Agency: Towards a Non-Anthropocentric Approach*, eds C. Knappett and L. Malafouris. New York: 79–96.

Bibliography

Kastelic, J. (1999) 'The Alcestis sarcophagus and the Orestes sarcophagus in the Vatican and reliefs in Šempeter' *Arheološki Vestnik* 50: 259–286.
Keary, C. F. (1882) *Outlines of Primitive Belief among the Indo-European Races*. New York.
Keay, S. and Terrenato, N. (2001) *Italy and the West: Comparative Issues in Romanization*. Oxford.
Keightley, T. (1828) *The Fairy Mythology*. London.
— (1831) *The Mythology of Ancient Greece and Italy*. London.
Kennedy, D. (1982) 'Gallus and the *Culex*' *CQ* 32: 371–389.
Kenzo, T. and Noboru, K. (1965) *Ise: Prototype of Japanese Architecture*. Cambridge, MA.
Kindt, J. (2012) *Rethinking Greek Religion*. Cambridge.
King, R. J. (1863) 'Sacred trees and flowers' *QR* 227: 210–250.
Kleiner, D. E. E. (1992) *Roman Sculpture*. New Haven, CT.
Kluckhohn, C. (1961) *Anthropology and the Classics*. Providence.
Knapp, R. (2011) *Invisible Romans. Prostitutes, Outlaws, Slaves, Gladiators, Ordinary Men and Women: The Romans that History Forgot*. London.
Köves-Zulauf, T. (1978) 'Plinius d. Ä. und die römische Religion' *ANRW* 2.16: 187–288.
Kruschwitz, P. (2010) 'Writing on trees: restoring a lost facet of the Graeco-Roman epigraphic habit' *ZPE* 173: 45–62.
Lambrinoudakis, V. (2005) 'Consecration' *ThesCRA* 3: 303–346.
Lancelotti, M. G. (2002) *Attis, between Myth and History: King, Priest and God*. Leiden.
Lane, E. N. (1985) *Corpus Cultus Iovis Sabazii: The Other Monuments and Literary Evidence*, vol. II. Leiden.
— (1989) *Corpus Cultus Iovis Sabazii: Conclusions*, vol. III. Leiden.
Lane Fox, R. (1986) *Pagans and Christians*. London.
Lang, A. (1893) *Custom and Myth*. London.
— (1898) *The Making of Religion*. London.
Larson, J. (2001) *Greek Nymphs: Myth, Cult, Lore*. Oxford.
— (2010) 'A land full of gods: nature deities in Greek religion' in *A Companion to Greek Religion*, ed. D. Ogden. Oxford: 56–70.
Latte, K. (1967) *Römische Religionsgeschichte*. Munich.
Lawrence, T. E. (1926/1977) *Seven Pillars of Wisdom*. Harmondsworth.
Leach, E. W. (1988) *Rhetoric of Space: Literary and Artistic Representations of Landscape in Republican and Augustan Rome*. Princeton.
Lehoux, D. (2011) 'Natural knowledge in the classical world' in *Wrestling with Nature: From Omens to Science*, eds P. Harrison, R. L. Numbers and M. H. Shank. Chicago: 37–58.
— (2012) *What Did the Romans Know? An Enquiry into Science and Worldmaking*. Chicago.
Leigh, M. (1999) 'Lucan's Caesar and the sacred grove: deforestation and enlightenment in antiquity' in *Interpretare Lucano: miscellanea di studi*, eds P. Esposito and L. Nicastri. Naples: 167–205.

Bibliography

Lejeune, M. (1993) 'Enclos sacré' dans les épigraphes indigènes d'Italie' in *Les bois sacrés. Actes du colloque international organisé par le Centre Jean Bérard et l'École Pratique des Hauts Études (Ve section), Naples, 23–25 novembre 1989*, eds O. de Cazanove and J. Scheid. Naples: 93–101.

Lennon, J. J. (2014) *Pollution and Religion in Ancient Rome*. Cambridge.

Lessa, W. A. and Vogt, E. Z. (1972) 'General introduction' in *Reader in Comparative Religion: An Anthropological Approach*, eds W. A. Lessa and E. Z. Vogt. New York: 1–6.

Leunissen, M. (2010) *Explanation and Teleology in Aristotle's Science of Nature*. Cambridge.

Levene, D. S. (1993) *Religion in Livy*. Leiden.

Levi, D. (1947) *Antioch Mosaic Pavements*. Princeton.

Lévy-Bruhl, L. (1922) *La mentalité primitive*. Paris.

Lewis, J. R. (1999) *Witchcraft Today: An Encyclopedia of Wiccan and Neopagan Traditions*. Santa Barbara, CA.

Liebeschuetz, J. H. W. G. (1979) *Continuity and Change in Roman Religion*. Oxford.

Linder, M. and Scheid, J. (1993) 'Quand croire c'est faire. Le problème de la croyance dans la Rome ancienne' *Archives de Sciences Sociales des Religions* 81: 47–62.

Linders, T. and Nordquist, G. eds (1985) *Gifts to the Gods: Proceedings of the Uppsala Symposium*. Uppsala.

Linderski, J. (1995) *Roman Questions: Selected Papers*. Stuttgart.

(2007) *Roman Questions II: Selected Papers*. Stuttgart.

Lipka, M. (2009) *Roman Gods: A Conceptual Approach*. Leiden.

Lomas, K. (1996) *Roman Italy: 338 BC–AD 200: A Sourcebook*. London.

Lovejoy, A. O. and Boas, G. (1965) *Primitivism and Related Ideas in Antiquity*. New York.

Lovelock, J. (2009) *The Vanishing Face of Gaia: A Final Warning*. London.

Lowe, D. (2010) 'The symbolic value of grafting in ancient Rome' *TAPhA* 140: 461–488.

(2011) 'Tree worship, sacred groves and Roman antiquities in the *Aeneid*' *PVS* 27: 99–128.

Lubbock, J. (1870) *The Origin of Civilisation and the Primitive Condition of Man: Mental and Social Condition of Savages*. London.

Lugli, G. (1946) *Roma antica: il centro monumentale*. Rome.

MacBain, B. (1982) *Prodigy and Expiation: A Study in Religion and Politics in Republican Rome*. Brussels.

MacDougall, E. B. ed. (1987) *Ancient Roman Villa Gardens: Dumbarton Oaks Colloquium on the History of Landscape Architecture X*. Washington, DC.

McKay, K. J. (1962) *Erysichthon: A Callimachean Comedy*. Leiden.

McLennan, J. F. (1869–1870) 'The worship of animals and plants' *Fortnightly Review* 4: 407–427, 562–582; 7: 194–216.

Maguinness, W. S. (1953) *Virgil: 'Aeneid' Book XII*. London.

Bibliography

Malay, H. and Sayor, M. H. (2004) 'A new confession to Zeus "from Twin Oaks"' *Epigraphica Anatolia* 37: 183–184.

Malinowski, B. (1935) *Coral Gardens and their Magic: A Study of the Methods of Tilling the Soil and of Agricultural Rites in the Trobriand Islands* (2 vols.). London.

Mannhardt, W. (1875) *Wald- und Feldkulte*, vol. I. Berlin.

(1877) *Wald- und Feldkulte*, vol. II. Berlin.

Marett, R. R. (1914) *The Threshold of Religion*. London.

Marinatos, N. and Hägg, R. (1993) *Greek Sanctuaries: New Approaches*. London.

Marks, R. (2004) 'Of kings, crowns and boundary stones: Cipus and the *hasta Romuli* in *Metamorphoses* 15' *TAPhA* 134: 107–131.

Marlow, H. (2009) *Biblical Prophets and Contemporary Environmental Ethics: Re-Reading Amos, Hosea and First Isaiah*. Oxford.

Marsden, W. (1783) *The History of Sumatra: containing an account of the government, laws, customs, and manners of the native inhabitants, with a description of the natural productions, and a relation of the ancient political state of that island*. London.

Martens, M. (2004) 'Re-thinking sacred "rubbish": the ritual deposits of the temple of Mithras at Tienen' *JRA* 17: 333–353.

Mattingly, D. J. (1997) 'Dialogues of power and experience in the Roman empire' in *Dialogues in Roman Imperialism: Power, Discourse, and Discrepant Experience in the Roman Empire*, ed. D. J. Mattingly. Portsmouth, RI: 7–24.

Mazzoni, C. (2010) *She-Wolf: The Story of a Roman Icon*. Cambridge.

Mehl, A. (2011) *Roman Historiography: An Introduction to its Basic Aspects and Development*, trans. H.-F. Mueller. Oxford.

Meiggs, R. (1982) *Trees and Timber in the Ancient Mediterranean World*. Oxford.

Metropilou, E. (1996) 'The goddess Cybele in funerary banquets and with an equestrian hero' in *Essays in Memory of M. J. Vermaseren*, ed. E. N. Lane. Leiden: 135–165.

Millett, M. (2002) 'Romanization: historical issues and archaeological interpretation' in *The Early Roman Empire in the West*, eds T. Blagg and M. Millett. Oxford: 35–41.

Mitchell, S. (1993) *Anatolia: Land, Men, and Gods in Asia Minor*. Oxford.

Moatti, C. (1997) *La raison de Rome: naissance de l'esprit critique à la fin de la République (IIe–Ier siècle avant Jésus-Christ)*. Paris.

Momigliano, A. (1987) *On Pagans, Jews and Christians*. Middletown, CT.

Mommsen, T. (1899/1955) *Römisches Strafrecht*. Graz.

Morales, H. (2007) *Classical Mythology: A Very Short Introduction*. Oxford.

Morford, M. P. O., Lenardon, R. J. and Sham, M. eds (2011) *Classical Mythology*. Oxford.

Morgan, G. (2000) 'Omens in Tacitus' *Histories* I–III' in *Divination and Portents in the Roman World*, eds R. L. Wildfang and J. Isager. Odense: 25–42.

Morgan, T. (2007) *Popular Morality in the Early Roman Empire*. Cambridge.

Bibliography

Mueller, H.-F. (2002) *Roman Religion in Valerius Maximus*. London.
Müller, F. M. (1901) *Lectures on the Origin and Growth of Religion, as Illustrated by the Religions of India*. London.
Murphy, T. (2004) *Pliny the Elder's 'Natural History': The Empire in the Encylopedia*. Oxford.
Myers, K. S. (2005) 'Docta otia: garden ownership and configuration of leisure in Statius and Pliny the Younger' *Arethusa* 38: 103–129.
Nadeau, Y. (2010) 'Naulochus and Actium, the fleets of Paris and Aeneas, and the tree-felling of C. Iulius Caesar Erysichthon' in *Studies in Latin Literature and Roman History XV*, ed. C. Deroux. Brussels: 219–239.
Naiden, F. S. (2013) *Smoke Signals for the Gods: Ancient Greek Sacrifice from the Archaic through Roman Periods*. Oxford.
Nash, E. (1962) *Pictorial Dictionary of Ancient Rome* (2 vols.). London.
Nasrallah, L. S. (2010) *Christian Responses to Roman Art and Architecture*. Cambridge.
Nilsson, M. P. (1925) *A History of Greek Religion*, trans. F. J. Fielden. Oxford.
Nisbet, R. G. (1939) *De domo sua*. Oxford.
 (1987) 'The oak and the axe: symbolism in Seneca *Hercules Oetaeus* 1618ff.' in *Homo Viator: Classical Essays for John Bramble*, eds M. Whitby, P. Hardie and M. Whitby. Bristol: 243–252.
Nisbet, R. G. and Rudd, N. (2004) *A Commentary on Horace, 'Odes', Book III*. Oxford.
Nock, A. D. (1972) *Essays on Religion and the Ancient World*. Cambridge, MA.
Norman, A. F. (2000) *Antioch as a Centre of Hellenic Culture as Observed by Libanius*. Liverpool.
North, J. A. (1994) 'The development of religious pluralism' in *The Jews among Pagans and Christians in the Roman Empire*, eds J. Lieu, J. North and T. Rajak. London: 174–193.
 (1995) 'Religion and rusticity' in *Urban Society in Roman Italy*, eds T. J. Cornell and K. Lomas. London: 135–150.
Ogilvie, R. M. (1969) *The Romans and Their Gods in the Age of Augustus*. London.
Oldenberg, H. F. (1875) '*De sacris fratrum Arvalium quaestiones*.' PhD thesis, Berlin.
Orlin, E. M. (1996) *Temples, Religion and Politics in the Roman Republic*. Leiden.
 (2010) *Foreign Cults in Rome: Creating a Roman Empire*. Oxford.
Orr, D. G. (1978) 'Roman domestic religion: the evidence of the household shrines' *ANRW* 2.16: 1557–1591.
Osborne, R. ed. (2004) *The Object of Dedication*. London.
Osborne, R. & Vout, C. (2010) 'A Revolution in Roman History?' *JRS* 100: 233–245.
Östenberg, I. (2009) *Staging the World: Spoils, Captives, and Representations in the Roman Triumphal Procession*. Oxford.

Bibliography

Otto, R. (1923) *The Idea of the Holy: An Inquiry into the Non-Rational Factor in the Idea of the Divine, and its Relation to the Rational*, trans. J. W. Harvey. Oxford.
Ouseley, W. (1819) *Travels in the East; more particularly Persia*. London.
Overmark Juul, L. (2010) *Oracular Tales in Pausanias*. Odense.
Paladino, I. (1988) *Fratres Arvales: storia di un collegio sacerdotale romano*. Rome.
Palm, T. (1948) *Trädkult*. Lund.
Palmer, R. E. A. (1974) *Roman Religion and Roman Empire*. Philadelphia.
Panciera, S. (2006) *Epigrafi, epigrafia, epigrafisti: scritti vari editi e inediti. (1956–2005) con note complementari e indici*. Rome.
Panetta, M. R. ed. (2004) *Pompeii: The History, Life and Art of the Buried City*. Vercelli.
Paparazzo, E. (2011) 'Philosophy and science in the Elder Pliny's *Naturalis historia*' in *Pliny the Elder: Themes and Contexts*, eds R. K. Gibson and R. Morello. Leiden: 89–111.
Papazarkadas, N. (2011) *Sacred and Public Land in Ancient Athens*. Oxford.
Parke, H. W. (1967) *The Oracles of Zeus: Dodona, Olympia, Ammon*. Oxford.
Parker, R. (1983) *Miasma: Pollution and Purification in Early Greek Religion*. Oxford.
(2004) 'Greek dedications I' *ThesCRA* 1: 269–281.
(2005) *Polytheism and Society at Athens*. Oxford.
Parkes, R. (2012) *Statius, 'Thebaid' 4: Edited with an Introduction, Translation and Commentary*. Oxford.
Pasoli, A. (1950) *Acta fratrum Arvalium quae post annum MDCCCLXXIV reperta sunt*. Bologna.
Pedley, J. (2005) *Sanctuaries and the Sacred in the Ancient Greek World*. Cambridge.
Peters, W. J. T. (1963) *Landscape in Romano-Campanian Mural Painting*. Assen, the Netherlands.
Petersen, E. (1908) 'Lupa capitolina' *Klio* 8: 440–456.
Petrain, D. (2000) 'Hylas and Silva: etymological wordplay in Propertius 1.20' *HSCP* 100: 409–421.
Petsalis-Diomidis, A. (2010) *Truly beyond Wonders: Aelius Aristides and the Cult of Asklepios*. Oxford.
Pettazzoni, R. (1946) 'Regnator omnium deus' *SMSR* 20: 142–156.
Petzl, G. (1978) 'Inschriften aus der Umgebung von Saittai (I)' *ZPE* 30: 249–273.
(1998) *Die Beichtinschriften im Römischen Kleinasien und der Fromme und Gerechte Gott*. Opladen.
Pfister, F. (1937) 'Numen' *RE* 17: 1273–1291.
Phillips, C. R. (1992) 'Roman religion and literary studies of Ovid's *Fasti*' *Arethusa* 25: 55–80.
(2000) 'Misconceptualising classical mythology' in *Oxford Readings in Greek Religion*, ed. R. G. A. Buxton. Oxford: 344–358.

Bibliography

(2011) 'Approaching Roman religion: the case for *Wissenschaftsgeschichte*' in *A Companion to Roman Religion*, ed. J. Rüpke. Oxford: 10–28.
Phillips, O. C. (1968) 'Lucan's grove' *CPh* 63: 296–300.
Philpot, J. H. (1897) *The Sacred Tree*. London.
Pietrangeli, C. (1939) *Spoletium (Spoleto): regio VI, Umbria*. Rome.
Pirenne-Delforge, V. (2008) *Retour à la source: Pausanias et la religion grecque*. Liège.
Platt, V. (2011) *Facing the Gods: Epiphany and Representation in Graeco-Roman Art, Literature and Religion*. Cambridge.
Polo, F. (2011) 'Consuls as curatores pacis deorum' in *Consuls and res publica: Holding High Office in the Roman Republic*, ed. H. Beck. Cambridge: 97–115.
Powell, J. (2007) 'Unfair to Caecilius? Ciceronian dialogue techniques in Minucius Felix' in *Severan Culture*, eds S. Swain, S. Harrison and J. Elsner. Cambridge: 177–189.
Prescendi, F. (2007) *Décrire et comprendre le sacrifice: les reflexions des Romains sur leur propre religion à partir de la littérature antiquaire*. Stuttgart.
Pretzler, M. (2007) *Pausanias: Travel Writing in Ancient Greece*. London.
Preus, J. S. (1987) *Explaining Religion: Criticism and Theory from Bodin to Freud*. New Haven, CT.
Price, S. R. F. (1984) *Rituals and Power: The Roman Imperial Cult in Asia Minor*. Cambridge.
(1999) *Religions of the Ancient Greeks*. Cambridge.
Pritchett, W. K. (1998) *Pausanias Periegetes*. Amsterdam.
Pugliese Carratelli, G. ed. (1999) *Pompei: pitture e mosaici IX*. Rome.
Purcell, N. (2005) 'Romans in the Roman world' in *The Cambridge Companion to the Age of Augustus*, ed. K. Galinksy. Cambridge: 85–105.
Quartarone, L. (2002) 'Roman forests, Vergilian trees: our ambiguous relationship with nature' in *Thinking about the Environment: Our Debt to the Classical and Medieval Past*, eds T. M. Robinson and L. Westra. Oxford: 59–71.
Rackham, H. (1945) *Pliny 'Natural History' XII–XVI*. Cambridge, MA.
(1950) *Pliny 'Natural History' XVII–XIX*. Cambridge, MA.
Rappaport, R. (1968) *Pigs for the Ancestors: Ritual in the Ecology of a New Guinea People*. New Haven, CT.
Rasmussen, S. W. (2000) 'Cicero's stand on prodigies: a non-existent dilemma?' in *Divination and Portents in the Roman World*, eds R. L. Longfang and J. Isager. Odense: 9–24.
(2003) *Public Portents in Republican Rome*. Rome.
Rawson, E. (1971) 'Prodigy lists and the use of the *Annales Maximi*' *CQ* 21: 158–169.
(1985) *Intellectual Life in the Late Roman Republic*. London.
Reckford, K. J. (1974) 'Some trees in Virgil and Tolkien' in *Perspectives of Roman Poetry: A Classics Symposium*, eds G. Luck and K. Galinsky. Austin, TX: 57–91.

Bibliography

Reggiani, A. M. (1998) *Tivoli: il santuario di Ercole Vincitore*. Milan.
Renfrew, C. and Zubrow, E. B. W. eds (1994) *The Ancient Mind: Elements of Cognitive Archaeology*. Cambridge.
Rhodes, P. J. and Osborne, R. eds (2003) *Greek Historical Inscriptions: 404–323 BC*. Oxford.
Richlin, A. (1992) 'Reading Ovid's rapes' in *Pornography and Representation in Greece and Rome*, ed. A. Richlin. Oxford: 158–179.
Richter, O. (1916) 'Indigitamenta' *RE* 9: 1334–1367.
Ridgway, B. S. (2002) *Hellenistic Sculpture III: The Styles of ca. 100–31 BC*. Madison, WI.
Ripollès, P. P. (2005) 'Coinage and identity in the Roman Provinces: Spain' in *Coinage and Identity in the Roman Provinces*, eds C. Howgego, V. Heuchert and A. Burnett. Oxford: 79–93.
Rives, J. B. (2007) *Religion in the Roman Empire*. Oxford.
(2012) 'Control of the sacred in Roman law' in *Law and Religion in the Roman Republic*, ed. O. Tellegen-Couperus. Leiden: 165–180.
Robert, L. (1983) 'Documents d'Asie Mineure' *BCH* 107: 497–599.
Robertson Smith, W. (1889) *Lectures on the Religion of the Semites*. New York.
Robinson, T. M. and Westra, L. eds (2002) *Thinking about the Environment: Our Debt to the Classical and Medieval Past*. Oxford.
Rose, H. J. (1926) *Primitive Culture in Italy*. London.
(1934) *Concerning Parallels*. Oxford.
(1935) 'Numen inest: "animism" in Greek and Roman religion' *HTR* 28: 237–257.
(1948) *Ancient Roman Religion*. London.
Rosenberger, V. (2011) 'Republican *nobiles*: controlling the *res publica*' in *A Companion to Roman Religion*, ed. J. Rüpke. Oxford: 292–303.
Rothblatt, S. (1968) *The Revolution of the Dons*. Cambridge.
Rouse, W. H. D. (1902) *Greek Votive Offerings: An Essay in the History of Greek Religion*. Cambridge.
Rüpke, J. (2007) *Religion of the Romans*, trans. R. Gordon. Cambridge.
ed. (2011a) *A Companion to Roman Religion*. Oxford.
(2011b) 'Roman religion and the religion of empire: some reflections on method' in *The Religious History of the Roman Empire: Pagans, Jews, and Christians*, eds J. A. North and S. R. F. Price. Oxford: 9–36.
(2012) *Religion in Republican Rome: Rationalization and Religious Change*. Philadelphia.
Rutherford, I. (2001) 'Tourism and the sacred: Pausanias and the traditions of Greek pilgrimage' in *Pausanias: Travel and Memory in Roman Greece*, eds S. E. Alcock, J. F. Cherry and J. Elsner. Oxford: 40–52.
Rutledge, S. H. (2012) *Ancient Rome as a Museum: Power, Identity, and the Culture of Collecting*. Oxford.
Ryberg, I. S. (1955) *Rites of the State Religion in Roman Art*. Rome.
Sabbatucci, D. (1952) 'Sacer' *SMSR* 23: 91–101.
Salzman-Mitchell, P. B. (2005) *A Web of Fantasies: Gaze, Image, and Gender in Ovid's 'Metamorphoses'*. Columbus, OH.

Bibliography

Sanctis, G. de. (1910) 'La leggenda della lupa e dei Gemelli' *RFIC* 38: 71–85.
Sandbach, F. H. (1975) *The Stoics*. London.
Schama, S. (1995) *Landscape and Memory*. London.
Scheid, J. (1981) 'Le délit religieux dans la rome tardo-républicaine' in *Le délit religieux dans la cité antique: table ronde: Rome, 6–7 avril 1978*, ed. M. Torelli. Rome: 117–171.
— (1987) 'Polytheism impossible; or, the empty gods: reasons behind a void in the history of Roman religion' *History and Anthropology* 3: 303–325.
— (1990) *Romulus et ses frères: le collège des frères arvales, modèle du culte public dans la Rome des empereurs*. Rome.
— (1993) 'Lucus, nemus: qu'est-ce qu' un bois sacré?' in *Les bois sacrés. Actes du colloque international organisé par le Centre Jean Bérard et l'École Pratique des Hauts Études (Ve section), Naples, 23–25 novembre 1989*, eds O. de Cazanove and J. Scheid. Naples: 13–20.
— (1996) 'Sacrifice, Roman' *OCD³*: 1345–1346.
— (1998) *Recherches archéologiques à La Magliana. Commentarii fratrum arvalium qui supersunt: les copies épigraphiques des protocoles annuels de la confrérie arvale (21 av.–304 ap. J.-C.)*. Rome.
— (2003a) *An Introduction to Roman Religion*, trans. J. Lloyd. Edinburgh.
— (2003b) 'Hierarchy and structure in Roman polytheism: Roman methods of conceiving action' in *Roman Religion*, ed. C. Ando. Edinburgh: 164–192.
— (2005) *Quand faire, c'est croire: les rites sacrificiels des Romains*. Paris.
— (2006) 'Oral tradition and written tradition in the formation of sacred law in Rome' in *Religion and Law in Classical and Christian Rome*, eds C. Ando and J. Rüpke. Stuttgart: 14–33.
— (2007) 'Sacrifices for gods and ancestors' in *A Companion to Roman Religion*, ed. J. Rüpke. Oxford: 263–272.
— (2012a) 'L'oubli du comparatisme dans certaines approches récentes des religions antiques' in *Comparer en histoire des religions antiques: controverses et propositions*, ed. C. Calame and B. Lincoln. Liège: 111–121.
— (2012b) 'Roman animal sacrifice and the system of being' in *Greek and Roman Animal Sacrifice: Ancient Victims, Modern Observers*, eds C. A. Faraone and F. S. Naiden. Cambridge: 84–98.
Scheid, J. and Linder, M. (1993) 'Quand croire c'est faire: le problème de la croyance dans la Rome ancienne' *Archives des Sciences Sociales des Religions* 81: 47–61.
Schilling, R. (1969) 'Dea Dia dans la liturgie des frères arvales' in *Hommages à Marcel Renaud*, vol. II, ed. J. Bibauw. Brussels: 675–679.
— (1979) *Rites, cultes, dieux de Rome*. Paris.
Schnabel, E. J. (2003) 'Divine tyranny and public humiliation: a suggestion for the interpretation of the Lydian and Phrygian confession inscriptions' *Novum Testamentum* 45: 160–188.
Schrijvers, P. H. (2006) 'Silius Italicus and the Roman sublime' in *Flavian Poetry*, eds R. R. Nauta, H.-J. van Dam and J. J. L. Smolenaars. Leiden: 97–111.

Bibliography

Scranton, R. L. (1967) *The Architecture of the Sanctuary of Apollo Hylates at Kourion*. Philadelphia.

Scullard, H. H. (1981) *Festivals and Ceremonies of the Roman Republic*. London.

Sedley, D. N. (1989) 'Philosophical allegiance in the Greco-Roman world' in *Philosophia togata: Essays on Philosophy and Roman Society*, ed. M. Griffin and J. Barnes. Oxford: 97–119.

(2007) *Creationism and its Critics in Antiquity*. Berkeley, CA.

Seeland, K. ed. (1997) *Nature is Culture: Indigenous Knowledge and Socio-Cultural Aspects of Trees and Forests in Non-European Cultures*. London.

Segal, C. P. (1973) 'Tacitus and poetic history: the end of *Annals* XIII' *Ramus* 2: 107–126.

Seidensticker, A. (1886) *Waldgeschichte des Alterthums: ein Handbuch für akademische Vorlesungen etc.* Frankfurt.

Sharpe, E. J. (1975) *Comparative Religion: A History*. London.

Simmons, M. B. (1995) *Arnobius of Sicca: Religious Conflict and Competition in the Age of Diocletian*. Oxford.

Sloman, A. (1906) *A Grammar of Classical Latin*. Cambridge.

Smith, C. (2007) 'Pliny the Elder and archaic Rome' in *Vita Vigilia est: Essays in Honour of Barbara Levick*, eds E. Bispham and G. Rowe. London: 147–170.

Smith, J. Z. (1973) 'When the bough breaks' *History of Religions* 12: 342–371.

(1982) 'The bare facts of ritual' in *Imagining Religion: From Babylon to Jonestown*, ed. J. Z. Smith. Chicago: 53–65.

(1990) *Drudgery Divine: On the Comparison of Early Christianities and the Religions of Late Antiquity*. London.

(1998) 'Religion, religions, religious' in *Critical Terms for Religious Studies*, ed. M. C. Taylor. Chicago: 269–284.

(2002) 'Manna, mana everywhere and /_/_/_/' in *Radical Interpretation in Religion*, ed. N. K. Frankenberry. Cambridge: 188–212.

(2004) 'The topography of the sacred' in *Relating Religion: Essays in the Study of Religion*, ed. J. Z. Smith. Chicago: 101–116.

Smith, R. R. R. (1985) Review of *Typology and Structure of Roman Historical Reliefs* *JRS* 75: 225–228.

Smith, R. S. and Trzaskoma, S. M. (2007) *Apollodorus' 'Library' and Hyginus' 'Fabulae': Two Handbooks of Greek Mythology*. Indianapolis.

Soren, D. (1987) *The Sanctuary of Apollo Hylates at Kourion, Cyprus*. Tucson, AZ.

Sourvinou-Inwood, C. (2000) 'What is polis religion?' in *Oxford Readings in Greek Religion*, ed. R. Buxton. Oxford: 13–37.

(2005) 'Hylas, the nymphs, Dionysos and others: myth, ritual, ethnicity', Martin P. Nilsson Lecture on Greek Religion, delivered 1997 at the Swedish Institute at Athens, Stockholm.

Spaltenstein, F. (1986) *Commentaire des 'Punica' des Silius Italicus: livres 1 à 8*. Geneva.

(2002) *Commentaire des 'Argonautica' de Valérius Flaccus: livres 1 et 2*. Brussels.

Bibliography

Spano, G. (1910) 'Pompei: relazione sulle scoperte avvenute dal 1 gennaio al 30 giugno 1910' *Notizie degli Scavi di Antichità* 7: 437–486.
Spawforth, A. (2012) *Greece and the Augustan Cultural Revolution*. Cambridge.
Stackelberg, K. T. von. (2009) *The Roman Garden: Space, Sense and Society*. London.
Stancliffe, C. (1983) *St. Martin and his Hagiographer: History and Miracle in Sulpicius Severus*. Oxford.
Stara-Tedde, G. (1905) 'I boschi sacri dell' Antica Roma', *BCAR* 33: 189–232.
Steiner, D. T. (2001) *Images in Mind: Statues in Archaic and Classical Greek Literature and Thought*. Princeton.
Steiner, G. (1955) 'The skepticism of Pliny the Elder' *CW* 48: 137–143.
Stewart, P. (2003) *Statues in Roman Society: Representation and Response*. Oxford.
Stocking, G. W. (1987) *Victorian Anthropology*. Oxford.
  (1995) *After Tylor: British Social Anthropology, 1888–1951*. London.
Stone, C. D. (1972) 'Should trees have standing? Toward legal rights for natural objects' *Southern California Law Review* 45: 450–487.
Straten, F. T. van. (1981) 'Gifts for the gods' in *Faith, Hope and Worship*, ed. H. S. Versnel. Leiden: 65–151.
Stubbings, F. H. (1946) 'Xerxes and the plane-tree' *G&R* 44: 63–67.
Susini, G. (1973) *The Roman Stonecutter: An Introduction to Latin Epigraphy*. Oxford.
Swain, S. (1996) *Hellenism and Empire: Language, Classicism, and Power in the Greek World, AD 50–250*. Oxford.
Tarrant, R. (2012) *Virgil 'Aeneid' Book XII*. Cambridge.
Tarver, T. (1994) 'Varro, Caesar and the Roman calendar: a study in late Republican religion' in *Religion and Superstition in Latin Literature*, ed. A. H. Sommerstein. Bari: 39–57.
Tatum, W. J. (1999) 'Roman religion: fragments and further questions' in *Veritatis amicitiaeque causa: Essays in Honor of Anna Lydia Motto and John R. Clark*, eds S. N. Byrne and E. P. Cueva. Wauconda, IL: 273–291.
Taylor, J. W. (1979) 'Tree worship' *Mankind Quarterly* 20: 79–142.
Taylor, L. R. (1912) *The Cults of Ostia*. Baltimore.
Thanos, C. A. (2003) 'Mt. Ida in mythology and classical antiquity: a plant scientist's approach' in *Book of Proceedings, First National Symposium on the Past, Present and Future of the Kazdağlari Mountains*. Ankara: 87–102.
Thiselton-Dyer, T. F. (1889) *The Folk-Lore of Plants*. London.
Thomas, R. F. (1988a) 'Tree violation and ambivalence in Virgil' *TAPhA* 118: 261–273.
  (1988b) *'Georgics': Virgil, Books 1–2*. Cambridge.
Thome, G. (1992) 'Crime and punishment, guilt and expiation: Roman thought and vocabulary' *Acta Classica* 35: 73–98.
Thommen, L. (2012) *An Environmental History of Ancient Greece and Rome*, trans. P. Hill. Cambridge.

Bibliography

Tomlinson, R. A. (1976) *Greek Sanctuaries*. New York.
Torelli, M. (1982) *Typology and Structure of Roman Historical Reliefs*. Ann Arbor, MI.
Tran Tam Tinh, V. (1964) *Essai sur le culte d'Isis à Pompéi*. Paris.
Tromp, S. (1921) *De Romanorum Piaculis*. Leiden.
Turcan, R. (1997) *The Cults of the Roman Empire*, trans. A. Nevill. Oxford.
  (2000) *The Gods of Ancient Rome*, trans. A. Nevill. Edinburgh.
Tylor, E. B. (1871a) *Primitive Culture: Researches into the Development of Mythology, Philosophy, Religion, Art, and Custom*, vol. I. London.
  (1871b) *Primitive Culture: Researches into the Development of Mythology, Philosophy, Religion, Art, and Custom*, vol. II. London.
  (1873) *Primitive Culture: Researches into the Development of Mythology, Philosophy, Religion, Language, Art, and Custom*, vol. II. London.
Vermaseren, M. J. (1977a) *Cybele and Attis: the Myth and the Cult*, trans. A. M. H. Lemmers. London.
  (1977b) *Corpus cultus Cybelae Attidisque*. Leiden.
Versnel, H. S. ed. (1981) *Faith, Hope and Worship: Aspects of Religious Mentality in the Ancient World*. Leiden.
  (2011) *Coping with the Gods: Wayward Readings in Greek Theology*. Leiden.
Veyne, P. (1988) *Did the Greeks Believe in their Myths? An Essay on the Constitutive Imagination*, trans. P. Wissing. Chicago.
Vigourt, A. (2001) *Les présages impériaux d'Auguste à Domitien*. Paris.
Visser, M. W. de. (1903) *Die Nicht Menschengestaltigen Götter der Griechen*. Leiden.
Vries, J. de. (1984) 'Theories concerning "nature myths"' in *Sacred Narrative: Readings in the Theory of Myth*, ed. A. Dundes. London: 30–40.
Wagenvoort, H. (1947) *Roman Dynamism*. Oxford.
Walker-Bynum, C. (2011) *Christian Materiality: An Essay on Religion in Late Medieval Europe*. Cambridge.
Wallace-Hadrill, A. (1982) 'The Golden Age and sin in Augustan ideology' *P&P* 95: 19–36.
  (1990) 'Pliny the Elder and man's unnatural history' *G&R* 37: 80–96.
  (1996) *Houses and Society in Pompeii and Herculaneum*. Princeton.
  (2005) 'Mutatas formas: the Augustan transformation of Roman knowledge' in *The Cambridge Companion to the Age of Augustus*, ed. K. Galinsky. Cambridge: 55–84.
  (2008) *Rome's Cultural Revolution*. Cambridge.
Warde-Fowler, W. (1899) *The Roman Festivals of the Period of the Republic*. London.
  (1911) *The Religious Experience of the Roman People*. London.
  (1914) *Roman Ideas of Deity in the Last Century before the Christian Era*. London.
Waring, J. B. (1870) *An Essay on the Mythological Significance of Tree and Serpent Worship*. Ramsgate.
Warrior, V. (2006) *Roman Religion*. Cambridge.
Watson, A. (1992) *The State, Law and Religion: Pagan Rome*. Oxford.
Watts, D. (1991) *Christians and Pagans in Roman Britain*. London.

Bibliography

Webster, J. (1996) 'Roman imperialism and the "post imperial age"' in *Roman Imperialism: Post-Colonial Perspectives*, eds J. Webster and N. Cooper. Leicester: 1–17.

Weinstock, S. (1949) 'H. J. Rose, *Ancient Roman Religion*' *JRS* 39: 166–167.

Welch, K. E. (2007) *The Roman Amphitheatre: From its Origins to the Colosseum*. Cambridge.

Wendel, C. (1935) *Scholia in Ap. Rhodium vetera*. Berlin.

Weniger, L. (1919) *Altgriechischer Baumkultus*. Leipzig.

Whaling, F. (1984) 'Comparative approaches' in *Contemporary Approaches to the Study of Religion*, vol. I., ed. F. Whaling. Berlin: 165–295.

White, C. (2000) *Early Christian Latin Poets*. London.

White, K. D. (1967) *Agricultural Implements of the Roman World*. Cambridge.

White, L., Jr (1967) 'The historical roots of our ecological crisis' *Science* 155: 1203–1207, repr. in Glotfelty, C. and Fromm, H. eds (1996) *The Ecocriticism Reader: Landmarks in Literary Ecology*. London: 3–14.

White, M. J. (2003) 'Stoic natural philosophy (physics and cosmology)' in *The Cambridge Companion to the Stoics*, ed. B. Inwood. Cambridge: 124–152.

Whitehouse, R. D. (1996) 'Ritual objects: archaeological joke or neglected evidence?' in *Approaches to the Study of Ritual: Italy and the Ancient Mediterranean*, ed. J. B. Wilkins. London: 9–30.

Wijsman, H. J. W. (1996) *Valerius Flaccus 'Argonautica', Book V: A Commentary*. Leiden.

Wildfang, R. L. and Isager, J. eds (2000) *Divination and Portents in the Roman World*. Odense.

Winstanley, D. A. (1940) *Early Victorian Cambridge*. Cambridge.

Wiseman, T. P. (1994) *Historiography and Imagination: Eight Essays on Roman Culture*. Exeter.

(1995) *Remus: A Roman Myth*. Cambridge.

(2008) *Unwritten Rome*. Exeter.

(2009) *Remembering the Roman People: Essays on Late-Republican Politics and Literature*. Oxford.

Wissowa, G. (1896) 'Arvales fratres' *RE* 2.2: 1463–1486.

(1912) *Religion und Kultus der Römer*. Munich.

Wobst, M. M. (2000) 'Agency in (spite of) material culture' in *Agency in Archaeology*, eds M.-A. Dobres and J. E. Robb. London: 40–50.

Woodard, R. D. (2006) *Indo-European Sacred Space: Vedic and Roman Cult*. Urbana, IL.

Woodford, S. (2003) *Images of Myths in Classical Antiquity*. Cambridge.

Woolf, G. (1994) 'Becoming Roman, staying Greek: culture, identity and the civilizing process in the Roman east' *PCPhS* 40: 116–143.

(1997a) 'Beyond Romans and natives' *World Archaeology* 28: 339–350.

Bibliography

(1997b) 'Polis-religion and its alternatives in the Roman provinces' in *Römische Reichsreligion und Provinzialreligion*, eds H. Cancik and J. Rüpke. Tübingen: 71–84.

(1998) *Becoming Roman: The Origins of Provincial Civilization in Gaul*. Cambridge.

(2001) 'Representation as cult: the case of the Jupiter columns' in *Religion in den germanischen Provinzen Roms*, eds W. Spickermann, H. Cancik and J. Rüpke. Tübingen: 117–134.

(2009) 'Found in translation: the religion of the Roman diaspora' in *Ritual Dynamics and Religious Change in the Roman Empire: Proceedings of the Eighth Workshop of the International Network Impact of Empire, Heidelberg, July 5–7, 2007*, eds O. Hekster, S. Schmidt-Hofner and C. Witschel. Leiden: 239–252.

Young, R. (1985) *Darwin's Metaphor: Nature's Place in Victorian Culture*. Cambridge.

Zaidman, L. B. and Schmitt Pantel, P. (1992) *Religion in the Ancient Greek City*, trans. P. Cartledge. Cambridge.

Zanker, P. (1988) *The Power of Images in the Age of Augustus*, trans. A. Shapiro. Ann Arbor, MI.

Zetzel, J. E. G. (2005) *Marginal Scholarship and Textual Deviance: The 'Commentum Cornuti' and the Early Scholia on Persius*. London.

Zissos, A. (2008) *Valerius Flaccus' 'Argonautica' Book 1: Edited with Introduction, Translation and Commentary*. Oxford.

(2009) 'Navigating power: Valerius Flaccus' *Argonautica*' in *Writing Politics in Imperial Rome*, eds W. J. Dominik, J. Garthwaite and P. A. Roche. Leiden: 351–366.

INDEX

Adolenda Coinquenda, 165–170, 293
Adolenda Conmolenda Deferunda, 15, 163–168, 292
Aeneas, 52, 93–94, 127n23
agency, of trees, 27, 173–177, 199–200, see also portents, arboreal
animism, 26, 43–49, 50–62, 66–70, 72–73, 177, see also mana, numen
preanimism, 58
Apollo, see also laurel
of the Cornels, 131, 238–239
of the Plane, 238
arboricultural care
and the *ficus Ruminalis*, 116–118
for sacred trees, 121, 133–152, 293
assumed sacrilege, 133–134
violence of, 134
Aristotle, on plant life, 175–176
Artemis
of the Cedar, 238, 242, 260–261, 293
of the Laurel, 238–239
of the Nut Tree, 238, 241–242
Saviour, 79–81
Asclepius, see also grove(s), of Asclepius
of the Agnus Castus, 238, 242, 260
ash, see Silvanus, half shut up in sacred ash
Athena, see also olive, produced by Athena
of the Cypress, 238, 241–243
of the Ivy, 238
statue of, attached to bronze palm, 264–265
Attus Navius, 102–109
Augustus, see also palm, on altar of Augustus at Tarraco
revives a holm oak on Capri, 218–219
transplants a palm sapling, 217, 260

Baumkultus, see tree worship
Baumseele, see tree souls
beech, see also *fagutal*, see Jupiter, Fagutalis
fagus deus, 239, 241, 244
belief, 9–11
Boetticher, C. G. W., 34–35, 39n39, 52, 58n114, 113n80, 121, 127, 263
Boscotrecase, 271–273, 279

casa Romuli, 115–118, 161
Cato, *Agr.* 139–140, 60–61, 67, 137–140, 143–144, 147–148, 151
columns, 259
in relationship with trees, 262n81, 277
comparative religion, 29–31
evolutionary model, 29–30, 35–37
fall from grace, 63–65
implications for the Church, 35–37
Protestant-centric approach, 37–39
confession inscriptions, 244–249
cornel, 118, 204, see also Apollo, of the Cornels
once Romulus' spear, 204
cross worship, 74–76
Cybele, 253–254, 257–258, 283–286, see also pine, in relationship with Cybele
cypress, 210–211, 252–253, see also Athena, of the Cypress

Daphne, 51, 54, 60, 197, 222, 233–234, 290–291, 293
at Antioch the Great, 290–291
Darwin, see comparative religion, evolutionary model
Dea Dia, see grove of Dea Dia, see pruning

Index

Dea Dia (*cont.*)
   major festival of, 137
   meaning of name, 148–149n91
dendrophori, 253–254, 258
Dionysus, *see also* pine, in relationship with Dionysus
   of the Fig, 239, 243–244
   of the Ivy, 238
   wooden statues of, 81–83, 292
Dowden, K., 10, 69–70, 134, 231–232, 269
dryads, *see* hamadryads and dryads
Dumézil, G., 65, 140n55, 180–181

epithets
   arboreal, 237–254
     Pausanias' penchant for, 238–241, 249–250
     scholarship on, 237–238, 250–251
Erysichthon, 52–54, 60, 122–124, 126, 191–192, 196
Evander, 13, 61, 67, 186–187

fagutal, 239, *see also* Jupiter, Fagutalis
Faunus/i, 93–95, 185, 187–188, 230
fetishism, 40–41, *see also* tree worship, Protestant-centric constructions of
ficus Navia, 103–109, 119–120
ficus Romula / Romularis, 116
ficus Ruminalis, 3, 9, 12, 61, 100–120, 121, 255
   on the *Anaglypha Traiana*, 255
   and arboricultural care, 116–118
   authenticity of, 111–112
   location of, 101–102
   and material vulnerability, 116–120
   and memory, 112–115, 118–120
   Pliny the Elder on, 100–120
   portentous behaviour, 111–112, 216
   sacrality of, 112–120
fig, *see also* Dionysus, of the Fig, *ficus Navia*, *ficus Romula / Romularis*, *ficus Ruminalis*
   on altar of Jupiter on Capitol, 215
   associations of, 215
   milky sap, 289–290
   in the roof of Dea Dia's temple, 15, 163–164
   at shrine of Rumina, 289–290
   upsets a statue of Silvanus, 164
foliage, 77, 96–97, 111, 233, 293
folklore, 31–33, 37
fratres Arvales, 135–136, *see also* grove of Dea Dia
Frazer, J. G., 2, 17, 25, 37n31, 42, 44, 48, 49, 52, 55

gerundives, 15, 139–140, 165–167
Golden Age, 11–14, 85, 125n14, 186–187, 269
grove of Dea Dia, 137–140, 163–165, 171–172
   arboreal crises, 152–171
   iron presumed 'taboo', 144–145
   nature of inscriptional evidence, 135–136
grove(s), *see* Evander, Lucina
   animistic explanations of, 127
   at Antioch the Great, 290–291
   of Apollo of the Cornels, 239
   of Asclepius, 129–130
   assumed inviolable, 126–128
   assumed sacred, 126–128
   of Jupiter Ammon, 83–87
   sacred to Diana, 231–232
   of Zeus Sabazius and Artemis Anaeitis, 248

hamadryads and dryads, 46, 53–54, 190–196
   animistic interpretations of, 46, 53–54, 190
   coeval with trees, 190–193
   varied relationships with trees, 190–196
Harpocrates, 276–277
Helen of the Tree, 238, 241
Hercules, 256–258, *see also* poplar, in relationship with Hercules
   in fresco from *casa* VII.9.47, 256–258
   in fresco from Oplontis, 224–226
   in garden of the Hesperides, 224–225, 258
   introduces white poplar and wild olive, 226
   plants two oaks, 226
   and his rerooting club, 204

Index

tree-hugger, 224–226, 293
and the wild olive, 98–99, 226
holm oak, 100, 218, 231, 260
humanisation of trees, 196–199
bleeding or in pain, 52–53, 122–125

imperial cult, 153–154, 217–223
inviolability
of groves, *see* grove(s), assumed inviolable
of sacred objects, 3–4
of sacred trees, *see* sacred trees
in contemporary scholarship on Roman religion, assumed inviolable
Isis, 257, *see also* Pompeii, frescoes from temple of Isis

Jupiter, *see also* oak, in relationship with Jupiter
Ammon, 83–87
Fagutalis, 239, 241–242, 293
Feretrius, 62
jurists, 3–9

Latinus, *see* laurel(s), in Latinus' palace
laurel, 214–215
badly burned in the Arval grove, 157–159
in Latinus' palace, 96–97, 228
in relationship with Apollo, 228–231, 233–235, 266–267, 290–291, 293
lightning strikes, 9, 104–105, 109, 119, 135, 155, *see also* puteal
lotus, 98, 100, 124, 288–289
Lucina, 288–289
lucus, *see also* grove(s)
as understood by Scheid, 136–137, 148–150
etymology of, 148–150

mana, 47, 59, 68–69, 179
Mannhardt, W., 32, 46, 52–54
memory, *see ficus Ruminalis*, and memory
metamorphoses, arboreal, 124, 196–197, 233–234, *see also* Daphne
Dryope, 193
Minerva, *see* olive, in relationship with Minerva

myrtle, 98, 216
and Artemis Saviour, 79–81, 83
in relationship with Venus, 228–231, 233, 242
statue of Aphrodite, made of, 263–264

neopaganism, 1–2
numen, 177–190, *see also mana*
aligned with *mana*, 59, 179
associated with trees, 85–86, 184–190, 291
history of scholarship on, 177–183
narrative of word's development, 179–180
new approach to, 183–184
numen Augustum, 181–183
numen inest, 184–186
undefinability, 183–184
understood as impersonal force, 178, 180, 182
nymphs, 289, *see also* hamadryads and dryads

oak, 130–131, 189, 199, *see also* Erysichthon, *see also* Zeus of the Twin Oaks
beam in Argo, 92–93
Dodonian, 33, 92–93, 122
in relationship with Jupiter, 62, 228–233, 236–237, 282–283
olive, 98–99
grove, which crossed the road, 212
produced by Athena, 98, 99, 212
in relationship with Minerva, 228–231
wild, 93–95, 98–99, 212, 226, 289, *see also* Faunus, Hercules
Oplontis, 224–226, *see also* Hercules
Ovid
Fast. 3.295–296, 67, 184–185
Metamorphoses, 51–52, 196–197

palm, 99, 217
on altar of Augustus at Tarraco, 15–16, 217–223, 291
on altar of Jupiter on the Capitol, 215
bronze, at Delos, 259
bronze, at Delphi, 15, 259, 264–265, 292
spared by Julius Caesar, 217

Index

palm (*cont.*)
  in temple of Victory at Tralles, 213–214
Pan, 228, *see also* pine, in relationship with Pan
plants a tree, 259
Pausanias, 24–25, *see also* epithets, Pausanias' penchant for, statues, of the divine, Pausanias' interest in
peach, 214–215
penates, 3, 217, 260, 293
Philpot, J. H., 26, 41, 47, 49, 53
piacula, 140–144, 291
pine
  cut down by St Martin, 73
  dedicated to Diana, 228
  in relationship with Cybele, 228–231, 234, 284–286
  in relationship with Dionysus, 234–236
  in relationship with Pan, 233–234, 286
  in relationship with Poseidon, 234–236
  in relationship with Priapus, 286
plane(s), 209, 228, 253, 260, *see* Apollo, of the Plane, *see* sacrifice, wine pouring on trees
  at Aulis, 95–96, 293
  at Delphi, planted by Agamemnon, 98–99
  honour for, 89–91
Pliny, *Nat.* 12.1–3, 13, 67, 187–188, 230–231
Polydorus, 33, 52, 54, 60
Pompeii
  fresco from *casa* IX. 2. 16, 277–278
  fresco from *casa* VII. 9. 47, 256–258
  frescoes from temple of Isis, 273–277
  tree root cavity excavations, 266–268
pons sublicius, 162
poplar, *see also* Zeus of the White Poplar
  and Dryope, 193
  in relationship with Heliades, 196–197, 234
  in relationship with Hercules, 228–231, 234
  white turns into black variety, 207
porta sacra, 271–276
portents
  arboreal, 111–112, 155–157, 199–223, 264

blurring of natural and divine causation, 155–157, 205–211, 293
interpretation, 213–217
'natural vs unnatural', 201–202, 205–211
Pliny the Elder on, 205–210
self-resurrecting trees, 208–211
technical sense, 200
Priapus, 228, 257n68, 262n82, 279–280, 286, 293,
  see also pine, in relationship with Priapus
pruning
  coinquere and *conlucare*, 137–139
  in the grove of Dea Dia, 137–152, 170–171
  purpose of, 148–152
  timing of, 150–151
puteal, 104–105

Roman culture and religion
  models for approaching, 21–22
  my methodological approach to, 19–22, 25
Roman Greece, 22–25
Roman religion, contemporary scholarship on
  decline of animism, 65–66
  and the environment, 17–19, 293–294
  animistic interpretations, 18
  assumed simplistic, 17–19
  legalism, 4–9, 142–143
  warnings against Christianocentric approach, 65–66, 70
Roman religion, early scholarship on
  evolutionary approach, 57–58
  obsession with animism, *numina* and tree spirits, 58–62
  overlap with comparativists, 54–62
  Christianocentric approach, 57–58
  Roman religion aligned with Catholicism, 50–51
  Roman religion understood as primitive, 50–51
Romulus, 103, 114, 117
  and Remus, 107, 110, 112–113, 116
  and a rerooting cornel spear, 118, 204

331

Index

Rose, H. J., 58–59, 64–65, 165, 179–181, 184
Rumina, 27, 116, 289–290

sacer, 3–6
sacrality, 3–9
  consecration model, 3–8
  divine property model, 3–8
  flexible and organic approach, 112–120, 292–293
  legalistic approach, 3–9, 121–122
  of the natural world, 5–7
sacred trees
  in cult space, 266–291
  exceptionally old, 98–100
  felling, implications of, 128–132, 244–249
  and the other, 83–84, 279–280
  physical treatment of, 157–162, 171–172, *see also* arboricultural care, vulnerability of trees
  and rusticity, 13–14
  struck by lightning, 155
  struggling or in decline, 93–96, 107, 111–112, 152–162
  understood as consecrated, 227–228, 231–233
sacred trees in comparativist scholarship
  animistic interpretations of, 26, 43–49, 177
  evolutionary narrative, 47–49
  Roman exempla, 51–54
  huge enthusiasm for, 29–49
  especially in Germany, 31–32
  non-animistic explanations of, 42–43
sacred trees in contemporary scholarship on Roman religion
  animistic interpretations of, 26, 66–70
  evolutionary model, 69–70
  hostility towards matter, 69–70
  assumed inviolable, 121–126, 128–129
  assumed simplistic, 1–2, 11–14, 66
sacred trees in early scholarship on Roman religion
  animistic interpretations of, 26, 50–62
  evolutionary model, 62
  hostility towards matter, 61–62
sacred trees in the apologists
  animistic interpretations of, 72–73

sacrifice, 140–141, 171–172, *see also* imperial cult, *piacula*
  piacular pigs, 137–138
  sacrificial prepositions, 153–154, 292
  strues and *fercta*, 154–155
  wine pouring on trees, 89–91
sacro-idyllic landscapes, 268–273
  trees in, 270–277
Seneca, *Ep.* 41.3, 67, 186–187
Servius
  on hamadryads and dryads, 192
  on oaks and groves, 231–232
Silvanus, 15, 62, 77, 134, 164, 228, 251–254, 266, 293
  and Cyparissus, 252
  Dendrophorus, 253–254
  half shut up in sacred ash, 15, 87–89
Silvestris, 253
sive deus sive dea, see Cato, *Agr.* 139–140
Sondergötter, 18, 163–168
Spoleto inscription (*CIL* 11.4766), 127–128, 148, 151
statues
  made from trees, 81–83, 88–89
  of the divine
    Pausanias' interest in, 80–81
    scholarly approaches to, 80–81, 262–263, 265
  of trees, 255–259
statues and trees
  tree worship aligned with Catholic idolatry, 39–41
  trees as primitive temples and statues, 35
  trees blurring with statues, 255–265
  in Roman cultural discourse, 261–262
  primitivism, 261–262
Stoicism, 202–203
  influence of in the Roman world, 202–204
  influence on Pliny the Elder, 203–204
storms, 153, 155–158, 236
stumps, *see* sacred trees, struggling or in decline
survivals, 31–33

theological thinking, 9–19
Theophrastus, 208–210

332

Index

totemism, 43
tree huggers
  Hercules, 224–226
  Passienus Crispus, 91
tree souls, 52–54, 166, 190
tree spirits, 43–49, 58–61, 67–68
tree types, *see also* portents, arboreal
  identification in Roman painting, 226
  in relationship with particular deities, 187–188, 227–237
tree worship
  blurring with worship of deities, 79–89
  glimpses of in the Roman world, 72–92
  Protestant-centric constructions of, 39–42, 47–48, 84
trees
  wrapped with wreaths or ribbons, 13, 72, 122, 224–226
Turnus, 93–95
Tylor, E. B., 26, 33, 36, 38, 41, 43–44, 53–54, 77

Venus, 94, 257, *see also* myrtle, in relationship with Venus
  of the Myrtle, 239
Vesta, temple of, 282–283
Vestal Virgins, 90n35, 164, 282–283
villa dei Papiri, Herculaneum
  wooden furniture fragments, 284–287
vulnerability of trees, 27, 77, *see also ficus Ruminalis* and material vulnerability, sacred trees, struggling or in decline

white poplar, *see* Hercules, Zeus
willow, 208–210
wreaths, 98, 226, 277–278, 289

Zeus
  of the Twin Oaks, 131–132, 244–249
  of the white poplar, 237–240, 243

333